THE ROLE OF THE PUBLIC BUREAUCRACY IN POLICY IMPLEMENTATION IN FIVE ASEAN COUNTRIES

This pioneering book addresses an important gap in the literature by comparing the role of the public bureaucracies in policy implementation in Indonesia, Malaysia, the Philippines, Singapore and Vietnam. It highlights the importance of the policy context, especially the commitment of the government in allocating the necessary resources and the support of the implementers, as well as the public bureaucracy's effectiveness, as the critical factors responsible for effective policy implementation. The comparative analysis shows that the public bureaucracies in Singapore and Malaysia are more effective in policy implementation than their counterparts in Indonesia, the Philippines and Vietnam because of their favourable policy contexts and higher level of organizational effectiveness. The focus on policy context and the public bureaucracy's role in the policy-making process and its implementation of two ASEAN policies will be of interest to policy-makers, civil servants, scholars and students concerned with enhancing policy implementation in the ASEAN countries.

JON S. T. QUAH is a retired Professor of Political Science at the National University of Singapore and an Anti-Corruption Consultant based in Singapore. He was a Vice-President of the Asian Association for Public Administration (2010–2012) and co-editor of the *Asian Journal of Political Science*. He has published extensively on corruption and public administration in Asian countries.

INTEGRATION THROUGH LAW

The Role of Law and the Rule of Law in ASEAN Integration

General Editors
J. H. H. Weiler, European University Institute
Tan Hsien-Li, National University of Singapore

The Association of Southeast Asian Nations (ASEAN), comprising the ten member states of Brunei Darussalam, Cambodia, Indonesia, Lao PDR, Malaysia, Myanmar, Philippines, Singapore, Thailand and Vietnam, has undertaken intensified integration into the ASEAN Community through the Rule of Law and Institutions in its 2007 Charter. This innovative book series evaluates the community-building processes of ASEAN to date and offers a conceptual and policy toolkit for broader Asian thinking and planning of different legal and institutional models of economic and political regional integration in the region. Participating scholars have been divided up into six separate thematic strands. The books combine a mix of Asian and Western scholars.

Centre for International Law, National University of Singapore (CIL-NUS)

The Centre for International Law (CIL) was established in 2009 at the National University of Singapore's Bukit Timah Campus in response to the growing need for international law expertise and capacity building in the Asia-Pacific region. CIL is a university-wide research centre that focuses on multidisciplinary research and works with other NUS or external centres of research and academic excellence. In particular, CIL collaborates very closely with the NUS Faculty of Law.

THE ROLE OF THE PUBLIC BUREAUCRACY IN POLICY IMPLEMENTATION IN FIVE ASEAN COUNTRIES

Edited by

JON S. T. QUAH

CAMBRIDGE
UNIVERSITY PRESS

CAMBRIDGE
UNIVERSITY PRESS

University Printing House, Cambridge CB2 8BS, United Kingdom

Cambridge University Press is part of the University of Cambridge.

It furthers the University's mission by disseminating knowledge in the pursuit of education, learning and research at the highest international levels of excellence.

www.cambridge.org
Information on this title: www.cambridge.org/9781107545175

First published 2016

A catalogue record for this publication is available from the British Library

Library of Congress Cataloguing in Publication data
The role of the public bureaucracy in policy implementation in five Asean countries / edited by Jon S. T. Quah.
pages cm. – (Integration through law: the role of law and the rule of law in Asean integration)
ISBN 978-1-107-54517-5 (Paperback)
1. Public policy–Southeast Asia. 2. Bureaucracy–Southeast Asia. 3. Public administration–Southeast Asia. 4. Southeast Asia–Politics and government. I. Quah, Jon S. T.
JF1525.P6R65 2015
320.60959–dc23 2015020014

ISBN 978-1-107-54517-5 Paperback

CONTENTS

TABLES

CONTRIBUTORS

Nik Rosnah Wan Abdullah, PhD is Deputy Dean and professor at the Tun Abdul Razak School of Government, University Abdul Razak in Kuala Lumpur, Malaysia. She was a senior international fellow at the Institute for Policy Studies, Johns Hopkins University; a senior visiting fellow at the Lee Kuan Yew School of Public Policy, National University of Singapore; Head of Department of Administrative Studies and Politics at the Faculty of Economics and Administration, University of Malaya; and Executive Director of the International Institute of Public Administration (INPUMA). She has published extensively on regulatory reform, health sector reform, public policy and governance.

Jairo Acuña-Alfaro is Policy Advisor on Core Government Functions and Public Service Excellence at the United Nations Development Programme (UNDP) in New York. From October 2007 to December 2014, he was Policy Advisor on Public Administration Reform and Anti-Corruption at UNDP Vietnam. In that capacity he helped develop several policies regarding public sector and civil service reforms and provided policy advice for the formulation and approval of the civil service law and new alternatives to measure governance and public administration performance. He was a Ronaldo Falconer Scholar at

St Antony's College, Oxford and a recipient of a British Chevening Scholarship.

David Seth Jones, PhD is a retired academic and currently a consultant in public procurement. He was formerly Associate Professor of Public Policy at the University of Brunei Darussalam and Associate Professor of Political Science at the National University of Singapore. He was also an adjunct professor at the Singapore Management University and Local Director (Singapore), Master in Public Administration Programme, Australian National University and Civil Service College, Singapore. He has published extensively on public policy and administration, public finance, government procurement and land administration. He has also undertaken many consultancy projects in these areas in various Southeast Asian countries.

Giulio Napolitano, PhD is Professor of Administrative Law at the Department of Law, Roma Tre University. He was a visiting and programme affiliate scholar at the Max Planck Institut of Heidelberg and at the New York University School of Law. He is a member of the Inaugural Council of the International Society of Public Law Society and of the Board of Editors of the *European Public Law Review*. He has published extensively in the fields of theoretical foundations of administrative law, comparative administrative law, regulation and anti-trust, economic analysis of public law and global governance.

Agus Pramusinto, PhD is a professor of public administration and director of the graduate programme in public policy and administration at the Faculty of Social and Political Sciences, Gadja Mada University in Indonesia. He received his MA and PhD degrees from the Australian National University. He is involved in research and consultancy projects on administrative reform for local governments and national ministries in Indonesia. He has published extensively in national and international journals and is participating in the Asian Leadership and Management Development Project in six Asian countries initiated by the National Graduate Institute for Policy Studies in Tokyo, Japan.

Jon S. T. Quah, PhD is a retired professor of political science at the National University of Singapore and an anti-corruption consultant based in Singapore. His major books include *Curbing Corruption in Asia: A Comparative Study of Six Countries* (2003); *Combating Corruption Singapore-Style: Lessons for Other Asian Countries* (2007); *Public Administration Singapore-Style* (2010); *Taiwan's Anti-Corruption Strategy: Suggestions for Reform* (2010); *Curbing Corruption in Asian Countries: An Impossible Dream?* (2011; 2013); *Minimizing Corruption in China: Is this an Impossible Dream?* (2013); and (as editor) *Different Paths to Curbing Corruption: Lessons from Denmark, Finland, Hong Kong, New Zealand and Singapore* (2013).

Vicente Chua Reyes, Jr, PhD is a lecturer of social science at the Faculty of Education, University of New England in Armidale, New South Wales, Australia. He is an executive committee member of the Educational Research Association of Singapore, a fellow of the Centre for Chinese

Studies in Taiwan and a visiting academic at the Institute of Education, University of London. His research interests focus on the political economy of education reform, corruption, educational leadership, policy learning and implementation. His latest book is *Mapping the Terrain of Education Reform: Global Trends and Local Responses in the Philippines* (2015).

Anh Tran, PhD is an assistant professor at the School of Public and Environmental Affairs, Indiana University, specializing in governance issues of developing countries. His research focuses on transparency, tax evasion, corruption, political networks and their economic and social outcomes. His articles have appeared in *American Political Science Review*, *Journal of Financial Economics*, *Journal of Law and Economics* and *Journal of Public Economics*. Tran frequently works as a consultant for reform initiatives by national governments, the United Nations and the World Bank. He has participated in UNDP's Academic Fellowships, Asia Foundation's Emerging Leaders Programme and the Vietnamese Prime Minister's Research Council.

GENERAL EDITORS' PREFACE

This monograph is published within the context of a wide-ranging research project entitled, Integration Through Law: The Role of Law and the Rule of Law in ASEAN Integration (ITL), undertaken by the Centre for International Law at the National University of Singapore and directed by J. H. H. Weiler and Tan Hsien-Li.

The Preamble to the ASEAN Charter concludes with a single decision: "We, the Peoples of the Member States of the Association of Southeast Asian Nations ... [h]ereby decide to establish, through this Charter, the legal and institutional framework for ASEAN." For the first time in its history of over four decades, the Legal and the Institutional were brought to the forefront of ASEAN discourse.

The gravitas of the medium, a Charter: the substantive ambition of its content, the creation of three interlocking Communities, and the turn to law and institutions as instruments for realization provide ample justification for this wide-ranging project, to which this monograph is one contribution, examining ASEAN in a comparative context.

That same substantive and, indeed, political ambition means that any single study, illuminating as it may be, will cover but a fraction of the phenomena. Our modus operandi in this project was to create teams of researchers from Asia and elsewhere who would contribute individual monographs within an overall framework which we had designed.

The project framework, involving several thematic clusters within each monograph, is thus determined by the framework and the place of each monograph within it.

As regards the specific content, however, the authors were free, indeed encouraged, to define their own understanding of the problem and their own methodology and reach their own conclusions. The thematic structure of the entire project may be found at the end of this Preface.

The project as a whole, and each monograph within it, display several methodological sensibilities. First, law, in our view, can only be understood and evaluated when situated in its political and economic context. Thus, the first studies in the overall project design are intended to provide the political, economic, cultural and historical context against which one must understand ASEAN and are written by specialists in these respective disciplines. This context, to a greater or lesser degree, also informs the sensibility of each monograph. There are no "black letter law" studies to be found in this project and, indeed, even in the most technical of areas we encouraged our authors to make their writing accessible to readers of diverse disciplines.

Comparative experience suggests that the success of achieving some of the more ambitious objectives outlined in Article 1 of the Charter will depend in no small measure on the effectiveness of legal principles, legal rules and legal institutions.

This is particularly true as regards the success of establishing "an ASEAN Community comprising the ASEAN Security Community, the ASEAN Economic Community and the ASEAN Socio-Cultural Community as provided for in the

Bali Declaration of ASEAN Concord II". Article 2(2)(n) stipulates the commitment of ASEAN Member States to act in accordance with the principle of "adherence to multilateral trade rules and ASEAN's rules-based regimes for effective implementation of economic commitments and progressive reduction towards elimination of all barriers to regional economic integration." The ASEAN Member States therefore envisage that rules of law and the Rule of Law will become a major feature in the future of ASEAN.

Although, as seen, the Charter understands itself as providing an institutional and legal framework for ASEAN, the question of the "role of law and the rule of law" is not advocacy but a genuine enquiry in the various substantive areas of the project as to:

- the substantive legal principles and substantive rules of the various ASEAN communities;
- the procedural legal principles and rules governing institutional structures and decision-making processes;
- implementation, enforcement and dispute settlement.

One should not expect a mechanical application of this scheme in each study; rather, a sensibility that refuses to content itself with legal enactments as such and looks to a "living" notion of law and institutions is ubiquitous in all the studies. Likewise, the project is sensitive to "non Law." It variously attempts to locate the appropriate province of the law in this experience. That is, not only the role of law, but also the areas that are and should remain outside the reach of legal institutionalization with due sensitivity to ASEAN and Asian particularism and political and cultural identities.

The project, and the monographs of which it is made, are not normatively thick. They do not advocate. They are designed, for the most part, to offer reflection, discuss the pros and cons, and in this way enrich public awareness, deepen understanding of different options and in that respect contribute indirectly to policymaking.

This decisive development of ASEAN has been accompanied by a growing Asian interest in various legal and institutional forms of transnational economic and political cooperation, notably the various voices discussing and showing an interest in an East Asia Integration project. The number of Free Trade Agreements (FTAs) and Regional Trade Agreements (RTAs) has increased from six in 1991 to 166 in 2013, with a further 62 in various stages of negotiations.

Methodologically, the project and many of the monographs are comparative in their orientation. Comparative law is one of the few real-life laboratories that we have in which to assess and understand the operation of different legal and institutional models designed to tackle similar objectives and problems. One should not need to put one's own hand in the fire to learn that it scorches. With that in mind a couple of monographs offer both conceptual reflection and pragmatic "tool boxing" on some of the key elements featuring in all regional integration systems.

Comparative law is in part about divergence: it is a potent tool and means to understand one's own uniqueness. One understands better the uniqueness of Apples by comparing them to Oranges. You understand better the specialness of a Toyota by comparing it to a Ford.

Comparative law is also about convergence: it is a potent tool and means to understand how what are seemingly different phenomena are part of a broader trend, an insight which may enhance both self-understanding and policy potentialities.

Although many studies in the project could have almost immediate policy implications, as would the project as a whole, this is not its only or even principal purpose. There is a rich theory of federalism which covers many countries around the world. There is an equally rich theory of European integration, which has been associated with the advent Union. There is also considerable learning on Free Trade Areas and the like.

To date, the study of the legal aspects of ASEAN specifically and other forms of Asian legal integration has been derivative of, and dependent on, theoretical and conceptual insight which were developed in different contexts.

One principal objective of ITL and these monographs will be to put in place the building blocks for an authentic body of ASEAN and Asian integration theory developed in, and with sensitivity to, the particularities and peculiarities of the region and continent. A theory and conceptual framework of Asian legal integration will signal the coming of age of research of and in the region itself.

Although the monographs form part of an overarching project, we asked our authors to write each as a "standalone" – not assuming that their readers would have consulted any of the other titles. Indeed, the project is rich and few will read all monographs. We encourage readers to pick and choose from the various monographs and design their own menu. There is, on occasion, some overlap in providing, for example, background information on ASEAN in different studies. That is not only inevitable but desirable in a project of this amplitude.

The world is increasingly witnessing a phenomenon of interlocking regional organization where the experience of one feeds on the others. In some way, the intellectual, disciplinary and comparative sensibility of this project is a microcosm of the world it describes.

The range of topics covered in this series comprises:

The General Architecture and Aspirations of ASEAN
The Governance and Management of ASEAN: Instruments, Institutions, Monitoring, Compliance and Dispute Resolution
Legal Regimes in ASEAN
The ASEAN Economic Community
ASEAN and the World
The Substantive Law of ASEAN

PREFACE

This book is one of the products of the 'Integration Through Law: The ASEAN Way in a Comparative Context' Project or the ASEAN Integration Through Law (ITL) Project sponsored by the Centre for International Law (CIL) at the National University of Singapore (NUS). The ASEAN ITL Project is directed by Professor J. H. H. Weiler, President of the European University Institute in Florence, Italy and Professor of Law at NUS, with the assistance of Dr Tan Hsien-Li, Senior CIL Research Fellow, as the Executive Director.

I was invited by Professor Weiler on 30 June 2011 to be the principal investigator for the Governance and Management Research Group's project on the role of the public bureaucracy in policy implementation in the Association of Southeast Asian Nations (ASEAN) countries. The ASEAN was formed on 8 August 1967 by the five member states of Indonesia, Malaysia, the Philippines, Singapore and Thailand. The number of member states has gradually increased to ten from 1984 to 1999 with the addition of Brunei Darussalam in January 1984, Vietnam in July 1995, Lao People's Democratic Republic and Myanmar in July 1997 and Cambodia in April 1999. As resource and time constraints did not permit the group to conduct research on all the ten member countries, the decision was made after consulting the project leaders to focus on the role of the public bureaucracy in policy implementation in Indonesia, Malaysia, the Philippines, Singapore and Vietnam.

I would like to thank all the contributors for accepting my invitation to write the chapters in this book and for attending the two research workshops in Singapore on 14 October 2011 and 17–18 July 2012. Two important decisions were made at the first research workshop in October 2011. First, all the authors agreed to use the six variables identified by Van Meter and Van Horn to analyse the public bureaucracy's role in policy implementation in the five ASEAN countries.

The second important decision made at the October 2011 workshop was to illustrate the public bureaucracy's role in implementing ASEAN policies in the five countries by focusing on two case studies. Three criteria were used to select the two case studies of ASEAN policies: (1) an 'effective' policy should be selected to understand why it has been successfully implemented; (2) an 'ineffective' policy should be selected to understand why it has encountered problems in implementation; and (3) the two policies selected should be similar for the five countries so as to facilitate comparison and to help identify the reasons for success or failure in implementing these policies.

Before the October 2011 research workshop, I had consulted some officials at the ASEAN Secretariat in Jakarta to seek their views on which ASEAN policies could be selected as examples of effective and ineffective implementation. I discussed the suggestions of these officials with the authors at the October 2011 workshop and the group decided, after further consultation with the ASEAN Secretariat officials, to focus on the ASEAN Cosmetic Directive

(ACD) as an example of an effective policy and the ASEAN Ministerial Meeting on Transactional Crime/Senior Officials Meeting on Transactional Crime (AMMTC/SOMTC) as an example of a policy which has encountered problems in implementation.

The second drafts of the five country studies were presented at the second research workshop in July 2012 in Singapore. At the Internal Plenary for the ASEAN ITL Project held in Singapore on 22 August 2012, four presentations were made by members of the group. Jon Quah presented his paper which provided a comparative overview of the public bureaucracy's role in policy implementation in the five ASEAN countries. David Seth Jones presented his country report on Singapore, and was followed by Vicente Chua Reyes, Jr, who presented the Philippines country report. The group concluded its progress report with Giulio Napolitano's presentation on the problem of asymmetric compliance in policy implementation in the European Union (EU) countries and its relevance for the five ASEAN countries.

All the contributors would like to thank Professor J. H. H. Weiler and Dr Tan Hsien-Li for supporting the publication of this book by Cambridge University Press, and for their constructive feedback on the earlier drafts of the various chapters. As the editor, I am grateful to the contributors for their cooperation in submitting their draft chapters to me on time and for making the necessary revisions according to the feedback provided on these chapters. In this regard, I wish to thank David Seth Jones and Giulio Napolitano for their kind assistance in reviewing the earlier drafts of the country chapters.

On behalf of the contributors, I would like to record my appreciation to Ms Geraldine Ng, CIL's Senior Manager for Events and Programmes, for making the excellent arrangements that facilitated discussion among the participants and ensured the success of the two workshops in Singapore in October 2011 and July 2012. All the contributors would also like to thank Ms Renee Chan, CIL's Finance Manager, for her kind assistance in facilitating the reimbursement of their travel expenses and honoraria.

My fellow contributors and I are most grateful to the ASEAN ITL Project's Executive Director, Dr Tan Hsien-Li, for her continuous support and understanding during the past three and a half years. She has always replied promptly to our queries and requests by email, whether from Florence, New York or Singapore, with the requested information or relevant advice.

Finally, I would like to thank Claire Wood and her colleagues at Cambridge University Press for facilitating the copy-editing of the manuscript and publication of the book.

Chapter 1

The role of the public bureaucracy in policy implementation in five ASEAN countries: a comparative overview

Jon S. T. Quah

1.1 Introduction

The Parable of the Owl and the Centipede

In the forest there lived a centipede who developed foot problems, and for a centipede that means a lot of pain. He asked the other animals what he could do about it, and no one had any suggestion except that he ask the Wise Old Owl.

So he went to the Wise Old Owl. 'Wise Old Owl, Wise Old Owl', he said. 'Tell me what I can do about my aching feet.' The Wise Old Owl considered the problem and said, 'Go back to your home and turn into a fish.' Since a fish has no feet, that seemed like good advice, so the centipede went home and tried it out. But, no matter how hard he tried, he couldn't turn into a fish. He asked the other animals how to do it and none of them knew.

Again he limped back to the Wise Old Owl. 'Wise Old Owl, Wise Old Owl', he said. 'I have tried very hard, every way I can think of, to turn into a fish, but I can't. Please, Wise Old Owl, Wise Old Owl, tell me how to do it.'

> *The Wise Old Owl looked annoyed. 'You don't understand my situation. I don't know* ***how*** *to do anything like that; I just make policy.'*
>
> (Steve Sachs, Attorney General of Maryland, quoted in Young 1983: 39)

This parable captures accurately the relative ease of formulating a policy on the one hand, as well as the difficulties encountered in policy implementation on the other hand. In their analysis of policy implementation in the Third World, Bertsch, Clark and Wood (1986: 472) observe that many governments 'operate under administrative, economic, and political constraints that virtually guarantee failure at the point where the policy is applied to the society'. Caiden (1976: 142–64) describes implementation as the 'Achilles' heel' of administrative reform and identifies twelve reasons for the failure of policy implementation in the developing countries.

Perhaps the most comprehensive analysis of the difficulties encountered in implementing policies is provided by Chase (1979: 386–435) who has identified forty-four obstacles to the implementation of human services programmes. In their pioneering book, *Implementation*, Pressman and Wildavsky (1973: xiii) contend that 'implementation, under the best of circumstances, is exceedingly difficult'. The obstacles to effective implementation in Third World countries are many and include lack of qualified personnel, lack of political support for the implementers and implementing agencies, insufficient direction and control from political leaders, severe lack of funds available to meet the costs of implementing projects and programmes, resistance to the policy itself, corruption, and social indiscipline (Quah 1984: 118).

1.2 Review of literature

A review of the literature on policy implementation reveals four important trends. First, there has been a growing interest in implementation studies in the United States dating from the 1970s and 1980s. Majone and Wildavsky (1984: 163) have described the study of implementation in the United States as 'a growth industry'. The pioneering work of Pressman and Wildavsky (1973) in analysing the difficulties encountered by the Economic Development Administration in implementing the Oakland Project was followed by Bardach (1977), Radin (1977), Van Horn (1979), Brigham and Brown (1980), Edwards (1980; 1984), Nakamura and Smallwood (1980), Williams (1980), Mazmanian and Sabatier (1981; 1983), Mann (1982), Levin and Ferman (1985), May and Williams (1986), Ripley and Franklin (1986), Shumavon and Hibbeln (1986), Frazier (1992) and Peck and Six (2006).

The second trend is the focus on comparative studies on policy implementation in the United States and other countries. The case studies on implementation compiled by Lewis and Wallace (1984) focus on race relations, employment and industrial strategy in the United Kingdom, cutting public expenditure in California, and two chapters on the European Community. The two comparative chapters deal with defence collaboration and education in the United Kingdom and the United States. Meyer (1993) compares the problems in implementing economic development projects in the United Kingdom and the United States. Echeverri-Gent (1993) has compared the implementation of government policy towards the rural poor in India and the United States. Rose-Ackerman

(1995) analyses the implementation of environmental policy in Germany and the United States and argues that policy-makers in both countries can learn from each other's experiences. Similarly, Lehmann (2000) compares environmental policy implementation in Germany and the United States by analysing the detailed negotiations between industry, regulating agencies and third parties in both countries. The implementation of European Union environmental policy in Germany, Great Britain and Greece is compared in Heinelt et al. (2001). Berg (1999) examines the implementation of the European fisheries law in the Netherlands and the United Kingdom. The most recent example is the comparison of policy implementation in the Defense Advanced Research Projects Agency (DARPA) of the US Department of Defense with Japan's Ministry of International Trade and Industry (MITI) by Jordan and Koinis (2014).

The third trend is that there is still a significant research gap on policy implementation in Asian countries in spite of the research that has been done so far. The first reader on implementation in twelve Asian countries, edited by Iglesias (1976), focuses on agriculture and rural development in Malaysia, Nepal, Philippines and Sri Lanka; infrastructure and industrial development in India, Indonesia and Japan; housing and urban development in Hong Kong, Singapore and Thailand; and social development in Iran and South Korea. All the case studies were prepared by local scholars from the twelve countries. In his introduction, Iglesias (1976: xxvii) explained that the approach of his book was based on 'the need to examine the dynamics and the environmental and historical contexts impinging on the implementation process' especially the role of such factors as 'structure, leadership, support, resources and technology'. While the public bureaucracy's role in implementation was analysed in a few case studies, it was generally not emphasized in Iglesias's book as a whole.

Unlike Iglesias's pioneering volume, Grindle's (1980) reader consists of nine case studies on implementation in the Third World that are written by American scholars. Of the seven countries represented in the book, two are from Africa (Kenya and Zambia), four from Latin America (Brazil, Colombia, Mexico and Peru), and India is the only Asian country represented. The case studies in Grindle's book focus on rural electrification, health care and rural development in India; cooperative policy in Zambia; housing policy in Brazil, Colombia and Kenya; agrarian reform in Peru; and agricultural development in Mexico. According to Grindle (1980: 20), these case studies focus on 'what went wrong' in policy implementation and Grindle makes recommendations for 'avoiding similar outcomes in other contexts'.

The third major work is Warwick's (1982) excellent comparative study of the implementation of population policies in these eight countries: Dominican Republic, Egypt, Haiti, India, Kenya, Lebanon, Mexico and the Philippines. Warwick's book is an important contribution to the literature on policy implementation for three reasons. First, there is an explicit focus on the 'key actors in implementation: top-level officials, field implementers, opinion leaders' in Warwick's comparative analysis of implementation of population policies (6). Second, Warwick (1982: 163) emphasizes the 'significance of clients' because they 'can speed, slow, stop, or redirect implementation' of a service delivery programme. Finally, Warwick's book illustrates that it is possible and useful for scholars from different countries to collaborate on a cross-national project. As the project manager, Warwick worked closely with sixteen collaborators from the eight participating countries.

Five years later, a special issue of the *Southeast Asian Journal of Social Science* was devoted to 'The Public Bureaucracy and Policy Implementation in Asia'. This special issue, edited by Quah (1987a), focused on the public bureaucracy's role in policy implementation in Hong Kong, India, Indonesia, the Philippines, Singapore and Thailand. The articles on Hong Kong, Indonesia and the Philippines were written by three foreign scholars familiar with the public bureaucracies in these countries (Scott 1987; Warwick 1987; Richter 1987). The other three articles, on India, Singapore and Thailand, were authored by local scholars (Jain 1987; Quah 1987c; Voradej and Likhit 1987). All six articles adopted a common analytical framework and focused on: the policy context, a profile of the civil service and civil servants, the policy-making process with emphasis on policy implementation, evaluation of the public bureaucracy's role in policy implementation and lessons to be drawn from the country's experience in policy implementation. An analysis of the six country studies shows that Hong Kong and Singapore were effective in policy implementation because of their governments' commitment and support and their effective public bureaucracies. In contrast, India, the Philippines and Thailand were ineffective in policy implementation because of the lack of governmental commitment and the ineffectiveness of their public bureaucracies (Quah 1987b: xv). However, according to Warwick (1987: 53), Indonesia occupied an intermediate position as its bureaucracy was ineffective in policy implementation if judged by conventional criteria, but if field criteria were used, then the Indonesian civil service was effective in policy implementation.

The fourth trend is that research on policy implementation in Asian countries has focused on case or country studies rather than comparative cross-national studies. China and the Philippines are the two Asian countries where the most research has been undertaken on policy implementation. For China, the studies are: Ross 1984; White 1985; Zweig 1985 ; Lampton 1987; Manion 1991; Chung 1993; Lee 1993; Chow 1994; Sinkule and Ortolano 1995; Lee 1997; Hsu 1998; Huang 1998; Yu 1999; Chan 2001; Zheng, Lu and White 2009; Burns and Zhou 2010; Gobel 2011; and Ahlers 2014. Similarly, in the case of the Philippines, research on policy implementation has been conducted by Varela (1976); Hanisch (1977; 1978); Wurfel (1977); Richter (1980; 1982); Ledesma and Tizon-Montinola (1988); Tadem (1993); Riedinger (1995); Reyes (2007; 2009a; 2009b); and Brillantes and Flores (2011). Other Asian countries where research has been done on policy implementation include: Bangladesh (Barenstein 1994), Hong Kong (Scott 1986; 2005), India (Vepa 1974; Jain 1984; Bussell 2012), Indonesia (Emmerson 1978; Rohdewohld 2003; Synnerstrom 2007; Prasojo 2011; Brata 2014; Suhardiman 2015), Japan (Muramatsu and Krauss 1984; Cothran 1987), Malaysia (Ness 1967; Puthucheary 1970; Esman 1972; Shamsul 1983; Nik Rosnah 2011), Singapore (Jones 1998; 2001; Neo and Chen 2007; Quah 1982a; 2010), Thailand (Kraiyudht 1989; Leoseng and Zimmermann 2005; Thandee 1985) and Vietnam (Fritzen 2005; Acuña-Alfaro 2009; Davidsen et al. 2009; Poon, Nguyen and Do 2009; Hausman 2010; Acuña-Alfaro and Do 2010).

While there is a plethora of country studies on policy implementation, there are few comparative studies on policy implementation in Asian countries. The pioneering study by Gable and Springer (1976) analysed the implementation of rice production programmes in Indonesia, the Philippines, South Korea and Thailand. In his Foreword, Riggs considers Gable and Springer's book as 'a major landmark' because it has made 'an extremely important and truly original contribution to the fields of comparative and development administration' (p. xxiii). Springer and Gable (1980) continued their comparative research on the four rice production programmes by analysing the impact of informal relations on organizational rewards. Cheema and Rondelli (1983) and Rondinelli (1983) have focused on the implementation of decentralization programmes in Asian countries. Cloete (2000) compared the effectiveness of the public bureaucracies in delivering public services in Indonesia, Malaysia, the Philippines, Singapore and Thailand. Finally, Quah (1982b) examined the implementation of anti-corruption measures in Indonesia, Malaysia, the Philippines, Singapore and Thailand. His most recent work focuses on the implementation of anti-corruption measures in these ten Asian countries: Hong Kong SAR, India, Indonesia, Japan, Mongolia, the Philippines, Singapore, South Korea, Taiwan and Thailand (Quah 2011).

1.3 Purpose and approach

The review of literature in section 1.2 has shown that research on policy implementation has focused on country studies that outnumber the comparative studies. The ASEAN Integration Through Law (ITL) Project's focus on the public bureaucracy's role in policy implementation in Indonesia, Malaysia, the Philippines, Singapore and Vietnam is therefore timely and appropriate as it addresses the significant research gap on policy implementation in these five ASEAN countries. The purpose of this chapter is to provide a comparative overview of the role of the public bureaucracies in policy implementation in these countries. This comparative overview is based on the five country studies in Chapters 2–6 in this book and the relevant published literature.

Van Meter and Van Horn's model of the policy implementation process is adopted as the framework for analysing the public bureaucracy's role in the five countries because of their focus on both public and private individuals and their emphasis on the importance of the policy context. Van Meter and Van Horn (1975: 447) define policy implementation as: 'those actions by public and private individuals (or groups) that are directed at the achievement of objectives set forth in prior policy decisions'. Their model focuses on the 'economic, social, and political conditions' or policy context and the following five aspects: (1) definition of policy standards and objectives; (2) policy resources; (3) interorganizational communication and enforcement activities; (4) characteristics of the implementing agencies; and (5) disposition of the implementers (462–74).

Before proceeding to analyse the public bureaucracy's role in policy implementation in the five countries, it is necessary to describe their policy context, the profile of their public bureaucracies and their role in policy formulation.

To illustrate the public bureaucracies' role in policy implementation, the penultimate section of this chapter evaluates the implementation of the ASEAN Cosmetic Directive (ACD) and the ASEAN Declaration on Transnational Crime of 1997, which is administered by the ASEAN Ministerial Meeting on Transnational Crime (AMMTC) and the Senior Officials Meeting on Transnational Crime (SOMTC) in the five ASEAN countries. These two different policies are selected as case studies to demonstrate the different levels of effectiveness of the public bureaucracies in policy implementation in the five countries. The concluding section identifies the factors responsible for effective policy implementation in the five ASEAN countries and explains why they have been more effective in implementing the ACD than the AMMTC/SOMTC.

1.4 Policy context

The policy context refers to all those aspects of the environment in the five ASEAN countries that influence the formulation, implementation and evaluation of public policies. The most comprehensive definition of 'policy context' is provided by Leichter (1979: 41–2) who defines 'policy context' in terms of the interaction between the thirty-seven situational, structural, cultural and environmental factors that influence the public policy-making process.

Why is policy context important in the formulation and implementation of public policies? Warwick (1979: 296–310) has found that the socio-historical and political contexts shaped both the contents and process of policy formulation and the implementation of population programmes in Egypt, Kenya, Mexico and the Philippines. Honadle (1999: 2) contends that context is important for environmental policy for three reasons. First, context determines the substance of a policy because 'a policy that is appropriate in one locale may lead to disastrous results in another'. Second, context influences policy formulation because 'without contextual sensitivity, effective policies may never be developed'. Third, contextual maps are needed for policy implementation because 'context stands in the way of the transformation of pronouncement into performance, and context changes over time'.

The policy context refers to the geographical, historical, economic, demographic, political and legal aspects of a country's environment that influence the nature and style of public policy formulation and implementation. A country's policy context can promote or hinder the public bureaucracy's role in policy implementation depending on whether the contextual factors are conducive or hostile to the implementation of public policies. Caiden (1969: 166–83) has identified seven 'outstanding universal obstacles' to administrative reform, namely geography, history, technology, culture, economy, society and polity, which can promote or hinder its public bureaucracy's role in policy implementation. Similarly, Spector (2012: 275) concludes from the application of his framework for assessing corruption in Honduras, Senegal, Timor-Leste and Ukraine that 'context can make a big difference in the capacity of countries, as well as their motivation, to seriously address corruption problems'.

The following five aspects of the policy context can assist or hinder the public bureaucracy's role in policy implementation.

1. *Size of the country.* The public bureaucracy in a large country or archipelago will encounter more difficulties in policy implementation in the provinces or outer islands than the public bureaucracy in a small country.
2. *Colonial legacy.* Is the colonial legacy positive or negative for the public bureaucracy's role in policy implementation in terms of promoting meritocracy, developing infrastructure and investing in the educational system?
3. *Gross domestic product per capita.* The public bureaucracy in a poor country will have more difficulty in policy implementation than will the public bureaucracy in an affluent country if the former does not have adequate financial and technical resources.
4. *Size of the population.* The public bureaucracy in a country with a small population will encounter less difficulty in policy implementation than will the public bureaucracy in a country with a large population.
5. *Nature of the political system.* The public bureaucracy in a stable, democratic and incorrupt political system with rule of law will be more effective in policy implementation than its counterpart in an unstable, authoritarian and corrupt political system without rule of law (Quah 2011: 30–1).

1.4.1 Geography

In terms of land area, Indonesia is the largest archipelago in the world, with 17,508 islands covering 1,904,443 sq. km.

Table 1.1 *The policy context in the five ASEAN countries*

Country	Land area (sq. km)	Colonial legacy	GDP per capita (2013)	Population (2013)	Political system
Indonesia	1,904,443	Dutch	US$3,510	248 million	presidential democracy
Malaysia	332,665	British	US$10,548	29.6 million	constitutional monarchy
Philippines	300,000	Spanish; US	US$2,790	97.5 million	presidential democracy
Singapore	716	British	US$54,776	5.4 million	parliamentary democracy
Vietnam	331,114	French	US$1,902	89.7 million	communist state

Sources: The Economist 2013: 160, 178, 196, 240; Schwab 2014: 401–2.

Table 1.1 shows that Malaysia is the second largest country, followed by Vietnam, the Philippines and Singapore, which has the smallest land area of 716 sq. km. This means that Indonesia is 2,660 times larger than Singapore, more than six times larger than the Philippines and almost six times larger than Vietnam and Malaysia. Like Indonesia, the Philippines is an archipelago of 7,107 islands, and highly fragmented, with its islands spread over 1,295,000 sq. km of ocean.

Among the five countries, Indonesia faces the most difficult challenges in implementing the government's policies across its vast domain, which stretches for 5,120 km from east to west, and for nearly 2,000 km from north to south (Sidik 2007: 23). Furthermore, its geographical location between the Tropic of Cancer and the Tropic of Capricorn makes Indonesia vulnerable to earthquakes, tsunamis, tropical cyclones and floods (Frost 2002: 25). Apart from causing serious economic and physical damage and casualties, the frequency of these natural disasters hinders policy implementation in Indonesia.

Similarly, the archipelagic nature of the Philippines has resulted in 'considerable fragmentation' and its mountainous nature has made 'intra-island interaction more difficult', especially in Mindanao (Timberman 1991: 4). Like Indonesia, the Philippines is also vulnerable to earthquakes as it has twenty-two active volcanoes, and experiences more than twenty typhoons a year (Bankoff 2005: 165). The fragmented nature of the Philippines and its vulnerability to earthquakes and typhoons has made the task of policy implementation more difficult for the public bureaucracy, especially in the provinces and rural areas.

In its SWOT (Strengths, Weaknesses, Opportunities and Threats) study of seven Asian countries, the Political and Economic Risk Consultancy (PERC) (2011: 24–6) found that the Philippines has the highest natural disaster disruption potential (9/10), followed by Indonesia (8/10), Vietnam (7/10) and Malaysia (3/10). Singapore was excluded from the study and is not affected by earthquakes or typhoons because of its favourable geographical location. Table 1.2 confirms that Indonesia was the most severely affected by natural disasters during 2000–2009, followed by the Philippines, Vietnam and Malaysia, in descending order. This means that the vulnerability of these countries to natural disasters is an important constraint affecting their public bureaucracies' capacity in policy implementation.

Table 1.2 *Disaster statistics in four Asian countries, 2000–2009*

Country	Disasters	Deaths	Persons affected	Cost of damage
Indonesia	154	179,875	11,748,000	US$12,573,740
Philippines	146	9,535	50,152,000	US$2,225,040
Vietnam	82	3,533	20,914,000	US$5,055,210
Malaysia	34	267	461,000	US$1,501,000

Source: PERC 2011: 24.

1.4.2 *Colonial legacy*

Tan (2000: 21) contends that the colonial heritage of the Asian countries is an important factor influencing their subsequent development. According to Tan:

> While the city states of Singapore and Hong Kong, and the other East Asian countries (South Korea and Taiwan) benefited from their colonial heritage in terms of infrastructural development, educational attainment and commercial development, the same cannot be said of other South and Southeast Asian countries . . . Where colonies were acquired for the expansion of trade (as in Singapore and Hong Kong), or for the production of food (as in South Korea and Taiwan), the colonial powers often made large investment in infrastructure, education and agriculture. This was less likely to be the case where colonies were acquired primarily to extract raw materials, or to produce cash crops for exports. (Tan 2000: 19)

The impact of the colonial legacy on the public bureaucracies' role in policy implementation varies in the five ASEAN countries depending on the colonizers. In terms of their former colonial backgrounds, Indonesia was colonized by the Dutch, Malaysia and Singapore by the British, the Philippines by the Spanish and the Americans, and Vietnam by the French. Darling (1979: 242–3) has argued that the degree of harshness of the Western colonization process was low for the Philippines and Malaya (including Singapore), and high for Indonesia and Vietnam.

The Dutch colonial legacy in Indonesia was negative for three reasons. First, as the Dutch were interested in Indonesia for its raw materials and spices, they did not invest in infrastructure or educate the local population (Tan 2000: 13). Second, the Dutch system of indirect rule in Indonesia was a farce as all the native rulers 'were reduced to mere servants of the colonial administration, inferior in everything except matters of ceremony' (Pluvier 1974: 14). Third, unlike the British, the Dutch did not introduce the tradition of meritocracy as they did not rely on merit to recruit the local civil servants, who were instead selected by hereditary succession (Quah 2011: 361). Consequently, as Warwick (1978: 3) has astutely observed, 'the Dutch left behind no workable model of public administration, and had done little to train Indonesians for responsible positions'. Indeed, the lack of a meritocratic tradition in the Indonesian public bureaucracy, which is reflected in the importance of patronage in the recruitment and promotion of civil servants, has increased the vulnerability of the public bureaucrats to corruption and undermines their capacity to implement public policies effectively (Quah 2011: 363).

By contrast, the British colonial legacy in Malaysia and Singapore has been much more positive than the Dutch colonial legacy in Indonesia. Realizing the importance of infrastructure in transport and communications, and an educated population for international trade, the British 'invested heavily in roads, railways and harbours, and educated the local populations in their colonies in the language of international trade, science and technology, English' (Tan 2000: 11). The British built a modern transport system from the north of the Malayan peninsula to the south in Singapore, which served as the major port through which raw materials were shipped, and manufactured goods were imported. Accordingly, extensive port and storage facilities, ship-chandlery and bunkering facilities, and banking and insurance industries were developed by the British to service the many ships passing through Singapore and to provide financial services for the importers and exporters. More importantly, the British system of justice and public administration was established in Malaya and Singapore to provide the legal and administrative framework for commerce (Tan 2000: 12). Treisman (2000: 31–2, 46) found that former British colonies with common law legal systems had significantly lower perceived corruption because of their 'superior administration of justice' and their 'preoccupation with procedural fairness even at the expense of social hierarchy'.

Perhaps the most important reform introduced by the British colonial government in Singapore was the introduction of meritocracy, with the establishment of the Public Service Commission (PSC) on 1 January 1951 to ensure that the recruitment and promotion of civil servants was based on merit and to accelerate the pace of localization in the civil service. The People's Action Party (PAP) government, which assumed power after winning the May 1959 general election, has retained the PSC to attract the 'best and brightest' Singaporeans to join the civil service by awarding scholarships to the best students in each cohort (Quah 2010: 74, 91).

The PSC was formed in the Federation of Malaya on 31 August 1957, ten years after the original recommendation by the *Report of the Public Services Salaries Commission of Malaya, 1947* (Tilman 1961: 183–8). However, the merit principle has not been adhered to fully in Malaysia because of the introduction in 1952 by the British colonial government of the quota system which specified the recruitment of one non-Malay candidate for every four Malay candidates admitted into the Malayan Civil Service (MCS). The *raison d'être* for the quota system was to preserve the special position of the Malays by ensuring their dominance in the MCS (Puthucheary 1978: 47, 53–4). According to the Constitution of Malaysia, there should be no discrimination against citizens 'on the ground only of religion, race, descent or place of birth . . . in the appointment to any office or employment under a public authority' except in the case of the reservation of positions in the Administrative and Diplomatic Service (ADS) for the indigenous group, i.e., the Malays or *Bumiputeras* (quoted in Elyas 1980: 256). Thus, the quota system not only gives rise to 'protective discrimination' for the *Bumiputeras* but also ensures that they will be recruited in adequate numbers in the MCS.

The Philippines was colonized by the Spanish for 333 years, from 1565 to 1898, and by the Americans for forty-eight years, from 1898 to 1946. The Spanish colonial administration was concerned with commercial profit and spreading their religion. Corruption was introduced to the Philippines by the Spanish as the 'low salaries and poor working conditions of the bureaucrats and the many opportunities available for corrupt behaviour contributed to the widespread corruption in the colonial bureaucracy' (Quah 1982b: 158). A public office was viewed as a grant or favour from the king during the Spanish colonial period and 'many bureaucrats actually treated the transaction as a business – selling an office at a profit and buying a more lucrative one' (Endriga 1979: 247–9). Indeed, according to Corpuz (1957: 129), the most serious weakness of the Spanish colonial bureaucracy was the 'internal moral corruption of its members'.

Unlike the Spanish, the Americans adopted a secular colonial policy that provided Filipinos with more opportunities for participating in the affairs of their country. This was reflected in the establishment of a modern civil service by the Americans and their efforts to localize it. The First Philippine Commission recommended the creation of an efficient and non-partisan civil service in 1899. On 19 September 1900, the Second Philippine Commission passed an act for the establishment and maintenance of an efficient and honest civil service in the Philippines (Corpuz 1957: 191). Thus, an important legacy of American colonial rule is the introduction of meritocracy in the Philippines. Furthermore, the American colonial bureaucracy was incorrupt because the bureaucrats received higher salaries and corrupt officials were promptly prosecuted (Endriga 1979: 254). However, these two positive aspects of American colonial rule in the Philippines have not endured following the attainment of independence in July 1946 because the contemporary public bureaucracy is afflicted by rampant corruption and relies on patronage rather than merit in the recruitment and promotion of civil servants. Indeed, *utang na loob*, or 'debt of gratitude', encourages nepotism in the Philippines because public officials readily perform favours for their relatives, including the appointment of unqualified persons (Quah 2011: 132).

The French consolidated their influence in Indochina from the middle of the nineteenth century and in 1887 a unified French colonial administration was established in Indochina which marked the culmination of French colonial rule in Southeast Asia. They monopolized economic activity in Indochina and controlled most of its finance and trade. In 1906, they introduced French education and also established tertiary education. Unlike the British, the French 'did little to develop their Southeast Asian colonies, and concentrated on the export of primary products from these territories' (Tan 2000: 15). By contrast with the British, who were 'more concerned with training efficient bureaucracies than in developing democratic political institutions', the French introduced political and administrative institutions in Indochina by imposing 'a complex system of direct and indirect colonial rule which transferred few important government skills to indigenous persons' (Darling 1979: 128, 131). The French did not train and promote Vietnamese civil servants to higher-level administrative positions except 'in the field where they had little actual authority or responsibility commensurate with their positions'. Consequently, the departure of the French administrative personnel when Vietnam became independent left a huge vacuum because the Vietnamese officials who replaced them had little administrative experience (Rose and Vu 1961: 1). In short, apart from introducing education, the French did not invest in infrastructure, introduce meritocracy or provide training for the Vietnamese civil servants. Von der Mehden's (1969: 22) criticism of the 'poor preparation for self-government' by most colonial administrations applies to the French colonial legacy in Vietnam.

1.4.3 *Economic development*

Table 1.1 demonstrates the disparity in level of economic development among the five ASEAN countries as reflected in their GDP per capita, which ranges from US$1,902 for Vietnam to US$54,776 for Singapore. This means that Singapore is about twenty-eight times richer than Vietnam, almost twenty times richer than the Philippines, nearly sixteen times richer than Indonesia and more than five times richer than Malaysia. As policies cannot be implemented without financial resources, the public bureaucracies in Singapore and Malaysia are provided with sufficient budgets to implement their public policies in view of their higher GDP per capita. On the other hand, the lower GDP per capita of Indonesia, the Philippines and Vietnam means that their public bureaucracies have not been allocated with adequate financial resources for policy implementation. For example, the budgets of the military and police in Indonesia provide only about one-third of the funds needed by them. Consequently, military and police personnel are forced to meet the shortfall in expenditure by relying on extorting payments from private corporations and involvement in illegal logging, mining, fishing, cattle rustling, smuggling, gambling, narcotics and prostitution (Crouch 2003: 21).

1.4.4 *Population*

The size of the population in a country is an important factor influencing the magnitude of its problems. Indonesia's population of 248 million is the fourth largest in the world, after China, India and the United States, and is forty-six times larger than Singapore's population of 5.4 million. The Philippines has a population of 97.5 million, followed by Vietnam's population of 89.7 million and Malaysia's population of 29.6 million.

1.4.5 *Political system*

In terms of their political systems, Indonesia and the Philippines are presidential democracies, Malaysia is a constitutional monarchy, Singapore is a parliamentary democracy and Vietnam is a communist state. The World Bank's governance indicator on voice and accountability refers to 'the extent of which citizens can participate in the selection of their governments; and the independence of the media, which monitor those in authority and hold them accountable for their actions' (Kaufmann, Kraay and Mastruzzi 2004: 3). Table 1.3 shows that even though four of these countries are democracies, their percentile ranks for voice and accountability are not high, with the Philippines having an average percentile rank of 49.8, followed by Singapore (46.5), Indonesia (41.1) and Malaysia (36.8). As Vietnam is a

Table 1.3 *Voice and accountability in the five ASEAN countries, 1996–2013*

Year	Indonesia	Malaysia	Philippines	Singapore	Vietnam
1996	23.6	50.0	55.8	55.3	16.8
1998	17.3	40.9	60.1	54.3	9.1
2000	34.1	39.9	53.4	54.3	12.0
2002	39.4	36.5	52.4	49.5	8.2
2003	37.0	33.2	51.4	42.3	6.7
2004	40.4	41.3	51.0	49.0	8.7
2005	45.2	42.8	48.6	51.4	8.7
2006	43.3	32.2	45.2	35.6	7.7
2007	46.6	32.2	45.2	35.6	8.2
2008	46.6	30.3	44.7	37.0	8.2
2009	46.9	31.8	48.3	40.8	8.1
2010	47.9	33.6	48.3	40.8	8.5
2011	47.9	32.4	47.4	46.9	8.5
2012	51.2	37.9	46.9	53.1	9.5
2013	48.8	37.4	47.9	52.1	11.8
Averages	41.1	36.8	49.8	46.5	9.4

Source: compiled from World Bank 2014a.

communist state, it is not surprising that it has the lowest average percentile rank of 9.4.

The World Bank's governance indicator of political stability and absence of violence or terrorism focuses on the 'perceptions of the likelihood that the government in power will be stabilized or overthrown by possibly unconstitutional and/or violent means, including domestic violence and terrorism' (Kaufmann, Kraay and Mastruzzi 2004: 3). Table 1.4 confirms that Singapore is the most politically stable country, with an average percentile rank of 88.2, followed by Vietnam

Table 1.4 *Political stability in the five ASEAN countries, 1996–2013*

Year	Indonesia	Malaysia	Philippines	Singapore	Vietnam
1996	13.0	62.0	30.3	85.1	58.7
1998	6.3	39.4	32.7	75.0	54.3
2000	3.4	47.6	11.1	81.3	58.7
2002	8.7	61.1	18.8	88.5	54.8
2003	2.9	60.1	7.2	76.4	48.1
2004	4.3	56.7	5.3	86.5	51.0
2005	7.2	64.9	13.5	87.0	61.5
2006	9.6	54.3	8.2	93.8	57.2
2007	13.0	50.0	8.2	89.9	52.9
2008	15.3	46.9	8.1	96.2	49.8
2009	20.9	42.2	5.7	89.6	52.1
2010	20.8	51.9	5.2	89.6	50.9
2011	22.2	49.5	9.9	91.0	53.3
2012	28.0	44.1	14.2	96.7	54.5
2013	28.9	47.9	16.6	95.7	55.9
Averages	13.6	51.9	13.0	88.2	54.2

Source: compiled from World Bank 2014a.

(54.2 percentile rank), Malaysia (51.9 percentile rank), Indonesia (13.6 percentile rank) and the Philippines (13.0 percentile rank).

The perceived level of corruption in the five ASEAN countries is ascertained by their performance on these five indicators: (1) World Bank's control of corruption indicator in 2013; (2) Transparency International's Corruption Perceptions Index (CPI) rank and score in 2014; (3) PERC's rank and score in its 2014 survey on corruption; (4) *Global Competitiveness Report*'s Public trust of politicians score in 2014; and (5) World Bank's ease of doing business rank in 2014. Table 1.5 provides details of the perceived level of corruption in the five ASEAN countries according to these five indicators. Table 1.5 shows that Singapore is perceived to be the least corrupt, followed by Malaysia, the Philippines, Vietnam and Indonesia, in descending order.

According to Kaufmann, Kraay and Mastruzzi (2004: 4), the rule of law focuses on those indicators that 'measure the extent to which agents have confidence in and abide by the rules of society', namely 'perceptions of the incidence of crime, the effectiveness and predictability of the judiciary, and the enforceability of contracts'. These indicators measure a society's success in 'developing an environment in which fair and predictable rules form the basis for economic and social interactions, and importantly, the extent to which property rights are protected'. Table 1.6 shows that, in terms of the rule of law, Singapore ranks first, with 92.5 percentile rank, followed by Malaysia (64.7 percentile rank), the Philippines (39.6 percentile rank), Vietnam (39.4 percentile rank) and Indonesia (29.7 percentile rank).

In sum, as shown in Table 1.7, Singapore has the most stable and least corrupt political system with the highest degree of rule of law. The political systems of Malaysia and Vietnam are second and third in terms of political stability, perceived level of corruption and the rule of law. Finally, among the five ASEAN countries, the Philippines and Indonesia are politically unstable and perceived to be very corrupt countries with a low degree of rule of law.

Table 1.5 *Perceived level of corruption in the five ASEAN countries, 2013–2014*

Country	**World Bank's control of corruption indicator (2013)**	**Transparency International's Corruption Perceptions Index rank and score[a] (2014)**	**Political and Economic Risk Consultancy's (PERC) rank and score[b] (2014)**	***Global Competitiveness Report*'s Public trust of politicians score[c] (2014)**	**World Bank's ease of doing business rank (2014)**
Indonesia	31.6	107th (34)	15th (8.85)	37th (3.6)	120th
Malaysia	68.4	50th (52)	7th (5.25)	17th (4.7)	6th
Philippines	43.5	85th (38)	11th (7.85)	89th (2.6)	108th
Singapore	96.7	7th (84)	1st (0.74)	1st (6.2)	1st
Vietnam	36.8	119th (31)	14th (8.73)	49th (3.4)	99th
Number of countries	215	175	16	144	189

[a] The CPI score ranges from 0 (highly corrupt) to 100 (very clean).

[b] The PERC score ranges from 0 (least corrupt) to 10 (most corrupt).

[c] The public trust of politicians score ranges from 1 (very low) to 7 (very high).

Sources: Transparency International 2014; *Asian Intelligence* 2014: 4; World Bank 2013: 3; 2014a; and Schwab 2014: 409.

Table 1.6 *Rule of law in the five ASEAN countries, 1996–2013*

Year	Indonesia	Malaysia	Philippines	Singapore	Vietnam
1996	39.7	65.1	50.7	89.5	37.3
1998	27.3	61.2	52.2	90.0	39.2
2000	28.7	60.8	38.3	87.6	41.6
2002	20.1	64.1	38.3	90.9	34.0
2003	20.6	67.9	36.4	93.3	38.3
2004	25.4	68.4	34.4	94.7	37.8
2005	25.4	65.6	42.1	95.7	45.9
2006	28.2	65.6	44.0	92.3	42.1
2007	30.6	64.6	39.2	92.3	42.6
2008	31.3	61.1	36.1	92.3	41.3
2009	34.6	64.5	34.1	91.9	39.8
2010	31.8	65.9	33.6	92.9	34.6
2011	31.9	64.8	35.7	93.4	39.4
2012	34.1	65.9	36.5	95.7	37.9
2013	36.5	64.5	41.7	95.3	39.3
Averages	29.7	64.7	39.6	92.5	39.4

Source: compiled from World Bank 2014a.

Table 1.7 *Ranking of the five ASEAN countries for political stability, perceived level of corruption and rule of law*

Country	Political stability rank	Corruption rank	Rule of law rank	Overall rank
Singapore	1st	1st	1st	1st
Malaysia	3rd	2nd	2nd	2nd
Vietnam	2nd	4th	4th	3rd
Philippines	5th	3rd	3rd	4th
Indonesia	4th	5th	5th	5th

Sources: compiled from Tables 1.4, 1.5 and 1.6.

1.4.6 Legal system

Before proceeding to describe the profile of the public bureaucracies in the five ASEAN countries, it is necessary to provide a brief description of their legal systems, which have been influenced by their colonial heritage. As mentioned earlier, Indonesia was colonized by the Dutch, Malaysia and Singapore by the British, the Philippines by the Spanish and the Americans, and Vietnam by the French.

Indonesia has a 'pluralistic legal system' which has been influenced by *adat* law, *syariah* law and Dutch colonial law and statutes. Before the advent of the Dutch in 1602, the various groups in the Indonesian archipelago were administered according to *adat* or customary law and *syariah* or Islamic law. Dutch colonial rule from 1602 to 1945 introduced the civil law system to Indonesia and the 'natives were governed by the prevailing *adat* law and *syariah* law, and correspondingly the Europeans and foreign Orientals were governed by Dutch law'. The Dutch colonial laws remained after the attainment of independence on 17 August 1945 and coexist with *adat* law and Islamic law (Rajenthran 2002: 2–3).

The Indonesian legal system consists of the 1945 Constitution, followed by the decrees of the *Majelis Permusyarawatan Rakyat* (MPR or People's Consultative Assembly) and the laws or statutes enacted by the *Dewan Perwakilan Rakyat* (DPR or House of Representatives), and ratified by the President. These laws authorize the government to regulate the detailed implementation of certain areas covered by them in the form of government regulations, which are passed by the Cabinet or by the President himself in the name of the

Cabinet. Furthermore, Presidential Decrees and Presidential Instructions provide detailed stipulations with legal impact for administrative activities, while Ministerial Decrees are detailed guidelines for the administration in specific or technical fields (Rohdewohld 1995: 18). Law No. 8 of Year 1974 on 'Fundamentals of Civil Service' replaced Law No. 18 of Year 1961 on 'Main Provisions of Civil Service' and gave the President the authority to administer civilian public servants (Manurung 1980: 137).

Malaysia is a constitutional monarchy and parliamentary democracy based on the Westminster model. As a former British colony, English common law and rules of equity were adopted under the Civil Law Act of 1956 and further developed by the Malaysian courts according with local circumstances. The written Federal Constitution is the supreme law of the land and recognizes Islam as the official religion but also guarantees freedom of religion and other rights. While the majority of the population is Muslim, *syariah* law is applied only in personal matters to Muslims who use the *syariah* courts. Customary law in West Malaysia includes Malay customary law, Hindu law and *syariah* law, while its counterpart in East Malaysia consists of Malay customary law, native customary law and Chinese and Hindu customary law (World Bank 2011: 2–3).

The Federal Constitution of Malaysia covers such essential aspects of the public services as appointment, dismissal, reduction in rank, secondment and protection of pension rights. Civil servants derive their executive authority from ministers where the law allows a delegation of powers. Delegation is done by gazette notification and is covered by the Delegation Ordinance. In their executive and administrative actions, civil servants are responsible to their respective ministers. Civil servants are also endowed with authority by legislation as provided by article 39 of the Federal Constitution (Elyas 1980: 255–6).

As the Philippines was colonized by the Spanish and the Americans, its legal system is a combination of continental civil law and the Anglo-American common law system. For example, the Revised Penal Code is mostly derived from Spanish criminal law while the commercial laws are based on US laws. The 1987 Constitution is also modelled after the US Constitution. The laws enacted by Congress are called 'Republic Acts' followed by their appropriate number. Regulatory agencies and departments of the government under the executive branch also issue implementing rules or administrative regulations to implement the laws passed by Congress. These agencies or departments derive their authority through delegation by Congress (Bautista 2010).

Furthermore, authority over and responsibility for operations may be delegated to bureau directors and regional directors to ensure the effective implementation of plans and programmes. However, the extent of such delegation is influenced by the need for economy, efficiency and effective implementation of national and local programmes according to the policies and standards developed by the departments. The regional field offices are the operating arms of the bureaus and are directly responsible to the bureau director for their operations (Tendero 2000: 68).

As a former British colony, it is not surprising that 'the main influence of the Singapore's legal system' is the

English common law tradition (Bell 1999: 12). However, with the attainment of independence in August 1965, there has been a gradual movement towards developing an 'autochthonous' legal system by adopting those legal practices or norms which are compatible with Singapore's cultural, social and economic requirements, especially during the late 1980s, and after the appointment of Yong Pung How as the Chief Justice in September 1990 (Tan and Chan 2011). Hence, Singapore's legal system relies on both common law (for contract, trust and equity, property and tort law) and parliamentary statutes (for criminal, company and family law).

The legal framework of the Singapore Civil Service (SCS) can be found in Part IX of the Constitution of Singapore, which focuses on the public service in Articles 102–119. Articles 105–110 specify the number, tenure and terms of service of the PSC members and their functions. Singapore's system of administrative law requires ministers, civil servants and public agencies to act fairly and in accordance with the law. Civil servants are required to follow the administrative and financial procedures described in the five instructional manuals. Those civil servants who fail to comply with the instructions in these manuals will face disciplinary action (Lee 1980: 443).

Vietnam's legal system is the product of its imperial institutions, French colonial rule and the Soviet system of socialist administration. The Le Dynasty adopted Confucianism as the state ideology in the fifteenth century and the Vietnamese state was organized on the three pillars of the emperor, Confucian ideology and bureaucracy. The French maintained two parallel administrative and legal systems by applying French law to French citizens and Vietnamese law to Vietnamese citizens. The French colonial administration relied on law as the primary written record of government policy and implementation required a complex administrative and judicial system. French legalism had lingered for some years after independence but by the late 1970s it was displaced by the imported Soviet system of socialist administration (Gillespie 2002: 173–5).

The 1992 Constitution of Vietnam replaced revolutionary tradition with constitutional order and party organs were required to operate within the framework of the law. The National Assembly was exalted as the paramount state institution. Public administration reform was initiated in the mid-1990s and Article 1 of the Ordinance on Public Employees 1998 defined public employees as 'Vietnamese citizens who are on the State payroll and get paid from the State budget'. This broad definition consists not only of those employed in ministries, people's committees and local government, but also includes elected National Assembly delegates, army, police and teachers (Gillespie 2002: 175–6). The administrative laws in Vietnam include: the Ordinance on Dealing with Administrative Breaches; Ordinance on Resolution on Administrative Proceedings; Law on Customs; and Law on local administrative agencies.

1.5 Profile of the public bureaucracies

In his book, *The ICS: The Indian Civil Service*, Blunt (1937: 1) used the term 'civil service' to differentiate the civilian employees of the English East India Company from those working in military, maritime and ecclesiastical organizations. Similarly, Pyper (1995: 1) describes civil servants as those who 'work for the "civil" as opposed to the military, ministerial or judicial arms of the state'. This means that 'members of the armed forces, government ministers and judges are not civil servants'. However, as the meaning of 'civil service' differs in the five ASEAN countries, the preferred term for this chapter and book is 'public bureaucracies', which refers to the governmental bureaucracies (Peabody and Rourke 1965: 803) in these countries and includes not only the civil service but also the statutory boards or public enterprises.

Malaysia's definition of the public service is the most comprehensive as it includes teachers, doctors, nurses, police, military officers and administrators at the federal, state and local governments. According to Article 132 of the Federal Constitution, the Malaysian public service consists of: (1) the Armed Forces, (2) the Judicial and the Legal Service, (3) the General Public Service of the Federation, (4) the Police Force, (5) the Railway Service, (6) the Joint Public Services, (7) the State Public Service and (8) the Education Service. The statutory boards and local authorities are also included as part of the public service because of their adoption of the same procedures for appointments, remuneration and terms and conditions of their service. Hence, it is not surprising that while Malaysia with 1.2 million civil servants in 2010 is ranked fourth, it has the most bureaucrats per 1,000 of the population with a ratio of 43 bureaucrats for every thousand Malaysians (see Table 1.8).

On the other hand, Singapore's public bureaucracy is the smallest with a total of 138,720 members in 2013 consisting

Table 1.8 *Size of the five ASEAN public bureaucracies, 2009–2013*

Country	**Number of bureaucrats**	**Population**	**Number of bureaucrats per 1,000 population**
Indonesia	4,375,009 (2014)	248 million (2013)	17.6
Malaysia	1,200,000 (2010)	27.9 million (2010)	43.0
Philippines	1,312,508 (2010)	93.6 million (2010)	14.0
Singapore	138,720 (2013)	5.4 million (2013)	25.7
Vietnam	1,900,000 (2009)	88.1 million (2009)	21.6

Sources: BKN 2014; Ali 2013: 31; Philippine Civil Service Commission 2010: 1; Department of Statistics 2014: 9, 63; Poon, Nguyen and Do 2009: 206; and Schwab 2011: 385; 2014: 401.

of 81,508 civil servants and 57,212 employees of the sixty-six statutory boards (Department of Statistics 2014: 63). Unlike the other four ASEAN countries, doctors and nurses are no longer considered as civil servants after the corporatization of the government hospitals in Singapore. Even though Singapore has the smallest public bureaucracy, it is ranked second after Malaysia with 25.7 bureaucrats per 1,000 of the population. While Indonesia has the largest public bureaucracy with 4,375,009 public officials, it has only 17.6 bureaucrats per 1,000 of the population. Vietnam's public bureaucracy in 2009 consisted of 1,900,000 officials, with 1,400,000 persons working in public service delivery agencies, 300,000 persons employed at the central, provincial and district levels, and 200,000 commune officials (Poon, Nguyen and Do 2009: 206). Vietnam is ranked third with 21.6 bureaucrats per 1,000 of the population. In 2010, the Philippines public bureaucracy had a total of 1,312,508 employees, with 834,327 persons (63.6 per cent) working in national government agencies, 383,422 persons (29.2 per cent) employed by local government units and 94,759 persons (7.2 per cent) working in government-owned and government-controlled corporations (Philippine Civil Service Commission 2010: 1). However, with its population of 93.6 million persons in 2010, the Philippines is ranked fifth with 14 bureaucrats per 1,000 of the population.

How effective are the public bureaucracies in the five ASEAN countries? Table 1.9 shows that, according to the World Bank's governance indicator on government effectiveness,[1] from 1996 to 2013, Singapore is the most effective with an average percentage rank of 98.9, followed by Malaysia (82.2 percentile rank), Vietnam (43.6 percentile rank), Indonesia (42.5 percentile rank) and the Philippines (40.6 percentile rank).

If the five ASEAN public bureaucracies are ranked in terms of their regulatory quality,[2] Table 1.10 confirms that

[1] Kaufmann, Kraay and Mastruzzi (2004: 3) define government effectiveness as 'the quality of public service provision, the quality of the bureaucracy, the competence of civil servants, the independence of the civil service from political pressures, and the credibility of the government's commitment to policies'.

[2] Regulatory quality refers to 'the incidence of market-unfriendly policies such as price controls or inadequate bank supervision, as well as perceptions of the burdens imposed by excessive regulation in areas such as foreign trade and business development' (Kaufmann, Kraay and Mastruzzi 2004: 4).

Table 1.9 *Government effectiveness of the five ASEAN countries, 1996–2013*

Year	Indonesia	Malaysia	Philippines	Singapore	Vietnam
1996	37.1	76.1	49.8	100.0	34.6
1998	29.3	77.6	57.1	100.0	42.0
2000	44.9	82.4	50.2	100.0	38.5
2002	38.0	81.5	53.7	93.7	37.6
2003	37.6	84.9	56.6	96.6	39.0
2004	44.4	84.9	48.8	96.1	41.0
2005	38.5	83.9	56.1	99.0	48.8
2006	43.9	85.4	53.7	99.5	48.8
2007	46.1	86.9	54.9	100.0	47.6
2008	46.6	83.5	56.8	100.0	47.1
2009	46.9	79.4	54.1	100.0	47.8
2010	47.8	82.8	55.5	100.0	45.9
2011	46.4	81.0	57.8	99.5	47.4
2012	44.0	80.4	57.9	99.5	44.5
2013	45.5	81.8	56.9	99.5	44.0
Averages	42.5	82.2	40.6	98.9	43.6

Source: compiled from World Bank (2014a).

Singapore is again the most effective, followed by Malaysia, the Philippines, Indonesia and Vietnam, in descending order.

The World Bank's evaluation of the government effectiveness and regulatory quality of the five ASEAN public bureaucracies is confirmed by PERC's assessment of their effectiveness from 1998 to 2012. Table 1.11 shows that, according to PERC, Singapore's public bureaucracy is ranked first with an average score of 2.24 from 1998 to 2012, followed by Malaysia (6.51), the Philippines (7.79), Vietnam (8.13) and Indonesia (8.22).

In sum, the five ASEAN public bureaucracies vary considerably in terms of their size and effectiveness.

Table 1.10 *Regulatory quality of the five ASEAN countries, 1996–2013*

Year	Indonesia	Malaysia	Philippines	Singapore	Vietnam
1996	57.4	72.5	59.8	100.0	28.4
1998	36.8	68.6	62.7	100.0	24.0
2000	41.7	68.1	56.9	100.0	22.1
2002	27.0	67.6	50.0	100.0	23.0
2003	20.6	68.1	52.5	99.0	29.4
2004	25.0	67.2	45.1	99.0	30.4
2005	31.4	68.6	51.5	99.5	28.4
2006	43.1	66.7	50.5	98.0	28.9
2007	41.7	68.0	51.5	98.1	31.1
2008	43.2	62.6	52.4	99.0	30.1
2009	39.7	61.7	50.7	97.6	29.2
2010	37.8	70.8	45.0	98.1	28.2
2011	40.8	71.1	44.5	96.2	31.3
2012	43.1	69.9	51.7	100.0	27.3
2013	46.4	72.2	51.7	100.0	28.2
Averages	38.4	68.2	51.8	99.0	28.0

Source: compiled from World Bank (2014a).

Singapore has the smallest but most effective public bureaucracy according to three indicators. Malaysia's public bureaucracy of 1.2 million employees is the second most effective after Singapore. On the other hand, the larger public bureaucracies of the Philippines, Vietnam and Indonesia are less effective than their counterparts in Singapore and Malaysia.

1.6 Policy formulation

Policy formulation is the first stage of the policy-making process, which 'involves the development of pertinent and acceptable proposed courses of action for dealing with public

Table 1.11 *PERC's effectiveness of the five ASEAN public bureaucracies, 1998–2012*

Year	Indonesia	Malaysia	Philippines	Singapore	Vietnam
		0 (most effective) – 10 (least effective)			
1998	7.91	6.14	7.00	2.73	9.25
2002	8.33	6.86	8.25	1.70	7.88
2004	7.25	7.00	7.42	1.63	8.14
2007	8.65	6.50	7.60	2.42	7.41
2009	8.50	6.21	8.33	2.45	7.60
2010	8.59	6.97	8.37	2.53	8.13
2012	8.37	5.89	7.57	2.25	8.54
Averages	8.22	6.51	7.79	2.24	8.13

Sources: Wong 2004; Hussain 2009; Lanka Business 2010 and *Economic Times* 2012.

problems' (Anderson 1979: 63). There are five steps in the policy formulation process: (1) the definition of the problem by the relevant policy-makers (usually the political leaders); (2) the identification of the causes of the problem; (3) the identification of the various alternatives for resolving the problem; (4) the selection of the most satisfactory alternative; (5) the operationalization of the selected alternative in terms of a particular policy or set of policies (Quah 1984: 113).

The Cabinet is the key institution responsible for policy formulation in the five ASEAN countries, although its role has evolved in tandem with political developments there. In Indonesia, the Cabinet formulates the President's policies for the thirty-four ministries during his five-year term of office. Chapter V, Article 17 of Law 1945 stipulates that: (1) the President receives assistance from ministers; (2) ministers are appointed and dismissed by the President; (3) every minister is responsible for certain portfolios within the government administration; (4) laws regulate the formation, reforms and dissolution of the state ministries. In Chapter 2, Agus Pramusinto observes that policy formulation in Indonesia during the post-Suharto era requires more time because the democratization of the political system has resulted in the demand for public consultation and the representation of more political parties in the National Assembly. Unlike the New Order regime of President Suharto, who relied on INPRES (*Instruksi Presiden* or Presidential Instruction) to expedite the policy formulation process, his successors cannot use the same mechanism. The senior civil servants in each ministry, especially the Secretary-General, Director-General and Inspector-General, are responsible for implementing the policies formulated by their minister. The other actors that have influenced the formulation of policies during the Reformation period are the international donor agencies, non-governmental organizations (NGOs) and the mass media, especially television and newspapers.

In Malaysia, the Cabinet is assisted in its role of policy formulation by the Prime Minister's Department, which coordinates the policies of the twenty-six ministries through the Cabinet Secretariat and the Chief Secretary, who is the Prime Minister's main adviser. The other three important agencies are: (1) the Economic Planning Unit (EPU), which formulates and evaluates the economic development plans; (2) the Implementation Coordination Unit (ICU), which ensures the efficiency of development projects and is an important source of policy initiatives; and (3) the

Malaysian Administrative Modernization and Management Planning Unit (MAMPU), which initiates reforms to enhance the quality, efficiency and effectiveness in the public service and serves as an inspectorate to oversee the implementation of administrative reforms in the state and federal agencies.

In the Philippines, executive power is vested in the President according to Article VII, Section 1 of the 1987 Constitution. This means that the President also has control over all the executive departments, bureaus and offices (Manuel 1999: 93). He is the chief administrator responsible for running the government as well as the chief domestic policy-maker who identifies the priorities for local development (Brillantes 1988: 129). However, the President's power has been curbed by the 1987 Constitution, which reacted to the abuses perpetuated by President Ferdinand Marcos during his imposition of martial law from 1972 to 1986, by introducing severe limitations on the presidency in order to 'prevent the rise of another Marcos' (Brillantes 1988: 128). The President is assisted in policy formulation by the Cabinet and the Presidential Management Staff (PMS), which was created by Executive Order No. 130 of 30 January 1987 as the primary government agency responsible for assisting the President in the overall management of the development process. The PMS 'translates presidential insights into operational terms' by providing data required for policy formulation, coordinating work with other government agencies, identifying alternative solutions and recommending these to the President (Tendero 2000: 91–4).

In Singapore, the Cabinet is the supreme policy-making body as it has 'the general direction and control of the government and is collectively responsible to Parliament' (Article 24[2] of the Constitution of the Republic of Singapore). Each minster has control of and direction of the civil servants in his ministry. The symbiotic relationship between a minister and his civil servants in policy formulation is described explicitly in *Instruction Manual* 4 thus:

> Ministers must be provided not only with information but also with considered advice on which they formulate policies and make important decisions. Civil servants are thus expected to provide the basis upon which important decisions are made and implemented by the Government. They are also expected to implement the decisions of Ministers in the most efficient manner. (quoted in Quah 1984: 113–14)

Thus, when policies are formulated at the political level by a minister or by the Cabinet as a whole, the role of the civil servants is to provide the necessary information, advice and past experience to the Cabinet, which will then discuss and evaluate the cabinet paper submitted by the civil servants before recommending an appropriate policy. When policies are not formulated at the cabinet level, they can result from the initiative of the civil servants, who are responsible for identifying the policy problem and the policy alternatives for dealing with it. For example, officials from the Ministry of Home Affairs received feedback from doctors regarding cases of young persons who had developed signs of brain damage from glue sniffing. Consequently, the Ministry recommended the launching of a national campaign against glue sniffing in February 1985. However, such instances of policy formulation by senior civil servants are few and constitute the exception rather than the rule (Quah 1984: 115). Indeed, the civil servants in Singapore usually behave as 'a trained apolitical body of professionals giving expert advice on, and carrying out the efficient implementation of, policy' (Kawin 1975: 335).

In addition to the political leaders and senior civil servants, the various elite groups in Singapore influence policy formulation in two ways. The first method is through their membership on statutory boards and advisory committees that provide technical information and assistance, 'review and make recommendations regarding proposed policy and programme changes and suggest new measures for official consideration'. Secondly, the elite groups also influence policy formulation through their participation in the chambers of commerce, trade associations and professional societies (Kawin 1975: 354–5). In their study 'Who runs Singapore?', George and Leow (1998: 36) identified 107 individuals 'holding full-time office in the executive, the civil service, the uniformed services, statutory boards, and government-owned corporations on January 1, 1998'. In 1999, the power elite in Singapore consisted of '226 individuals with 42 per cent from the bureaucratic elite, 41.6 per cent from the political elite, and 16.4 per cent from the business elite' (Quah 2001: 311).

Perhaps the most important change in policy-making in Singapore during the more than five decades under the PAP government is the change in leadership style from a paternalistic style under Prime Minister Lee Kuan Yew (June 1959 to November 1990) to a consultative style under Prime Minister Goh Chok Tong (November 1990 to August 2004) and Prime Minister Lee Hsien Loong (from August 2004).

As Lee Kuan Yew's successor, Goh Chok Tong softened Lee's authoritarian style by adopting a more consultative approach in policy-making and retained the policy on meritocracy, introduced competitive salaries for the public sector and improved the quality of service in the public bureaucracy (Quah 2009: 59). Indeed, Goh's successor, Lee Hsien Loong, has further consolidated the consultative style of leadership and continued with the same policies.

As Vietnam is a communist state, it is not surprising that the 'Party leads and the Government implements' and the Politburo is responsible for policy formulation. Policy-making in Vietnam is formalistic as policy-makers are reactive rather than proactive in responding to policy issues. Policy formulation also focuses on the issuing of laws, decrees and resolutions without considering their implementation. The public bureaucracy is hierarchically structured with emphasis on seniority. According to Jairo Acuña-Alfaro and Anh Tran in Chapter 6, the government has shown its commitment to public sector reform through the recently approved Resolution 30c on the State Administration Reform Master Programme for 2011–2020, which has emphasized (1) the clearer definition of roles and responsibilities of the line ministries and implementing agencies; (2) the development of human resources; and (3) the improvement of public service delivery.

1.7 The public bureaucracy's role in policy implementation

Van Meter and Van Horn (1975: 474–83) have hypothesized that effective policy implementation depends not only on favourable economic, social and political conditions (or policy context) but also on the clarity of the policy standards and objectives and their communication to the implementers, the availability of policy resources, the effectiveness of the implementing agencies and the disposition of the implementers. In other words, effective policy implementation requires the proper communication of policy standards and objectives to the implementers, capable implementing agencies and supportive implementers.

In Indonesia, policy standards and objectives are formulated by the ministries responsible for implementing the policies without relying on performance measurement. The government introduced performance-based budgeting in 2003, which requires every agency to establish performance management for budget allocation and to submit a Government Institution Performance Accountability Report describing its achievements during the year. Prasojo (2011: 101–2) contends that the performance management rules are ineffective because they are not used to evaluate individual performance, which is based on abstract indicators like loyalty and leadership, and the subjective evaluation of subordinates by the head of the agency. For cross-sectoral programmes, the relevant ministries are jointly responsible for defining the policy standards and objectives. However, the lack of a clear-cut division of authority between ministries has resulted in significant policy overlaps in the large ministries. Pramusinto observes in Chapter 2 that the lack of clarity in the division of labour between the central government and local governments has contributed to the overlapping authority between them and the following three problems: (1) conflict in regulations between laws on local governments and sectoral laws; (2) efforts by sectoral ministries to de-concentrate activities devolved to local governments; (3) cases where provincial governments have interfered in the affairs of the district or city governments.

As indicated by Nik Rosnah Wan Abdullah in Chapter 3, the Government Transformation Programme (GTP) was launched in Malaysia in 2009 to improve the government's effectiveness in public service delivery and to enhance the country's living standards. Key performance indicators (KPIs) were identified for these six national key result areas: crime prevention, reducing government corruption, increasing access to quality education, improving the living standards for low income groups, upgrading rural infrastructure and improving public transportation. The introduction of the KPIs has 'galvanized' the public bureaucracy from its inertia. While it is too early to evaluate the GTP's effectiveness, its inaugural annual report for 2010 provides evidence of the government's commitment to deliver positive outcomes.

In Singapore, according to David Seth Jones in Chapter 5, policy standards and objectives are determined by performance measurement as the implementing agencies systematically evaluate their performance by means of KPIs since the introduction of Budgeting for Results (BFR) in 1996. Performance data on the ministries and statutory boards are provided on their websites or in their annual reports. The performance indicators employed focus on the output in terms of the amount of work done and the standard of service provided, as well as on the attainment of the policy goals. Performance measurement provides managers, senior civil servants, political leaders and the public with precise information on an agency's performance in policy implementation and service delivery and feedback on the required improvements.

In Chapter 6, Acuña-Alfaro and Tran identify the three main institutions in policy implementation in Vietnam as: the Communist Party of Vietnam (CPV), which leads, the government, which implements, and the Vietnam Fatherland Front, which mobilizes. The public bureaucracy's capacity has been adversely affected by the long period of political conflict and war from 1945 to 1975. It has evolved from a mandarin system under French colonial rule to a cadre system under communist rule, and from a centrally planned economy to a socialist-oriented market economy since 1995. Consequently, the public bureaucracy is characterized by these three enduring features: (1) a mandarin structure rather than a civil service to serve the public; (2) a Soviet-style central planning cadre system which does not distinguish civil servants from other public officials; and (3) one-party rule of the CPV (Poon, Nguyen and Do 2009: 205). Thus, the policy standards and objectives are determined by the CPV without relying on any performance measurement system. Unlike the other four ASEAN countries, Vietnam is a communist state under the absolute control of the CPV, which is responsible for the development and implementation of personnel policies of the cadres and civil servants. This means that, unlike their politically neutral counterparts in Indonesia, Malaysia, the Philippines and Singapore, most Vietnamese public officials and civil servants are party members who remain loyal to its goals and ideology (Acuña-Alfaro and Do 2010: 348).

Van Meter and Van Horn (1975: 465) have also emphasized the importance of the availability of policy resources for facilitating effective policy implementation. In Indonesia, policy resources refer to financial resources, human resources and implementation rules. During the New Order regime, the National Planning Board (*Bappenas*) was responsible for determining financial resources but this role was transferred to the Ministry of Finance and the National Assembly during the post Suharto Reformation era. In Chapter 2, Pramusinto contends that the tendency for ministries to increase their employees results in overstaffing and inefficiency. Furthermore, there is also a vast disparity in the quality and quantity of human resources between the Ministry of Finance and *Bappenas*, which has attracted talented personnel, and the other ministries. A similar disparity in human resources is manifested among the regional governments, and those regions with lower-quality human resources remain backward as they face formidable obstacles in transforming knowledge and work culture from other areas. Finally, policy implementation in Indonesia also depends on the implementing regulations because laws approved by the National Assembly do not necessarily become effective policies if there are no implementing regulations such as presidential regulations, government regulations or ministerial decisions.

In the Philippines, Richter (1987: 65) has highlighted 'the dire scarcity of financial resources to commit to vital policy sectors', which makes its public bureaucracy 'very dependent on external aid' in policy implementation. Apart from resource scarcity, the public bureaucracy is also afflicted with rampant corruption, which is a serious obstacle to effective policy implementation. As the public bureaucracy has not been effective in delivering services, Reyes argues in Chapter 4 that NGOs and international organizations have emerged as alternative agents of service delivery to meet the deficit in provision of services by the government agencies.

In Singapore, Jones observes in Chapter 5 that the implementing agencies are usually provided with adequate financial and human resources to ensure effective implementation because its strong economic growth and efficient system of tax collection have generated substantial revenue and a budget surplus. The Block Vote Budget Allocation System (BVBAS) was introduced in 1989 to delegate budget allocations in a ministry to its permanent secretary. Thus, ministries can allocate operational spending according to the funding needs of their programmes, and transfer funds from one programme to another. This flexibility reduces the possibility of overfunding or underfunding programmes. Even though funding is available, the managers in the ministries and statutory boards are expected to make savings, avoid waste and secure a greater return for each dollar spent in the procurement of physical resources. The emphasis on cost savings in statutory boards is reflected in their adoption of accrual accounting, which provides their managers with information on the full costs of their programmes to enable them to make savings where necessary.

Third, Van Meter and Van Horn (1975: 465–6) contend that effective policy implementation requires that policy standards and objectives must be stated clearly so that the implementers will 'know what is expected of them'. Consequently, effective implementation is more likely to occur if policy standards and objectives are clearly stated and communicated accurately and consistently to the implementers. In Indonesia, intra-organization communication within the public bureaucracy is hierarchical and top down, which means that the subordinates implement the policy standards and objectives communicated to them by their superiors. Rohdewohld (2003: 264) has identified the 'hierarchical and patrimonial working culture that was not conducive to creating an internal culture of critical thinking and self-reflection' as an important deficiency of the Indonesian public bureaucracy. Indeed, the subordinates only provide information, advice and recommendations if requested by their superiors. However, Pramusinto notes in Chapter 2 that there has been a shift from a hierarchical to a more egalitarian style of communication between superior and subordinate officers in Indonesia during the past decade.

Pramusinto also observes in Chapter 2 that the thirty-four ministries in Indonesia rely on meetings to communicate with each other instead of electronic mail, not only because of the limited availability of computers in government offices outside Java but more importantly because officials attending meetings within or outside Java receive travelling and *per diem* allowances, which are important supplements to their low salaries. As officials usually inflate their travelling expenses, it is not surprising that the Financial Audit Board has reported that misuse of the budget for office travel has increased from Rp 73.5 billion (US$7.35 million) in 2009 to Rp 89.5 billion (US$8.95 million) in 2010.

In Singapore, Jones describes the process of policy formulation and policy implementation in Chapter 5 as being characterized by communication and cooperation between different public agencies and between the latter and external agencies. Inter-ministerial and inter-agency committees and working groups are formed to examine policy and operational issues and to make recommendations. The membership of these committees and groups is drawn from ministers and senior- and mid-level personnel from various ministries, who work together in collecting and analysing evidence, and submitting proposals. Furthermore, statutory boards are responsible for implementing many regulations and for administering such support services as the provision of loans, grants and subsidies to business firms and the public. The decentralized system of implementation by statutory boards reflects the need for greater operational autonomy in those areas where operational decisions require specialist and professional expertise.

The characteristics of implementing agencies and the disposition of the implementers are the two remaining variables influencing the public bureaucracy's role in policy implementation (Van Meter and Van Horn 1975: 470–3). A comparison of the importance of these two factors in Indonesia and Singapore will demonstrate clearly the different levels of effectiveness of their public bureaucracies in policy implementation.

In Chapter 5, Jones observes that over 70 per cent of the 138,720 persons employed in the ministries and statutory boards in Singapore are involved in these aspects of policy implementation: operational management and supervision, technical support, service delivery, enforcement, support and day-to-day administration. He contends that the personnel of the implementing agencies are highly competent because of the emphasis on meritocracy and the importance of training. As staff members are required to undergo professional training and skills upgrading, the Civil Service College offers many courses dealing with policy implementation issues. After the introduction of 'Public Service for the 21st Century' (PS21) in May 1995, the importance of training in the public bureaucracy was recognized with the implementation of a new training policy in November 1996 which entitled every civil servant or employee of a statutory board to a minimum of 100 hours of training a year or 12.5 days (with eight hours of training daily) by 2000 (Quah 2010: 159–60).

In addition to being highly competent, the implementers in Singapore are supportive and have interpreted and applied policy in a manner that is consistent with the policy objectives. This means that policies are translated consistently into more detailed and specific requirements through implementing regulations, statutory orders, notices, guidelines, manuals and circulars. While discretion is permitted when professional judgement is required or when special cases arise, Jones contends in Chapter 5 that there is no evidence of implementers who have rejected or hindered policy implementation. To enhance the disposition of the implementers in Singapore, the quality of customer service in the public bureaucracy has been improved through greater transparency and reduction of red tape.

In April 1991, the Service Improvement Unit was formed to reduce red tape and improve service in the public bureaucracy through the appointment of senior bureaucrats as quality service managers to handle complaints from the public. In May 1995, PS21 was launched to enhance the quality of service in the public bureaucracy and to prepare their members to welcome and accept change (Quah 2010: 8). The Cut Waste Panel (CWP) was established in September 2003 to reduce wastage and make savings in the delivery of public services by obtaining feedback from the public. Those suggestions that were accepted by the CWP since its inception have resulted in cost savings of SGD11.5 million. The reliance on e-government as manifested in the wide range of online services made available to the public has resulted in greater transparency and streamlining. The improvement of customer service in the public bureaucracy has resulted in the streamlining of bureaucratic regulations and procedures for the business sector and Singapore being consistently ranked first on the World Bank's *Doing Business* surveys from 2007 to 2015. In 2015, Singapore was ranked first among the 189 economies on the ease of doing business (World Bank 2014b: 4).

By contrast, in Chapter 2, Pramusinto attributes the ineffectiveness of Indonesia's implementing agencies to their incompetent staff, the disparity in span of control among ministries and their vulnerability to political pressures from members of the National Assembly. First, in terms of competence, there is a wide gap between the leadership and their subordinates. The street-level bureaucrats fail to implement policies as required by their superiors either because of their lack of understanding of the policies or their vested interests in ensuring that the policies are not implemented. Public officials are incompetent because of 'the continuing mismatch between administrative tasks and the skills and experience of staff', which is caused by (1) the inadequate analysis of the functions, workloads and human resource requirements of government agencies, and (2) the fact that most civil servants have received only a secondary school education as no more than 25 per cent of them are university graduates (Rohdewohld 2003: 265).

The incompetence of civil servants is also the result of the following problems encountered in implementing their training, namely the lack of cooperation and coordination among the various training agencies; the uneven quality of the training programmes; the difficulty in retaining trained personnel; and the inadequate funding provided for training. Moreover, it is difficult to monitor the attitudes and discipline of the civil servants because of 'the absence of performance standards, the low salary, and affiliation-related promotion' (Prasojo 2010: 119–21). Hence, it is difficult to motivate public officials to enforce regulations because officials who do not perform as expected are not punished.

The second reason for the ineffectiveness of the implementing agencies in Indonesia is the vast difference in size of the ministries, which has resulted in a wider span of control in the larger ministries like the Ministry of Finance, where a senior official at echelon I supervises ten times more subordinates than his counterpart in the smaller Ministry of Development Planning (MDP). The disparity in span of control is even greater among echelon II officials in the Ministry of Education who supervise more than fifty subordinates each in contrast with their MDP colleagues, who supervise only three colleagues each.

Third, the implementing agencies in Indonesia are ineffective because the appointment of ministers and the size of the budget allocation for ministries are influenced by political considerations since both aspects are determined by the National Assembly. As the support of the National Assembly is important for approving the budget allocation for ministries, agencies which are in conflict with it usually have their budget allocations reduced. For example, the conflict between the Ombudsman and the National Assembly resulted in a severe reduction of the Ombudsman's budget for 2011.

Compounding the problem of ineffective implementing agencies in Indonesia is the cautious disposition of the implementers. According to Pramusinto, in Chapter 2, the implementers are cautious and only take action if they are backed by the regulations. Indeed, in the absence of regulations, the implementers lack the courage to initiate action, even when the issue involves the public interest, because they face legal action for making mistakes in implementation. Consequently, the implementers avoid high-risk activities and focus instead on safe activities and comfort zones. Similarly, the 'lack of awareness, commitment and capacity' of the implementers constitutes a fundamental obstacle for the effective implementation of public sector reform in Indonesia. Furthermore, the 'deeply rooted political cooptation' of the public bureaucracy by political parties has given rise to 'intense resistance from politicians and bureaucrats alike against the bureaucratic reform'. This means that such reforms do not result in changing the mind sets and attitudes of the civil servants because they view the reforms in terms of providing incentives like additional expenditure for themselves and their agencies (Prasojo 2011: 119–20).

In the Philippines, de Guzman, Brillantes and Pacho (1988: 196–202) have identified those multiple problems which have hindered the public bureaucracy's role in policy implementation: duplication and overlapping of functions; inadequate coordination; rampant corruption; red tape and inefficiency; cumbersome and complicated procedures; ineffective administration of public enterprises; inadequacy of the communication system; the practice of creating 'adhocracies'; and problems in personnel administration. As a good communication system is required for effective policy formulation and implementation, an inter-agency technical committee on monitoring and evaluation found in 1982 that the communication system was characterized by these weaknesses: (1) the existence of unnecessary channels of communication; (2) inadequate control measures for verifying the accuracy of information or reports submitted; (3) the generation of unnecessary reports which management did not use; (4) delayed reporting and non-submission of reports by regional offices; (5) the unreliability and inaccuracy of reports; and (6) the lack of communication facilities and opportunities. Finally, the public bureaucracy in the Philippines is also afflicted by these personnel problems: overstaffing of agencies at both the national and local levels; erosion of the merit principle in recruiting and promoting personnel; the low salaries of civil servants; frequent transfer of personnel; and widespread corruption.

Similarly, the evaluation of the Philippine public bureaucracy by public administration scholars and practitioners in 2005 identified five major problems. The first problem was the political interference or intrusion in the recruitment and selection of members of the career executive service. Second, the low salaries of civil servants make it difficult for the public bureaucracy to recruit and retain talented personnel. Third, rampant corruption in the public bureaucracy reflects the lack of public accountability and erodes the quality of service delivery. Fourth, the public bureaucracy's poor performance culture is reflected in the 'lack of work ethic' and 'lack of responsiveness' in terms of service delivery. The fifth problem is the lack of a rational basis for staffing the public bureaucracy, resulting in overstaffing in some agencies and understaffing in other agencies (Brillantes and Sonco 2010: 230–2).

Riedinger's analysis of the implementation of the Comprehensive Agrarian Reform Law (Republic Act 6657), which was enacted in June 1988, has highlighted the leadership problems in the Department of Agrarian Reform (DAR) and the occurrence of many valuation scandals. The various nominees for the position of secretary of the DAR during Aquino's presidency were inexperienced in agrarian reform and their nominations were often 'delayed, if not derailed'. The most notable scandal was the overvaluation of the 1,888-hectare Garchitorena Estate, which was purchased by Sharp International Marketing Inc. in April 1988 for P3.014 million. Sharp International offered the estate to the DAR in May 1988 for P56 million. The DAR officials increased the valuation of the estate to P62.725 million in December 1988. However, the valuation was disputed by the staff of the Land Bank of the Philippines and its president rejected the order for payment in April 1989. The Garchitorena scandal and other overvaluations revealed 'several serious defects' in the Voluntary Offer to Sell Programme and the agrarian reform programme (Riedinger 1995: 177–83).

In Chapter 4, Reyes has identified 'systemic weaknesses' and 'ubiquitous corruption' as the two major obstacles to effective policy implementation in the Philippines. In his comparative analysis of the implementation of the Textbook Development Programme (TDP) and the Programme on Basic Education (PROBE), Reyes (2009b: 206–9) found that the operational demands, nature and availability of resources, and power and shared authority were the critical variables determining the level of effectiveness of the implementation of both programmes. The TDP's implementation was 'discordant and fragmented' and its prevailing conditions contributed to 'a dysfunctional bureaucracy typified by irregular transactions that made it prone to corruption and implementation failure'. By contrast, PROBE's implementation linkages were functional and most of its fellows were highly committed to the programme, which was also strengthened by the Teacher Support Units in schools and the professional growth and development of its participants (Reyes 2009b: 217–18).

According to Acuña-Alfaro and Tran in Chapter 6, the effectiveness of the Vietnamese public bureaucracy in policy implementation is adversely affected by four problems. First, the eight criteria[3] used in the performance appraisal

[3] The eight criteria are 'compliance with the state's law and policies, work results, compliance with work and organization regulations, cooperation at work, truthfulness, ethics, attitude towards learning, and attitude towards serving people' (Poon, Nguyen and Do 2009: 217 n. 1).

system are general and do not permit a 'meaningful assessment of actual staff performance'. Second, it is difficult to enforce disciplinary action against incompetent civil servants because of the cultural tendency in Vietnam of not wanting to give offence and the difficulty in removing them in the career-based lifelong employment system (Poon, Nguyen and Do 2009: 217). Third, the limited capacity of Vietnamese civil servants was revealed in a study by the Institute of State and Law which found that: (1) 60 per cent to 70 per cent of civil servants were not trained in state management issues; (2) half of the senior commune personnel had only primary or secondary education; (3) 79 per cent of key commune staff did not receive professional training in state management. Fourth, the low salaries in the public bureaucracy have not only increased the incentive for corruption but also contributed to the brain drain of civil servants to the private sector, and the phenomenon of holding multiple jobs among them. During 2003–2007, more than 16,000 civil servants from the central and provincial governments left for more lucrative private sector jobs, including 6,400 officials from Ho Chi Minh City (Poon, Nguyen and Do 2009: 214). The proportion of civil servants holding several jobs is the highest in public administration services (37 per cent), education (32.4 per cent) and health (10.1 per cent), with an average of 14.4 per cent for all state employees (Acuña-Alfaro 2009: 10).

1.8 Two case studies of policy implementation

The two case studies to be discussed in this section are the ASEAN Cosmetic Directive (ACD) and the ASEAN

Ministerial Meeting on Transnational Crime/ Senior Officials Meeting on Transnational Crime (AMMTC/SOMTC). However, before analysing these case studies, it is necessary to provide a description of the ministries responsible for implementing ASEAN matters in the five countries.

1.8.1 Ministries responsible for implementing ASEAN matters

The Ministry of Foreign Affairs (MFA) is usually the lead ministry in the five ASEAN countries that is responsible for dealing with ASEAN matters and implementing ASEAN agreements, working together with other relevant ministries depending on the issues.

In Indonesia, the MFA has a Directorate General of ASEAN Cooperation which formulates and implements policies and standardization in technical and political relations abroad within the framework of ASEAN cooperation. Its specific functions are: (1) formulating and implementing policies in foreign relations as part of ASEAN cooperation; (2) negotiating with other ASEAN member states; (3) preparing standards, norms, guidelines, criteria and procedures for ASEAN cooperation; (4) providing technical assistance and evaluation; (5) administration of the Directorate General.

The Directorate General of ASEAN Cooperation consists of the Secretariat and these four directorates: (1) Directorate of ASEAN Political Security Cooperation; (2) Directorate of ASEAN Economic Cooperation; (3) Directorate of ASEAN Functional Cooperation; (4) Directorate of Dialogue Partners and Inter-Regional Affairs. The Directorate of

ASEAN Functional Cooperation assists the Directorate General of ASEAN Cooperation to formulate and implement projects and activities in human resources, the ASEAN foundation, information, culture, education, science and technology, environment and social development. Its staff members are also responsible for attending the meetings of the ASEAN council in these eight areas and coordinating the outcomes of these meetings, as well as the conducting of training and supervision in administration, implementing the tasks of the Directorate and the preparation of reports (Ministry of Foreign Affairs, Indonesia 2014).

In Malaysia, the ASEAN Department of the MFA was renamed the ASEAN-Malaysia National Secretariat (AMNS), which serves as the 'national focal point' by coordinating with other ministries and agencies on ASEAN matters to enhance regional cooperation within the ASEAN framework. The AMNS is headed by a Director-General and consists of these four divisions: the ASEAN Political Security Community Division (APSCD), ASEAN Economic Community Division (AECD), ASEAN Socio-Cultural Community Division (ASCCD) and ASEAN External Relations Division (AERD). Each division is led by a Deputy Director-General.

The main objective of the AMNS is to ensure that Malaysia's interests in various activities of ASEAN cooperation are preserved through increased mutual understanding between Malaysia and other ASEAN member states and ASEAN dialogue partners and enhanced cooperation in political-security, economic and socio-cultural fields. The AMNS's major functions are: (1) hosting summits, meetings, conferences and seminars related to ASEAN on a rotational basis; (2) representing Malaysia in ASEAN meetings at the level of Heads of State/Ministers and officers in official or unofficial forums for exchange of views and coordination of national positions on specific issues and in respective areas of cooperation; (3) participating in ASEAN forums with the dialogue partners and other external linkages to strengthen cooperation with these countries; (4) coordinating the implementation of ASEAN-related decisions and activities in Malaysia; (5) serving as the depository for information on ASEAN in Malaysia; (6) promoting ASEAN identity and awareness in Malaysia; (7) supporting the work of Malaysia's Permanent Mission to ASEAN in Jakarta (Ministry of Foreign Affairs, Malaysia 2014).

In the Philippines, the Office of the Undersecretary for Policy in the Department of Foreign Affairs (DFA) advises and assists the Secretary of Foreign Affairs on matters concerning the formulation and execution of Philippine foreign policy, particularly on bilateral, regional and international political and security issues. It is divided into six offices, with each office being responsible for ASEAN affairs, Asia and Pacific affairs, American affairs, European affairs, Middle East and African affairs, and United Nations and other international organizations (Department of Foreign Affairs, Philippines 2014a). The Office of ASEAN Affairs serves as the ASEAN National Secretariat of the Philippines and is divided into these five divisions: summitries and ASEAN Coordinating Council (ACC); ASEAN Political Security Community (APSC); ASEAN Economic Community (AEC); ASEAN Socio-Cultural Community (ASCC); and external relations (Department of Foreign Affairs, Philippines 2014b). It is responsible for organizing and implementing ASEAN-related activities at the country level and as well as for the country's participation in ASEAN affairs. It also provides policy guidance and staff support in negotiations, coordination, supervision, monitoring, integration, reporting and operations of the national government in ASEAN (culture360.org 2014).

In Singapore, the MFA has eighteen directorates, including an ASEAN Directorate, which is staffed with seventeen members and is responsible for dealing with ASEAN matters. The ASEAN Directorate is divided into the Directorate Support Centre and these three branches: ASEAN Political Security Community Branch, ASEAN Economic Community Branch and ASEAN Socio-Cultural Community Branch (Ministry of Foreign Affairs, Singapore 2014). Among the other fourteen ministries, only the Ministry of Trade and Industry has an ASEAN Division dealing with ASEAN integration issues and ASEAN external relations, and the Ministry of Environment and Water Resources has listed ASEAN and International Environmental Matters as one of its subjects.

In Vietnam, the MFA has thirty-two departments, including the ASEAN Department, which is responsible for dealing with ASEAN matters (Ministry of Foreign Affairs, Vietnam 2012). The MFA was appointed by the Vietnamese Prime Minister on 4 February 2009 as the national coordinator for regional cooperation for building an ASEAN community and implementing the ASEAN charter. As the National ASEAN Secretariat, the MFA's task is to enhance coordination of action in formulating and implementing national policies regarding ASEAN cooperation. The Minister of Foreign Affairs is responsible for chairing the ASEAN Coordinating

Council and the ASEAN Political Security Community Council, while the Minister of Industry and Trade chairs the ASEAN Economic Community Council, and the Minister of Labour, War Invalids and Social Affairs is the chairperson of the ASEAN Socio-Cultural Community Council.

1.8.2 *The ASEAN Cosmetic Directive*

The ACD was signed by the ASEAN countries in September 2003 and came into effect on 1 January 2008. Its objective is to protect consumers in the ASEAN countries from the health hazards posed by cosmetics products by conducting post-market surveillance of these products instead of relying of pre-market approval. Each ASEAN country has to incorporate the ACD into its domestic laws, but it has the discretion to amplify and interpret the ACD provisions for implementation.

The ACD is implemented in Indonesia by these five agencies: the MFA, which deals with cooperation with the other ASEAN countries; the Ministry of Health (MOH), which formulates the regulations; the Food and Drugs Inspection Board (FDIB), which is responsible for inspecting the implementation of regulations; the Ministry of Industry, which provides guidance and promotes industrial development; and the police, which enforces the regulations. However, as shown in Chapter 2 by Pramusinto, the implementation of the ACD in Indonesia has encountered five problems. First, the ACD is supported by large companies but not by small and medium-sized enterprises (SMEs), which lack the capacity to implement the ACD. Similarly, the ACD has been supported by the MOH but not by some ministries. Third, rampant corruption in the public bureaucracy has resulted in extortion of the owners of SMEs by the police and the FDIB. Fourth, there is weak coordination between the police and FDIB in implementing the ACD. The final problem is the FDIB's limited budget for implementing the ACD.

In Malaysia, the ACD is implemented by the Enforcement Division of the Ministry of Health, the National Pharmaceutical Control Bureau (NPCB), and the Department of Standards Malaysia of the Ministry of Science and Technology. Nik Rosnah contends in Chapter 3 that there are no major problems in implementing the ACD in Malaysia as the problems identified are: the high manufacturing and overhead costs for the cosmetics industry; minimizing the differences in implementing the ACD among the ASEAN countries by coordinating with the ASEAN Cosmetics Association; and providing the authorized personnel with the technical knowledge and experience on product contents and knowledge on the ACD guidelines for conducting the notification process.

In the Philippines, the Food and Drugs Administration (FDA) in the Department of Health is the key agency responsible for implementing the ACD. According to Reyes in Chapter 4, the implementation of the ACD in the Philippines suffers from three problems. The first major problem is the FDA's inadequacies as manifested in its lack of competent staff and capable leaders. Consequently, the Chamber of Cosmetics Industry of the Philippines has provided professional training for the FDA field and central officers without charging fees in 2003. Secondly, as in the case of Indonesia, SMEs have also faced problems in implementing the ACD because the increase in production costs has reduced their competitiveness. Thirdly, the widespread corruption in the Bureau of Customs and the FDA has hindered the ACD's implementation.

In the case of Singapore, the Health Sciences Authority (HSA) is the statutory board responsible for implementing the ACD, which was incorporated into Singapore law in 2007 with the enactment of the Health Products Act, and the issue of the Health Products (Cosmetic Products – ASEAN Cosmetic Directive) Regulations, 2007. The Health Products Regulation Group (HPRG) of the HSA handles the day-to-day implementation and enforcement of the ACD. However, the monitoring of the cosmetics industry to ensure its compliance with the ACD is done by the Cosmetic Control Unit in the Complementary Health Products Branch of the HPRG. The HSA takes enforcement action when a product is found to be unsafe, or when the ACD guidelines and the HSA regulations are violated. Finally, the HSA cooperates with the Cosmetic, Toiletry and Fragrance Association of Singapore (CTFAS) to conduct workshops and informal tea sessions to familiarize manufacturers and distributors with the ACD requirements and HSA regulations.

In Chapter 5, Jones provides five reasons for the effective implementation of the ACD in Singapore. First, the HSA's cosmetics laboratory has the required resources and expertise for testing cosmetics products. Second, Singapore's economic affluence has increased the demand for cosmetics products. Third, the effective partnership between the HSA and the CTFAS in educational outreach activities provides useful feedback to the HSA to enhance the ACD's implementation. Fourth, the HSA's extensive experience in regulating other health products for many years has been a tremendous asset in implementing the ACD. The final reason for the HSA's effectiveness is the withdrawing of harmful products from the market and issuing warnings instead of employing tough enforcement measures.

In Vietnam, the ACD is implemented by many agencies including the MOH, which is the ministry responsible for regulating the cosmetics sector from January 1997, and the Ministry of Science and Technology, the Ministry of Environment, the Market Management Agency of the Ministry of Industry and Trade, the Customs Department, the Police Department and the Drug Administration of Vietnam. Like Indonesia and the Philippines, the implementation of the ACD in Vietnam has also encountered problems. Acuña-Alfaro and Tran have identified in Chapter 6 the five problems faced by the Vietnamese public bureaucracy in implementing the ACD. The first problem was the challenge of convincing the managers of cosmetics companies to accept the change from pre-market approval to post-market surveillance. Secondly, as the ACD was written in English, its contents must be translated accurately into Vietnamese. The third problem was that financial resources were not allocated properly for the ACD's implementation. Fourth, there was a shortage of management staff to meet the inspection requirements of the ACD. Finally, SMEs had limited financial and human resources to implement the ACD. Table 1.12 summarizes the discussion of the ACD by identifying the implementing agencies in the five ASEAN countries.

Table 1.12 *Implementing agencies of the ACD in the five ASEAN countries*

Country	Implementing agencies
Indonesia	Ministry of Foreign Affairs, Ministry of Health, Food and Drugs Inspection Board, Ministry of Industry, Police
Malaysia	Enforcement Division, Ministry of Health, National Pharmaceutical Control Bureau, Department of Standards Malaysia
Philippines	Food and Drugs Administration, Ministry of Health, Chamber of Cosmetics Industry of the Philippines
Singapore	Health Sciences Authority, Cosmetic, Toiletry and Fragrance Association of Singapore
Vietnam	Ministry of Health, Ministry of Science and Technology, Ministry of Environment, Market Management Agency of the Ministry of Industry and Trade, Customs Department, Police Department and Drug Administration of Vietnam

1.8.3 The AMMTC/SOMTC

Unlike the ACD, the AMMTC/SOMTC is multi-faceted and covers various issues. In 1997, the ASEAN Declaration on Transnational Crime was signed by the ASEAN countries to combat transnational crime. This was followed by the ASEAN Plan of Action to Combat Transnational Crime in 1999, and the Work Programme to Implement the ASEAN Plan of Action to Combat Transnational Crime in 2002. The 1997 ASEAN Declaration on Transnational Crime focuses on the following eight aspects: terrorism, trafficking in persons, sea piracy, drug trafficking, money laundering and terrorism financing, cyber-crime, economic crime and arms smuggling. The AMMTC was convened in November 1997 to implement the ASEAN agreements on transnational crime. It is supported by the SOMTC, which meets annually to coordinate and cooperate with other ASEAN bodies dealing with transnational crime. The AMMTC/SOMTC has recommended that the ASEAN countries enhance their efforts in combating transnational crime by sharing intelligence, tracking and deporting wanted persons and conducting joint operations.

In his analysis of the implementation of the AMMTC/SOMTC in Indonesia in Chapter 2, Pramusinto focuses on the fight against terrorism and human trafficking. The three major agencies involved in countering terrorism are the National Counter-Terrorism Board, the Financial Transaction Reports and Analysis Centre and Densus 88. Pramusinto contends that Indonesia has been more effective in combating terrorism than human trafficking because of these four factors: (1) the consensus among the implementing agencies regarding the importance of taking concerted action against terrorists; (2) the provision of adequate funding by the government to enable the implementing agencies to perform their functions; (3) the efficient coordination among the stakeholders; (4) the support received from non-governmental organizations, especially religious organizations. Conversely, the Indonesian public bureaucracy has been ineffective in its efforts to curb trafficking in persons because of the lack of consensus in resolving the problems, the lower priority and limited budget allocation, the weak coordination and cooperation among government agencies and the limited support from religious organizations.

In Malaysia, the AMMTC/SOMTC is implemented by these agencies: the Ministry of Home Affairs (the key agency),

Bank Negara Malaysia, Labour Department, Royal Malaysian Police, Royal Customs Department, Ministry of Finance, and the National Anti-Narcotics Agency. Nik Rosnah contends in Chapter 3 that while Malaysia has introduced adequate and stringent laws for combating such transnational crimes as drug trafficking and human trafficking, it still needs the cooperation of other ASEAN countries to combat transnational crime effectively. As bilateral agency-to-agency contact is the most effective way of sharing information, the ASEAN countries should enhance their efforts in combating transnational crime by sharing more information with each other.

Reyes has devoted his analysis of the implementation of the AMMTC/SOMTC in Chapter 4 to the serious problem of human trafficking in the Philippines. The major agencies involved in dealing with transnational crime include: Department of Justice and Department of Social Work (which are the co-chairs), Department of Foreign Affairs, Department of Labour and Employment, Philippine Overseas Employment Agency, Bureau of Immigration, Philippine National Police, and National Commission on the Role of Filipino Women. He has identified these four problems in combating human trafficking in the Philippines: (1) the difficulty in obtaining funds; (2) 'capacity-building fatigue' among civil society representatives; (3) rampant corruption among the law enforcement agencies, especially in human trafficking; and (4) the provisions of the AMMTC/SOMTC are not binding.

In Singapore, the major agencies responsible for implementing the AMMTC/SOMTC are the Ministry of Home Affairs, the Central Narcotics Bureau, the Monetary Authority of Singapore and the Commercial Affairs

Department and Criminal Investigation Department of the Singapore Police Force. In Chapter 5, Jones observes that the Singapore government has developed the institutional capacity to ensure the effective enforcement for combating transnational crime in accordance with the stipulations in the ASEAN agreements. This involved the establishment of specialist agencies, the formulation of detailed operational measures and the adherence to systematic and rigorous procedures of surveillance and investigation. Furthermore, the Singapore government has taken seriously its responsibilities under the ASEAN agreements on transnational crime and has implemented its obligations effectively because of its commitment to ensure that Singapore remains free from crime, and its extensive experience in combating transnational crime before the advent of the AMMTC/SOMTC. While Singapore has curbed crime effectively within its territory, it still requires the cooperation of the other ASEAN countries to succeed in curbing such transnational crimes as terrorism, drug trafficking and human trafficking.

In Vietnam, there are many agencies involved in implementing the AMMTC/SOMTC, namely Ministry of Public Security (the lead agency), Ministry of National Defence, Customs Department, Ministry of Foreign Affairs, Financial Intelligence Unit, Ministry of Finance, Supreme People's Procuracy and Ministry of Communication and Information. According to Acuña-Alfaro and Tran in Chapter 6, the four problems encountered by these agencies in implementing the AMMTC/SOMTC are: (1) the enforcement mechanisms are ineffective; (2) there are few staff members who are proficient in English and have the required technical skills; (3) the dominance of political factors as bilateral cooperation between Vietnam, China, Laos and Cambodia is more effective than with other countries; and (4) there are problems of coordination among the implementing agencies and between Vietnam and the other ASEAN countries. Table 1.13 identifies the various agencies responsible for implementing the AMMTC/SOMTC in the five ASEAN countries.

Table 1.13 *Implementing agencies of the AMMTC/SOMTC in the five ASEAN countries*

Country	Implementing Agencies
Indonesia	National Counter-Terrorism Board, Financial Transaction Reports and Analysis Centre, Densus 88 (for counterterrorism)
Malaysia	Ministry of Home Affairs, Bank Negara Malaysia, Labour Department, Royal Malaysian Police, Royal Customs Department, Ministry of Finance and National Anti-Narcotics Agency
Philippines	Department of Justice, Department of Social Work, Department of Foreign Affairs, Department of Labour and Employment, Philippine Overseas Employment Agency, Bureau of Immigration, Philippine National Police and National Commission on the Role of Filipino Women (for human trafficking)
Singapore	Ministry of Home Affairs, Central Narcotics Bureau, Monetary Authority of Singapore, Commercial Affairs Department and Criminal Investigation Department of the Singapore Police Force
Vietnam	Ministry of Public Security, Ministry of National Defence, Customs Department, Ministry of Foreign Affairs, Financial Intelligence Unit, Ministry of Finance, Supreme People's Procuracy and Ministry of Communication and Information.

1.9 Conclusion

1.9.1 Major findings

Two major findings can be drawn from the preceding analysis. First, the effectiveness of the public bureaucracies in policy implementation in the five ASEAN countries depends on (1) whether the policy context is favourable or unfavourable, and (2) whether the public bureaucracy is effective or ineffective. This means that a country with a favourable policy context and an effective public bureaucracy will be more effective in policy implementation than a country with an unfavourable policy context and an ineffective public bureaucracy. Table 1.14 shows that Singapore is the most effective in policy implementation because of its favourable policy context and its effective public bureaucracy. Conversely, Indonesia is the least effective in policy implementation because of its unfavourable policy context and its ineffective public bureaucracy. Malaysia, Vietnam and the Philippines occupy intermediate positions between Singapore and Indonesia and are ranked second, third and fourth respectively, depending on the nature of their policy contexts and the levels of effectiveness of their public bureaucracies.

Table 1.14 *Effectiveness of the five ASEAN public bureaucracies in policy implementation*

Public bureaucracies				
most effective				least effective
Singapore	Malaysia	Vietnam	Philippines	Indonesia
favourable policy context			unfavourable policy context	

Second, the comparison of the implementation of the ACD and AMMTC/SOMTC by the five ASEAN countries shows that their public bureaucracies have been more effective in implementing the ACD than the AMMTC/SOMTC, for three reasons. First, the ACD focuses on a single issue while the AMMTC/SOMTC deals with eight types of transnational crime. Second, the narrower scope of the ACD means that fewer agencies are involved in its implementation in contrast with the implementation of the AMMTC/SOMTC, which requires more implementing agencies because of their wider scope. Finally, while both policies have encountered problems in implementation, the problems in implementing the AMMTC/SOMTC are more serious than those faced in implementing the ACD (See Table 1.15). In short, the five ASEAN countries have been more effective in implementing the ACD than the AMMTC/SOMTC because the former involves a single issue and fewer implementing agencies, and has encountered fewer implementation problems than the latter.

1.9.2 *Implications for further research*

What are the implications of this comparative study for further research on the role of the public bureaucracies in policy implementation in the ASEAN countries? As the purpose of this book is to address the research gap on the dearth of comparative studies on policy implementation in the ASEAN countries, what have we learnt from the five country studies presented in Chapters 2–6?

First, the experiences of the five public bureaucracies in policy implementation confirm the importance of the

Table 1.15 *Comparing the implementation of the ACD and AMMTC/ SOMTC*

Variable	ASEAN Cosmetic Directive	AMMTC/SOMTC
Number of issues	single	multiple
Number of implementing agencies	few	many
Implementation problems	1. SMEs lack capacity 2. Limited budgets of implementing agencies 3. Corruption	1. Limited capacity and budgets of enforcement agencies 2. Lack of goal consensus in dealing with some problems 3. Coordination problems 4. Corruption

favourability of their policy contexts, which is reflected most importantly in the political will or commitment of the governments and implementers in ensuring the success or failure of policy implementation. In their model, Van Meter and Van Horn (1975: 465) indicate that policies not only provide the standards and objectives for evaluating implementation but also 'make available resources which facilitate their administration'. Policy resources include 'funds or other incentives in the program that might encourage or facilitate effective implementation'.

If the incumbent government is committed to a policy it will allocate sufficient budget, personnel and other resources to ensure that the policy will be implemented. Conversely, the government's lack of political will is reflected in the limited financial and human resources allocated for implementing the policy. In many Third World countries, policies are not implemented effectively because they are 'highly problematic' and not provided with sufficient resources (Cleaves 1980: 292).

Indeed, the importance of allocating sufficient resources to ensure effective policy implementation is clearly illustrated in the experiences of the five countries. For example, in Chapter 2, Pramusinto contends that an important factor for Indonesia's success in combating terrorism is the substantial budget allocated for anti-terrorism efforts. On the other hand, the limited budget provided by the Indonesian government has undermined the effectiveness of its efforts in preventing trafficking in persons. In Malaysia, Nik Rosnah reports in Chapter 3 that the government has made more progress in curbing drug trafficking than human trafficking mainly because it has allocated more resources to the former than the latter. In Chapter 4, Reyes laments the fact that government agencies in the Philippines have not been provided with adequate resources to implement the guidelines of the AMMTC/SOMTC. Similarly, Acuña-Alfaro and Tran have observed in Chapter 6 that inadequate financial resources were allocated to the government agencies in Vietnam for implementing the ACD. By contrast, Singapore's affluence and strong revenue flows, according to Jones in Chapter 5, enable the government to provide the public bureaucracy with the human and financial resources needed to ensure that policies are implemented effectively.

Apart from the provision of adequate resources by the government, the other important dimension of political will, which is sometimes neglected, is the disposition of the implementers. Van Meter and Van Horn (1975: 472) contend that the 'ability and willingness' of the implementers to implement the policy depends on 'their cognition (comprehension, understanding) of the policy, the direction of their response to it (acceptance, neutrality, rejection), and the intensity of that response'. Implementers refuse to execute policies if they reject the policy objectives that offend their personal values or undermine their self-interest. The worst case scenario occurs when the implementers' 'intense negative preferences' lead to 'outright and open defiance of the program's objectives' (473). In extreme cases, the implementers can initiate measures to sabotage policy implementation.

In Chapter 5, Jones observes that civil servants in Singapore are highly competent and supportive and implement policies according to the stated objectives. As corruption is also not a serious problem in Singapore, the implementers have not rejected or hindered the implementation of policies. On the other hand, civil servants in Indonesia, according to Pramusinto, in Chapter 2, are less competent and adopt a cautious attitude in policy implementation for fear of making mistakes and facing legal action. In Chapter 4, Reyes indicates that the FDA's efforts in implementing the ACD have been hindered by its lack of capable leaders and competent personnel. Similarly, as pointed out by Acuña-Alfaro and Tran in Chapter 6, civil servants in Vietnam are incompetent because of their limited capacity and the difficulties faced in taking disciplinary action against them. As Vietnamese civil servants are also poorly paid and not punished for poor performance, there is no incentive for them to ensure that policies are effectively implemented.

Second, the policy content and whether a policy is 'more or less problematic' is another important factor determining the success or failure of policy implementation. Van Meter and Van Horn (1975: 461–2) assert that 'implementation will be most successful where only marginal change is required and goal consensus is high'. Conversely, policies requiring major change but having low goal consensus will not be implemented effectively. According to Peter S. Cleaves (1980: 287), a policy becomes 'more problematic' when it involves 'complex technical features, comprehensive change from status quo, multi-actor targets, multi-goal objectives, ambiguous or unclear goals, and long duration'. As 'more problematic' policies require 'a large amount of physical and material resources for implementation', policymakers should not be surprised by policy failure if they attempt to implement 'an extremely complicated policy with very few resources' (Cleaves 1980: 287–8).

The comparative analysis of the implementation of the ACD and AMMTC/SOMTC in the five ASEAN countries in Chapters 2–6 confirms the validity of the above arguments by the three scholars. The ACD is 'less problematic' than the AMMTC/SOMTC because it has these features: 'simple technical features, marginal change from status quo, one-actor target, one-goal objective, clearly stated goals and short duration' (Cleaves 1980: 287). In other words, while the implementation of the ACD has encountered some problems in Indonesia, the Philippines and Vietnam, these problems pale in comparison to the more intractable problems encountered in the implementation of the AMMTC/SOMTC in these countries. The wider scope of the AMMTC/SOMTC with the involvement of multiple agencies within each country and the necessity for cooperation and sharing of data among these agencies as well as the lack of goal consensus among the policy-makers explain, for example, why human trafficking remains a serious problem in the five ASEAN countries.

Drawing from the experiences of the five countries in implementing the ACD and AMMTC/SOMTC, the policy-makers in all the ASEAN countries and the ASEAN Secretariat should take into account the nature of those policies being implemented and allocate the budget and personnel required for their effective implementation. Consequently, they should not initiate the implementation of 'more problematic' policies if there is insufficient goal consensus and if the governments lack the political will to allocate the necessary financial and human resources for effective implementation.

Finally, the success or failure of policy implementation is also determined by the level of effectiveness of the public bureaucracies in the five ASEAN countries. According to Van Meter and Van Horn (1975: 480), 'successful implementation is also a function of the implementing organization's capacity to do what it is expected to do'. Furthermore, they posit that an agency's 'ability to implement policy may be hindered by such factors as overworked and poorly trained staffs, insufficient information and financial resources, or impossible time constraints'. In other words, the public bureaucracy will be ineffective in policy implementation if it is afflicted by capability problems.

Table 1.9 shows that Singapore is the most effective, according to its performance on the World Bank's indicator on government effectiveness from 1996–2013, followed by Malaysia, Vietnam, Indonesia and the Philippines, in descending order. Similarly, the PERC's evaluation of the effectiveness of the five public bureaucracies from 1998 to 2012 in Table 1.11 confirms that Singapore and Malaysia are more effective than the Philippines, Vietnam and Indonesia. As Singapore and Malaysia have effective public bureaucracies, it is not surprising that they are more effective in policy implementation than their less effective counterparts in Vietnam, Indonesia and the Philippines.

As benchmarking provides policy-makers with a tool for evaluating a national programme and enables them to learn about successful programmes in other countries, Richard Rose (2005: 35) suggests that if policies are ineffective, 'benchmarking will stimulate policy-makers to introduce improvements by learning from the best practices in other countries'. Following Rose's recommendation, the policy-makers, especially the senior civil servants involved in policy implementation in Indonesia, the Philippines and Vietnam, as well as their counterparts in Brunei Darussalam, Cambodia, Lao PDR, Myanmar and Thailand, should learn the best practices in policy implementation adopted by Singapore and Malaysia. The ASEAN Secretariat in Jakarta could facilitate this process of policy learning and transfer by organizing an annual regional workshop on best practices in policy implementation for senior civil servants in the member states to learn from the successful experiences of Singapore and Malaysia.

References

Acuña-Alfaro, J. (ed.) 2009. *Reforming Public Administration in Vietnam: Current Situation and Recommendations*. Hanoi: National Political Publishing House.

Acuña-Alfaro, J. and Do, T. H. 2010. 'Reforming the Public Sector in Vietnam'. In P. S. Kim (ed.), *Civil Service System and Civil Service Reform in ASEAN Member Countries and Korea*. Seoul: Daeyoung Moonhwasa Publishing Company, pp. 347–88.

Ahlers, A. L. 2014. *Rural Policy Implementation in Contemporary China: New Socialist Countryside*. London: Routledge.

Ali, M. 2013. 'Efficiency, Wages, Public Service Motivation and Effort in Malaysia: An Empirical Case Study of *Universiti Sains Malaysia*', PhD thesis, Murdoch University.

Amara, R. and Siedentopf, H. (eds) 1980. *Asian Civil Service: Developments and Trends*. Kuala Lumpur: Asian and Pacific Development Administration Centre.

Anderson, J. E. 1979. *Public Policy-Making*, 2nd edn. New York: Holt, Rinehart and Winston.

Asian Intelligence 2014. 'Regional Overview', 895 (19 March): 1–5.

Badan Kepegawaian Nasional (BKN) 2014. *Statistik Pegawai Negeri Sipil*. Jakarta: *Pemerintah Republik Indonesia*.

Bankoff, G. 2005. 'Profiting from Disasters: Corruption, Hazard, and Society in the Philippines'. In N. Tarling (ed.), *Corruption and Good Governance in Asia*. London: Routledge, pp. 165–85.

Bardach, E. 1977. *The Implementation Game: What Happens after a Bill Becomes a Law*. Cambridge, MA: MIT Press.

Barenstein, J. 1994. *Overcoming Fuzzy Governance in Bangladesh: Policy Implementation in Least Developed Countries*. Dhaka: The University Press Ltd.

Bautista, R., Jr 2010. 'The Philippine Legal System', available at: https://suite.io/renato-bautista-jr/36zn2j3 (accessed 30 December 2014).

Bell, G. F. 1999. 'The Singapore Legal System in Context – Whither the Concept of the National Legal System'. In K. Y. L. Tan (ed.), *The Singapore Legal System*, 2nd edn. Singapore: Singapore University Press, pp. 1–25.

Berg, A. 1999. *Implementing and Enforcing European Fisheries Law: The Implementation and the Enforcement of the Common Fisheries Policy in the Netherlands and the United Kingdom.* The Hague: Kluwer Law International.

Bertsch, G. K., Clark, R. P. and Wood, D. M. 1986. *Comparing Political Systems: Power and Policy in Three Worlds.* New York: Macmillan Publishing Company.

Blunt, E. 1937. *The ICS: The Indian Civil Service.* London: Faber and Faber.

Brata, R. A. 2014. *Why Did Anticorruption Policy Fail? A Study of Anticorruption Policy Implementation Failure in Indonesia.* Charlotte, NC: Information Age Publishing.

Brigham, J. and Brown, D. W. 1980. *Policy Implementation: Penalties or Incentives?* Beverly Hills, CA: Sage Publications.

Brillantes, A. B., Jr 1988. 'The Executive'. In R. P. de Guzman and M. A. Reforma (eds), *Government and Politics of the Philippines.* Singapore: Oxford University Press, pp. 113–31.

Brillantes, A. B., Jr and Flores, H. P. 2011. 'Public Sector Reform in the Philippines'. In P. S. Kim (ed.), *Public Sector Reform in ASEAN Member Countries and Korea.* Seoul: Daeyoung Moonhwasa Publishing Company, pp. 228–66.

Brillantes, A. B., Jr and Sonco II, J. O. T. 2010. 'Civil Service Reforms in the Philippines: Its Many Faces, Leadership and Politics'. In P. S. Kim (ed.), *Civil Service System and Civil Service Reform in ASEAN Member Countries and Korea.* Seoul: Daeyoung Moonhwasa Publishing Company, pp. 210–52.

Burns, J. P. and Zhou, Z. 2010. *Performance Management in the Government of the People's Republic of China: Accountability and Control in the Implementation of Public Policy*. Paris: OECD Publishing.

Bussell, J. 2012. *Corruption and Reform in India: Public Services in the Digital Age*. Cambridge: Cambridge University Press.

Caiden, G. E. 1969. *Administrative Reform*. London: Allen Lane.

1976. 'Implementation – The Achilles Heel of Administrative Reform'. In A. F. Leemans (ed.), *The Management of Change*. The Hague: Martinus Nijhoff, pp. 142–64.

Chan, A. L. 2001. *Mao's Crusade: Politics and Policy Implementation in China's Great Leap Forward*. Oxford: Oxford University Press.

Chase, G. 1979. 'Implementing a Human Service Program: How Hard Will it Be?', *Public Policy*, 27(4): 385–435.

Cheema, G. S. and Rondinelli, D. A. (eds) 1983. *Implementing Decentralization Programmes in Asia: Local Capacity for Rural Development*. Nagoya: United Nations Centre for Regional Development.

Chow, K. W. 1994. 'Policy Formulation and Implementation in China: Issues and Implications'. In J. S. Jun (ed.), *Development in the Asia Pacific: A Public Policy Perspective*. Berlin: Walter de Gruyter, pp. 449–74.

Chung, J. H. 1993. 'The Politics of Policy Implementation in Post-Mao China: Central Control and Provincial Autonomy under Decentralization', PhD thesis, University of Michigan.

Cleaves, P. S. 1980. 'Implementation amidst Scarcity and Apathy: Political Power and Policy Design'. In M. S. Grindle (ed.), *Politics and Policy Implementation in the Third World*. Princeton, NJ: Princeton University Press;, pp. 281–303.

Cloete, F. 2000. *At Full Speed the Tiger Cubs Stumbled: Lessons from South East Asia about Sustainable Public Service Delivery*. Pretoria: Human Sciences Research Council Press.

Corpuz, O. D. 1957. *The Bureaucracy in the Philippines*. Manila: Institute of Public Administration, University of the Philippines.

Cothran, D. A. 1987. 'Japanese Bureaucrats and Policy Implementation: Lessons for America?', *Policy Studies Review*, 6(3): 439–58.

Crouch, H. 2003. 'Political Update 2002: Megawati's Holding Operation'. In E. Aspinall and G. Fealy (eds), *Local Power and Politics in Indonesia: Decentralization and Democratization*. Singapore: Institute of Southeast Asian Studies, pp. 15–34.

culture360.org 2014. 'ASEAN Affairs Office', available at: http://culture360.asef.org/organisation/asean-affairs-office/ (accessed 30 December 2014).

Darling, F. C. 1979. *The Westernization of Asia: A Comparative Political Analysis*. Cambridge, MA: Schenkman Publishing Company.

Davidsen, S., Ha, N. V., Giao, H. N., Vasavakul, T. and Garrido, M. A. 2009. *Implementation Assessment of the Anti-Corruption Law: How Far Has Vietnam Come at the Sector Level? A Case Study of the Construction Sector*. Copenhagen: Danish International Development Agency.

de Guzman, R. P., Brillantes, A. B., Jr and Pacho, A. G. 1988. 'The Bureaucracy'. In R. P. de Guzman and M. A. Reforma (eds), *Government and Politics of the Philippines*. Singapore: Oxford University Press, pp. 180–206.

Department of Foreign Affairs (DFA) Philippines 2014a. 'Organizational Structure', available at: http://web.archive.org/web/20141106212405/https://www.dfa.gov.ph/index.php/articles/organizational-structure (accessed 30 December 2014).

2014b. 'Home Office Personnel Directory', available at: http://web.archive.org/web/20141106212331/https://www.dfa.gov.ph/index.php/transparency/name-of-officials (accessed 30 December 2014).

Department of Statistics 2014. *Yearbook of Statistics, Singapore 2014*. Singapore: Ministry of Trade and Industry.

Echeverri-Gent, J. 1993. *The State and the Poor: Public Policy and Political Development in India and the United States*. Berkeley, CA: University of California Press.

Economic Times 2012. 'Indian Bureaucracy Rates Worst in Asia, Says a Political and Economic Risk Consultancy Report'. 11 January.

The Economist 2013. *Pocket World in Figures, 2014 Edition*. London: Profile Books.

Edwards, G. C. 1980. *Implementing Public Policy*. Washington, DC: Congressional Quarterly Press.

(ed.) 1984. *Public Policy Implementation*. Greenwich: JAI Press.

Elyas. B. O. 1980. 'The Civil Service Systems in Malaysia'. In R. Amara and H. Siedentopf (eds), *Asian Civil Service: Developments and Trends*. Kuala Lumpur: Asian and Pacific Development Administration Centre, pp. 249–99.

Emmerson, D. K. 1978. 'The Bureaucracy in Political Context: Weakness in Strength'. In K. D. Jackson and L. W. Pye (eds), *Political Power and Communications in Indonesia*. Berkeley, CA: University of California Press, pp. 82–136.

Endriga, J. N. 1979. 'Historical Notes on Graft and Corruption in the Philippines', *Philippine Journal on Public Administration*, 23(3–4): 241–54.

Esman, M. 1972. *Administration and Development in Malaysia*. Ithaca, NY: Cornell University Press.

Frazier, M. 1992. *Implementing State Government Export Programs*. New York: Praeger.

Fritzen, S. 2005. 'The "Misery" of Implementation: Governance, Institutions and Anti-Corruption in Vietnam'. In N. Tarling (ed.), *Corruption and Good Governance in Asia*. London: Routledge, pp. 98–120.

Frost, N. 2002. *Indonesia*. Oxford: Oxfam Publishing.

Gable, R. W. and Springer, J. F. 1976. *Administering Agricultural Development in Asia: A Comparative Analysis of Four National Programs*. Boulder, CO: Westview Press.

George, C. and Leow, J. 1998. 'Who Runs Singapore?', *Sunday Times*, 26 April, p. 36.

Gillespie, J. 2002. 'The Political-Legal Culture of Anti-Corruption Reforms in Vietnam'. In T. Lindsey and H. Dick (eds), *Corruption in Asia: Rethinking the Governance Paradigm*. Annandale: Federation Press, pp. 167–200.

Gobel, C. 2011. 'Uneven Policy Implementation in Rural China', *China Journal*, 65: 53–76.

Grindle, M. S. (ed.) (1980). *Politics and Policy Implementation in the Third World*. Princeton, NJ: Princeton University Press.

Hanisch, R. 1977. 'Decision-making Processes and Problems of Implementation of the Land Reform in the Philippines (Part I)', *Asia Quarterly*, 4: 305–22.

1978. 'Decision-making Processes and Problems of Implementation of the Land Reform in the Philippines (Part II)', *Asia Quarterly*, 5(1): 3–38.

Hausman, D. 2010. 'Policy Leaps and Implementation Obstacles: Civil Service Reform in Vietnam, 1998–2009', Innovations for Successful Societies. Princeton, NJ: Princeton University.

Heinelt, H., Malek, T., Smith, R. and Toller, A. E. (eds) 2001. *European Union Environment Policy and New Forms of Governance: A Study of the Implementation of the Environmental Impact Assessment Directive and the Eco-management and Audit Scheme Regulation in Three Member States*. Aldershot: Ashgate.

Honadle, G. 1999. *How Context Matters: Linking Environmental Policy to People and Place*. West Hartford, CT: Kumarian Press.

Hsu, P. S. C. 1998. 'Policy Implementation under Dual Decentralization in the People's Republic of China, 1979–1995: Coalitions, Institutions, and International Economic Links', PhD thesis, University of Denver.

Huang, J. 1998. 'Special Zoning Strategy in the People's Republic of China: State Capacity and Policy Implementation', PhD thesis, University of Tennessee.

Hussain, Z. 2009. 'PERC: Recession Could Test Singapore's Civil Service', *Straits Times*, 5 June, p. C5.

Iglesias, G. U. (ed.) 1976. *Implementation: The Problem of Achieving Results. A Casebook on Asian Experiences*. Manila: Eastern Regional Organization for Public Administration.

Jain, R. B. 1984. 'Parliament and Policy in India', *Asian Journal of Public Administration*, 6(2): 127–52.

1987. 'The Role of Bureaucracy in Policy Development and Implementation in India', *Southeast Asian Journal of Social Science*, 15(2): 20–39.

Jones, D. S. 1998. 'Law Enforcement in Singapore: An Analysis of the Compliance Strategy', *Asian Journal of Public Administration*, 20(1): 30–56.

2001. 'Inspection and Enforcement Strategies in Singapore: Food Safety, Pollution Control and Industrial Safety'. In L. Low and D. Johnston (eds), *Singapore Inc.: Public Policy Options in the Third Millennium*. Singapore: Asia Pacific Press, pp. 179–203.

Jordan, L. S. and Koinis, K. 2014. *Flexible Implementation: A Key to Asia's Transformation*. Honolulu: East-West Center Policy Studies, 70.

Kaufmann, D., Kraay, A. and Mastruzzi, M. 2004. 'Governance Matters III: Governance Indicators for 1996–2002'. Washington, DC: World Bank.

Kawin, W. 1975. 'Singapore's Foreign Policy: A Study of the Foreign Policy System of a City-State', PhD thesis, Georgetown University.

Kim, P. S. (ed.) 2010. *Civil Service System and Civil Service Reform in ASEAN Member Countries and Korea*. Seoul: Daeyoung Moonhwasa Publishing Company.

(ed.) 2011. *Public Sector Reform in ASEAN Member Countries and Korea*. Seoul: Daeyoung Moonhwasa Publishing Company.

Kraiyudht, D. 1989. *Privatization: An Analysis of the Concept and its Implementation in Thailand*. Bangkok: Thailand Development Research Institute Foundation.

Lampton, D. M. (ed.) 1987. *Policy Implementation in Post-Mao China*. Berkeley, CA: University of California Press.

Lanka Business. 2010. 'Civil Service: India, Indonesia Worst for Red Tape', 2 June.

Ledesma, A. J. and Tizon-Montinola, Maria Lourdes (eds) 1988. *The Implementation of Agrarian Reform in Negros: Issues, Problems, and Experiences*. Bacolod City: Social Research Center, University of St. La Salle.

Lee, B. H. 1980. 'The Public Personnel System in Singapore'. In R. Amara and H. Siedentopf (eds), *Asian Civil Service: Developments and Trends*. Kuala Lumpur: Asian and Pacific Development Administration Centre, pp. 431–79.

Lee, J. Z. 1993. 'Central-local Political Relationships in Post-Mao China: A Study of Recruitment Policy Implementation in Wuhan', PhD thesis, Ohio State University.

Lee, P. N. S. 1997. 'Policy Implementation in Reform China: The Case of Retirement Insurance'. Institute of Asia-Pacific Studies, Chinese University of Hong Kong, Occasional Paper 67. Hong Kong.

Lehmann, M. A. 2000. *Negotiating Environmental Quality: Policy Implementation in Germany and the United States*. Cheltenham: Edward Elgar.

Leichter, H. M. 1979. *A Comparative Approach to Policy Analysis: Health Care in Four Nations*. Cambridge: Cambridge University Press.

Leosong, M. and Zimmermann, W. 2005. 'Limits to Environmental Policy Implementation: The Case of User Charge Implementation in Thailand', *International Public Management Review*, 6(1): 23–58.

Levin, M. A. and Ferman, B. 1985. *The Political Hand: Policy Implementation and Youth Employment Programs*. New York: Pergamon Press.

Lewis, D. and Wallace, H. (eds) 1984. *Policies into Practice: National and International Case Studies in Implementation*. London: Heinemann Educational Books.

Majone, G. and Wildavsky, A. 1984. 'Implementation as Evolution (1979)'. In J. L. Pressman and A. Wildavsky (eds), *Implementation*. 3rd edn. Berkeley, CA: University of California Press, pp. 163–80.

Manion, M. 1991. 'Policy Implementation in the People's Republic of China: Authoritative Decisions versus Individual Interests', *Journal of Asian Studies*, 50(2): 253–79.

Mann, D. E. (ed.) 1982. *Environmental Policy Implementation*. Lexington, MA: D.C. Heath.

Manuel, M. J. 1999. 'Philippine Government and its Separation and Coordination of Powers'. In L. N. Yu-Jose (ed.), *Politics and Governance: Theory and Practice in the Philippine Context*. Quezon City: Department of Political Science, Ateneo de Manila University, pp. 77–116.

Manurung, C. 1980. 'The Public Personnel System in Indonesia'. In R. Amara and H. Siedentopf (eds), *Asian Civil Service: Developments and Trends*. Kuala Lumpur: Asian and Pacific Development Administration Centre, pp. 131–77.

May, P. J. and Williams, W. 1986. *Disaster Policy Implementation: Managing Programs under Shared Governance*. New York: Plenum Press.

Mazmanian, D. A. and Sabatier, P. A. (eds) 1981. *Effective Policy Implementation*. Lexington, MA: Lexington Books.

1983. *Implementation and Public Policy*. Glenview, IL: Scott, Foresman and Company.

Meyer, P. B. (ed.) 1993. *Comparative Studies in Local Economic Development: Problems in Policy Implementation*. Westport, CT: Greenwood Press.

Ministry of Foreign Affairs (MFA), Indonesia 2014. 'Directorate General of ASEAN Cooperation'. Jakarta, available at: www.kemlu.go.id/Pages/Orgz.aspx?IDP=4&l=en (accessed 30 December 2014).

Ministry of Foreign Affairs (MFA), Malaysia 2014. 'ASEAN-Malaysia National Secretariat'. Putrajaya, available at: www.kln.gov.my/web/guest/dd-asean_malaysia (accessed 30 December 2014).

Ministry of Foreign Affairs (MFA), Singapore 2014. 'ASEAN Directorate'. Singapore, available at: http://app.sgdi.gov.sg/ (accessed 30 December 2014).

Ministry of Foreign Affairs (MFA), Vietnam 2012. 'Organizational Structure'. Hanoi, available at: www.mofahcm.gov.vn/vi/mofa/bng_vietnam/nr070622153725/ (accessed 30 December 2014).

Muramatsu, M. and Krauss, E. S. 1984. 'Bureaucrats and Politicians in Policy-making: The Case of Japan', *American Political Science Review*, 78(1): 126–46.

Nakamura, R. T. and Smallwood, F. 1980. *The Politics of Policy Implementation*. New York: St Martin's Press.

Neo, B. S. and Chen, G. 2007. *Dynamic Governance: Embedding Culture, Capabilities and Change in Singapore*. Singapore: World Scientific Publishing.

Ness, G. D. 1967. *Bureaucracy and Rural Development in Malaysia*. Berkeley, CA: University of California Press.

Nik Rosnah, Wan Abdullah 2011. 'public sector Reform in Malaysia'. In P. S. Kim (ed.), *Public Sector Reform in ASEAN Member Countries and Korea*. Seoul: Daeyoung Moonhwasa Publishing Company, pp. 160–87.

Peabody, R. L. and Rourke, F. E. 1965. 'Public Bureaucracies'. In J. G. March (ed.), *Handbook of Organizations*. Chicago, IL: Rand McNally, pp. 802–37.

Peck, E. and Six, Perri. 2006. *Beyond Delivery: Policy Implementation as Sense-making and Settlement*. New York: Palgrave Macmillan.

Philippine Civil Service Commission 2010. *'Inventory of Government Personnel'*. Quezon City.

Pluvier, J. 1974. *South-East Asia from Colonialism to Independence*. Kuala Lumpur: Oxford University Press.

Political and Economic Risk Consultancy (PERC) 2011. *Emerging Asia SWOT Report*. Hong Kong.

Poon, Y., Nguyen, K. H. and Do, X. T. 2009. 'The Reform of the Civil Service System as Viet Nam Moves into the Middle-income Country Category'. In J. Acuña-Alfaro (ed.), *Reforming Public Administration in Vietnam: Current Situation and Recommendations*. Hanoi: National Political Publishing House, pp. 199–251.

Prasojo, E. 2010. 'A Review of Civil Service System and Civil Service Reform in Indonesia'. In P. S. Kim (ed.), *Civil Service System and Civil Service Reform in ASEAN Member Countries and Korea*. Seoul: Daeyoung Moonhwasa Publishing Company, pp. 89–125.

2011. 'Exploring Public Sector Reform in Indonesia'. In P. S. Kim (ed.), *Public Sector Reform in ASEAN Member Countries and Korea*. Seoul: Daeyoung Moonhwasa Publishing Company, pp. 82–128.

Pressman, J. L. and Wildavsky, A. B. 1973. *Implementation.* Berkeley, CA: University of California.

Puthucheary, M. 1970. 'The Operations Room in Malaysia as a Technique in Administrative Reform'. In H. B. Lee and A. G. Samonte (eds), *Administrative Reforms in Asia.* Manila: Eastern Regional Organization for Public Administration, pp. 165–98.

1978. *The Politics of Administration: The Malaysian Experience.* Kuala Lumpur: Oxford University Press.

Pyper, R. 1995. *The British Civil Service.* London: Prentice Hall/ Harvester Wheatsheaf.

Quah, J. S. T. 1982a. 'The Public Bureaucracy and National Development in Singapore'. In K. K. Tummala (ed.), *Administrative Systems Abroad.* Washington, DC: University Press of America, pp. 42–75.

1982b. 'Bureaucratic Corruption in the ASEAN Countries: A Comparative Analysis of their Anti-Corruption Strategies', *Journal of Southeast Asian Studies*, 13(1): 153–77.

1984. 'The Public Policy-Making Process in Singapore', *Asian Journal of Public Administration*, 6(2): 108–26.

(ed.) 1987a. 'The Public Bureaucracy and Policy Implementation in Asia', Special Issue, *Southeast Asian Journal of Social Science*, 15(2).

1987b. 'Public Bureaucracy and Policy Implementation in Asia: An Introduction', *Southeast Asia Journal of Social Science*, 15(2): vii–xvi.

1987c. 'Public Bureaucracy and Policy Implementation in Singapore', *Southeast Asian Journal of Social Science*, 15(2): 77–95.

2001. 'Singapore: Meritocratic City-State'. In J. Funston (ed.), *Government and Politics in Southeast Asia.* Singapore: Institute of Southeast Asian Studies, pp. 291–327.

2009. 'Public Administration: Change in Style and Continuity in Policy'. In B. Welsh, J. Chin, A. Mahiznan and T. H. Tan (eds),

Impressions of the Goh Chok Tong Years in Singapore. Singapore: NUS Press, pp. 50–60.

2010. *Public Administration Singapore-Style*. Bingley: Emerald Group Publishing.

2011. *Curbing Corruption in Asian Countries: An Impossible Dream?* Bingley: Emerald Group Publishing.

Radin, B. A. 1977. *Implementation, Change, and the Federal Bureaucracy: School Desegregation Policy in H[ealth]E[ducation and] W[elfare], 1964–1968*. New York: Teachers College Press.

Rajenthran, A. 2002. 'Indonesia: An Overview of the Legal Framework for Foreign Direct Investment', Economic and Finance Paper No. 4, Institute of Southeast Asian Studies, Singapore.

Reyes, V. C. 2007. 'Corruption and Policy Implementation in the Philippines: A Comparative Analysis of the Teacher Training and Textbook Delivery Programmes', *Asian Journal of Political Science*, 15(1): 97–125.

2009a. 'Case Study of Implementation amidst Corruption Linkages: The National Textbook Delivery Programme (TDP) of the Philippine Department of Education', *Journal of Educational Policy*, 24(4): 515–35.

2009b. *Corruption and Implementation: Case Studies in Philippine Public Administration*. Quezon City: National College of Public Administration and Governance, University of the Philippines.

Richter, L. K. 1980. 'Priorities in National Development: A Comparative Analysis of Philippine Policy Implementation under Martial Law', *Philippine Journal of Public Administration*, 24(1): 1–25.

1982. 'Bureaucracy by Decree: Public Administration in the Philippines'. In K. K. Tummala (ed.), *Administrative Systems Abroad*. Washington, DC: University Press of America, pp. 76–95.

1987. 'Public Bureaucracy in Post-Marcos Philippines', *Southeast Asian Journal of Social Science*, 15(2): 57–76.

Riedinger, J. M. 1995. *Agrarian Reform in the Philippines: Democratic Transitions and Redistributive Reform*. Stanford, CA: Stanford University Press.

Ripley, R. B. and Franklin, G. A. 1986. *Policy Implementation and Bureaucracy*, 2nd edn. Chicago, IL: Dorsey Press.

Rohdewohld, R. 1995. *Public Administration in Indonesia*. Melbourne: Montech.

2003. 'Decentralization and the Indonesian Bureaucracy: Major Changes, Minor Impact?' In E. Aspinall and G. Fealy (eds), *Local Power and Politics in Indonesia: Decentralization and Democratization*. Singapore: Institute of Southeast Asian Studies, pp. 259–74.

Rondinelli, D. A. 1983. 'Implementing Decentralization Programmes in Asia: A Comparative Analysis', *Public Administration and Development*, 2(3): 181–203.

Rose, D. L. and Vu, V. H. 1961. *The Vietnamese Civil Service System*. East Lansing, MI: Vietnam Advisory Group, Michigan State University.

Rose, R. 2005. *Learning from Comparative Public Policy: A Practical Guide*. London: Routledge.

Rose-Ackerman, S. 1995. *Controlling Environmental Policy: The Limits of Public Law in Germany and the United States*. New Haven, CT: Yale University Press.

Ross, L. 1984. 'The Implementation of Environmental Policy in China: A Comparative Analysis', *Administration and Society*, 15(4): 489–516.

Schwab, K. (ed.) 2011. *The Global Competitiveness Report, 2011–2012*. Geneva: World Economic Forum.

(ed.) 2014. *The Global Competitiveness Report, 2014–2015*. Geneva: World Economic Forum.

Scott, I. 1986. 'Policy-making in a Turbulent Environment: The Case of Hong Kong', *International Review of Administrative Sciences*, 52(4): 447–69.

1987. 'Policy Implementation in Hong Kong', *Southeast Asian Journal of Social Science*, 15(2): 1–19.

2005. *Public Administration in Hong Kong: Regime Change and its Impact on the Public Sector*. Singapore: Marshall Cavendish Academic.

Shamsul, A. B. 1983. 'The Politics of Poverty Eradication: The Implementation of Development Projects in a Malaysian District', *Pacific Affairs*, 56(3): 455–76.

Shumavon, D. H. and Hibbeln, H. K. (eds). 1986. *Administrative Discretion and Public Policy Implementation*. New York: Praeger.

Sidik, M. 2007. *A New Perspective of Intergovernmental Fiscal Relations: Lessons from Indonesia's Experience*. Jakarta: Ripelge.

Sinkule, B. J. and Ortolano, L. 1995. *Implementing Environmental Policy in China*. Westport, CT: Praeger.

Spector, B. I. 2012. *Detecting Corruption in Developing Countries: Identifying Causes/Strategies for Action*. Sterling, VA: Kumarian Press.

Springer, J. F. and Gable, R. W. 1980. 'The Impact of Informal Relations on Organizational Rewards: Comparing Bureaucracies in Southeast Asia', *Comparative Politics*, 12(2): 191–210.

Suhardiman, D. 2015. *Bureaucracy and Development: Reflections from the Indonesian Water Sector*. Singapore: Institute of Southeast Asian Studies.

Synnerstrom, S. 2007. 'The Civil Service: Towards Efficiency, Effectiveness and Honesty'. In R. H. McLeod and A. MacIntyre (eds), *Indonesia: Democracy and the Promise of Good Governance*. Singapore: Institute of Southeast Asian Studies, pp. 159–77.

Tadem, E. C. 1993. 'Agrarian Reform Implementation in the Philippines: Disabling a Centerpiece Program'. In J. I. A. Angeles (ed.), *International Conference on Agrarian Reform: Proceedings and Documentation*. Quezon City: Conference Secretariat, pp. 79–109.

Tan, E. and Chan, G. 2011. 'Overview: Chapter 1. The Singapore Legal System', SingaporeLaw.sg, available at: www.singaporelaw.sg/sglaw/laws-of-singapore/overview/chapter-1 (accessed 10 December 2014).

Tan, G. 2000. *Asian Development: An Introduction to Economic, Social and Political Change in Asia*. Singapore: Times Academic Press.

Tarling, N. (ed.) 2005. *Corruption and Good Governance in Asia*. London: Routledge.

Tendero, A. P. 2000. *Theory and Practice of Public Administration in the Philippines*. Mandaluyong City: Fiscal Administration Foundation Inc.

Thandee, D. 1985. *Politics of Policy Implementation: A Case Study of Rural Development in Thailand*. Bangkok: Social Research Institute, Chulalongkorn University.

Tilman, R. O. 1961. 'Public Service Commission in the Federation of Malaya', *Journal of Asian Studies*, 20(2): 181–96.

Timberman, D. G. 1991. *A Changeless Land: Continuity and Change in Philippine Politics*. Singapore: Institute of Southeast Asian Studies.

Transparency International 2014. 'Corruption Perceptions Index 2014: Results', available at: www.transparency.org/cpi2014/results (accessed 10 December 2014).

Treisman, D. 2000. *The Causes of Corruption: A Cross-National Study*. Los Angeles, CA: Department of Political Science, University of California at Los Angeles.

Van Horn, C. E. 1979. *Policy Implementation in the Federal System: National Goals and Local Implementers*. Lexington, MA: D.C. Heath.

Van Meter, D. S. and Van Horn, C. E. 1975. 'The Policy Implementation Process: A Conceptual Framework', *Administration and Society*, 6(4): 445–88.

Varela, A. P. 1976. 'Family Planning in the Philippines: Assessment of Program Implementation', *Philippine Journal of Public Administration*, 20(3): 236–60.

Vepa, R. K. 1974. 'Implementation – The Problem of Achieving Results', *Indian Journal of Public Administration*, 20(2): 257–92.

Von der Mehden, F. R. 1969. *Politics of the Developing Nations*, 2nd edn. Englewood Cliffs, NJ: Prentice-Hall.

Voradej, C. and Likhit, D. 1987. 'Policy Implementation in the Thai Public Bureaucracy', *Southeast Asian Journal of Social Science*, 15(2): 96–106.

Warwick, D. P. 1978. 'Civil Service Reform in Indonesia: Problems and Possibilities', unpublished confidential report, Harvard Institute for International Development, Cambridge, MA.

1979. 'Cultural Values and Population Policies: Cases and Contexts'. In J. D. Montgomery, H. D. Lasswell and J. S. Migdal (eds), *Patterns of Policy: Comparative and Longitudinal Studies of Population Events*. New Brunswick, NJ: Transaction Books, pp. 295–337.

1982. *Bitter Pills: Population Policies and their Implementation in Eight Developing Countries*. Cambridge: Cambridge University Press.

1987. 'The Effectiveness of the Indonesian Civil Service', *Southeast Asian Journal of Social Science*, 15(2): 40–56.

White, B. T. 1985. 'Population Policy and Rural Reform in China, 1977–1984: Policy Implementation and Interdependency at the Local Level', PhD thesis, Ohio University.

Williams, W. 1980. *The Implementation Perspective: A Guide for Managing Social Service Delivery Programs*. Berkeley, CA: University of California Press.

Wong, J. W. P. 2004. 'Hong Kong Civil Service Continues to Impress', Hong Kong: Civil Service Bureau, 3 August.

World Bank 2011. *Malaysia, Court Backlog and Delay Reduction Program: A Progress Report*. Washington, DC: World Bank.

2013. *Doing Business 2014: Understanding Regulations for Small and Medium Size Enterprises*. Washington, DC: World Bank.

2014a. 'Worldwide Governance Indicators, 2013', available at: http://info.worldbank.org/governance/wgi/index.aspx#reports (accessed 10 December 2014).

2014b. *Doing Business 2015: Going Beyond Efficiency*. Washington, DC: World Bank.

Wurfel, D. 1977. *Philippine Agrarian Policy Today: Implementation and Political Impact*. Occasional Paper No. 46. Institute of Southeast Asian Studies, Singapore.

Young, J. D. 1983. 'Implementation: Key to Reform', *Bureaucrat*, 12(1): 35–40.

Yu, Q. Y. 1999. *The Implementation of China's Science and Technology Policy*. Westport, CT: Quorum.

Zheng, Y., Lu, Y. and White, L. T. (eds) 2009. *Politics of Modern China*, vol. 1, *Policy-making and Policy Implementation*. New York: Routledge.

Zweig, D. 1985. 'Strategies of Policy Implementation: Policy "Winds" and Brigade Accounting in Rural China, 1968–1978', *World Politics*, 37: 267–93.

Chapter 2

Weak central authority and fragmented bureaucracy: a study of policy implementation in Indonesia

Agus Pramusinto

2.1 Introduction

The aim of this chapter is to analyse the role of the civil service in policy implementation in Indonesia. The civil service has played a pivotal role in the development process during the initial phase of Indonesia's independence, the nation-building phase and the process of socio-economic development that followed (Bachtiar 1972). Many terms are used by scholars to describe the role of the civil service in Indonesia, including bureaucratic polity (Jackson 1978), bureaucratic state (Emmerson 1983), bureaucratic authoritarian regime (King 1982), *beamtenstaat* (McVey 1982) and patrimonial bureaucracy (Crouch 1979).

The use of these concepts is still relevant for a good understanding of practices that characterized the conduct of the Indonesian government and bureaucracy until the late 1990s, before the implementation of the subsequent political reforms. Decision-making was very effective due to the dominance of the public bureaucracy with the support of ABRI (*Angkatan Bersenjata Republik Indonesia* or Indonesian Army) and the then ruling political party, Golkar (*Golongan*

Karya or Functional Group). However, forces outside the state were relatively weak and this ensured that the state had ample autonomy in formulating and implementing policies without interference from the non-state actors. Despite the positive aspects of the Suharto regime, there were many administrative problems such as corruption, lack of capacity of the local bureaucrats and the central government's limitations in accommodating local problems.

As the rapid pace of political development during the last decade has induced major changes in the impact of political actors on public policy, it is necessary to revisit studies that portrayed the public bureaucracy as a dominant force in Indonesia, especially during the New Order[1] regime. Previous studies have shown that the role of public bureaucracy in Indonesia was very strong. This chapter focuses on the shift from a hegemonic political party system during the New Order regime to a multi-party system that began to emerge in the wake of its collapse, and addresses two questions. First, to what extent have political changes affected the role of the civil service in policy formulation and implementation in Indonesia? Second, what has been the impact of these political changes on the nature of policy formulation and implementation in Indonesia?

To analyse policy implementation in Indonesia, this chapter relies on the framework introduced by Van Meter and

[1] *Order Baru* (New Order) refers to the period when Suharto was the President, from 1966 to May 1998. Suharto replaced Soekarno's regime (1945–66), which is called *Orde Lama* (Old Order). The Reformation era is the regime that took over after Suharto's fall in May 1998.

Van Horn (1975: 462–74). Indonesia's policy context and the role of its public bureaucracy in the policy formulation and implementation are discussed before analysing in depth the two case studies on the implementation of the ASEAN Cosmetic Directive (ACD) and the ASEAN Ministerial Meeting on Transnational Crime/Senior Officials Meeting on Transnational Crime (AMMTC/SOMTC).

2.2 Indonesia's policy context

2.2.1 Geography

Indonesia is the world's largest archipelago, with more than 17,508 islands, which stretches for more than 5,000 km from Sabang in the West to Merauke in the East, with a land area of 1,904,443 sq. km (*The Economist* 2013: 160). Its vast geographic area is also mirrored by its variety of communications and transportation facilities. Unlike Java Island, which has relatively excellent land and air transport and communications, Papua, which is mountainous, has limited good communications and transportation infrastructure and facilities. The poor accessibility conditions in regions outside Java make policy implementation difficult because regional government officials take a long time to reach remote areas. Furthermore, in relation to handling issues with the central government and ministries in Jakarta, daily flights are not always available in these areas.[2]

[2] It usually takes more than eight hours to travel from one district to another in Papua and requires a four-wheel-drive vehicle. Some areas require the use of small boats, which do not operate daily as their availability depends on the state of the waves and tides.

There are three time zones in Indonesia: East, Central and West Indonesia Standard Time. Jakarta and cities in Sumatra, Java and Kalimantan are seven hours ahead of GMT, while Bali, Sulawesi and Nusa Tengara Barat and Nusa Tenggara Timur are eight hours ahead of GMT. Maluku and Papua in the eastern part of Indonesia are nine hours ahead of GMT. The time difference complicates the public service delivery process which involves the central government agencies in Jakarta and the regional agencies. For example, when the government office opens in Papua at 8 a.m., the respective ministerial office in Jakarta is not opened until two hours later. However, when the regional government office closes at 4 p.m., the Jakarta ministerial office remains open for another two hours. This means that decisions made in Jakarta at 4 p.m. are communicated to the Papua regional government on the following day because of the time difference.

2.2.2 *Formative historical experiences*

During the pre-colonial era Indonesia consisted of many kingdoms, each of which had its full sovereignty and state administrative system. Historical records show that the Majapahit Kingdom controlled virtually all the area that falls within the Indonesian archipelago for nearly half a century. The Majapahit Kingdom collapsed in 1471 and was succeeded by small kingdoms based on Islam.

The Portuguese were the first Europeans to reach Indonesia. In 1522 they built a fort in Ternate and subsequently established a stranglehold over the spice markets in the region (Furnivall 1944: 14–17; Ricklefs 1993). Not long after that, the Dutch arrived and colonized Indonesia for over 350 years after the withdrawal of the Portuguese. The year 1597 marked the beginning of what is referred to as 'wild' or 'unregulated' voyages. The United East India Company, *Vereenigde Oost-Indische Compagnie* (VOC) was awarded a charter as a quasi-sovereign power, which laid the foundation for the permanent presence of the Netherlands India (Cribb 1994).

The Netherlands surrendered unconditionally to the Japanese on 9 March 1942. The policy which the Japanese implemented was to reduce the influence of the West, coupled with measures to mobilize the Indonesian population to support their efforts to win the war. From the structural perspective, Japan tried to leave the existing structure of government intact as long as there were no contradictions with the rules they put in place. The entire European administrative corps was dismissed (Walker 1968: 111).

By and large, the 350 years of Dutch colonial rule and the three and a half years of the Japanese Occupation had a negative impact on the Indonesian public bureaucracy. Both Dutch and Japanese colonial rule did not introduce meritocracy to improve the public bureaucracy in Indonesia. On the contrary, the VOC was notorious for rampant corruption, which today has become the dominant culture in the Indonesian public bureaucracy. In other words, Dutch colonial rule did not introduce a tradition of meritocracy in the civil service, which constitutes an important cause of corruption in Indonesia today (Quah 2011: 360–3). Such a negative legacy can be contrasted with the good education system and clean bureaucracy which Britain bequeathed to Hong Kong and Singapore.

2.2.3 *Economy*

Indonesia is endowed with many natural resources. Historical records show that many countries such as Portugal, the Netherlands, Britain and Japan came in turn to Indonesia attracted by the possibility of wresting control of and exploiting the country's abundant resources.

For several decades during the independence era, the performance of the economy continued to fluctuate. Soekarno, who emphasized nation building during early phases of the post-independence era, did little to improve the economy. When Suharto assumed the reins of power in 1965, the economy was in bad shape because 60 per cent to 70 per cent of the population was poor. Suharto introduced the 'development trilogy' of growth, stabilization and equity, and elevated the Indonesian economy to become an emerging economy and one of the New Asian Tigers. The economy grew by an average of 6 per cent to 7 per cent per year (Hill 1994: 63). The rise in GDP per capita was even more spectacular, increasing from US$70 in 1969 to US$1,080 in 1996 (Basri 2003: 53). The development of the agricultural sector through the intensification and 'extensification' programmes increased rice production from 12.1 million tons in 1969 to 25.8 million tons in 1984. During the span of two decades, sustained economic growth led to economic development, which in turn induced a reduction in poverty from 40 per cent to 11 per cent (Utomo 2003: 159). According to the *Badan Pusat Statistik* (BPS)

(2014), Indonesia's GDP per capita in 2013 was Rp 36,508,486.32 (US$3,650).

The middle of 1997 was a bleak period because the financial crunch affected Indonesia adversely, and the situation deteriorated into a fully fledged economic crisis. The value of the Rupiah against the US$ depreciated drastically from Rp 2,470 in July 1997 to Rp 15,000 in February 1998. Consequently, inflation soared to 34.2 per cent per year, rising further to 47 per cent in April 1998 and hovered around 59 per cent in July 1998 (Utomo 2003: 159). In 1998, inflation was 77.63 per cent on average and economic growth decreased by −13.13 per cent. The economic crisis in turn generated a political crisis which eventually forced Suharto to relinquish power in May 1998. This economic crisis has created difficulties in implementing various policies and programmes because of the limited government budget (Table 2.1).

2.2.4 *Demography*

Based on the 2010 population census, Indonesia has a population of 237,556,363 persons, consisting of 119,507,580 males and 118,048,783 females (*Badan Pusat Statistik* 2011). It is estimated that Indonesia's population has reached 250 million in 2014 (*Badan Pusat Statistik* 2014). It should be noted that Indonesia's population is almost equal to the combined population of the other nine members of ASEAN. Population distribution differs widely by island. Java island, which covers only 7 per cent of the total area in Indonesia (126,700 sq. km), has nearly 60 per cent of the total population (about 136 million) (*Badan Pusat Statistik* 2012).

Table 2.1 *Growth, inflation and unemployment in Indonesia, 1998–2013*

Year	Growth (%)	Inflation (%)	Unemployment (%)	President
1998	−13.13	77.63	5.46	Habibie
1999	0.85	2.01	6.63	Gus Dur
2000	4.92	9.35	6.08	Gus Dur
2001	3.45	12.55	8.10	Megawati
2002	4.50	10.03	9.06	Megawati
2003	4.78	5.06	9.67	Megawati
2004	5.03	6.04	9.86	Susilo Bambang Yudhoyono
2005	5.68	17.11	10.26	Susilo Bambang Yudhoyono
2006	5.5	6.60	10.28	Susilo Bambang Yudhoyono
2007	6.3	6.59	9.1	Susilo Bambang Yudhoyono
2008	6.2	11.06	8.39	Susilo Bambang Yudhoyono
2009	4.55	2.78	8.14	Susilo Bambang Yudhoyono
2010	5.90	6.96	7.41	Susilo Bambang Yudhoyono
2011	6.98	3.79	6.56	Susilo Bambang Yudhoyono
2012	6.85	4.30	6.25	Susilo Bambang Yudhoyono
2013	6.25	8.38	6.25	Susilo Bambang Yudhoyono

Source: compiled from BPS 2000; 2005; 2010; 2014.

Indonesia has a highly diverse population in terms of ethnicity, with attendant regional languages such as Java, Sunda, Batak, Padang, Bali, Makassar and Ambon, with more than 725 local languages. Moreover, there is also a variety of immigrants who are minorities and descendants of the Chinese, Indians and Arabs. With respect to religious affiliation, based on the 2010 Population Census, Indonesia has the largest Muslim population in the world, with 87.18 per cent practising Islam, followed by Protestants (6.96 per cent), Catholics (2.90 per cent), Hindus (1.69 per cent), Buddhists (0.4 per cent) and those professing other religions (0.1 per cent) (*Badan Pusat Statistik* 2011). However, Indonesia is not an Islamic state that uses *syariah* law as its legal foundation.

For various reasons, the existing differences have not degenerated into centrifugal forces. First, the Indonesian language, which originated from the *Melayu* (Malay) language, is the national language. Second, many people have roots in various ethnic groups that have commonalities. For example, Batak ethnicity in Sumatra, which is predominantly Christian, has common features with Manado ethnicity (Sulawesi), Ambon ethnicity (Maluku), Flores ethnicity (NTT) and Papua ethnicity. Meanwhile, those of Aceh ethnicity, who are predominantly Muslims, have close ties with those ethnic groups professing Islam from Java, Minang (West Sumatra), Banjar (West Kalimantan), Makassar and Bugis (South Sulawesi), Lombok (West Nusa Tenggara) and Fak-Fak (Papua).

The diverse demography also influences the effectiveness of policy formulation and implementation. Religious groups such as *Muhammadiyah* and *Nahdatul Ulama* serve as strong pressure groups for certain political issues to accelerate the policy-making process. In terms of ethnicity, local ethnic values appear to be incompatible with the modern values of bureaucracy. Assisting their relatives from their clan group to have a job may be a positive value for some ethnic groups but such assistance is against the practice of meritocracy.

2.2.5 *Political system*

The 1945 Constitution is the highest law of the land, which bestows sovereignty in its entirety to the general public. Subsequently, the 1945 Constitution separates the powers of state to seven State Institutions, which have equal position vis-à-vis one another, inter alia, the President, MPR (*Majelis Permusyawaratan Rakyat* or People's Consultative Assembly), DPR (*Dewan Perwakilan Rakyat* or House of Representatives), DPD (*Dewan Perwakilan Daerah* or Regional Representatives Assembly), BPK (*Badan Pemeriksa Keuangan* or Financial Audit Board), MK (*Mahkamah Konstitusi* or Constitutional Court) and MA (*Mahkamah Agung* or the Supreme Court). So far, the 1945 Constitution has undergone four amendments. One important element in the fourth amendment concerns the MPR, which hitherto was the highest state institution in Indonesia, but today has equal powers and position with the President, DPR, DPD, MA, MK and BPK (*Kementerian Sekretariat Negera* 2014).

New state institutions, which came into being in the wake of the 1998 reformation made possible by the third amendment to the 1945 Constitution, include the DPD and

MK, based on Law No. 24/2003. Meanwhile, there are other institutions, such as the KY (*Komisi Yudisial* or Judicial Commission), ORI (Ombudsman *Republik Indonesia*), UKP4 (*Unit Kerja Presiden bidang Pengawasan dan Pengendalian Pembangunan* or Presidential Work Unit of Supervision and Control of Development) and KPK (*Komisi Pemberantasan Korupsi* or Corruption Eradication Commission), which were created during the Reformation era. These institutions play a vital role in promoting good governance as well as enhancing the performance of government institutions.

Besides the abovementioned formal structural aspects, the political system in Indonesia has evolved during the past sixty-five years. During 1950–1957, Indonesia had a well-functioning parliamentary democratic system. Regrettably, the protracted conflicts among political parties as well as between the central government and provincial governments became one of the distinguishing features of that period. From 1957 to 1965, Indonesia embraced a guided democracy, which espoused a very strong central government vis-à-vis the regional governments (Thoha 2005). The adoption of the centralized political system was induced by a spate of secessionist guerrilla movements which were a consequence of the liberal democratic system.

Subsequently, during Suharto's reign, Indonesia embraced the *Pancasila* democracy idea which was embodied in Suharto as the sole authority in Indonesia. Suharto remained in power for thirty-two years with the support of the senior military officers who occupied key positions as ministers, governors, regional government heads and village heads.

He adopted a centralized administration and bureaucratic system based in Jakarta. For economic planning, Suharto was also supported by prominent technocrats, who were called the 'Berkeley Mafia' as they graduated from the University of California at Berkeley. Political stability was achieved through the imposition of strong restrictions on political party activities and public involvement in politics, which created the 'floating mass'.

New Order politics under Suharto was characterized by hegemonic politics in which the Golkar Party was dominant. The United Development Party, *Partai Persatuan Pembangunan* (PPP) and the Indonesian Democratic Party (*Partai Demokrasi Indonesia* or PDI) were limited to serving superficial political roles as they lacked the capacity to stage strong opposition against Golkar and Suharto. Table 2.2 shows that during the six elections from 1971 to 1997 Golkar was the unanimous winner because of the support it had received from three key forces at the time, which were the public bureaucracy, military and non-civil servants.

Table 2.2 *Indonesian election results, 1971–1997*

Party	1971	1977	1982	1987	1992	1997
Golkar	62.80	62.11	64.34	73.16	68.1	74.51
Partai Persatuan Pembangunan	27.11	29.29	27.78	15.97	17.0	22.43
Partai Demokrasi Indonesia	10.09	8.60	7.88	10.87	14.9	3.06

Source: Suryadinata 2007: 336.

Since Suharto's downfall, Indonesia has experienced significant political reforms because the number of political parties increased from three to forty-eight as a direct consequence of the strong democratization process. In 1999, the dominance of Golkar in Indonesia's politics ended when power was transferred to the PDI-P. Table 2.3 shows that the PDI-P won 153 seats, followed by Golkar (120 seats), PPP (58 seats), PKB (51 seats), PAN (34 seats), PBB (13 seats) and PKS (7 seats). In 2004, another surprise shook the political establishment when the Demokrat party, under the stewardship of President Susilo Bambang Yudhoyono (SBY), won the elections (see Table 2.3). In 2014, Joko Widodo, supported by KIH (*Koalisi Indonesia Hebat* or Great Indonesia Coalition), obtained 53.15 per cent of the votes against Prabowo Subiyanto, who was supported by the KMP (*Koalisi Merah Putih* or Red White Coalition), with 46.85 per cent of the votes.

The above changes had significant implications for the political decision-making process in the National Assembly. During Suharto's regime, a presidential system was created, which enabled him to wield strong executive authority. However, since his downfall, the increase in the number of political parties means that the political system has moved toward a parliamentary system. The strong position of the National Assembly vis-à-vis the President has transformed the focus of the political system from the executive to the legislature.

In 1999, the Indonesian government led by President Habibie issued Laws No. 22 and 25/1999 on Regional Government. These laws replaced Law No. 5/1974 on government in regions, which had created a highly centralized system. President Habibie also introduced freedom of speech, giving

Table 2.3 *Results of the parliamentary elections, 1999–2014*

Party	Number of seats and percentage (1999)	Number of seats and percentage (2004)	Number of seats and percentage (2009)	Number of seats and percentage (2014)
Golkar	120 (25.97%)	128 (23.27%)	107 (19.11%)	91 (16.25%)
PDI-P	153 (33.12%)	109 (19.82%)	95 (16.96%)	109 (19.46%)
PKB	51 (11.03%)	52 (9.45%)	27 (4.82%)	47 (8.39%)
PPP	58 (12.55%)	58 (10.54%)	37 (6.61%)	39 (6.96%)
PD	–	57 (10.36%)	150 (26.78%)	61 (10.89%)
PKS	7 (1.51%)	45 (8.18%)	57 (10.18%)	40 (7.14%)
PAN	34 (7.36%)	52 (9.45%)	43 (7.68%)	49 (8.75%)
PBB	13 (2.81%)	11 (2.00%)	–	–
PBR	–	13 (2.36%)	–	–
PDS	–	12 (2.18%)	–	–
PKPB	–	2 (0.36%)	–	–
Others	26 (5.63%)	11 (2.00%)	–	–
Hanura	–	–	18 (3.21%)	16 (2.86%)
Gerindra	–	–	26 (4.64%)	73 (13.03%)
Nasdem	–	–	–	35 (6.25%)
Total seats	462	550	560	560

Note: PAN (*Partai Amanat Nasional*, National Mandate Party); Partai Nasdem (*Partai Nasional Demokrat*, National Democracy Party); Partai Gerindra (*Partai Gerakan Indonesia Raya*, Great Indonesia Movement Party); *Partai Golkar* (*Partai Golongan Karya*, Functional Groups Party); Partai Hanura (*Partai Hati Nurani Rakyat*, People's Conscience Party); PBB (*Partai Bulan Bintang*, Moon and Star Party); PBR (*Partai Bintang Reformasi*, Reformed Star Party); PD (*Partai Demokrat*, Democratic Party); PDIP-P (*Partai Demokrasi Indonesia-Perjuangan*, Indonesian Democratic Party-Struggle); PDS (*Partai Damai Sejahtera*, Peaceful and Prosperous Party); PKB (*Partai Kebangkitan Bangsa*, Nation Awakening Party); PKPB (*Partai Karya Peduli Bangsa*, Concern for the Nation Party); PKS (*Partai Keadilan Sejahtera*, Justice and Prosperous Party); PPP (*Partai Persatuan Pembangunan*, United Development Party).

more room for the people to express their aspirations without being threatened by the government.

2.2.6 *Legal system and administrative law*

In general, the legal system in Indonesia is influenced by three systems: the Dutch colonial system, the monarchy and the national system, which came into being after the country attained independence on 17 August 1945. While the legal system in Indonesia is closer to Continental Europe, it also draws some positive elements from the Anglo Saxon nations. Some commercial laws follow the Dutch system but other laws, including Banking Law (amended in 1998), Company Law (1995) and Capital Market Law (1995), are based on the national legal code. The legal system is based on Civil Law combined with customary law, and modified by various sovereign laws passed by the legislature, Presidential decrees and government decrees or regulations.

Administrative law in Indonesia adheres to these two principles: (1) public officials use law as the basis for the execution of their functions; and (2) the state, according to State Administrative Law, constitutes the highest legal subject. Consequently, all administrative activities and actions must

Notes to Table 2.3 (*cont.*)
PKPB (*Partai Karya Peduli Bangsa*) did not fulfil the parliamentary threshold of 2.5 per cent in the 2009 election. PD (*Partai Demokrat*) was established in 2004, Partai Hanura (*Partai Hati Nurani Rakyat*) and Partai Gerindra (*Partai Gerakan Indonesia Raya*) in 2009 and Partai Nasdem (*Partai Nasional Demokrat*) in 2014.
Sources: Suryadinata 2002: 220–3, Wiratna 2004: 143 and KPU 2014.

be based both directly and indirectly on the provisions of the law (Kansil and Kansil 2005: 186).

2.3 Profile of the civil service

2.3.1 Historical evolution

The history of the civil service can be traced to the Dutch occupation of Indonesia 400 years ago. In 1932, when the Dutch government had total control of Indonesia, the civil service employed 85,708 Indonesians and 17,034 Europeans (Bachtiar 1972: 431). The number of civil servants increased to 415,627 in 1957 and to 1,674,871 in 1974. During the next ten years, the number of employees in the civil service swelled to 2,785,646 by 1984 (Logsdon 1992: 228).

The role of the civil service in Indonesia depends on the nature of the politics of the day. A strong sense of neutrality and professionalism, which should be the most important features of the civil service, are absent in Indonesia. This was very much the case during the Old Order regime (1945–1965) when political parties strove to wrest interest and influence the civil service, as well as during the New Order era government when it became a main pillar and support of the regime. The civil service was used by Golkar to mobilize votes in directing general elections.

When the Kingdoms held sway, the civil service was an extension of the palace establishment and was charged with the main task of delivering services to the King. The ruler considered and used public administration as a personal issue. Salaries for subordinates bore semblance to presents which depended on the whims of the King. Civil servants were officials and employees of the King and could treat members of the general public in accordance with their wishes or whims.

The rising trend of democratization has influenced the terminologies used to refer to the civil service. *Pangreh Praja* was used to refer to the civil service during the early phases of post independent Indonesia, a term which denoted mastery and control of power (Thoha 2005). The terminology used is akin to the public bureaucracy during the Kingdom era, which reflected a hierarchical relationship between the King (superior) and his subordinates. Even though there was not much change in practice during the New Era regime, the terminology used to refer to civil servants changed to *Pamong Praja*, which meant that the civil service was the protector and sustainer of members of the general public. The latest term, *Pelayan Publik* (public servants), denotes a bureaucracy which is obliged to be ready to deliver services to members of the general public (Dwiyanto 2012b).

2.3.2 *Current size and composition*

The Indonesian civil service today consists of administration employees, teachers, lecturers, doctors and nurses. In 2011, the civil service employed 4,646,351 persons consisting of 2,455,072 males (52.84 per cent) and 2,191,279 females (47.16 per cent). Thus, the ratio of males to females in the civil service in 2011 was 1.12 to 1. Tables 2.4 and 2.5 show the growth in the number and composition of servants per 1,000 population.

Table 2.4 *Growth of Indonesian Civil Service, 1950–2014*

Year	Number of civil servants	Civil servants per 1,000 population
1950	303,500	3.7
1960	393,000	4.1
1970	515,000	4.4
1980	2,047,000	13.9
1992	4,009,000	21.8
2011	4,646,351	19.4
2014	4,375,009	17.5

Sources: Rohdewohld 1995: 94 and BKN 2012; 2014.

Table 2.5 *Indonesian Civil Service by age and gender, October 2011*

Age group	Male	Percentage	Female	Percentage	Totals
18–20	2,787	62.90	1,644	37.10	4,431
21–25	67,477	38.69	106,923	61.31	174.400
26–30	223,273	43.58	289,036	56.42	512,309
31–35	276,093	47.56	304,483	52.44	580,576
36–40	302,674	50.83	292,738	49.17	595,412
41–45	446,888	52.82	399,139	47.18	846,027
46–50	533,999	56.19	416,293	43.81	950,292
51–55	462,724	62.84	273,632	37.16	736,356
56–60	132,112	55.92	104,141	44.08	236,253
61–65	6,665	67.95	3,143	32.05	9,808
65+	380	78.03	107	21.97	487
Totals	2,455,072	52.84	2,191,279	47.16	4,646,351

Source: Badan Kepegawaian Nasional 2012.

Between 1950 and 2011, the number of civil servants has increased by fifteen times. In addition, the number of civil servants available to deliver services has increased significantly from 3.7 to 21.8 civil servants per 1,000 population during

1950–1992. By 2014, the number of civil servants had decreased to 4,375,009, or 17.5 civil servants per 1,000 population.

In accordance with the job structure, the Indonesian Civil Service consists of structural, general and special functional positions. Structural positions refer to those jobs that have subordinates who are accountable to their superiors. In the Ministry, the Secretary-General and Director-General are the highest structural positions, while at the provincial or district levels, the regional secretary constitutes the highest position.

Meanwhile, special functional positions, which do not have subordinates or superiors, include jobs such as medical doctors, nurses, lecturers and teachers. There are 2,323,095 Indonesian civil servants occupying special functional positions in 2014. General functional positions, on the other hand, are those civil servants who do not have structural positions and provide general administrative services. In 2014, the Indonesian civil service employed 1,751,331 persons in general functional positions (Table 2.6).

MENPAN-RB (*Kementrian Pemberdayaan Aparatur Negara dan Reformasi Birokrasi* or the Ministry of State

Table 2.6 *Distribution of Indonesian Civil Service by position, 2012–2014*

Position	**2012**	**2013**	**2014**
Structural	238,462	277,745	308,583
Special functional	2,252,090	2,328,671	2,323,095
General functional	1,977,430	1,756,389	1,751,331

Source: Badan Kepegawaian Nasional 2014.

Apparatus Empowerment and Bureaucratic Reforms) is responsible for conducting bureaucratic reform by providing guidance to national ministries and regional governments. The BKN (*Badan Kepegawaian Nasional* or National Civil Service Agency) is charged with the administration of the civil service at the national level, while BKD (*Badan Kepegawaian Daerah* or Regional Civil Service Agency) at the Provincial and District Government plays a similar role at the level of the province and district respectively.

LAN (*Lembaga Administrasi Negara* or National Institute of Public Administration) and the *Badan Diklat* (*Badan Pendidikan dan Latihan* or the Agency for Education and Training) at the provincial and district levels, are charged with conducting the education and training of civil servants at the provincial and district levels. The authority for conducting education and training is streamlined. The *Diklatpim* I (*Pendidikan dan Pelatihan Kepemimpinan* or Leadership Training Grade I), which constitutes the highest level, is carried out by LAN, the Provincial *Badan Diklat*, which is an accredited agency, is charged with conducting *Diklatpim* II at the level of the province. Meanwhile, accredited District/City *Badan Diklat* are charged with carrying out *Diklatpim* III and IV.

Law No. 43/1999 on State Civil Service stipulates that the management of employees requires the formation of the State Civil Service Commission (*Komisi Kepegawaian Negara*), which consists of a representative of the government, academics and representatives of the general public. However, more than fifteen years since the Law was enacted, the formation of the commission remains elusive. The long delay has been attributed to conflicts of interest in the ministry. There are fears that the existence of the commission will reduce the authority of the MENPAN-RB and BKN.

The civil service continues to be highly susceptible to corruption, as reflected in Indonesia's consistently poor rankings on Transparency International's Corruption Perceptions Index (Quah 2011: 391). The process of recruiting employees in local government has often been exploited to perpetuate corruption. Efforts to enhance the merit recruitment system have not significantly reduced the incidence of corruption, which still reaches millions of Rupiah. Public officials often have to pay for the opportunity to participate as well as pass the training exercises, which they are required to undertake in order to obtain a certificate that is a prerequisite to occupy strategic positions. A female public servant who wishes to move to another place to follow her husband has to pay a bribe to facilitate her transfer. This condition has undermined meritocracy and hindered the implementation process. As the 'investment' of obtaining the strategic position is expensive, bureaucrats often demand large bribes from those persons applying for business, building and work permits. Corruption is also common in public procurement with the inflation of project budgets (Pramusinto 2005).

2.3.3 *Salary and benefits of civil servants*

The current Indonesian system is a combination of single-scale and multiple-scale systems. The single-scale system involves a payment system that gives a certain level of salary to heads of all families who fall under the same grade, without taking into consideration the nature of the job and attendant responsibility. However, a multiple-scale system considers the nature of the job, the workload and the responsibilities associated with the job.

Every year, the Indonesian government issues a government regulation which increases the basic salaries. In accordance with PP No. 34/20014, the minimum basic salary for civil servants (Grade Ia with no work experience) is Rp 1,402,400 (US$140.24) while the basic salary for the highest grade (Grade IVe with working experience of thirty-two years) is Rp 5,302,100 (US$530.20). Table 2.7 shows that the basic salary of civil servants in Indonesia is extremely low. The highest educational attainment of Grade I civil servants is elementary school and junior school. Grade II employees are those with a high school education, while grade III civil servants have bachelor's or graduate degrees.

In addition to the basic salary, civil servants earn various allowances, including family allowance, food allowance, job allowance (for structural and functional positions),

Table 2.7 *Basic monthly salary for civil servants in Indonesia, 2014*

Grade	a	b	c	d	e
			thousands of rupiahs		
I	1,402.4	1,531.5	1,596.3	1,663.8	–
	2,098.6	2,221.9	2,315.8	2,413.8	
II	1,816.9	1,984.2	2,068.1	2,155.6	–
	3,031.1	3,159.3	3,293.0	3,432.3	
III	2,317.6	2,415.6	2,517.8	2,624.3	–
	3,806.3	3,967.3	4,135.2	4,310.1	
IV	2,735.3	2,851.0	2,971.6	3,097.3	3,228.3
	4,492.4	4,682.4	4,880.5	5,086.9	5,302.1

Source: Government Regulation No. 34/2014.

incentives for getting involved in project activities, allowance for being a committee member, and others. For example, with respect to the functional allowance for university lecturers, the implementation of the certification policy means that a university professor earns three times his basic salary, which amounts to Rp 13 million (US$1,300).

With a civil service characterized by a low salary remuneration system, civil servants in Indonesia are often compelled to undertake various activities to make ends meet. A strategy known as 'projectism' is often adopted by civil servants to transform routine activities into projects so that they can receive honoraria in their capacity as project implementers (Rohdewohld 1995: 102). They also convene frequent meetings to receive honoraria for attending these meetings. Making office trips is also a common practice, as these trips entitle civil servants to receive additional transport allowances. Consequently, there are usually more organizing committee members than the number of people invited for the meetings. For example, the twenty-four members of the organizing committee of a ministry invited twenty officials to attend a meeting.

In 1999, the Indonesian Government issued Law No. 22 on Local Governance, which has become an important determinant in managing the country. The central government devolved all governmental functions to local governments except for security and defence, foreign relations, fiscal and monetary policies, religion and judiciary. Provincial, district and city governments become autonomous and the central government becomes weak in controlling them. Implementing the central government's policies in local governments has become a serious problem.

2.4 Policy formulation

2.4.1 *Problem definition by the policy-makers*

There is a significant shift in the policy formulation process since the onset of reforms implemented during the Reformation era. Policy formulation during the New Order regime was dominated by the public bureaucracy, drawing on much support from the technocrats and the military playing the role of development stabilizers (Jackson 1978; King 1982). The public bureaucracy formulated the laws, which were easily approved by the National Assembly. President Suharto authoritatively used the INPRES (*Instruksi Presiden* or Presidential Instruction) mechanism to accelerate the policy formulation process. At the technical level, the experts and bureaucrats formulated the policies. Although the policy formulation was swift, the policy content was problematic due to lack of appropriateness between the central government's policies and the local aspirations. The policy formulation process was also manipulated by Suharto for the sake of his family and crony interests. For example, Suharto issued INPRES No. 2/1996 on National Car Policy and INPRES No. 1/1992 on Clove Support and Marketing Board for the benefit of his son.

During the Reformation era, policy formulation followed a lengthy process of public consultation. However, members of the National Assembly are now drawn from many political parties instead of a single political force. Consequently, the policy formulation takes longer. The INPRES mechanism, which Suharto had used to expedite the policy formulation process, is no longer online or allowed for his successors.

The process of revising laws in the National Assembly requires more time because of the long agenda list. From 2005 to 2011, the National Assembly had more than 300 draft laws on its agenda, which were beyond its capacity of revising thirty laws a year from its previous target of seventy laws a year. In 2012, the DPR was able to complete just thirty laws from a target of sixty-nine laws (*Kompas* 2012b). The delay in completing laws is attributed to the lack of time allocated for the completion of all legislation. Consequently, the completion of each law takes longer than expected (Nurbaningsih 2012). The National Assembly cannot create timely laws to respond to all important issues in society because of these reasons: whether or not the issue is on the agenda, when it is on the agenda and whether the draft legislation can be discussed immediately.

2.4.2 *Role of the Cabinet*

Chapter V, Article 17, Law 1945 stipulates that: (1) the President receives assistance from ministers; (2) ministers are appointed and dismissed by the President; (3) every minister is charged with certain portfolios within the government administration; and (4) laws regulate the formation, changes and the dissolution of the state ministries.

The Indonesian Cabinet consists of ministers who assist the President. Ministerial positions are political appointments, and ministers are accountable to the President. There are thirty-four ministries in the First United Indonesia Cabinet. However, the multi-party system means that ministers are drawn from various political parties. Political parties in the coalition represented in the Cabinet include: Democratic Party, Justice Party, National Awakening Party, National Mandate Party, Golkar Party and United Development Party. However, the Indonesia Democratic Party for Struggle, which was able to garner substantial votes in the 2009 general elections, opted to remain in the opposition. Some ministers in the Cabinet are professionals and do not have political party affiliation.

The *Kabinet Kerja* (Cabinet of Work) under President Joko Widodo inaugurated on 27 October 2014 consists of eighteen professionals and sixteen politicians. Political parties supporting him have obtained some cabinet seats. It was not an easy task for him to avoid some pressures from the political parties to accommodate some candidates. He relied on the *Pusat Pelaporan Analisis Transaki Keuangan* (PPATK) and KPK to select cabinet members who were not involved in corruption. Thus, ministers representing political parties in the Cabinet are accountable to the President and their parties. Such a condition complicates decision-making for the President as he may not dismiss a cabinet minister who fails to perform. Whenever a cabinet reshuffle is in the offing, political parties engage in bargaining as well as providing protection and defence for ministers who represent them in the Cabinet. For instance, during the 2011 cabinet reshuffle, several ministers, who were alleged to be corrupt, were retained by SBY to keep the coalition intact even though the general public had called for their dismissal and replacement.

The role of the Cabinet in the Indonesian government is to formulate presidential policies for each ministry. Ministries translate the vision and missions of the President for five years, which are drawn from the pledges made during election campaigns into policies. These policies are incorporated into the RPJMN (*Rencana Pembangunan Jangka Menengah Nasional* or the National Medium-Term Development Plan), which serves as a guideline. Formally, all development plans are distributed within each ministry as well as integrated across all ministries. However, the implementation of the RPJMN has been hindered by the interests of sectoral ministries. Moreover, there is no clear linkage between planning in the central government and the provincial and local governments.

2.4.3 *Role of senior civil servants*

Senior civil servants in Indonesia consist of echelon I officials, including the Secretary-General, Director-General and Inspector-General. These officials are career employees who are recruited into the civil service based on a merit system. They are responsible for implementing policies that are formulated by the ministers. The Secretariat-General serves as a supporting agency to ensure that the activities of the ministry are run smoothly. The Directorate-General is the implementing agency responsible for executing the policies of the minister. The Inspectorate-General is the agency responsible for supervising the execution of the ministry's activities. For instance, education policy is handled by two Director-Generals: the Director-General for Advanced Education and the Director-General for Elementary and Junior School Education.

During the New Order regime, many military officials were appointed as senior civil servants to strengthen the public bureaucracy's role in policy implementation. After the Reformation era, these positions are occupied by senior bureaucrats without a military background. However, as some ministries are controlled by political parties, their senior officials are appointed on the basis of political affiliation.

2.4.4 *Role of other policy actors*

In a democratic system, non-state actors play an important role. Some of the key non-state actors include donor agencies, non-governmental organizations (NGOs) and the mass media. Though they are not part of the government, these actors have substantial influence.

2.4.4.1 Donor and international agencies

Donor agencies have played a very important role in influencing public policy changes in Indonesia. Some of the donor agencies include, among others, the World Bank, which during the 1967–1998 period disbursed substantial funds to the tune of US$24 billion (Hutagalung 2009). Other United Nations agencies, such as UNDP, ILO, UNICEF, and donor agencies like USAID, AusAID, GTZ, CIDA and JICA have also played an important role in the process of formulating regulatory frameworks, laws and other lower-tier regulations. It is evident that almost all laws and regulations created by the central government are supported and facilitated by these agencies.

2.4.4.2 Non-governmental organizations

NGOs play an important role in the process of social and economic development in Indonesia (Eldridge 1995). Their important role testifies to the relations between the state and its citizens. The onset of democracy has enhanced the involvement of the NGOs in areas that are extremely sensitive for public officials. They have, for instance, criticized various government policies, ranging from the implementation system and budgeting to policy implementation. According to the *Direktori Organisasi Kemasyarakatan* 2009 (*Community Organizations Directory*), Indonesia had 405 large NGOs, spread across different parts of the country, in 2009. Examples of these NGOs include: YLBH (*Yayasan Lembaga Bantuan Hukum* or Legal Aid Institute Foundation), Walhi (*Wahana Lingkungan Hidup Indonesia* or Indonesian Environmental Network), ICW (Indonesian Corruption Watch) and FITRA (*Forum Indonesia untuk Transparansi Anggaran* or Indonesian Forum for Budget Transparency).

2.4.4.3 Television and newspapers

Mass media have played a crucial role in influencing significant changes in Indonesia's political system and its public policies. Suharto's New Order regime imposed stringent restrictions on news reporting by the mass media. Newspapers which were bold enough to criticize government failures were forced to cease operations. During the Reformation era, the freedom of media guaranteed space for virtually boundless criticism of government policies as well as public officials. Today, Indonesia has more than ten television stations. The current intensive television coverage of issues of the day is in part influenced by the majority ownership stakes of individuals with political party affiliation. Metro television is the television station owned by Surya Paloh, who is a Golkar functionary, but has now established *Partai Nasdem* (*Partai Nasional Demokrat* or the National Democratic Party). Aburizal Bakri, head of the Golkar party, has a majority stake in TVOne and ANTV, and other private television stations (Sitepu 2011).

Besides broadcasting news reports on government policies, these television stations often stage political debates or talk shows with prominent critical leaders as well as giving viewers an opportunity to make comments through telephone calls. For instance, the current issue concerning the government's plan to raise the fuel price has received serious media attention, as reflected in the intensity of news coverage and live debates. Undoubtedly, the debates generated by the mass media have enriched and lengthened the policy-making process.

2.5 The civil service's role in policy implementation

2.5.1 Definition of policy standards and objectives

The public bureaucracy is responsible for determining the policy standards and objectives. Each ministry is responsible for formulating its own policy standards and objectives but the standards and targets of cross-sectoral programmes are determined by the relevant ministries.

The problem of policy standards and targets faced by ministries is attributed to the absence of a clear-cut division of authority, both horizontally between one ministry and other ministries as well as between the central government and local governments (provinces and districts or cities). Policy overlap has become a common feature in most large ministries. According to the MENPAN-RB, the organizational structure of the public bureaucracy is too large, which generates the problem of overlap among ministries and agencies (*Kompas* 2010). For example, Professor Agus Dwiyanto of Gadjah Mada University was asked to undertake the same assignment by two sub-directorates in the Ministry of Home Affairs (Dwiyanto 2012b).

From the vertical perspective, there is still lack of clarity in the division of power and authority between the central government and local governments. Despite the fact that the government has issued Government Regulation No. 38/2007, the problem of overlapping authority between the central government and provincial, district and city governments still exists. Many programmes initiated by district governments in accordance with their powers entrusted to them through devolution overlap with those programmes implemented by ministries in their capacity as agents of the central government. The existence of an overlap in power or authority between different levels of government has resulted in these three problems: (1) conflicting regulations between laws on local governments and sectoral laws; (2) efforts by the sectoral ministries to de-concentrate activities which were devolved to local governments; and (3) cases where the provincial governments meddle in the affairs of district or city governments (Dwiyanto 2012a).

2.5.2 *Policy resources*

In the context of the Indonesian public bureaucracy, policy resources consist of financial resources, human resources, implementation rules and other resources. Every sector or ministry often attempts to obtain resources that are tailored to strengthen their organizations. During the New Order regime, the National Planning Board *(Bappenas)* was responsible for determining financial resources, while during the post Suharto Reformation era, the Ministry of Finance and political decisions made in the National Assembly have assumed this role.

For human resources, there is a tendency to increase the number of organizations and employees. The increase in the number of agencies and personnel has often led to inefficiency. For example, the number of directorate generals and directors in every ministry has increased. Besides, organizations at the local government level have also experienced an increase simply because central government assistance requires the establishment of a new organizational structure (*Kompas* 2012a). Whenever there is a new programme or activity, agencies often try to increase the number of temporary employees. Unfortunately, the process of recruiting temporary and contract workers is often not based on merit as it involves such underhand methods as cronyism and using project funds for their remuneration. The expectation is that during the recruitment process of civil servants such employees receive precedence over the new applicants.

The disparity in the quality and quantity of human resources among ministries constitutes a very serious problem.

Some ministries such as the Ministry of Finance and Planning or *Bappenas* have very high quality human resources compared with other ministries. The pattern of recruitment employs higher standards (GPA, TOEFL and *Tes Potensi Akademik* or Academic Potential Test), making it possible to attract employees with high development potential. In general, employees in the two ministries are able to pursue advanced education both within the country and abroad for masters' degrees and even doctorates. The disparity in the quality of human resources between the central government and local governments has become more apparent. This is attested by the differential treatment with respect to TOEFL and TPA requirements, which *Bappenas* has adopted in selecting participants in training exercises drawn from the central government and regional governments. The parochial understanding of regional autonomy has helped to widen the disparity. The mobility of employees from one region to another as well as between the central government and regional governments has been severely restricted. Consequently, according to Pohan (*Bappenas* 2011), primordialism has increased as emphasis is being placed on prioritizing the interests of '*Putra Daerah*' (local indigenous people) in recruitment and promotion. Regions that have low-quality human resources remain backward as they face formidable obstacles in transforming knowledge and work culture from other areas. To that end, the draft revision for Law No. 43/1999 is expected to provide an opportunity for officials at the district or city government level to enhance their careers and promotion in other districts and provinces as well as at the central government and Jakarta (Thoha 2012).

As policy implementation depends on the implementing regulations, laws approved by the National Assembly do not necessarily become effective policies as long as there are no implementing regulations such as Presidential regulations, government regulations or ministerial decisions. Furthermore, the time lag between enacting laws and the issuance of implementing regulations can take years. The government usually opts not to use its mandate to issue implementing regulations if it considers the regulation or law detrimental to its interests. A good example was Law No. 5/1974[3] that was delayed for more than twenty years before it was implemented.

2.5.3 *Inter-organizational communication and enforcement activities*

Inter-organizational communication in the Indonesian public bureaucracy is both hierarchical and top down. The domination of superiors over subordinates leaves little room for open communication between them. In general, the subordinates are expected to implement the rules that are approved by their superiors. Information, advice and recommendations from subordinates are conveyed to superiors if demanded. Over the past ten years, hierarchical communication has shifted towards becoming more egalitarian. Subordinates can now convey their views to their superiors and there is

[3] This law focuses on local government. However, its implementation depends on several regulations issued by the central government and needs clear functional assignment among the three different levels of government based on government regulations.

also more openness shown by superiors to their subordinates. This shift is related to the demand by members of the public as users of services for public officials to democratize service delivery. This trend has also become apparent outside the public bureaucracy.

Communication among public agencies occurs in a conventional manner, that is, through routine meetings involving many ministries. However, as the officials attending these meetings are not authorized to make decisions for their ministries, they cannot resolve differences of opinion. Furthermore, information technology is not used fully as a medium for communication because not all officials have the ability or willingness to do so. Sharing data that facilitates access to information is rarely done because of limited technology and the selfish and fragmented behaviour among the officials of ministries. Moreover, communication and coordination usually means meetings with the relevant officials without the sharing of data.

Indonesia is ranked 106th among 193 countries on the United Nations E-Government Survey for 2014, with a score of 0.4487, which is below the world average score of 0.4712 (UNPACS 2014). There is also a difference in understanding of and skills in using computers among the public officials in Java and those outside Java. The availability of computers in government offices in regions outside Java is limited and their use is confined to typing letters. Several regional government employees interviewed by telephone informed the author that the ratio of computer availability was 60 per cent to 70 per cent higher than the number of employees. However, while the employees know how to use computers, their use of

Table 2.8 *Travel budget for Civil Service, 2009–2011*

Budget allocation for travel	**2009**	**2010**	**2011**
		trillion rupiah	
National budget	2.9	16.2	20.9 (proposed)
Revised national budget	12.7	19.5	24.5 (agreed)
Realization	15.2	n/a	n/a

Source: Kedaulatan Rakyat 2012.

computers is limited to typing letters, and saving and processing data (Aziz 2012; Nuryanto 2012; Siswanti 2012).

Government officials spend a great deal of money travelling to attend meetings, from the regions to Jakarta and vice versa. They reap financial rewards because travelling allowances provide additional income for them. Table 2.8 shows that the budget for office travelling expenses for 2011 was Rp 24.5 trillion (US$2.45 billion) and larger than the 2010 budget. The government submitted a budget proposal of Rp 20.9 trillion (US$2.09 billion) but the amount approved by the government and DPR was Rp 24.5 trillion (US$ 2.45 billion). The Financial Audit Board reported that misuse of the budget for office travel amounted to Rp 73.5 billion (US$7.35 million) in 2009 and Rp 89.5 billion (US$8.95 million) in 2010 (*Kedaulatan Rakyat* 2012). For the 2015 budget, President Joko Widodo has reduced the travel budget from Rp 41 trillion (US$4,100 billion) to Rp 16 trillion (US$1,600 billion) (*Kompas* 2014).

With regards to enforcement, there is as yet no clear action taken against those public officials who underperform. The reward and punishment system does not apply to the public bureaucracy, and hence has no bearing on one's pace of promotion or demotion. In general, in the Indonesian public bureaucracy, the application of individual performance measurement has never been undertaken. Consequently, evaluating the extent to which performance has attained the target every year for every individual employee cannot be done because the targets at the individual level are not implemented (Sutrisno 2012). Hence, the evaluation system to determine whether a programme or activity generates output or outcome for future improvement is rarely done.

Punishment is meted to an individual when he or she is found to have committed such serious offences as corruption. The civil service continues to be highly susceptible to corruption. However, petty corruption such as bribing officers to expedite the issuance of permits is not considered a serious offence. Furthermore, it is difficult to prove whether an individual is corrupt in the Indonesian public bureaucracy. Petty corruption involving the misuse of the office travel budget is rampant in Indonesia (Table 2.9). For example, a public

Table 2.9 *Misuse of travel budget in selected Indonesian ministries*

Ministry	**Amount of misused budget**
	billion rupiah
National Education	14.0
Cultural and Tourism	12.8
Social Affairs	10.0
Forestry	7.9

Source: Kedaulatan Rakyat 2012.

official travelling to and from the regions for two days inflates his claim to the host office by submitting a form for travel expenses for three to four persons for four to five days instead. Though such practice is a manifestation of the misuse of public funds, as long as all documents are in order from an administrative standpoint it is not viewed as corruption because administratively all the documents are available. There is still no law on the reversal of burden of proof where the official has to prove where his money comes from.

2.5.4 *Characteristics of implementing agencies*

2.5.4.1 Competence and size of agency staff

The competence of staff is an important precondition for policy implementation. In the context of the Indonesian public bureaucracy, there is a large gap between the leadership and staff as manifested in these three problems. First, for certain agencies, street level bureaucrats who have direct impact on the implementation of policy to the general public rarely execute policies based on the spirit of their leaders' decisions. This problem is attributed to the low capacity of understanding of street-level bureaucrats, which hampers their ability to implement policies as required by their leaders. However, street-level bureaucrats deliberately fail to implement policies because of their desire or interest in taking advantage of the shortcomings that arise. Consequently, leaders are often frustrated because subordinates fail to implement policies they have formulated. Unfortunately, there is no punishment for those who do not perform effectively in the public bureaucracy.

Secondly, there is a gap in capacity and authority of leaders and their subordinates. Some institutions have many young officials who have high leadership capacity but lack the authority to effect changes, and leaders who have the authority but lack the required capacity. The failure of these young officials to apply their ideas to efforts that are tailored to changing their organizations reduces their motivation.

Besides competence issues, the difference in the size of ministries is the third problem. An official at echelon I in the Ministry of Finance controls ten times the number of subordinates of an echelon I official in the Ministry of Development Planning (*Bappenas*) or MENPAN-RB. Another example is the stark contrast between an echelon II official in *Bappenas*, who has three subordinates, and an echelon II official in the Ministry of Finance and Ministry of Education, who controls more than fifty subordinates (Dwiyanto 2012b).

2.5.4.2 An agency's political resources

A ministry often constitutes an arena where the contestations of political parties or agencies occur. Some agencies are fraught with political interests, with the implication that choosing leadership often involves political transactions in the National Assembly. In the process of electing the leadership of the KPK (Corruption Eradication Commission), the selection committee prepared a list of candidates based on their rankings. However, that ranking was in abeyance during the selection tests for candidates in the National Assembly (*Tempo* 2014).

The support of the National Assembly is crucial for determining the size of budget allocation approved for a ministry. As an institution that is tasked with the budgeting function, the National Assembly is very powerful in determining the amount of budget allocation for some ministries. Moreover, the mechanism for determining the amount of budget allocation is riddled with political transactions rather than focusing on development needs and priorities. In addition, the size of budget allocation also depends on the intensity of the conflict of an organization with the National Assembly as illustrated in the case of the Ombudsman of the Republic of Indonesia. According to a member of the Ombudsman Commission, Commission II DPR agreed to allocate Rp 31.7 billion (US$3.1 million) in March 2011. However, the allocation of the budget for the Ombudsman could only be effected if certain conditions were met. 'Some culprits on the budget commission [*Badan Anggaran* or Budget Board] demanded Rp 9 billion (US$900,000), meaning that they wanted to be the implementers of projects.' The conflict between the Ombudsman and the National Assembly led to a drastic reduction in the Ombudsman's budget proposal that was submitted to the National Assembly (Sutrisno 2011).

2.5.4.3 Vitality of an organization

Organizational capacity also depends on the vitality of the organizational structure of the ministries. Furthermore, the networks of each ministry with agencies at the regional level also vary markedly. The Ministry of Internal Affairs has the strongest network as regional governments tend to have higher obedience or compliance with this ministry than with other ministries. For instance, the Ministry of National Planning has little influence on the Regional Planning Agency in comparison with the Ministry of Internal Affairs.

With respect to institutional relations, many agencies at the central government level have hierarchical relations with agencies at the regional level. Examples include the National Narcotics Agency with the Regional Narcotics Agencies at the province and district levels, and the National Disaster Management Board with the semi-autonomous Regional Disaster Management agencies. However, the National Employees Board does not have hierarchical relations with the regional employees' boards (Dwiyanto 2012a).

2.5.4.4 Disposition of the implementers

The degree to which public policy is implemented depends on the disposition of the implementers. Some of the questions that often arise concerning the public bureaucracy in Indonesia relate to the extent of the existing legal framework. The Indonesian public bureaucracy can only operate as long as it has the mandate. Without regulations, the bureaucrat lacks the courage to take action even in cases where the issue involves the public interest. There are no rules on discretion, which would give the bureaucrats a sense of security. Administrative mistakes made in the course of conducting public administration activities may have serious implications that result in legal actions taken against bureaucrats (Sutrisno 2012).

One district government head informed the author that he preferred not to conduct any activities in order to avoid being accused of corruption. Singular action by an official can result in his being accused of engaging in criminal activity. For example, if a district head carries out repairs or improvements on roads, which are the responsibility of the provincial government, he is liable to sanctions or actions, even though road improvements will benefit the general public by reducing the number of accidents. However, he does not think that he has done anything wrong as he has not done anything corrupt and perceives such an action to fall within his responsibility and accountability to the citizenry. What he has done is to serve the public and his actions follow the existing regulations. Such action would seem very appropriate given the fact that the provincial government, as the responsible party, does not have the budgetary allocation for such services. Some regions do not undertake innovations in public service delivery because such actions do not follow the approved procedures. Bureaucrats also have a tendency to seek out comfort zones and avoid high-risk activities.

2.6 Implementing the ASEAN Cosmetic Directive (ACD)

Indonesia has shown its leadership in the implementation of various ASEAN agreements. ASEAN continues to move towards an ASEAN Community 2015, with one vision, one identity and one community. However, it is not an easy task for Indonesia to face the challenges relating to the creation of the ASEAN Community. Indonesia may suffer because of its weak economic position compared with its neighbouring countries. For example, various ministries may not be prepared to deal with the challenges arising from the ASEAN Free Trade Area or ASEAN–China Free Trade Area.

In Indonesia, the Ministry of Foreign Affairs (MFA) is the most important institution in various regional and international cooperation agreements. The MFA is a hub for those international agencies which provide assistance for regional cooperation such as the ASEAN. It is also responsible for communicating and coordinating various programmes with the relevant ministries to implement the agreements.

The ACD agreement was signed in September 2003 during the 35th ASEAN Economic Ministers Meeting. The expectation was that the ASEAN member states would implement the provisions of the agreement within the stipulated period, with the deadline set for 1 January 2008. Malaysia, the Philippines, Singapore and Thailand had conducted a systematic Post Market Surveillance (PMS) system for cosmetics products marketed in their countries (Anis 2015). However, Indonesia, Cambodia and Myanmar suffered delays to such an extent that they were eventually unable to implement the ACD by the stipulated deadline of January 2008. For Indonesia, Fahmi Idris, then serving as Minister of Industry, pledged on 12 December 2008 during an exhibition of traditional medicine and cosmetics to implement the ACD by early 2010 at the latest (Suhendra 2008).

In 2010, the government issued several government regulations that indicated its commitment to implement the ACD. Such regulations included, among others, Ministry of Health Regulation (*Permenkes*) No. 1175/2010 on Permission for the Production of Cosmetics, *Permenkes* No. 1176/2010 on the Notification of Cosmetics and Regulation No. HK.03.1.23.12.10.11983 in 2010 (Mardjan 2012) issued by the BPOM (*Badan Pengawasan Obat dan Makanan* or the National Food and Drugs Inspection Board) on the criteria and methods of submitting the notification for cosmetics.

Permenkes No. 1175/Menkes/Per/VIII/2010 on Permission for the Production of Cosmetics was enacted on 20 August 2010. This permission to produce cosmetics is divided into two categories: category A, which entails permission for cosmetics industries with the capacity to produce all forms and types of cosmetics; and category B, which entails permission for the production of industrial cosmetics with the capacity to produce certain forms and types of cosmetics using simple technology. *Permenkes* No. 1176/Menkes/Per/VIII/2010 on the notification of cosmetics, which came into effect on 20 August 2010, stipulates that notification constitutes a form of permission to distribute and is considered approved if fourteen days elapse without the issuance of rejection. The regulation stipulates that every cosmetics producer, prior to marketing his or her products, is required to file a notification to the government in every ASEAN country where the product will be sold.

The fundamental difference between the ASEAN harmonization regime and the previous registration system is that the former does not require inspection prior to marketing the product as it relies on post-market surveillance (Mardjan 2012), while the latter requires inspection prior to the marketing of the product (pre-market approval). The reason for the change is the relatively low risk associated with cosmetics products as long as the producers fully comply with regulations. Such a condition is advantageous to the producer as it shortens the process of obtaining the licence to market the product, without the need for pre-market evaluation. Nonetheless, the existence of post-market surveillance, which takes the form of sampling and testing the quality and safety by the BPOM officials, ensures that the consumer is still protected. The cosmetics industry demands complete responsibility for the quality and safety of its products. Cosmetics companies are required to have a good understanding of all the provisions that are stipulated in the ACD as well as create a database of information and data on the safety of the raw materials used in the production of cosmetics products.

2.6.1 *Problems in implementing the ACD*

Issues relating to the implementation of the ACD in Indonesia involve these five agencies: (1) the MFA, which serves as the institution that handles the various issues related to cooperation with other countries; (2) the Ministry of Health in its capacity as the regulations-maker; (3) the BPOM in its capacity as the agency responsible for conducting inspections on the implementation of regulations; (4) the Ministry of Industry as the institution responsible for providing guidance and promoting industrial development; and (5) the police, which is responsible for enforcing the regulations.

The production of cosmetics in Indonesia has increased significantly in recent years. Despite the economic recession, the cosmetics sector has been able to register strong growth (Pathoni 2012). In 2006, the value of exports of cosmetics products in Indonesia amounted to US$79.5 million, and increased significantly to US$106.2 million in 2007. However, the value of imports of cosmetics products is still very high, and was valued at US$58.7 million and US$76.9 million in 2006 and 2007 respectively. The growth in the sales of cosmetics in 2011 was estimated to reach double digits compared with the 2010 figures. According to Putri Kusuma Wardhani, the general chairperson of PERKOSMI (*Persatuan Perusahaan Kosmetik Indonesia*, or the Association of Indonesian Cosmetics), the trade in cosmetics in 2010 was estimated as Rp 50–60 trillion (US$5–6 billion), two-thirds of which were produced domestically. Considering the favourable prospects of the cosmetics industry, L'Oreal cosmetics has invested Rp 900 billion (US$90 million) in Indonesia (*Kementerian Perindustrian* 2011).

The implementation of the ACD in Indonesia also depends on the perceptions of its stakeholders. The response to the ACD's existence tends to be varied. Large cosmetics companies such as the Martha Tilaar Group and *Mustika Ratu* are enthusiastic and hope that the implementation of the ACD will trigger an increase in sales by 20 per cent. The Martha Tilaar Group, which has been involved in the cosmetics business for forty years and controls 30 per cent of the country's cosmetics market, expects company sales to reach Rp 900 billion. The company has 6,000 employees and manages forty-four spas and thirty shops. It is the first company in Southeast Asia to obtain ISO 9000 and ISO 14000 certification for fulfilling the Good Manufacturing Standards (GMS) requirements. Furthermore, the PT *Mustika Ratu* company won the Indonesia Best Brand Award in 2010 for slimming and skin care products (Pathoni 2012).

According to the Chairperson of the BPOM, most cosmetics companies were not ready in 2012 to implement the ACD (Pathoni 2012). A similar view was expressed by the Head of Sub-Directorate of Downstream Chemical Industry, Ministry of Industry, to the effect that the existence of the

ACD constitutes a formidable challenge for small companies (Sudarto 2012). Similarly, Fahmi Idris, the Minister of Industry, contended that the small and medium-sized cosmetics producers were unable to implement the ACD. According to him, 85 per cent of the 630 cosmetics producers are small and medium-sized companies. Thus, most of the cosmetics companies in Indonesia are still weak and require empowerment to enhance their capacity to implement the ACD (Suhendra 2008).

Since 1 January 2011, when the ACD came into effect in Indonesia, the PERKOSMI of East Java province has been involved in making preparations to establish a Memorandum of Understanding with Airlangga University (UNAIR). PERKOSMI and the Faculty of Pharmacy of UNAIR have developed many programmes in various areas such as education, community research and development relating to testing the quality and safety of new cosmetics products, development and validation of methods, community counselling services relating to cosmetics and training in human resources development in cosmetics.

Five factors have undermined the implementation of the ACD. The first factor is the existence of different viewpoints among the government stakeholders. Not all the ministries consider the implementation of the ACD as a positive step. On the contrary, some ministries perceive that its implementation is detrimental to Indonesia's interests. An informant from the BPOM contended that the harmonization of regulations on cosmetics is detrimental to Indonesia's interests as Indonesia is a potential large market for cosmetics from other countries. The informant also noted that as the skin complexion of people and climate in various countries differ, the uncontrolled entry of foreign cosmetics products may end up causing harmful effects. This perspective is contrary to the view from the Ministry of Health, which considers the ACD as being very important and positive for the Indonesian cosmetics industry, and is an important advantage for enhancing the competitiveness of Indonesian cosmetics companies in other countries. However, the Ministry of Industry is relatively moderate as it recommends a phased approach in implementation starting with large companies that have relatively more advanced technology, after which small-scale companies will follow (Sudarto 2012).

Secondly, there are constraints in implementing the ACD for small-scale cosmetics companies in Indonesia. In general, many of these companies are still using traditional methods as they do not have modern technology to guarantee the quality of their products. In other words, if small companies are forced to produce their products based on the ACD standards they will face very high production costs, which in turn will make their products expensive. Consequently, the high prices of products will reduce the competitiveness of the products of small companies. Moreover, small companies face another constraint in the form of their low level of development of human resources. Many small companies employ traditional methods inherited from their parents to produce cosmetics products. Unfortunately, the Ministry of Industry does not have any plans to provide assistance to such companies in the foreseeable future. Consequently, Indonesia's economic situation has been exacerbated by the high level of unemployment and bankruptcy of small companies.

Thirdly, rampant corruption in the public bureaucracy is still a constraint in implementing the ACD. Expired permits have been used by several police officers to extort payments from businessmen. According to an informant, details of companies and expiry dates are not shared with the police since they may be used for extortion and bribes. Many cosmetics businessmen complain about the apparent lack of interest and willingness of the public bureaucracy to protect small companies. Officials of the BPOM and the police are in fact exploiting the existence of *Permenkes* No. 1175 and No. 1176 to siphon off money from the cosmetics companies. Based on these complaints, HM Ismail, Chairman of the Supervisory Team for the Regulations of Cosmetics, Drugs and Health in Indonesia, contends that victims of such extortion practices are mostly micro, small, and medium-sized enterprises. He regrets the fact that in signing up to free trade, Indonesia has not taken measures to protect and assist the development of domestic industries, but instead has contributed to complicating their activities and forcing them out of business. In his view, the problems started when the notification process or permission to market or distribute came into effect online with the support of the BPOM in 1 January 2011. According to Ismail, lodging complaints to the police is a very lengthy process, and it is likely that the victims of extortion end up aggravating the problem by taking such a course of action (*Suara Pembaruan* 2011).

Fourth, there is weak coordination among those agencies which are charged with handling ACD issues. Coordination between the BPOM and the police on the data on operational permission or licences of companies is very difficult. The police must have data in order to enforce the regulations, but the BPOM does not want to provide such data as it fears the possibility of moral hazard arising from efforts by the police to detect problems or mistakes that relate to those companies which delay the issuance of licences from the government (Sudarto 2012). The BPOM is concerned that if the police were to have access to data on permissions, such data could be misused, and result in providing the police with the means to extort payments from the cosmetics companies. In practice, businessmen often face difficulties whenever they have to deal with the public bureaucracy. Various permits take time to process, and such delay undermines or jeopardizes production and encourages businessmen to pay bribes to minimize the delay in processing permits. For example, it requires thirteen procedures and 158 days to get a construction permit in Indonesia (World Bank 2013: 198).

The fifth factor is the limited budget allocation for implementing the ACD. The Indonesian government faces budget constraints in implementing its policies. Simply put, each policy and regulation requires socialization to the implementing parties, which the government often fails to provide due to the absence of financial resources for the purpose. At the implementation phase of regulations, the government faces budgetary constraints in providing guidance to businessmen who lack sufficient capacity to implement the regulations. Such businessmen need capacity enhancement to increase their human resource capabilities and improve infrastructure and production technology. In 2011, the BPOM received Rp 300 billion (US$30 million) in additional funding which was earmarked for constructing laboratories and enhancing human resources. In future, once all the plans reach fruition, there will be four BPOM agencies at the centres in Banten, Tanjung Pinang, Manokwari and Solo (*Investor Daily Indonesia* 2010).

2.7 Implementing the ASEAN Ministerial Meeting on Transnational Crime (AMMTC)/ Senior Officials Meeting on Transnational Crime (SOMTC)

2.7.1 Countering terrorism

Indonesia is a lead shepherd in efforts to counter terrorism. The issue of countering terrorism assumed greater importance in the aftermath of the Bali bombing, which took place on 12 October 2002, killing 202 people, eighty-six of whom were Australian citizens. The bombing was linked to the *Jemaah Islamiyah* organization, which made terrorism a major issue for Indonesia, Malaysia and Singapore.

Follow-up efforts and implementation of the efforts to combat terrorism in Indonesia are manifested in the issuing of government regulations in lieu of the *Perpu* (*Peraturan Pemerintah Pengganti Undang-Undang* or Government Regulation Substituting Law) No. 2/2002 on Anti-Terrorism. In 2003, the government made improvements to the law, and later issued it as Law No. 15/2003 on combating terrorism crimes (Hariana and Irawan 2003). In addition, the government also established the National Counter-Terrorism Board (BNPT), which is directly accountable to the President through *Menkumham* (*Kementrian Hukum dan HAM* or

Coordinating Ministry for Politics, Legal Affairs, and Human Rights). The establishment of the BNPT was based on *Perpres* (*Peraturan Presiden*, Presidential Regulation) No. 46/2010, which constituted an upgrading of the *Desk Koordinasi Pemberantasan Teroris* (Coordinating Desk for Combating Terrorism).

With regards to money laundering and terrorism financing, the Indonesian government formed the PPATK (*Pusat Pelaporan Analisis Transaksi Keuangan* or Financial Transaction Reports and Analysis Centre). The agency is tasked with preventing and combating money laundering crimes as well as providing counter terrorism funding in Indonesia. From the legal perspective, the PPATK is based on Law No. 8/2010 and its creation indicates Indonesia's commitment to and involvement in efforts by other countries in the world to combat organized transnational crimes such as terrorism and money laundering.

The implementation of Law No. 15/2003 has since paved the way for the formation of Densus (*Detasemen Khusus* or Special Detachment) 88, which is designed as an anti-terrorism unit with the capability of handling terrorism threats ranging from financing to hijacking activities. With respect to performance, Densus 88 is considered to have had significant success in combating terrorism in Indonesia (rmol.co 2011). Success in combating terrorism in Indonesia is reflected in the arrest, detention and sentencing to death of the trio in the Bali I bombing on 10 November 2008: Amrozi, Ali Ghufran and Imam Samudra. Two other terrorists were also executed: Dr Azahari, a terrorist who was a Malaysian citizen, in Malang on 9 November 2005; and Noordin M. Top on 8 August 2009. The deaths of these two terrorists dealt a major blow to the terrorism network in South Philippines. Nonetheless, this does not mean that the war against terrorism has come to an end (RNW Indonesia 2009). In 2011, the notorious terrorist Umar Patek was arrested in Pakistan and later deported to Indonesia (Wardah 2011).

2.7.2 *Trafficking in persons*

Trafficking in persons has been a serious concern for many governments. Indonesia has signed but not ratified the United Nations Convention against Transactional Organized Crime (humantrafficking.org 2015a). According to Heyzer (2002), trafficking has increased by almost 50 per cent from 1995 to 2000. It has become a multi-billion dollar industry, involving individuals and large companies. In Southeast Asian countries, trafficking in persons, especially women and children, takes many forms, including such abuses as exploitative labour, child labour, recruitment practices into the sex industry, and servile marriages.

Although this issue has been seriously recognized, information about the trafficking of Indonesian women and children is limited. According to *Badan Reserse Kriminal Kepolisian* (Police Agency for Crime Detection), there were 492 cases of trafficking in persons involving 1,016 adults and 238 children from 2003 to 2007. However, the International Organization for Migration notes that there were around 3,024 victims from 2005 to 2008 (Rahayu 2011: 117).

On 30 December 2002, the Indonesian Government enacted the Indonesian National Plan of Action for the

Elimination of Trafficking in Women and Children (NPA). The NPA became the 'foundation and guidance for the government and the public in the implementation of the elimination of trafficking in women and children' (*Kementerian Pemberdayaan Perempuan* 2002: 4). In 2003, the Indonesian Parliament discussed anti-trafficking policy and it took four years to enact the Suppression of the Criminal Act of Trafficking in Persons Law in 2007. This became the first national legislation on human trafficking and provided a legal basis for anti-trafficking efforts in Indonesia.

Comparing the anti-trafficking and anti-terrorism efforts, it is clear that anti-trafficking in Indonesia has been unsuccessful. Indonesia was originally placed in Tier 3 of the US Department of State People Trafficking Chart and updated to Tier 2 in 2003 (US Department of State 2008: 142).[4] Up to 2011, the US government has kept Indonesia in Tier 2 (humantrafficking.org 2015b).

The Indonesian government maintains that the rate of unemployment is very high whereas the proportion of workers who are abused is small. The perceptions among policy-makers on the protection of children are diverse and fragmented, making it difficult to sustain the programme in the long term (UNICEF 2009: 38). It has therefore become a dilemma for Indonesia to cope with this problem seriously.

[4] Tier 2 is defined as 'not fully complying with the minimum standards, but making significant efforts to meet those minimum standards' while Tier 3 is defined as 'countries assessed as neither complying with the minimum standards nor making significant efforts to do so'.

2.7.3 *Success and failure of the AMMTC/SOMTC*

Four factors determine the performance of cooperation and integration of the police within each ASEAN nation as well as across national borders in combating terrorism. First, is the existence of common goals underlying the activities related to combating terrorism. There is no difference in perceptions about the need to combat such crimes as every country understands that international crimes constitute a common enemy. At the country level, there are no conflicting perceptions among policy-makers about the policies.

There are no differences in Indonesia in goal perceptions in combating terrorism, which has often been associated with Muslim groups that can be resolved by religious leaders. The two largest Muslim organizations in Indonesia, the *Nahdatul Ulama* and *Muhammadiyah*, consider terrorism as a crime, even if it is shrouded in religion. In fact, despite cases of human rights violation, the head of *Nahdatul Ulama*, Kyai Haji Hasyim Muzadi, supports and considers the existence of the Anti-Terrorism Law as justified. The need to observe and protect human rights should not take precedence over the rights of victims of terrorism perpetrated by terrorists (Santoso 2011).

With respect to the cases of trafficking in persons, the perception of various parties on the prevention and combating of the problem is rarely the same. Not all the parties involved have the same definition of trafficking in persons. In Indonesia, some manifestations of trafficking are also accepted practices so that they are not considered a bad thing (Rosenberg 2003: 11). To some extent, the variety of women and children trafficking ranges from the most negative things (sex exploitation) to normal activities (such as child labour).

Secondly, sufficient funding is a *sine qua non* for successful cooperation in combating terrorism. The Indonesian government spends a lot of money towards ASEAN cooperation within the AMMTC framework. The Ministry of Finance spent Rp 1 billion (US$100,000) for the transnational database in Singapore (Susilowati 2012). The Indonesian police allocated Rp 71 billion (US$7.1 million) in 2012 for combating terrorism. The Coordinating Ministry for Politics, Legal Affairs, and Security allocated Rp 225 billion (US$22.5 million) in 2011 for the BNPT to combat terrorism (Wikanto 2010). This amount is far larger than the Rp 2.1 billion (US$210,000) allocated by the Indonesian police for combating corruption (Saputra 2011). By contrast, the handling of trafficking in persons is not a high priority of the government of Indonesia as reflected in the limited budget allocation for preventing human trafficking (UNICEF 2009). The Ministry of Women Empowerment received only 0.06 per cent of the 2007 national budget (Sukma 2008: 18). This limited funding has contributed to the failure of the implementation of anti-trafficking in persons policies.

Third, coordination among the various public policy stakeholders influences the success or failure in policy implementation. There is relatively better coordination in the area of terrorism than in trafficking in persons. The involvement of many ministries has not led to the emergence of conflicts of interests. The police have not encountered difficulties in obtaining the support of the National Assembly for combating terrorism. However, there is weak coordination and cooperation in coping with trafficking persons among the different levels of government within the country (UNICEF 2009).

Fourth, the existence of support from non-government stakeholders is vital for preventing and combating terrorism. Religious organizations lend their support for combating terrorism as long as such measures do not cause the stigmatization of Muslims. Religious leaders drawn from a spectrum of religious organizations often meet in an effort to encourage the government to combat terrorism and instill public awareness that there is a link between terrorism and certain religions. However, for combating trafficking in persons, the support from religious organizations is limited since this is not an important issue or well understood. Moreover, the case of trafficking in persons has little international exposure in the media compared to the great deal of publicity on terrorism.

2.8 Conclusion

2.8.1 Summary of key findings

Indonesia is a vast country, with an extremely high degree of social, cultural and geographical complexity. Politically, the shift of power from the New Order era to the Reformation era has ushered in significant changes. The political system has shifted from one of hegemony to a fragmented multi-party system, a process that has affected the characteristics of the civil service and relations between the executive and legislature. The public policy process has also shifted from an emphasis on the executive to the legislature.

With respect to the economy, Indonesia has faced significant fluctuations in its economic growth. The 1997 financial crisis had devastating effects on the Indonesian economy. Consequently, Indonesia required a long time before its economy recovered. In line with that, changes in government structure in the wake of implementation of the decentralization policy have also affected the pattern of relations between the central government and regional governments as well as the pattern of coordination and communication. Consequently, the implementation of programmes has been undermined.

In the context of the civil service's role in policy formulation and implementation, the above changes have had a significant impact on the performance of the public bureaucracy. In the context of policy formulation, the process of enacting laws to respond to a certain policy is both protracted and complicated. Given the DPR's extremely limited capacity to make new legislation, the inclusion of any issue on the agenda requires a long process of negotiation in both the executive and legislature. If both parties consider the issue lacking in urgency, it is shelved and hence has little chance of being deliberated in the future. While the policy-making process during the New Order regime was technocratic and based on academic rationality and objectivity, it is necessary today to consider the political process through discussion with politicians and the general public. Moreover, the policy formulation process has become more difficult to control, even with those political parties which are allied with the government. Upon enacting the law, its implementation requires its translation into government regulations.

With respect to policy implementation, both the executive and public bureaucracy depend on Parliament, which has the authority to determine the budget expenditure to resolve any issues. Budget allocation in Parliament calls for bargaining and intensive negotiation. Moreover, at the level of the public bureaucracy, budgeting is still fragmented and contesting for budget allocations among the ministries is common. Setting the budget is no longer based on the need to find the solution to a problem, but is oriented towards strengthening each agency with its own interests. From the vertical standpoint, policy implementation is influenced by stronger powers vested in local governments making them difficult to work with and complicating the efforts of the central government to coordinate policies.

For the AMMTC/SOMTC, cooperation has been successful, especially in countering terrorism. The common perception among the various stakeholders is an important factor that has enhanced cooperation among the ASEAN countries. Terrorism is considered by all parties as a common problem, which has encouraged and galvanized serious action. However, the differences in perceptions among the various stakeholders have led to the failure in implementing the ACD and in efforts to reduce trafficking in persons.

The second important factor is coordination among the policy implementers. On the one hand, the failure in implementing the ACD is attributed to weak coordination. Each ministry has its own interests and those interests are difficult to consolidate. This condition is also influenced by the resistance of small and medium-sized enterprises that have direct relations with the policy-makers. In the implementation of the ACD and the anti-trafficking in persons policy, there are serious difficulties in the coordination of information and data. By contrast, the success of counter terrorism is largely due to strong coordination among the agencies.

Third, the size of budget allocation determines the success or failure of policy implementation. For the ACD and anti-trafficking in persons policy, the relevant agencies do not have sufficient budget or financial resources to implement the activities that fall under their jurisdiction. On the other hand, both the police and the BNPT have sufficient financial resources to combat terrorism. However, the size of budget allocation for the agencies depends on the degree to which members of the DPR consider the issue to be urgent. Furthermore, the urgency of these issues also depends on the importance attached by the general public, which accords higher priority to be given to terrorism because not many people are well informed about the ACD and trafficking in persons. As these two issues are rarely discussed in the newspapers or on television compared with terrorism, it is not surprising that public demands for a larger budget allocation for terrorism are stronger than those for the ACD and trafficking in persons.

2.8.2 The civil service's weaknesses in policy implementation

The Indonesian civil service has four weaknesses in policy implementation. First, the leadership has failed to direct the public bureaucracy. Differences in perception have also hampered policy implementation. The existence of strong or weak leadership plays an important role in determining the effectiveness of policy implementation. The public bureaucracy is led by ministers from various political parties and demands strong presidential leadership. If ministers do not perform according to expectations, the President has the prerogative to appoint and dismiss them with impunity. However, in many cases, President SBY did not dismiss his ministers for their poor performance.

Secondly, the high fragmentation of the public bureaucracy is reflected in 'sectoral egoism' in every agency, which undermines its performance in policy implementation. Every ministry has its own interests, which are accorded higher priority than the interests of other ministries. Whenever a policy is viewed as a threat to the ministry's interests, it is often rejected. In the context of the ACD's implementation, the responses of ministries constitute a zero sum game. A policy which imposes good discipline on the cosmetics making process supports the Ministry of Health's policy, but on the other hand jeopardizes the activities of those ministries which support the empowering of the small enterprises.

Third, the existence of a gap between the leaders and their subordinates has created a sense of 'paranoia' among civil servants. Conflicts between those civil servants with authority but who lack the capacity and capability and those civil servants with the capability and capacity but who lack the authority, also influence the performance of the public bureaucracy in policy implementation. The young bureaucrats who are idealistic and better educated have limited opportunities for formulating policies while the senior bureaucrats with less education have more power in policy formulation. This gap has not been conducive for creating a good environment for the bureaucrats.

Fourth, regional autonomy has led to changes in the institutional structure of the central government and regional governments. The central government often is no longer able to control agencies at the regional government level, which in turn has an adverse impact on policy implementation in the regions. The governor and district head or *Bupati* as regional government heads face a dilemma in dealing with the central government and regional government assembly (DPRD) because they are more inclined to support local political interests in the DPRD than the directives from the President. Moreover, decentralization is also hampered by the lack of trained officials at the provincial and district or city government levels.

2.8.3 Improving the civil service's role in policy implementation

First, it is necessary to strengthen executive leadership vis-à-vis parliamentary power. In the context of executive–legislature political relations which are dominated by the legislature, the role of the President is weak in policy formulation. Former President SBY, who had garnered the support of more than 60 per cent of the votes during the direct elections, found it difficult to muster enough votes in Parliament. Moreover, SBY's personality and cautious approach had weakened his position in policy-making. Thus, an institutional mechanism is needed to enable the executive to formulate policies in a rational-technocratic way without undue political intervention.

The new President Joko Widodo has been more decisive than his predecessor. He increased the price of petrol from Rp 6,500 (US$0.65) to Rp 8,500 (US$0.85) per litre to reduce the government subsidy. He has also forbidden all government officials to conduct meetings in hotels to enhance efficiency and decided to sink the ships coming from other countries that are illegally fishing. His decisions have created some resistance from university students and parliamentary members from the KMP, the hotel association, bureaucrats and other countries. However, Joko Widodo remains committed in making decisions which benefit the country.

Secondly, there is a need for strengthening bureaucratic leadership in order to eliminate sectoral parochialism (egoism) and to reform the public bureaucracy in general. So far, the administrative reform portfolio held under the MENPAN-RB's purview is not effective since the positions of other ministries are equal. Therefore, the role of the Vice President to lead the reform in the public bureaucracy is crucially needed.

Thirdly, there is a need for more efforts to enhance information technology for database development relevant to the issues assigned to the ministry. For example, information technology is important for the formulation and implementation of policies which need accurate and comprehensive data that can be delivered quickly. Such data can also enhance the coordination among ministries without conducting meetings, which are costly in terms of money and time.

Fourthly, it is necessary to revitalize human resources in the public bureaucracy. There is a wide gap between the senior leaders of the bureaucracy and developments in technology and communications as well as globalization. Not all leaders have the ability to follow ideas that are suggested by their young subordinates. Subordinates perceive their leaders as anachronistic and outdated but have the authority without the legitimacy to lead the public bureaucracy. By creating a more visionary leadership, the public bureaucracy will be able to respond swiftly to issues that are becoming more important in Indonesia and the other ASEAN countries by transforming the orientation of leadership training from local to global issues.

Finally, there is a need for institutional reorganization between the central and regional governments. With the policy of regional autonomy, the central government has limited capacity to coordinate its activities with the local governments. The central government needs to enhance its networking capacity with local governments to guarantee the success of its policy implementation. Strengthening the role of governor as the representative of the central government at the regional level is urgently needed for adoption to enable the central government to make policy implementation more effective.

References

Anis, T. 2015. 'Status of ACD Implementation and Pertinent Change to Malaysian Cosmetic Regulations'. PowerPoint presentation available at: http://portal.bpfk.gov.my/aeimages/File/COSMET

ICS/Status_of_ACD_implementation-_Anis_Talib.pdf (accessed 10 January 2015).

Aziz, A. 2012. Interview, 11 May.

Bachtiar, H. W. 1972. 'Bureaucracy and Nation Formation in Indonesia', *Bijdragen tot de Taal-, Land-en Volkenkunde*, 128(4): 430–49.

Badan Kepegawaian Nasional (BKN) 2012. *Statistik Pegawai Negeri Sipil*. Jakarta: *Pemerintah Republik Indonesia*.

2014. *Statistik Pegawai Negeri Sipil*. Jakarta: *Pemerintah Republik Indonesia*.

Badan Pusat Statistik (BPS) 2000. *Statistik Indonesia*. Jakarta: *Pemerintah Republik Indonesia*.

2005. *Statistik Indonesia*. Jakarta: *Pemerintah Republik Indonesia*.

2010. *Statistik Indonesia*. Jakarta: *Pemerintah Republik Indonesia*.

2011. *Statistik Indonesia*. Jakarta: *Pemerintah Republik Indonesia*.

2012. *Statistik Indonesia*. Jakarta: *Pemerintah Republik Indonesia*.

2013. *Statistik Indonesia*. Jakarta: *Pemerintah Republik Indonesia*.

2014. *Statistik Indonesia*. Jakarta: *Pemerintah Republik Indonesia*.

Bappenas 2011. '*Menuju Perencana Profesional*' [Toward Professional Planners], *Simpul Perencana*, 17(8): 20–5.

Basri, M. C. 2003. 'Indonesia's Economic Transformation: Before and During the Economic Crisis'. In A. Ananta (ed.), *The Indonesian Crisis: A Human Development Index*. Singapore: Institute of Southeast Asian Studies, pp. 53–75.

Cribb, R. 1994. 'Introduction: The Late Colonial State in Indonesia'. In R. Cribb (ed.), *The Late Colonial State in Indonesia: Political and Economic Foundations of the Netherlands Indies, 1880–1942*. Leiden: KITLV Press, pp. 1–10.

Crouch, H. 1979. 'Patrimonialism and Military Rule in Indonesia', *World Politics*, 31(4): 571–87.

Direktori Organisasi Kemasyarakatan 2009. Jakarta, available at: http://web.archive.org/web/20130810042913/http://www.kemen

dagri.go.id/media/documents/2010/03/10/f/i/file.pdf (accessed 10 January 2015).

Dwiyanto, A. 2012a. 'Pembagian Urusan Pemerintahan: Isu, Problema, dan Rekomendasi Kebijakan' [Functional Assignment: Issues, Problems and Policy Recommendations]. Paper presented at a focused group discussion held by the Deutsche Gesellschaft für Internationale Zusammenarbeit (GTZ) [German Technical Cooperation Agency], Jakarta, 5 April.

2012b. Interview, 10 May.

The Economist 2013. *Pocket World in Figures, 2014 Edition*. London: Profile Books.

Eldridge, P. J. 1995. *Non-governmental Organizations and Democratic Participation in Indonesia*. Kuala Lumpur: Oxford University Press.

Emmerson, D. K. 1983. 'Understanding the New Order: Bureaucratic Pluralism in Indonesia', *Asian Survey*, 23(11): 122–41.

Furnivall, J. S. 1944. *Netherlands India: A Case Study of Plural Economy*. Cambridge: Cambridge University Press.

Government Regulation No. 34/2014. Kenaikan Gaji Pegawai Negeri Sipil [Public Service Salary Increase], Jakarta.

Government Regulation No. 38/2007. Pembagian Urusan antara Pemerintah, Pemerintah Provinsi dan Pemerintah Kabupaten/Kota [Functional Assignment between Central Government, Province and District or City], Jakarta.

Hamid, T. B. 2012. Interview, 14 February.

Hariana, A. and Irawan, A. 2003. 'Perpu anti-terorisme disahkan menjadi undang-undang' [Anti-terrorism Act Becomes Law], 3 June, available at: www.indosiar.com/fokus/perpu-anti-terorisme-disahkan-menjadi-undang–undang_23834.html (accessed 10 January 2015).

Heyzer, N. 2002. 'Combating Trafficking in Women and Children: A Gender and Human Rights Framework'. Plenary Address, United Nations Development Fund for Women (UNIFEM) conference, 'The Human Rights Challenge of Globalization: Asia–Pacific–US: The Trafficking in Persons, especially Women and Children', Honolulu, Hawaii, 13–15 November.

Hill, H. 1994. 'The Economy'. In H. Hill (ed.), *Indonesia's New Order: The Dynamics of Socio-Economic Transformation*. Sydney: Allen & Unwin, pp. 54–122.

humantrafficking.org 2015a. (Washington, DC) 'Indonesia Best Practices', available at: www.humantrafficking.org/countries/indonesia/best_practices (accessed 10 January 2015).

2015b. (Washington, DC) 'Indonesia', available at: www.humantrafficking.org/countries/indonesia/ (accessed 10 January 2015).

Hutagalung, J. 2009. 'Peran Bank Dunia dan IMF dalam Perekonomian Indonesia Dulu dan Sekarang' [The Role of the World Bank and IMF in the Indonesian Economy: Past and Present]. In A. Abimanyu and A. Megantara (eds), *Era Baru Kebijakan Fiskal: Pemikiran, Konsep dan Implementasi* [The New Era of Fiscal Policy: Ideas, Concepts and Implementation]. Jakarta: PT Kompas Media Nusantara, pp. 426–44.

Investor Daily Indonesia 2010. '2011, Kosmetika beredar tanpa uji pre-market' [2011, Cosmetics Spread without Pre-Market Testing], 3 December, available at: www.investor.co.id/family/2011-kosmetika-beredar-tanpa-uji-pre-market/1217 (accessed 10 January 2015).

Jackson, K. D. 1978. 'Bureaucratic Polity: A Theoretical Framework for the Analysis of Power and Communications in Indonesia'. In K. D. Jackson and L. W. Pye (eds), *Political Power and Communications in Indonesia*. Berkeley, CA: University of California Press, pp. 3–42.

Kansil, C. S. T. and Kansil, C. (eds) 2005. *Modul Hukum Administrasi Negara*. Jakarta: Pradnya Paramita.

Kedaulatan Rakyat 2012. 'Perjalanan dinas PNS-DPR boros' [The Civil Servants' Travel Budget was Insufficient], 9 May.

Kementerian Pemberdayaan Perempuan (KPP) 2002. *Keputusan Presiden Republik Indonesia Nomor 88 Tahun 2002 tentang Rencana Aksi Nasional Penghapusan Perdagangan (Trafficking) Perempuan dan Anak [The Decision of the Government of Indonesia No. 88/2002 on the National Action Plan on Elimination on Women and Children Trafficking]*. Jakarta: Pemerintah Republik Indonesia.

Kementerian Perindustrian 2011. (Jakarta) 'Kenaikan harga katrol Perturbuhan Industri Kosmetik' [Price Increase Enhances Cosmetic Industry Growth], available at: www.kemenperin.go.id/artikel/1251/ (accessed 10 January 2015).

Kementerian Sekretariat Negara 2014. (Jakarta) 'The 1945 Constitution of the State of the Republic of Indonesia' (unofficial English translation), available at: www.setneg.go.id/images/stories/kepmen/legal_product/uud_1945.pdf (accessed 30 December 2014).

King, D. 1982. 'Indonesia's New Order as a Bureaucratic Polity, a Neo Patrimonial Regime or a Bureaucratic Authoritarian Regime: What Difference Does it Make?' In B. Anderson and A. Kahin (eds), *Interpreting Indonesian Politics: Thirteen Contributions to the Debate*. Ithaca, NY: Cornell Southeast Asia Program Publications, pp. 167–86.

Komisi Pemilihan Umum (KPU) 2014. (Jakarta) 'Partai politik peserta pemilu yang memenuhi dan tidak memenuhi ambang batas perolehan suara sah secara nasional dalam pemilihan umum Dewan Perwakilan Rakyat tahun 2014' [Political Parties Involved in the General Election Which Met or Did Not Meet the Threshold of National Valid Votes in the 2014 Parliamentary

Elections], 9 May, available at: www.kpu.go.id/koleksigambar/952014_ambang_Batas.pdf (accessed 10 January 2015).

Kompas 2010. 'Reformasi Birokrasi Masih Timbulkan Paradoks' [Reforms still Causing Paradox], 27 July, available at: http://nasional.kompas.com/read/2010/07/27/02435098/reformasi.birokrasi.masih.timbulkan.paradoks (accessed 10 January 2015).

2012a. 'Birokrasi Terlampau Gemuk' [Bureaucracy Too Fat], 3 May, available at: http://nasional.kompas.com/read/2012/05/03/10003045/Birokrasi. (accessed 10 January 2015).

2012b. 'Lagi-lagi, Kinerja Legislasi DPR Meleset dari Target' [Again, Parliament Legislation Performance Missed Target], 23 December, available at: http://nasional.kompas.com/read/2012/12/23/11195257/ (accessed 10 January 2015).

2014. 'Jokowi Pangkas Anggaran Dinas dan Rapat 2015 hingga Rp 16 Triliun' [Jokowi Cuts Budget for Meetings in 2015 to Rp 16 trillion], 24 November, available at: http://nasional.kompas.com/read/2014/11/24/14542781/ (accessed 10 January 2015).

Logsdon, M. G. 1992. 'Indonesia's Civil Service in the New Order: Consolidation, Growth, and Change', *Sojourn: Journal of Social Issues in Southeast Asia*, 7(2): 223–47.

McVey, R. T. 1982. 'The *Beamtenstaat* in Indonesia'. In B. Anderson and A. Kahin (eds), *Interpreting Indonesian Politics: Thirteen Contributions to the Debate*. Ithaca, NY: Cornell Southeast Asian Program Publication, pp. 137–48.

Mardjan, H. 2012. Interview, 14 February.

Nurbaningsih, E. 2012. Interview, 13 May.

Nuryanto, A. 2012. Interview, 11 May.

Pathoni, A. 2012. 'South East Asia – Strength in Diversity', cosmeticsbusiness.com, 31 May, available at www.cosmeticsbusiness.com/technical/article_page/South_East_Asia__strength_in_diversity/57169 (accessed 10 January 2015).

Pramusinto, A. 2005. 'The Dynamics of Change in Decentralization: Implications for Local Government–Business Relations: A Case Study of Decentralization in Sidoarjo, East Java, Indonesia', PhD thesis, Australian National University.

Quah, J. S. T. 2011. *Curbing Corruption in Asian Countries: An Impossible Dream?* Bingley: Emerald Group Publishing.

Rahayu, D. 2011. 'Perlindungan Hukum bagi Buruh Migran Terhadap Tindakan Perdagangan Perempuan', *Jurnal Hukum*, 18(1) (January): 115–35.

Ricklefs, M. C. 1993. *A History of Modern Indonesia since c.1300*. London: Macmillan.

rmol.co 2011. 'UU Antiterorisme Lahirkan Pelanggaran HAM' [Anti-terrorism Act Results in Human Rights Violations], 23 June, available at: www.rakyatmerdekaonline.com/read/2011/06/23/30954/UU-Antiterorisme-Lahirkan-Pelanggaran (accessed 10 January 2015).

RNW Indonesia 2009. 'Kematian Noordin M. Top tidak berarti terorisme tuntas' [Death of Noordin M. Top Does Not Mean the End of Terrorism], 18 September, available at: http://archief.rnw.nl/bahasa-indonesia/article/kematian-noordin-m-top-tidak-berarti-terorisme-tuntas (accessed 10 January 2015). No longer online.

Rohdewohld, R. 1995. *Public Administration in Indonesia*. Melbourne: Montech.

Rosenburg, R. (ed.) 2003. *Trafficking of Women and Children in Indonesia*. Jakarta: International Catholic Migration Commission and American Centre for International Labour Solidarity Report.

Santoso, B. 2011. 'Penanganan terorisme ala Hasyin Muzadi' [Combating Terrorism ala Hasyim Muzadi], *Gresnews*, 26 September, available at: www.gresnews.com/berita/Politik/1117269-penanganan-terorisme-ala-hasyim-muzadi/ (accessed 10 January 2015).

Saputra, A. 2011. 'Anggaran Polri untuk Teroris Lebih Besar Dibanding Berantas Korupsi' [Police Budget for Combating Terrorists More than for Fighting Corruption] *detiknews*, 12 October, available at: http://news.detik.com/read/2011/10/12/072118/1741983/10/anggaran-polri-untuk-teroris-lebih-besar-dibanding-berantas-korupsi (accessed 10 January 2015).

Siswanti, W. 2012. Interview, 11 May.

Sitepu, V. 2011. 'The Power Relations: Media and Politics of Contemporary Indonesia' (in Indonesian), personal blog, 29 October, available at: www.vinsensius.info/index.php/2011/10/ (accessed 10 January 2015).

Suara Pembaruan 2011. 'Menkes Didesak Cabut Peraturan Notifikasi Kosmetik' [Minister Urged to Revoke Cosmetic Notification Regulations], 28 February, available at: http://sp.beritasatu.com/home/menkes-didesak-cabut-peraturan-notifi kasi-kosmetik/4051 (accessed 10 January 2015).

Sudarto 2012. Interview, 31 January.

Suhendra 2008. 'RI Siap Terapkan ASEAN Cosmetic Directive di 2010' [RI Ready to Implement the ASEAN Cosmetic Directive in 2010], *detikfinance*, 16 December, available at: http://finance.detik.com/read/2008/12/16/112140/1054323/4/1/ (accessed 10 January 2015).

Sukma, R. 2008. 'The Securitization of Human Trafficking in Indonesia', *CSIS Working Papers* No. 162, pp. 1–24.

Suryadinata, L. 2002. *Elections and Politics in Indonesia*. Singapore: Institute of Southeast Asian Studies.

2007. 'The Decline of the Hegemonic Party System in Indonesia: Golkar after the Fall of Soeharto', *Contemporary Southeast Asia*, 29(2): 333–58.

Susilowati 2012. Interview, 12 February.

Sutrisno, E. D. 2011. 'Anggota Banggar DPR dan Ombudsman Sepakat Berdamai' [Banggar Members and Ombudsman

Agree to Terms], *detiknews*, 20 October, available at: http://news.detik.com/read/2011/10/20/165057/1748924/10 (accessed 10 January 2015).

2012. Interview, 11 May.

Tempo 2014. 'DPR Hambat Calon Ketua KPK, Menteri Angkat Tangan' [DPR Hinders Candidature of KPK Chairman, Minister Gives up], 25 November, available at: www.tempo.co/read/news/2014/11/25/078624337/DPR-Hambat-Calon-Ketua-KPK-Menteri-Angkat-Tangan (accessed 10 January 2015).

Thoha, M. 2005. *Politik dan Birokrasi di Indonesia*. Jakarta: Rajawali Press.

2012. Interview, 5 February.

UNICEF 2009. *Child Trafficking in East and South East Asia: Reversing the Trend*. Bangkok: UNICEF East Asia and Pacific Regional Office.

United Nations Public Administration Country Studies (UNPACS) 2014. (New York) 'Compare Countries: 2014 E-Government Development Index', Division for Public Administration and Development Management, available at http://unpan3.un.org/egovkb/en-us/Data/Compare-Countries (accessed 10 January 2015).

US Department of State 2008. *Trafficking in Persons Report, 2008*. Washington, DC: US Department of State.

Utomo, B. 2003. 'Health Status in Indonesia during the Economic Crisis'. In A. Ananta (ed.), *The Indonesian Crisis: A Human Development Index*. Singapore: Institute of Southeast Asian Studies, pp. 159–81.

Van Meter, D. S. and Van Horn, C. E. 1975. 'The Policy Implementation Process: A Conceptual Framework', *Administration and Society*, 6(4): 445–88.

Walker III, M. P., 1968. 'Administration and Local Government in Indonesia', PhD thesis, University of California.

Wardah, F. 2011. 'Tertangkapnya Umar Patek Akan Bantu Ungkap Jaringan Teroris Internasional' [Umar Patek's Arrest Will Reveal International Terrorist Network], *Voice of America Bahasa Indonesia*, 11 August, available at: www.voaindonesia.com/content/tertangkapnya-umar-patek-akan-bantu-ungkap-jaringan-teroris-internasional-127528573/96623.html (accessed 10 January 2015).

Wikanto, A. 2010. '2011, Anggaran pemberantasan terorisme Rp 225 miliar' [2011: Rp 225 billion Allocated for Combating Terrorism], *Kontan.co.id*, 4 October, available at: http://nasional.kontan.co.id/news/2011-anggaran-pemberantasan-terorisme-rp-225-miliar-1 (accessed 10 January 2015).

Wiratna, I. M. L. 2004. '*Perkembangan Politik Triwulan Kedua*' [The Second Quarterly Development of Political Situation], *Analisis CSIS*, 33(2): 143–55.

World Bank 2013. *Doing Business 2014: Understanding Regulations for Small and Medium Size Enterprises*. Washington, DC: World Bank.

Chapter 3

The public bureaucracy's role in policy implementation in Malaysia

Nik Rosnah Wan Abdullah

3.1 Introduction

The Malaysian public service plays a significant role in the country's economic and social development. More importantly, it has been instrumental in initiating the country's transformational efforts towards a high income nation. This chapter analyses the role of the public service in policy implementation in Malaysia, and assesses its effectiveness in implementing these two Association of Southeast Asian Nations (ASEAN) agreements: (1) the Agreement on the ASEAN Harmonized Cosmetic Regulatory Scheme, or the ASEAN Cosmetic Directive (ACD), which Malaysia signed together with the other ASEAN countries at the 35th ASEAN Economic Ministers Meeting in Cambodia in September 2003; and (2) combating transnational crime, as agreed under the ASEAN Ministerial Meeting on Transnational Crime (AMMTC) and the Senior Officials Meeting on Transnational Crime (SOMTC).

This chapter begins by describing Malaysia's policy context, followed by an analysis of the public bureaucracy's profile and its role in policy formulation. The implementation of the ACD and AMMTC/SOMTC is then analysed in depth before concluding the chapter with a summary of the major findings.

3.2 Malaysia's policy context

This section describes Malaysia's policy context in terms of its geography, formative historical experiences, economy, demography and political system as these factors affect the public bureaucracy's effectiveness in policy implementation.

3.2.1 Geography

Malaysia has a total land area of 332, 665 sq. km (*The Economist* 2013: 178) and consists of thirteen states, with eleven states located in Peninsular Malaysia, and the East Malaysian states of Sabah and Sarawak. These two states have a higher degree of local government and legislative autonomy than the West Malaysian states. Sabah and Sarawak have separate laws regulating the entry of citizens from other states in Malaysia, whereas, in Peninsular Malaysia, there are no restrictions on inter-state travel or migration, including visitors from East Malaysia. There are also separate land laws governing Sabah and Sarawak, as opposed to the National Land Code, which governs Peninsular Malaysia. The three main land laws are: (1) National Land Code (Act 56 of 1965) implemented in all states in Peninsular Malaysia; (2) Sarawak Land Code (Cap 81) implemented for Sarawak only; and (3) Sabah Land Ordinance (Cap 68) implemented for Sabah only.

3.2.2 Formative historical experiences

The Federation of Malaya was granted independence from Great Britain on 31 August 1957 with a relatively peaceful period of transition that was largely achieved by the granting of concessions to the main ethnic groups in Malaya, which included citizenship for the immigrant Chinese and Indians, while preserving the special position of the Malays as the indigenous group (Means 1998: 96). In September 1963, the Federation of Malaya became known as the Federation of Malaysia when Sabah, Sarawak and Singapore joined the Federation. Singapore separated from Malaysia in August 1965. During the British colonial rule in the nineteenth century, the development of rubber and tin industries brought about a large inflow of immigrants from China and India. By the 1920s, the population of Malaya was highly divided on ethnic lines, with the Malays, Chinese and Indians as the major ethnic groups (Means 1998: 96). At independence, the Malays, although the major group and politically powerful, were concentrated in the less developed states and rural areas and employed in the low-paid occupations and mainly in the agricultural sector where the per capita product was the lowest whilst the Chinese were concentrated in the urban centres, employed in mining, manufacturing and construction where per capita product was more than 150 per cent that of the agricultural sector and about 60 per cent higher than the economy's average (Ragayah 1988: 31).

Malaysia's government was established in the Federal Constitution, which preceded independence and included the social contract between the various races of the country which formed the bedrock of the constitution. The Federal Constitution through Article 153, Article 160 (2), Article 161A(6)(a) and Article 161A(6)(b) articulated the provision of the indigenous people with special rights and privileges in return for the citizenship of the Chinese and Indians immigrants. The constitution also serves as a rule book for the political conduct in the realm of multiple ethnic groups.

Malaysia's public bureaucracy in general was shaped by its colonial history on the one hand, and its socio-cultural and institutional setting on the other. The Malacca Sultanate in the fifteenth century has also influenced the administrative institutions. However, the foundation of the modern administration and governance was laid down during British colonial rule (1824–1957) through a variety of new administrative structures which subsequently became the key pillars of government administration.

The British also introduced meritocracy in 1957 with the establishment of the Public Service Commission and the strict process of recruitment into the Malayan civil service (MCS). At the same time, the British initiated the quota system of recruiting four Malay candidates for one non-Malay candidate based on affirmative action to increase the participation of the Malays, who were economically the disadvantaged group in the areas of education, employment and business. The Malay quota in the civil service was first introduced by the colonial government in 1952 as part of its policy of safeguarding the special position of the Malays in the administrative service. The specific aim was to prevent the possibility of the non-Malays outnumbering the Malays in the MCS (Marican 1979: 7). The practice of the Malay quota in the civil service is traced to the Federal Constitution and reinforced through the Article 153 of the Constitution which authorizes the continuation of this practice by permitting the reservation of posts for the Malays. Lee (2005: 212) points out that the constitutional provisions for affirmative action were set out as early as in the 1948 Federation of Malaya Agreement under British colonial rule. The quota system has resulted in a Malay dominated public service that is significantly under representative of all other ethnic groups.

3.2.3 *Economy*

When Malaysia was formed in September 1963, it was a relatively poor country, and had a small economy by any measure. In 1960, its GDP per capita was US$299, which increased to US$381 in 1969 (IMF 2011). After independence, Malaysia has successfully transformed its economy from an economy that was heavily reliant on the production of raw materials in the 1960s to a multi-sector economy driven by high technology and capital-intensive industries. Its major exports in 2011 included electronics (34.5 per cent), petroleum and products (9.9 per cent), palm oil (9.3 per cent) and chemical products (6.9 per cent). Malaysia is now an upper-middle-income country as its per capita GDP has increased from US$8,752 in 2010 to US$10,514 in 2013 (World Bank 2014a). It is also ranked as the twentieth most competitive nation among 144 countries in *The Global Competitiveness Report, 2014–2015* (Schwab 2014: 13).

A unique feature of Malaysia's economic restructuring was the New Economic Policy (NEP) which was introduced in 1971 after the 1969 race riots as a socio-economic affirmative action plan to forge national unity. The NEP was implemented from 1971 to 1990. As its overriding objective was national unity, the NEP employed a two-pronged strategy: poverty reduction regardless of race, and social restructuring to eliminate identification of race with economic function. The three areas targeted under the NEP were public higher education, government employment and private sector employment.

In terms of restructuring the economy, the target was to increase the *Bumiputeras'* share of corporate capital from 2.4 per cent to 30 per cent, the share of the Chinese, Indians and others was to increase from 34.3 per cent to 40 per cent, while that of foreigners would be reduced from 63.3 per cent to 30 per cent. The target represented a 30:40:30 ratio of distribution among the *Bumiputeras*, other Malaysians and foreigners. To reach this target, it was projected that the *Bumiputeras'* share would have to expand at the rapid rate of 30 per cent per annum while the equity shares of the Chinese and Indians had to expand by 15.4 per cent per annum. In support of the NEP, there were many other economic policy innovations since 1981, starting with the industrializing thrust to the Look East policy and privatization policy in 1983. Accordingly, the public sector also regulated businesses, by using legislative means and bureaucratic procedures and ethnic quotas for equity participation. The NEP ended in 1990, but the affirmative action-based policy was continued through the National Development Plans (NDP) (1991–2000), National Vision Policy (2001–2010) and the new Economic Model in 2010.

The achievements of the NEP are debated by some scholars. On the one hand, the NEP is viewed as a success story. Overall, other than a short period of severe economic recession during 1985–1986, the Malaysian economy has expanded tremendously since the 1970s and was considered as one of the ten fastest growing economies during 1965–1990, which serves as a real world example of the redistribution and growth process advocated by the World Bank (Snodgrass 2002: 11).

Jacob Meerman (2008: 77) has viewed Malaysia's economic growth as a paradox and asked how it could grow 'at more than 6 per cent annually for over three decades (1970–2006) despite three recessions, while investing a sizeable proportion of its resources in redressing ethnic disparity?' Furthermore, how could Malaysia transform itself in a generation from a rural primary producer to a partially industrialized, urban, middle-class country 'while implementing a deep, invasive, and costly social policy?' However, he concludes that 'aspects of the NEP and some of the government's strategic economic choices imposed high costs in financial losses and opportunities foregone' (Meerman 2008: 107).

For poverty reduction, according to official data, the percentage of households living below the poverty line across all ethnic groups has been reduced from 49.3 per cent in 1970 to 12.4 per cent in 1992. The poverty rate in Malaysia further declined from 3.8 per cent to 1.7 per cent from 2009 to 2012 (Economic Planning Unit 2013; *The Star* 2013). Ragayah (2014: 21), however, observed that although the policies pursued yielded a rapid rate of growth, at an average of about 6 per cent, there was relatively little reduction in the level of absolute poverty since the poor, particularly the *Bumiputeras*, remained trapped in their traditional, low-productivity rural occupations.

A remarkable feature of this economic expansion, as Ragayah (2014: 36) argues, is that the high growth rate throughout the period has also been accompanied by low inflationary rates. Aside from the period from 1973 to 1974, inflation rates have always been in single digits, and the average annual inflation rate between 1971 and August 2009 is less than 4.5 per cent. The NEP was also recognized as a catalyst for the development of Malay entrepreneurs that led to a burst of activities in the private sector beginning from the 1970s. *Bumiputeras'* equity ownership and trust agencies increased to 21.9 per cent from 1.5 per cent in 1969 (Malaysia 2010a: 403).

On the other hand, the NEP was most controversial and the government was criticized for practising economic discrimination towards the non-*Bumiputeras*. The NEP's promotion of ethnic Malay capital was alleged to involve intra-ethnic selective patronage, ostensibly in an attempt to identify, pick and groom 'winners' (Gomez and Jomo 1999: 24–74). The NEP has also been criticized for severely undermining 'inter-ethnic social cohesion' and inhibiting 'genuine entrepreneurial capacity' (Gomez, Savaranamuttu and Maznah 2013: 3). This weakness of the NEP has resulted in a brain drain with many Malaysians leaving the country for greener pastures abroad every year.

According to Gomez, Savaranamuttu and Maznah (2013: 9) the goals of the NEP had been 'achieved in part rather than in its entirety'. Poverty has been reduced but spatial disparities have worsened. Spatial inequalities, or disparities between beneficiaries in different regions, or between urban and rural beneficiaries, have increased because preferences that were 'designed to encourage *Bumiputera* entrepreneurship were disproportionately utilized by members of the targeted group in urban and prosperous rural areas'. Furthermore, the NEP's implementation had not helped develop rural enterprises, even though this was one of its objectives. Poor infrastructural support in the rural areas and the inability of the poor to access quality education were also responsible for exacerbating the problem (Gomez, Saravanamuttu and Maznah 2013: 10).

The most recent development is a bold approach under the New Economic Model to transform the Malaysian economy into a high-income country by 2020, through the Economic Transformation Programme (ETP), a comprehensive effort initiated by Prime Minister Najib Razak. To support the ETP, there is the Government Transformation Programme (GTP), which addresses these eight National Key Result Areas (NKRAs), namely reducing crime; fighting corruption; improving students outcomes; raising living standards of low-income households; improving rural infrastructure; ensuring access to clean water; improving urban public transport; and addressing the cost of living. Both the ETP and the GTP, which are under the concept of 'People First Performance Now', are the main agenda of Prime Minister Najib's administration (Malaysia 2010b).

3.2.4 Demography

According to the 2010 Population and Housing Census, Malaysia has a population of 28.3 million people of which 91.8 per cent are Malaysian citizens and 8.2 per cent are non-citizens, with some 22.5 million concentrated in Peninsular Malaysia and 5.8 million living in Sabah and Sarawak. The population, essentially a plural society, is characterized by deep ethnic divisions, with Malays (also known as the *Bumiputeras*, comprising mostly ethnic Malays as well as other indigenous ethnic minority groups like the Ibans, Kadazan-Dusuns, Kelabit, Bisayas, Melanaus and Bidayuhs) as the largest group, accounting for about 67.4 per cent of the total population, followed by the Chinese (24.6 per cent), Indians (7.3 per cent) and others (0.7 per cent) (Department of Statistics Malaysia 2011). In 2014, the total population was estimated as 30.1 million, with *Bumiputeras* at 68 per cent, Chinese 23.8 per cent, Indians 7.2 per cent and others 1 per cent (Department of Statistics Malaysia 2012: 7).

These ethnic divisions are compounded by language, religion, culture, economic, geographic and political differences along communal lines. The official language is *Bahasa Melayu*. However, there are many languages spoken by the various ethnic groups. The Chinese speak Mandarin and Chinese dialects such as Hakka, Hokkien, Cantonese, Teochew, Hainanese and Hokchiu (Lee and Tan 2000). The Indians speak Tamil, Urdu, Malayalee and Telugu. Islam is the official religion of Malaysia, but non-Muslims are allowed to practise their own religious beliefs (Article 11). The culture is a mélange mixture of different cultures. The Malays observe the Malay culture drawn from Arab and Persian influences dating back to more than 1,500 years ago, while the Chinese and the Indians observe their own cultures.

In relation to the public sector, the ethnic composition of the population is not well represented as it is dominated by the Malays. In 1969, before the introduction of the NEP, the Malays accounted for 64.5 per cent, Chinese 18.3 per cent, Indian 15.7 per cent and others 1.5 per cent in the public service (Lim 2013: 177). However, opponents of the government claimed that the number of civil servants of other ethnic groups is still lacking. Lim (2013: 190–4) argues that the quota policy in recruitment and promotion in the public service is a serious constraint affecting its effectiveness in policy implementation in Malaysia as the 'best and brightest' non-Malays avoid the civil service and work in the private sector or emigrate to Singapore, Australia and other countries.

In the economic sector the participation of ethnic groups illustrates a stark Chinese dominance. In 2005, thirty-four years after the NEP was introduced, in 1971, the Chinese who made up 27 per cent of the total population owned more than 70 per cent of commercial buildings (i.e., industrial premises, business complexes and hotels). In comparison, only 12 per cent of these buildings and premises are owned by *Bumiputeras*, who make up more than 65 per cent of the total population, while the Indians, who constitute 7.7 per cent of the total population, own 1.5 per cent (Shafii, Abidin and Ahmad 2009: 400). As Shafii, Abidin and Ahmad (2009: 400) argue, the ownership of business enterprises serves as an indicator for measuring the wealth disparity among the ethnic groups.

3.2.5 *Political system*

The Federation of Malaysia has a constitutional monarchy based on the British model. There are thirteen states, each headed by the hereditary rulers known as the sultans. In those states with no hereditary ruler (the former British Settlements of Penang, Malacca, Sabah and Sarawak), a governor or *Yang di Pertuan Negeri*, appointed by the *Yang di Pertuan Agong* or King, heads the state. Besides the thirteen states, there are three Federal Territories: Kuala Lumpur, the national capital city; Putrajaya, the administrative capital; and Labuan in Sabah, an off-shore financial centre.

The Parliament comprises the Supreme Head (*Yang di Pertuan Agong*). Under His Majesty are the three branches of government: the legislative, the executive and the judiciary. The legislative branch consists of the Senate (*Dewan Negara*) or the Upper House of the Federal Parliament and the House of Representatives (*Dewan Rakyat*). The *Dewan Rakyat* comprises 219 members (elected from single-member districts) while the *Dewan Negara* has seventy members (twenty-six elected by the thirteen state assemblies and forty-four appointed by the King on the Prime Minister's recommendation). Each state has its own constitution and a unicameral State Legislative Assembly (*Dewan Undangan Negeri*) whose members are elected for five years from constituencies based on population. The executive body at the state level is the State Executive Council (SEC). The SEC's chief executive is the *Menteri Besar* or Chief Minister and its members are from the state legislature appointed by the ruler or governor on the advice of the *Menteri Besar*. Each state is divided into districts, which are sub-divided into *mukims*. After independence on 16 September 1963, elections to parliament and state legislative assemblies in West Malaysia have been held simultaneously, with individual state elections held in Sabah and Sarawak.

The executive branch has the power to govern (at the federal or state level), and has the role of implementing the laws that are passed by the legislative body in the Parliament or the State Legislative Assembly. At the federal level, the executive branch is known as the Cabinet. According to the Federal Constitution (Article 39), the power of the executive lies in the hands of the *Yang di Pertuan Agong*. However, executive power is exercised by the Cabinet, Parliament or by any minister empowered by the Cabinet. The nine rulers (Sultans) of the Malay states and the governors or *Yang di Pertuan Negeri* form the Council of Rulers, which was officially established under Article 38 of the Constitution of Malaysia. Every five years, the rulers of the nine sultanates confer through the *Majlis Raja-Raja Melayu* (Conference of Rulers) to select one of their own as the Federal Head of State (the *Yang di Pertuan Agong*), basically a symbolic supreme ruler. The Conference of Rulers originates from the Council of Rulers for the Federated Malay States of Perak, Selangor, Negeri Sembilan and Pahang in 1897 during the British colonial period.

The thrust of the Malaysian political system has been to achieve consensus between the different ethnic groups, although it is frequently argued that certain political parties represent and promote the elite of a community (Sanusi, Mansor and Kuddus 2003: 17). Elections to determine the representation in Parliament are held regularly every five years, and the political party with the majority of seats forms the government. The National Alliance (*Barisan Nasional* or BN) has been the ruling party since 1957. The BN consists of the United Malays National Organization (UMNO), the dominant party that spearheaded Malaya's independence, the Malaysian Chinese Association (MCA), the Malaysian Indian Congress (MIC), *Parti Bersatu* Sabah, the Sarawak United People's Party and the other BN component parties.

This party system has endured for more than five decades in all twelve general elections since independence. At the heart of this success is the power-sharing formula forged through the BN, and its precursor, the Alliance, that allowed for pluralism in Malaysia's multi-racial society, enabling all races to be represented in government and able to coalesce competing ethnic demands by mediation between political parties, a political system characterized as 'an elite accommodation system' or what Lijphart (1977: 153) describes as a 'consociational' arrangement.

The central focus of the political system is on national unity and the aim has always been to enlarge the economic pie so that Malaysians of every ethnic group can have an equitable piece of it. Despite constant political tensions and occasional upheavals among political parties in the coalition, in contrast with many of the Third World countries, as Crouch (1996: 21) observed, Malaysia has experienced politics characterized by extraordinary continuity since its independence. Crouch's observation was true at least until the eleventh general election in 2004 when the ruling coalition won 198 seats, leaving the opposition far behind with only twenty-one seats. However, the results of the twelfth general elections held on 8 March 2008 indicate a deep political rift with an unprecedented setback for the ruling coalition as the opposition political parties made significant inroads and gained a momentous victory while the BN only managed to obtain

140 of the 222 parliamentary seats, slightly more than half the parliamentary seats in Peninsular Malaysia (51.5 per cent). The People's Alliance (*Pakatan Rakyat*), which is a coalition between the National Justice Party (*Party Keadilan Nasional*), the Pan-Islamic Party (PAS) and the Democratic Action Party (DAP), obtained eighty-two seats and made significant inroads in five states (Fernando 2013: 24). This is the only general election besides the one in 1969 where the BN failed to capture a two-thirds majority of the parliamentary seats.

Evaluation of Malaysia's political discourse shows how the BN's control and domination has created a form of political hegemony. Khoo (2005: 13) argues that since the Malays form the largest proportion of the electorate, and UMNO has always won the largest share of the BN's seats in Parliament, a crucial feature of this 'majoritarian' power-sharing arrangement is that the prime minister and his deputies are Malays, and Malays head the key ministries. He further argues that this affects public sector governance in two ways. First, the civil service became increasingly Malay-dominated in terms of staff recruitment, training, deployment and promotion at the higher administrative and professional levels. Second, as administration and regulations were increasingly ethnicized, an ethnic public sector–private sector divide emerged when the public sector applied ethnic quotas and targets to many socio-economic sectors (Khoo 2005: 18–19 and 26).

The national unity and economic focus is expressed in all of the national development plans of Malaysia, and the administrative and political context was shaped by the process of balancing and harmonizing the varied racial interests.

According to the World Bank, Malaysia's percentile rank on the governance indicator on political stability and absence of violence/terrorism has decreased from 62 in 1996 to 47.9 in 2013 (World Bank 2014b).

3.3 Profile of the Malaysian public service

The Malaysian Public Service is divided into the Federal Government, the State Governments, Federal Statutory Bodies, State Statutory Bodies, Local Governments, Town and District Councils, Kuala Lumpur City Hall and the Islamic Council of Malaysia. The Federal Government administers the whole of the Malaysian federation through the powers embodied in the Constitution of the Federation of Malaysia. The state government is empowered to rule and manage the administration at the state level with powers vested by the Federal Constitution as the highest laws of the land. Local government, while relatively autonomous in its functions and decision-making processes, falls under the jurisdiction of the respective state governments, with the Ministry of Housing and Local Government playing an advisory role. However, as observed by Jomo and Wee (2002: 29), the central government controls the returns of petroleum and gas sales from the oil-producing states of Terengganu, Sabah and Sarawak through the National Petroleum Act of 1974, and these three states receive only a mere 5 per cent of the royalty.

In policy-making, however, the central government often relies on the state-level apparatus to implement many of its policies and deliver services (Watts 1999: 37). In shouldering this responsibility the state governments recruit large numbers of civil servants. Watts (1999: 41) observes that although the federalist arrangements are 'relatively centralized legislatively, they are much more decentralized administratively', which confers upon the state-level governments a great deal of de facto autonomy in their policy directions.

Malaysia is the only country in Southeast Asia practising federalism as the other countries in the region have unitary systems. Federalism in Malaysia was characterized from the start by a 'high degree of centralization' (Watts 1999: 28). Briefly, powers were delineated across these three tiers: those held by the central government, those held at the state level and those to be exercised concurrently. The purview of the Federal Government, according to the Ninth Schedule of the Federal Constitution, stretches widely, from foreign affairs, defence, internal security, law and order, trade, commerce and industry as well as communications and transport, education and health. In addition, the Tenth Schedule of the Federal Constitution notes that 'income taxes, property and capital gains taxes, international trade taxes including production and consumption taxes' belong to the Federal Government, which then provides funds to the local councils in the form of a capitation grant (based on population size) and a state road grant. The role of the local councils is basically to provide services such as caring for the environment, public health and cleaning, enforcement and licensing, public amenities, social services, development and planning to its residents. The revenue of local government is derived mainly from assessment, rentals and licences, thus limiting their operational and development expenditures.

The federal administrative machinery consists of ministries, each with several departments and statutory bodies, headed by a Minister. The federal framework and the constitution, with twenty-six ministries and five central agencies, have created a strong central government headed by the Prime Minister that controls many budgetary and personnel matters and formulates national financial and economic policies (Sanusi, Mansor and Kuddus 2003: 43). Besides the ministries, the federal agencies also include the Ministry of Finance, the Economic Planning Unit (EPU), the Implementation Coordination Unit (ICU), the Public Service Department (PSD), the Public Service Commission (PSC) and the Malaysian Administrative Modernisation and Management Planning Unit (MAMPU). These are known as central agencies and are powerful as they are responsible for formulating the national financial and economic policies, the public sector human resource policies, and monitoring and supervising the implementation of these policies, and controlling the budgets.

Besides the Federal Government there are thirteen State Governments which implement state functions. At the state level is the state public service, organized along similar lines. The State Secretariat is the highest administrative office. The state government generates its own revenues and incurs its own expenditures. The lowest tier is local government, also known as the local authorities, which collectively refer to the administrative authorities that are smaller than the state authorities. Local government collects assessment taxes, creates rules in the form of by-laws, grants licences and permits for trade in its area of jurisdiction, provides basic amenities, collects and manages waste, and plans development in its area of jurisdiction. There are four types of local governments: the City Hall of Kuala Lumpur; the eleven city councils of each state capital; the thirty-six municipal councils; and the ninety-six district councils. These local governments receive financial grants from the state government and the federal government.

Government agencies consist of ministries, departments and statutory bodies. The statutory bodies, also known as public corporations, are created under the federal or state law for a particular business and placed under the control of the relevant ministries. Some examples of statutory bodies are the Malaysian Industrial Development Authority (MIDA), Inland Revenue Board, Malaysian Rubber Board, Malaysian Communications and Multimedia Commission, public universities and the state development corporation. Every statutory body is subjected to its own incorporation act, which sets out the purpose and specific powers of autonomy and functions. In terms of financial management, these statutory bodies have their own financial regulations and systems, with some dependent on government grants and others generating their own funds.

In 2014, at the federal level, there were 147 ministries and departments, 92 statutory bodies and 1 local council, whilst at the state level in Peninsular Malaysia there were 178 ministries or departments, 69 statutory bodies and 98 local councils. In Sabah, there were 39 ministries or departments, 13 statutory bodies and 22 local councils, while in Sarawak, there were 30 ministries or departments, 21 statutory bodies and 24 local councils (see Table 3.1).

Table 3.1 *Number of government agencies in Malaysia, 2014*

Agencies	Ministries / Departments	Statutory bodies	Local councils	Total (percentage)
Federal	147	92	1	240 (32.7%)
Peninsular Malaysia States	178	69	98	345 (47.0%)
Sabah	39	13	22	74 (10.0%)
Sarawak	30	21	24	75 (10.2%)
Totals	394	195	145	734 (100%)

Source: Organizational Division, Public Service Department, Malaysia.

3.3.1 Structure of the public service

The public service had 1.2 million employees in 2010, with 924,039 federal government employees (74.4 per cent), 113,998 state employees (9.2 per cent), 123,663 employees of federal statutory bodies (9.9 per cent), 18,838 employees of state statutory bodies (1.5 per cent) and 62,531 local government employees (5 per cent) (Ali 2013: 31). As outlined in Article 132 of the Federal Constitution, the public service covers twenty-eight schemes of service including the Federal Public Service, the State Public Service and the Joint Public Services, the Education Service, the Judiciary, the Legal Service and the Police and the Armed Forces.

Structurally, the public service is divided into several categories. In 1992, under the New Remuneration System, civil servants are categorized into four groups: Premier Group; Professional and Managerial Group; Support Group I; and Support Group II. The Premier Group or the *Jawatan Utama Sektor Awam* (JUSA) is the highest group and the most coveted in terms of salaries and perks. Members of the Premier Group are the leaders of the public service. The top civil servant is the Chief Secretary to the Government, *Ketua Setiausaha Negara* (KSN), who is also the Secretary to the Cabinet.

The public service is ethnically mainly composed of Malays with 25 per cent of non-Malays. This was partly the legacy of the British colonial policy of recruiting one non-Malay for every four competent Malay candidates under the quota system introduced in 1952, as well as the political 'bargaining' and the 'special privileges' in the Federal Constitution. The rationale for the quota system introduced by the British colonial government was to ensure that non-*Bumiputeras* do not outnumber the *Bumiputeras,* and that the merit criteria would result in the educationally disadvantaged group being under-represented in the public service.

Within the professional and managerial group is the MCS, presently known as *Perkhidmatan Tadbir dan Diplomatik* (PTD) (Administrative and Diplomatic Service). The Malayan Civil Service evolved through various phases until it was dissolved in 1966 after the formation of Malaysia and replaced by the Malaysian Home and Foreign Service. In 1972, the service was renamed as the PTD, and is often referred to as the premier service. It is a small service, and is recognized as the *crème de la crème* of the administration. The PTD has many things in its favour – the PTD officers hold extensive powers and key decision-making positions at the federal level or state level (Sarji 1996). Almost all strategic posts in the government at federal level, overseas, the states and district are headed by PTD officers. The government recruits about

400 officers annually into the PTD and the total strength is approximately 8,000 (Mohd Nasir 2010).

3.4 The public service's role in policy formulation

Before going into the role of the public service in policy formulation, it is useful first to understand the sources of policy initiatives. Policy formulation involves laws and regulations. At the start, it is helpful to understand how laws and regulations are made as that will also help us in understanding the role of the civil service in policy formulation. Therefore, it is necessary to examine the institutional machinery. The analysis in this chapter is based on the theoretical framework of Van Meter and Van Horn (1975: 447) who define policy implementation as 'those actions by public or private individuals (or groups) that are directed at the achievement of objectives set forth in prior policy decisions'. They view the implementation process as a top-down approach but stress their concerns about consensus, compliance and participation in policy formulation by subordinates. They have identified the importance of these six variables: (1) the policy standards and objectives; (2) the available resources and incentives; (3) the inter-organizational communication and enforcement activities; (4) the characteristics of the implementing agencies; (5) the economic, social and political conditions; and (6) the disposition of the implementers (Van Meter and Van Horn 1975: 462–74).

The institutional machinery consists of these central agencies: Ministry of Finance; EPU and the ICU of the Prime

Minister's Department; PSD; PSC; and MAMPU are the most significant institutions in policy-making, as these agencies set the policy standards and objectives mentioned by Van Meter and Van Horn. The EPU is responsible for the formulation of broad objectives, policies and strategies in development planning, and sets the policy standards and objectives. It coordinates and prepares development budgets, evaluates the progress of development plans and advises the government on economic issues. It plays a central role in managing the national economy and in overseeing national economic policies, namely the NEP and NDP. The ICU is responsible for ensuring the efficiency of development projects and is an important source of policy initiatives. The MAMPU is responsible for introducing reforms in the public service to increase the quality, efficiency and effectiveness in administration. It also acts as an inspectorate to oversee the implementation of administrative reforms in the state and federal agencies. Of significance is the PSD, which is responsible for all the civil service sub-systems except for recruitment and discipline, which falls under the purview of the PSC. The Ministry of Finance is another important ministry as the custodian of Malaysia's public finances.

The coordination and control by the above-mentioned central agencies encompass these important functions: examining and scrutinizing the estimated annual budgets of the state, public servant services scheme, public servant grades and positions; examining and scrutinizing the annual economic development programmes and projects of state, and also the five-yearly economic policy of the state; enforcing the financial regulations and public services;

coordinating the formulation and implementation of public policy, programmes and projects, as well as analysing and investigating public complaints and feedback with regard to the various governmental programmes and projects (Sanusi, Mansor and Kuddus 2003: 45–7). The central agencies not only provide the broad goal and specific performance assessment through the EPU but also ensure that there are resources and incentives through the MAMPU and the Ministry of Finance.

The Legislative branch is responsible for law-making. The Acts of Parliament are laws legislated by the Parliament which affect the country as a whole. The three tiers of government (federal, state and local) have their own jurisdictions in which laws are passed. The Malaysian legal system is mainly based on the common law. Its source is a mixed legal system of English common law, Islamic law and customary law; and a judicial review of legislative acts in the Supreme Court. Article 4(1) of the Malaysian Constitution states that the supreme law of the federation is the Constitution. The Constitution of Malaysia also provides for a unique dual justice system – the secular laws (criminal and civil) and the Islamic law or the *syariah* laws, which applies only to the Muslims and comes under the control of the *Syariah* Court. It covers matters such as marriage, divorce, adoption, wills and other offences under the Islamic law. The dual system of law is provided in Article 121(1A) of the Constitution of Malaysia. Federal laws, also known as Acts (of Parliament), are enacted by the Parliament of Malaysia and apply throughout the country. There are also state laws enacted by the State Legislative Assemblies that apply in the particular state. State laws are often referred to as enactments or ordinances. Article 75 of the Constitution provides that federal laws prevail over any inconsistent state laws, including *syariah* laws.

All international commitments must be transposed into domestic rules before they can take effect on individuals, companies or organizations to which the international agreements are aimed to influence. There are two methods by which international law may be incorporated into domestic law. The first is through legislation which may expressly enact the terms of a treaty or convention to which Malaysia may be a party or it may implicitly do so by requiring domestic law to be interpreted in accordance with a treaty or convention. The second method is through the common law process. Courts may, through the interpretation of domestic law, introduce principles of international law into the domestic system.

The policy-making process involves several stages, such as identifying the problems, planning, recommending and formulating suitable alternatives, legitimizing policies, implementing the suitable action policy, coordinating various activities in the implementation of the policy and evaluating the effectiveness of the policy. In general, the politicians, civil servants at the federal government and related relevant interest groups are the three main players in the policy-making process. The politicians (cabinet ministers and Members of Parliament) and senior government officials are the major players in ensuring the success of policy implementation. The public, through interest groups, put forth their ideas for the government's consideration.

The essential components of coordination within the government machinery lie at the federal level, two of which are the Cabinet and the Cabinet Committees. The most important councils are the National Development Council (NDC), the National Economic Council (NEC) and the National Security Council (NSC), which assist the Cabinet in dealing with such related fields as coordinating the implementation of development programmes and projects under the NDC, planning on economic aspects under the NEC and security aspects under the NSC. These councils are chaired by the Prime Minister himself. Furthermore, the National Development Planning Committee (NDPC), which is responsible for formulating the five-year development plans, evaluates and restructures all the development programmes drawn by various government ministries and agencies. The NDPC Chairman is the Secretary to the Government and the EPU serves as the NDPC Secretariat.

As the Federal Government has authority over macroeconomic policies, these policy initiatives are coordinated by the EPU, Ministry of Finance (MOF) and *Bank Negara Malaysia* (BNM or the Central Bank of Malaysia) with the involvement of those agencies responsible for the development of various sectors. The EPU coordinates the policy-making process through the Cabinet Secretariat. The formulation and mid-term reviews of the five-year development plans, and the Privatization Masterplan, are undertaken by the EPU. The designated post is the office of the Chief Secretary, who is the Chief Executive of the Prime Minister's Department and the Prime Minister's major adviser. As Secretary to the Cabinet, he coordinates the policies of the various ministries and ensures that the decisions of the Cabinet are implemented. As head of the civil service, he is responsible for the efficiency of the civil service and chairs the permanent committee meetings of the Secretary-Generals, the federal heads of Departments, and the Federal/State Liaison. Furthermore, the Inter-Agency Planning Group (IAPG) and the Technical Working Groups (TWGs) provide the technical support, which is supplemented by some ministries and departments.

In a normal federal system, there exists a reasonably equitable distribution of power, resources and revenue between the federal and state governments. However, Malaysia's administrative system is highly centralized. Loh (2010: 132) argues that the situation is entirely different in Malaysia because its constitutional design privileges the central over the state and local governments 'in terms of legislative jurisdictions as well as in revenue assignments'. This means that, as part of the federalist arrangement, the central government asserts its authority not only over foreign policy, defence, monetary policy and constitutional amendments, but also controls and taps resources that cuts across areas typically shared with or reserved for state-level government. However, the central government often relies on the state-level apparatus to implement many of its policies and deliver services (Watts 1999: 37). In shouldering this responsibility the state governments recruit large numbers of civil servants. As Watts (1999: 41) observes, although the federalist arrangements are 'relatively centralized legislatively, they are much more decentralized administratively', which confers upon state-level governments a degree of de facto autonomy over policy direction in the process of implementation.

The final arbiter on policy is the Cabinet. Policy papers submitted by the various ministries and government departments for consideration are presented to the Cabinet by the respective ministers. The Cabinet papers are prepared in consultation with the relevant ministries and departments whose views are incorporated. If there are dissenting views on the policy, the decision is left to the Cabinet. The Cabinet could instruct the relevant minister and the initiating agency to consider the matter and resubmit to the Cabinet. There are also councils, committees and task forces of the Cabinet – for example, the Cabinet Committee on Competitiveness and the National Implementation Task Force (NITF) – to vet specific areas of policy, particularly the economic policy.

Other relevant groups are the non-financial public enterprises and the government-linked companies (GLCs), which are agencies operating in the corporate environment in which the government has equity interests. Sources of policies can also come from the non-governmental bodies and the private sector. Representatives of private associations and commercial groups participate in the budget dialogue to provide views and recommendations to the government. Another source are the independent groups such as university academics and think tanks, which are also included in the policy-making loop. The Institute of Strategic and International Studies (ISIS), the Asian Leadership Institute (ASLI) and the Malaysian Institute of Economic Research (MIER) are some of the leading think tanks, which are partially funded by the government to conduct studies and make policy recommendations.

Public policies are finalized after several discussions at various levels, involving the setting up of internal committees at the departmental level, and sometimes if the memorandum requires comprehensive measures, the department appoints consultants, and conducts several brainstorming sessions involving individuals or representatives from the government agencies, private sector and non-governmental organizations (NGOs). The draft policy document is amended to satisfy the various sectors. Ministerial consent has to be acquired before the document is submitted to the central agency and in particular to the Cabinet.

After a policy draft has been developed, a memorandum to the Cabinet (recommendation paper) will be prepared. This is in line with the Order No. 1 of the Chief Secretary to the Cabinet 2000 entitled 'Guidelines for Preparing the Cabinet Paper and Implementation of the Cabinet Decision'. The memorandum may include comments from the related ministries and central agencies such as the MOF, EPU, ICU and the Attorney-General's Office. After these comments are taken into account, the responsible minister gives approval to forward the memorandum to the Cabinet weekly meeting (which is scheduled on every Wednesday) following clearance from the Cabinet Secretariat.

When the Cabinet approves the memorandum the decision is conveyed to the relevant ministries. The proposed measure may be expressed through other instruments such as statutory orders, regulations and guidelines (known as subsidiary legislation). It need not take the form of a parliamentary bill. The most important policy measures will be drafted as bills to be submitted to Parliament, while other measures will be drafted as statutory orders, regulations or guidelines. In the case of bills, the Ministry concerned proceeds to obtain a Notice of Presentation on the Bill to the House of

Representatives and the Senate for debate and approval in both Houses during the parliamentary session. The bill will be passed by both Houses (more than two-thirds of the votes) and will be submitted to His Majesty the *Yang di-Pertuan Agong* for the Royal Assent. The bill becomes law after being gazetted by the Parliament. Finally, the decision will be conveyed administratively to the related parties and through several high-level government meetings such as the State Executive Meeting, Meeting of Secretary-Generals of Ministries and Heads of Services, Meeting of Heads of Federal Departments, Meeting of Chief Executives of Federal Statutory Bodies, and Meeting of the Liaison Committee between the Federal and State Governments.

The implementation machinery is equally important to ensure the successful execution of the policies, and requires effective institutions, leadership, processes and mechanisms as well as good coordination and proper delivery systems. Generally, policy implementation is left to the lead agencies such as the various ministries and departments. Coordination among agencies is vital and is undertaken by the key agency responsible for the policy, such as the Ministry of Health (MOH) for policies concerning health, or the Ministry of Home Affairs (MOHA) for policies dealing with national security.

In relation to Van Meter and Van Horn's framework, policy implementation is assumed to occur at two levels: macro-implementation, where the centrally located actors devise a government programme; and micro-implementation, where the local level actors react to these plans and develop their own plans and implement them. They also suggest that these characteristics require the examination of coordination issues across institutions in the absence of operational authority. In the case of Malaysia, a system of oversight of policy implementation has been developed and occurs at different levels of government. This is related to Van Meter and Van Horn's reminder that policy implementation is a process involving multiple actors and organizations with important roles played by the clients or recipients.

The oversight of implementation varies according to the type of policy, the implementing agency, and the groups affected by the policy. At the parliamentary level, the progress of the implementation of policies, programmes and projects are debated. The implementation oversight is usually integrated within a planning framework, covering a medium- to long-term planning perspective. Within the civil service, the system of oversight involves the setting up of steering committees, councils or groups. Steering committees, usually led by technocrats, are responsible for specific areas of policy to ensure that the implementation progress is on track. The NITF, established in 2006, with the Prime Minister as Chairman, for example, oversees the implementation of the Ninth Malaysia Plan. There is also the PEMUDAH, a joint public–private sector committee to ensure the smooth implementation of policies and make recommendations for the improvement of the delivery system.

The public service also continuously reviews the implementation of policies in the context of broader economic and social performance and specific targets. Where polices fall short of the target, adjustments are made so that policies move in the direction of consolidating the public sector. As the Ministry of Information is responsible for policy presentation, public information officers stationed at the various ministries ensure that official news reaches the public through press conferences, press releases, ministerial interviews, interviews with senior officials and special launches.

On its part, the Malaysian public service has earned national and international acclaim for providing stability and contributing to the country's prosperity. The significant feature of the role of Malaysia's public service in policy-making is that it has created a strong mechanism that has become apparent over time, as recognized in the World Bank's governance indicator on government effectiveness. Malaysia's percentile rank for government effectiveness has improved from 76.1 in 1996 to 81.8 in 2013 (World Bank 2014b).

However, there have been significant obstacles to effective policy implementation. Being the major group in the population, the Malays have dominated the positions in the public service. The government has difficulty in attracting the other ethnic groups into the civil service, thus limiting the pool of high calibre candidates in the civil service. Lim (2013: 178–9) argues that since the NEP restructuring began in 1971 until 2005, the non-*Bumiputeras* have been under-represented in the total public service (see Table 3.2).

Lim (2013: 185–6) also argues that there is a strong perception that the practice of ethnic preference is not limited to recruitment but also includes promotion, as the disproportionate control of the Malays in the senior positions in the public service seems to suggest (see Tables 3.2 and 3.3). The negative effects on public service performance pertain to three

Table 3.2 *Ethnic representation in the Malaysian Public Service, 2005*

Ethnic group	Top management group		Professional and management group		Support group		Total public service	
	Number	Percentage	Number	Percentage	Number	Percentage	Number	Percentage
Malay	1,370	83.9	155,871	81.7	535,495	75.8	692,736	77.0
Other *Bumiputera*	23	1.4	6,156	3.2	63,649	9.0	69,828	7.8
Chinese	151	9.3	17,896	9.4	66,248	9.4	84,295	9.4
Indian	83	5.1	9,777	5.1	36,194	5.1	46,054	5.1
Others	5	0.3	1,203	0.6	5,129	0.7	6,337	0.7
Totals	1,632	100	190,903	100	706,715	100	899,250	100

Source: Oriental News, 8 December 2005, cited in Lim 2013: 180.

Table 3.3 *Ethnic representation in the Malaysian Public Service, 2009*

Ethnic group	Top management group		Management and professional group		Support group		Totals	
	Number	Percentage	Number	Percentage	Number	Percentage	Number	Percentage
Malay	1,360	79.3	212,733	74.6	718,132	76.7	932,225	76.2
Other *Bumiputera*	32	1.9	13,406	4.7	75,736	8.1	89,174	7.3
Chinese	165	9.6	30,415	10.7	42,259	4.5	72,875	6.0
Indian	120	7.0	14,468	5.1	35,552	3.8	50,140	4.1
Others	38	2.2	13,886	4.9	64,609	6.9	78,553	6.4
Totals	1,715	100	284,908	100	936,288	100	1,222,967	100

Source: Sin Chew Daily, 22 May 2010, cited in Lim 2013: 182.

basic aspects, as Lim (2013: 192–4) argues: responsiveness, effectiveness and efficiency. Research on representative bureaucracy in the United States has shown that public servants are often more responsive to their own ethnic group than to other ethnic groups, and may seem to suggest that partiality is bound to occur (Bradbury and Kellogh 2011). Although such systematic studies are lacking in Malaysia, some observers (Means 1972: 46–8; Shamsul 1996: 25) have pointed to the same problem which led to the erosion of public trust in the public service. As Abdullah Badawi, a former Prime Minister, commented, 'without the brightest minds conceptualizing, adapting, and driving public policies, good governance would remain an elusive ideal' (quoted in Lim 2013: 194). This view was supported by another minister, Rais Yatim (2006: 196–7) when he observed that 'the Cabinet formulates policies mainly pursuant to findings and submissions made by officials. However, as recent indications have shown, many of their considered opinions and findings have proven to be off-target.'

In response to the growing concern in the government over the calibre of civil servants, the PSC has recently stepped up the hiring of non-*Bumiputeras* into the public service. In 2009, the numbers recruited from other ethnic groups has increased (see Table 3.3). As Malays constitute the major group in the population, Malay domination in the public service would naturally persist.

Furthermore, evidence suggests that corruption is entrenched in the public service. Malaysia's ranking and score on Transparency International's Corruption Perceptions Index (CPI) seems to be declining. While the policy-making processes seem to be right, implementation is another story as it is impeded by corrupt practices. Despite the government's effort in combating corruption, the problem persists as reflected in Malaysia's perpetual backsliding position on the CPI. In 2008, Malaysia was ranked 47th among 178 countries. In 2009 and 2010, its position was 56th. In 2011, it was ranked 60th among 183 countries, a drop of four places from 2010, and its CPI score was 4.3 out of 10. However, Malaysia's ranking has improved from 54th position in 2012 to 50th position in 2014 (Transparency International 2014). Nevertheless, there are still concerns on issues of graft, as indicated in the Auditor-General's Report, particularly on the political front. Transparency International's *Global Corruption Barometer 2013* reported that the police and political parties were the most corrupt institutions in Malaysia (Hardoon and Heinrich 2013: 36).

3.5 Implementing the ASEAN Cosmetic Directive (ACD)

3.5.1 Regulatory authorities for controlling cosmetics products

The regulatory authorities are the Enforcement Division in the MOH and the *Biro Pengawalan Farmaseutikal Kebangsaan* (BPFK) or National Pharmaceutical Control Bureau (NPCB), formerly known as the National Pharmaceutical Control Laboratory, which was formed in October 1978.[1]

[1] The empirical data in this section are based on personal interviews and group discussions with two NPCB officials and one MOH official.

As the NPCB was established to implement quality control on pharmaceutical products, its main activities are to implement the registration scheme of drugs and cosmetics through laboratory tests, research and information from international bodies. The Enforcement Division in the MOH monitors the products in the market.

The policy standards and objectives are defined by the NPCB and Standards Malaysia, designated as the Malaysian Compliance Monitoring Authorities (CMAs) by the Malaysian government. The NPCB is the CMA for the non-clinical safety testing of test items contained in pharmaceutical products, cosmetics products, veterinary drugs and food additives, whereas Standards Malaysia is the CMA for the non-clinical safety testing of test items contained in industrial chemicals, pesticides, feed additives and biotechnology (non-pharmaceuticals). The NPCB is responsible for the enforcement of the Directive under Regulation 29 of the Control of Drugs and Cosmetics Regulations 1984 in June 2009. Beginning in 1985, the NPCB was tasked with ensuring the quality, efficacy and safety of pharmaceuticals through registration and licensing scheme (National Pharmaceutical Control Bureau 2014a).

3.5.2 *Legal framework for controlling cosmetics products*

The Malaysian government instituted the legal framework for control of cosmetics products through the combination of various laws, regulations and guidelines. The related laws, regulations and guidelines are (1) the Sale of Drugs Act 1952

(SODA); (2) Control of Drugs and Cosmetics Regulations 1984 (CDCR); (3) Control of Drugs and Cosmetics (amendment) Regulations 2007; and (4) Guidelines for Control of Cosmetic Products in Malaysia 2009. The CDCR contains information on the product notification, importation, sales and manufacturing. It was revised in May 2009 to transpose the ACD and came into force in January 2010. Presently the CDCR is again under revision, waiting for the Parliamentary gazette. Under the Control of Drugs and Cosmetics (amendment) Regulations 2007, the company or person responsible for placing a cosmetics product in the local market must notify the Director of Pharmaceutical Services (DPS) through the NPCB prior to product manufacture or importation (interview with a senior NPCB official). The NPCB serves as a secretariat to the DPS, which is responsible for the cosmetics product notification process.

The Guidelines for Control of Cosmetic Products includes regulatory information pertaining to the Cosmetic Advertising Code as well as cosmetics claims. These guidelines were prepared by the Cosmetic Technical Working Group (CTWG), comprising the NPCB and representatives from the cosmetics industry that consists of associations representing the cosmetics industries: (1) Cosmetic Toiletries and Fragrance Association of Malaysia (CTFAM) and (2) Federation of Malaysian Manufacturers–Malaysia Cosmetics and Toiletries Industry Group (FMM–MCTIG). The Guidelines for Control of Cosmetic Products in Malaysia are prepared in accordance with the ACD. The primary goal of the CTWG is to implement an efficient regulatory control system without compromising consumer safety. The requirements of the ACD are the fundamental principles of cosmetics product control: to ensure safety and quality and to regulate any claimed benefits of cosmetics products. The authority responsible for the regulation of cosmetics products lies with the DPS (group discussion with NPCB and MOH officials).

The Guidelines for Control of Cosmetic Products pertain to the Cosmetic Advertising Code and Cosmetic Claims Guidelines and cover: the regulation of cosmetics products; legal aspects of cosmetics control; legislation covering the manufacturer; notification procedure; post-market surveillance; cosmetics ingredients; labelling requirements; good manufacturing practices (GMP); authorization for manufacture, import or wholesale; test market sampling or aesthetic studies and in-house evaluation; reporting of adverse events; product recall, withdrawal; penalty; and the Cosmetic Advertising Code.

3.5.3 *Regulations and monitoring at work*

The implementation of the ACD came into force in Malaysia on 1 January 2008. The requirements of the ACD have been adapted and transposed into the Control of Drugs and Cosmetics (amendment) Regulations 2007 and the Guidelines for Control of Cosmetic Products. Prior to the ACD, from 2002 to the end of 2007, the control of cosmetics products was through pre-market registration for review and registration by the NPCB before the product could be manufactured, imported or sold in the country, and by conducting post-market surveillance. However, in conformance with the harmonization of cosmetics regulations in the ASEAN region, this system has been replaced by a notification procedure starting from 1 January 2008. Instead of registration, companies are now required only to notify or to declare their compliance with the ACD to the NPCB. The company responsible for placing a cosmetics product in the local market is required to submit a notification to the DPS through the NPCB prior to any marketing, manufacturing, importing or wholesaling of the product. A notification note should be printed out for every product and variant (if any) and will act as the authorization to carry out the above-mentioned activities. The cosmetics products must not contain any substance that may cause harm to the consumer when applied under normal or reasonably foreseeable conditions of use (interview with a senior NPCB official).

The system has been improved further such that the product holder or the manufacturer can now notify online the Centre for Post Registration of Products, under the Cosmetic Section of the NPCB, and the procedure has been reduced to three days instead of one month, as previously. The system can filter ingredients of the products to ensure that the dangerous ingredients do not exceed the allowable limit (interview with a senior NPCB official).

Another notable improvement to the system is that Malaysia has proposed a new initiative at the national level to establish a pool of safety experts for the cosmetics sector and will explore the possibility of extending it at the regional level. This is conducted through the establishment of the Cosmetic Safety Expert Committee (CoSEC) by the NPCB. The main functions of CoSEC are threefold: to compile and review the ingredients list, toxicological data, technical and safety issues related to cosmetic product/ingredients; to review the available technical data on cosmetics ingredients including the new and local botanical ingredients; and to review the relevant international standards on cosmetics and provide recommendations for possible adoption. CoSEC comprises members from the regulatory (NPCB), clinical experts, academia and cosmetics associations (group discussion with NPCB and MOH officials).

The NPCB conducts monitoring of cosmetics products through the Post Market Surveillance (PMS) programme to ensure that only safe products are being marketed. Action will be taken against cosmetics and toiletry products that are not compliant with the ACD. The PMS activities consist of screening of product formulation and information; audit of product information files (PIFs) for compliance with the regulations; sample collection, testing and monitoring of label compliance; audit of premises to ensure compliance with the ASEAN Guidelines for Cosmetic Good Manufacturing Practices; investigation of complaints; initiation of warning and information sharing system between ASEAN countries; monitoring of adverse reactions from cosmetics products; and monitoring of cosmetics advertisements. Some examples are the advertisements broadcast on television and radio, in magazines, newspapers, pamphlets, brochures and leaflets, online, on billboards, television programme slots, talk shows, on public transport, in testimonies and in advertorials (interview with a senior NPCB official).

Laboratory tests are conducted on products where doubts have been found in its ingredients, in particular whitening agents in cosmetics products (interview with a senior NPCB official). The laboratory is certified with MS ISO/IEC 17025: 2005 on 14 January 2010 (discussion with NPCB officials). Besides the ISO certification, the laboratory also has the Principles of Good Laboratory Practice (GLP) endorsement, a quality system concerned with the organizational process and the conditions under which non-clinical health and environment safety studies are planned, performed, monitored, recorded, archived and reported. The purpose of these Principles of GLP is to promote the development of high-quality data applied to the non-clinical safety testing of items contained in pharmaceutical products and cosmetics products. The purpose of testing these items is to obtain data on their properties and/or their safety with respect to human health and/or the environment. Non-clinical health and environmental safety studies covered by the Principles of GLP include work conducted in laboratories and greenhouses, and in the field. The GLP Compliance Programme ascertains whether the test facilities have implemented the requirements described in the documents of the Organisation for Economic Cooperation and Development (OECD) Series on Principles of Good Laboratory Practice and Compliance Monitoring (National Pharmaceutical Control Bureau 2014b).

From January to September 2009, a total of 26,306 cosmetics were notified. The audit priority is on high-risk products such as baby products, products to be used around the eyes and mucous membranes, whitening products, history of notification holders and manufacturer numbers. According to the Officer of the Enforcement Division, the MOH conducts surveillance and monitoring activities on products in the market on a regular basis. From January to September

Table 3.4 *Statistics on product sampling, January–September 2009*

Item	Number (per month)
Samples being targeted	50
Targeted samples received	292
Products passing the laboratory tests	222
Products failing the laboratory tests	19

Source: information provided by a Ministry of Health official.

2009, fifty-two complaints were received. Initially, product sampling was targeted at fifty samples per month. However, the workload proved to be much greater than forecast, as the NPCB undertook product sampling almost six times what had been predicted (see Table 3.4).

Common complaints included unsubstantiated claims, non-cosmetic claims, incomplete labelling and dissatisfied consumers (interview with a senior NPCB official). Product complaints are important in order to provide the authority to conduct surveillance and monitor product quality and safety in the market, as well as being a trigger to conduct audit and product sampling. The information in these complaints is shared with other regulatory agencies such as ASEAN Alert.

The NCPB has been vigorous in its regulatory activities. From 2008 to 2014, sixty-nine products were recalled from the market, as shown in Table 3.5. The recalled products are listed on the NCPB's website for the public's information.

The two regulatory bodies may be considered in the light of Van Meter and Van Horn's discussion on implementing agencies. The implementing agency, the NPCB, has its

Table 3.5 *Cancellation of notifications by the National Pharmaceutical Control Bureau, 2008–2014*

Year	Number of products
2008	6
2009	12
2010	12
2011	5
2012	12
2013	13
2014	9
Total	69

Source: National Pharmaceutical Control Bureau 2014c.

own legal framework for control and sets its own standards and objectives. To ensure the understanding of the laws it implements, the NPCB issues guidelines based on the recommendations of its technical working group. It also engages the cosmetics industry to ensure the continuous improvement of its system of monitoring, enforcement and advice. This is done through CoSEC, which provides technical support and promotes research into product safety. There is thus a good inter-organizational relationship between the NPCB and the leaders of the cosmetics industry.

The impartiality of the implementing agency is demonstrated through its due process in vigorous monitoring activities – ISO certification of its laboratories, the adoption of the GLP Compliance Programme as described in documents of the OECD Series on Principles of Good Laboratory Practice and Compliance Monitoring, product sampling which went beyond their targets, product screening, surveillance, cancellation of notifications, product recalls and sharing of information with other regulatory agencies such as ASEAN Alert.

It should be noted that the state administration, besides being an operating or implementing agency, complements the federal agencies. However, by itself, the state administration operates in a constrained manner because it does not have the manpower or the capacity to operate like those agencies at the federal level. It is more concerned with the delivery of services such as cleanliness, safety and health, facilities, schools, lamp posts and roads. Furthermore, the local government in general is constrained by inefficiency and lack of funds.

3.5.4 Challenges in implementing the ACD

It has now been seven years since the ACD has been implemented. On the part of the cosmetics industry, the challenges in addressing the ACD are the high cost of manufacturing and overheads – for example, ingredients, packaging materials, transportation and electricity – together with a shortage of workers (interview with an FMM official).

Another issue concerns the ways of coordinating the ASEAN Cosmetics Association members to ensure the elimination of differences in implementing the ACD among the different countries. There are different interpretations on the listing of ingredients among the countries. The third challenge is that authorized personnel must have technical knowledge and experience on product contents and be well versed in the ACD guidelines before conducting the notification process. An audit on product information is required for all notified products and made available when requested by the authority (interview with a senior NPCB official).

3.6 Implementing the ASEAN Ministerial Meeting on Transnational Crime (AMMTC)/ Senior Officials Meeting on Transnational Crime (SOMTC)

While many countries have taken steps to combat transnational crime, there are diverging views on how best to tackle these threats and differing levels of development among the ASEAN countries in their laws and enforcement.[2] To enhance the importance of cross-border cooperation, Malaysia has spearheaded the formulation of a regional Treaty on Mutual Legal Assistance in Criminal Matters to which all the ten ASEAN countries have become signatories. This treaty has been accepted as the ASEAN Treaty on Mutual Legal Assistance in Criminal Matters to assist in reducing the legal red tape and combating transnational crime and terrorism, and facilitates cross-border cooperation in criminal investigations and the gathering of evidence for court proceedings (personal correspondence with senior MOHA officials).

While there are at least nine types of transnational crime identified in the ASEAN Declaration on Transnational

[2] The empirical data in this section are based on personal correspondence with senior MOHA officials in Malaysia.

Crime, because of space constraints and for an in-depth discussion, this chapter will focus on two types of transnational crime: drug trafficking and trafficking in persons. These two types of transnational crime come under the purview of the MOHA.

3.6.1 Drug trafficking

As Malaysia occupies a strategic location, it is used as a transit point for drug trafficking to places such as Europe, Hong Kong, Taiwan, Singapore and Australia. While Malaysia itself is not a narcotic-producing country, the drugs are smuggled into the country mainly from the Golden Crescent (Iran–Pakistan–Afghanistan) and Golden Triangle (Laos–Thailand–Myanmar). Malaysia is a party to the 1988 United Nations Drug Convention (personal correspondence with a senior MOHA official).

The legislative tool to combat drug trafficking is the Dangerous Drugs Act 1952 and Dangerous Drugs Act (Amendment) 1975. In 1983, drugs were proclaimed as a national threat and a mandatory death penalty for drug offences was introduced. The measure still exists today. A National Drug Policy was formulated in 1996 with the objective of eliminating the supply of and demand for illicit drugs. This policy has three priorities: (1) preventing the smuggling of drugs into the country for local consumption; (2) reducing drug abuse; and (3) preventing the transit of drugs through Malaysia to third countries. The regulatory body is the National Anti-Narcotics Agency (AADK) and the Royal Malaysian Police through the Royal Malaysian Police Narcotics Criminal Investigations Division.

Under the ASEAN Framework, besides being a State Party to the ASEAN Declaration of Principles on Drug Abuse Control 1976, Malaysia is a member of the ASEAN Senior Officials on Drug Matters (ASOD) since it was established in 1984. It is also a member of the ASEAN–China Cooperative Operations in Response to Dangerous Drugs (ACCORD) 2000. Malaysia's commitment to eliminating drug trafficking is evident by it being also a State Party to the following three United Nations conventions: the Single Convention on Narcotic Drugs 1991; the Convention of Psychotropic Substances 1971; and the Convention Against Illicit Traffic in Narcotic Drugs and Psychotropic Substances 1988.

Between 2009 and 2011, 10,500 persons were arrested for drug trafficking in Malaysia, according to the MOHA (*The Star* 2012). Police statistics, as shown in Table 3.6, indicate that cases of drug trafficking are on the increase.

Despite the punitive anti-drug laws, the Deputy Home Affairs Minister, Datuk Abu Seman Yusop, indicated in April 2011 that, according to the latest police statistics, the

Table 3.6 *Drug-trafficking arrests in Malaysia, 2009–2011*

Year	**Number of arrests**
2009	2,955
2010	3,700
2011	3,845

Source: The Star 2012.

number of drugs-related crimes had increased by 25.58 per cent in a single year, from 2009 to 2010. In 2010, 157,756 persons were detained under the various anti-narcotics laws compared with 125,620 persons detained in 2009. A total of 42,133 persons were arrested from January to March 2011 (Bedi 2011). According to the Ministry of Foreign Affairs, 1,597 Malaysian citizens are held overseas for crimes committed abroad. In another newspaper report, a total of 889 Malaysian nationals are said to have been detained abroad for drug offences over the past ten years – the largest number of Malaysians detained abroad compared with those accused of other crimes committed overseas (mysinchew.com 2012). The government continues to promote ASEAN's 'Drug-Free by 2015' policy. Malaysia's anti-narcotics officials and police officers have the full support of senior government officials, but systemic problems with the legal system hinder the overall effectiveness of enforcement and interdiction efforts.

3.6.2 *Trafficking in persons*

There are an estimated 2 million documented and 2 million or more undocumented foreign workers in Malaysia. They migrate willingly to Malaysia from countries including Indonesia, Nepal, India, Thailand, China, the Philippines, Myanmar, Cambodia, Bangladesh, Pakistan and Vietnam in search of greater economic opportunities. Some of them subsequently encounter forced labour or debt bondage at the hands of their employers, employment agents or informal labour recruiters. While many of Malaysia's trafficking offenders are individual business persons, there are also large organized crime syndicates.

Malaysia has enacted a comprehensive Anti-Trafficking in Persons Act 2007 (Act 670), and acceded to the United Nations Protocol to Prevent, Suppress and Punish Trafficking in Persons, Especially Women and Children on 26 February 2009 (correspondence with a senior MOHA official). From 2008 to September 2011, 357 cases were brought to justice. The details of these cases are shown in Table 3.7.

Simultaneously, from 2008 to September 2011, a total of 2,151 cases, comprising men, women and children of various nationalities, were rescued. Out of these, 844 persons were identified as victims of trafficking and were placed under the care of shelter homes (see Table 3.8).

Realizing the close relation between trafficking in persons and migrant smuggling, Malaysia decided in 2010 to amend the Anti-Trafficking in Persons Act 2007, and the amendments came into force on 15 November 2011. The various amendments include incorporation of the migrant

Table 3.7 *Status of trafficking in persons cases brought to justice in Malaysia, 2008–2011*

Category of cases	2008	2009	2010	2011	Totals
Cases charged	8	141	191	17	357
Cases pending trial	3	81	150	17	251
Acquittal and discharged	2	23	22	2	49
Cases discharged not amounting to acquittal	1	9	–	–	10
Convictions	2	21	19	3	45

Source: information provided by a Ministry of Home Affairs official.

Table 3.8 *Identified victims of trafficking (men, women and children) in Malaysia, September 2011*

Category	Number
Men	259
Women	481
Children	104
Total	844

Source: information provided by a Ministry of Home Affairs official.

smuggling elements in the Trafficking Act, heavier penalties for both offences, and expansion of the roles of the Council for Anti-Trafficking in Persons (MAPO), which will monitor and regulate policies relating to both crimes as well as gazetting the Labour Department as an enforcement agency.

A five-year National Action Plan against Trafficking in Persons 2010–2015 was launched on 31 March 2010, a document that reflected the national efforts to combat trafficking in persons. The government hoped that the National Strategic Plan would give a clear perspective and direction in its mission to address the crimes of trafficking in persons, including people smuggling. The National Action Plan is based on these four core principles: policy, protection, prosecution and prevention. The thrust of the National Plan comprises five guiding principles pertaining to government ownership, human rights-based treatment of victims, civil society participation and inter-disciplinary coordination at all levels, including systemic evaluation and sustainability. The National Action Plan, however, does not provide the concrete guide to implementers, or guidance on the assessment of performance, following Van Meter and Van Horn's policy standards and objectives.

The MAPO was established in 2008. Following the Anti-Trafficking in Persons (Amendment) Act 2010, which also includes the smuggling of migrants, MAPO is now known as the Council for Anti-Trafficking in Persons and Anti-Smuggling of Migrants and is headed by the MOHA Secretary General. Its objective is to make Malaysia internationally accredited as being free of illegal activities in connection with human trafficking and the smuggling of migrants. Hence, its main function is to prevent and eradicate human trafficking and migrant smuggling crimes through the enforcement of the Anti-Trafficking in Persons (Amendment) Act 2010. However, records of MAPO's meetings are not made available to the public.

In 2008, Malaysia was placed in Tier 3 of the US Department of State People Trafficking Chart. Perceptions seemed to have improved in the 2010 and 2011 reports, which placed Malaysia in the watch list of Tier 2 of the Trafficking in Persons Report 2010 released by the US Department of State. The Trafficking in Persons Report ranks countries according to their level of compliance on the established minimum standards for the elimination of human trafficking. The US report highlighted the low rates of prosecution in Malaysia: the police and immigration officials investigated ninety-seven suspected trafficking cases in 2011 but initiated only sixteen prosecutions.

Various public awareness and educational campaigns were launched through seminars, workshops and widely disseminated brochures, and warnings are frequently published in the media, cautioning potential victims about overly lucrative job offers abroad. Starting in 2004, the Malaysian state-run television has broadcast documentaries on the victims of trafficking. Malaysia is also venturing into bilateral cooperation with Saudi Arabia, the United Kingdom, China, Vietnam, the Netherlands, Australia, United States and neighbouring countries to combat trafficking in persons. Malaysia and Thailand are working closely through multi-disciplinary team meetings that involve the Royal Malaysian Police, Malaysian Immigration and TENAGANITA (an NGO) and Thailand's police and Ministry of Social Development. This network has successfully worked on a few human trafficking cases.

3.6.3 Challenges in implementing the AMMTC/ SOMTC

The government has faced many problems attempting to tackle the issue of trafficking in persons, which involves trans-border crime with links to prostitution, drug trafficking and money laundering. First, most victims enter Malaysia as tourists and later get involved with human trafficking syndicates. Secondly, there is lack of public cooperation in providing information, and threats from the syndicates have discouraged victims from making reports. From 28 February to 30 May 2010, 1,447 persons were given interim protection orders under Section 44 (2) of Anti-Human Trafficking Act 2007. Among them, 338 were identified as victims of human trafficking and given protection orders under Section 51(3) of the same act (mysinchew.com 2010).

In addition, there seem to be ambiguities and confusion between trafficking in persons and migration. There is forced or involuntary migration, in which people are compelled to move out of their homes because of conflict, and voluntary migration, when people move out in search of better livelihoods. It is difficult clearly to differentiate between migration and trafficking in persons as the demarcation between the two is often not apparent and is a question of perception. Furthermore, most people who enter a country illegally are also engaged in illegal activities and the available statistics do not distinguish between smuggling and trafficking (Zarinah 2006: 56). According to Van Meter and Van Horn (1975: 472–3), the implementers must understand and accept the policy to ensure its implementation.

Zarinah (2006: 55) contends that the Malaysian government views the problem of trafficking in persons as smuggling and not trafficking because smuggling means that the transported persons have agreed to be transported. Thus, smuggled persons are considered as illegal immigrants rather than trafficked victims. Besides, the equivalent word in Malay does not distinguish between trafficking and smuggling. Consequently, trafficking issues are viewed as smuggling issues in Malaysia. The ambiguity of the issues and lack of clarity on the part of the implementers impede policy implementation, as argued by Van Meter and Van Horn. Furthermore, Malaysia has not ratified the United Nations Protocol to Prevent, Suppress and Punish Trafficking in Persons, Especially Women and Children although it has ratified the United Nations Convention Against Transnational Organized Crime, which, as Zarinah (2006: 56) observes, seems to indicate some resistance towards addressing the human trafficking problem.

Equally important are the available resources and incentives mentioned by Van Horn and Van Meter. The Labour Department was gazetted as the enforcement agency. However, there are no additional resources in terms of manpower and finances for monitoring purposes. As the added responsibility did not come together with any form of support in terms of resources, the monitoring task was sidelined. The inter-organizational communication and enforcement activities mentioned by Van Meter and Van Horn appear to be lacking in the case of combating human trafficking. The mere presence of law in the case of human trafficking cannot guarantee effective implementation. There must also be concrete guidance and specific standards in assessing the performance of the regulatory agencies following Van Meter and Van Horn's suggestion that there must be policy standards and objectives.

3.7 Conclusion

The preceding analysis of the role of Malaysia's public bureaucracy in policy formulation and implementation has shown: (1) a strong central structure and capacity for macro-economic and strategic policy-making, over and above the policy-making in each ministry, to facilitate consultation among the ministries; (2) mechanisms to analyse and debate policies within each ministry; and (3) institutional links to the stakeholders and the public at large outside the government to provide transparency and accountability, as well as to receive feedback on the policy or inputs for preparing policy proposals from interest groups and citizens. These structures help organize the workload of the Cabinet and facilitate the monitoring of policies that are implemented. Another exceptional feature of the role of Malaysia's public service in policy formulation is the detailed consideration of options that preceded implementation, the involvement of public and private sectors in the specific design of policies, and the bundling of related policy measures to overcome legislative and coordination problems. However, in policy implementation, there seem to be some obstacles in the delivery system of the public service, in part due to the skewed representation of one ethnic group that could undermine the continued effectiveness and efficiency of the public sector.

Implementation problems also arise from the interaction between policy and micro-level institutions. Central actors can only indirectly influence micro-level factors and autonomy at the local level is necessary to allow adaptation of policy to suit contextual factors, as is evident in the case study on human trafficking, where the policy is ambiguous, and there is confusion even at the very beginning between migration and trafficking in persons.

In addition, the disposition of the implementers to champion the policy can encourage implementation and make a significant difference in ensuring its successful implementation. The case study on the implementation of the ACD identifies the CDCR as the champion agent, the MOH as the champion institution and the Enforcement Division in the MOH and the NPCB as the 'implementation energizers'.

Furthermore, the NPCB also works together with the industry representatives and formulates industry guidelines to simplify the bureaucratic procedures. CoSEC is another important initiative that disseminates information on dangerous ingredients in cosmetics products to other member countries. There is also due diligence in monitoring activities.

In terms of combating transnational crime, Malaysia has introduced adequate and stringent laws, administrative procedures and regulations for the effective control over the trafficking of drugs and trafficking in persons. However, despite the existence of laws and regulatory frameworks, because of the sophisticated nature and mode of the illegal activities, combating transnational crime has not been easy for the regulatory agencies, and cannot be undertaken unilaterally. It needs continuous and collaborative efforts, both bilateral and multilateral among the ASEAN countries. From Malaysia's experience, in addressing the ever-growing transnational crime, bilateral agency-to-agency contact remains the most effective way of sharing information. The challenge is for all ASEAN Member states to allow the information to be shared on a wider scale for practical use.

References

Ali, M. 2013. 'Efficiency, Wages, Public Service Motivation and Effort in Malaysia: An Empirical Case Study of *Universiti Sains Malaysia*', PhD thesis, Murdoch University.

Bedi, Rashvinjeet S. 2011. 'Drugs Still the No. 1 Enemy', *The Star*, 15 May.

Bradbury, M. and Kellogh, J. E. 2011. 'Representative Bureaucracy: Assessing the Evidence on Active Representation', *American Review of Public Administration*, 41(2): 157–67.

Crouch, H. A. 1996. *Government and Society in Malaysia.* Ithaca, NY: Cornell University Press.

Department of Statistics, Malaysia 2011. (Putrajaya) *Population and Housing Census, Malaysia 2010*, available at: https://www.statistics.gov.my/portal/index.php?option=com_content&id=350 (accessed 30 December 2014).

2012. (Putrajaya) *Population Projections, Malaysia 2010–2040.* (Putrajaya) available at: https://www.statistics.gov.my/portal/download_Population/files/population_projections/Population_Projection_2010–2040.pdf (accessed 30 December 2014).

Economic Planning Unit 2013. (Putrajaya)'Household Income and Poverty, Table 6: Incidence of Poverty by Ethnicity, Strata and State, Malaysia, 1970–2012', available at: www.epu.gov.my/documents/10124/669145a4-1b34-4f04-9043-31b24d1c3442 (accessed 30 December 2014).

The Economist 2013. *Pocket World in Figures, 2014 Edition*. London: Profile Books.

Fernando, J. M. 2013. 'The Urban Drift in Kuala Lumpur in the 2008 General Election: A Return to the Old Ways?', *Malaysian Journal of Democracy and Election Studies*, 1(1): 24–41.

Gomez, E. T. and Jomo, K. S. 1999. *Malaysia's Political Economy: Politics, Patronage and Profits*. Cambridge: Cambridge University Press.

Gomez, E. T. and Saravanamuttu, J. (eds) 2013. *The New Economic Policy in Malaysia: Affirmative Action, Ethnic Inequalities and Social Justice*. Singapore: NUS Press and ISEAS Publishing.

Gomez, E. T., Saravanamuttu, J. and Maznah, M. 2013. 'Malaysia's New Economic Policy: Resolving Horizon Inequalities, Creating Inequities?' In E. T. Gomez and J. Saravanamuttu (eds)

2013. *The New Economic Policy in Malaysia: Affirmative Action, Ethnic Inequalities and Social Justice*. Singapore: NUS Press and ISEAS Publishing, pp. 1–28.

Hardoon, D. and Heinrich, F. 2013. *Global Corruption Barometer 2013*. Berlin: Transparency International.

International Monetary Fund (IMF), 2011. *World Economic Outlook (WEO) Tensions from the Two-speed Recovery: Unemployment, Commodities, and Capital Flows*. Washington, DC: IMF.

Jomo, K. S. and Wee, C. H. 2002. *The Political Economy of Malaysian Federalism: Economic Development, Public Policy and Conflict Containment*. Helsinki: United Nations University, World Institute for Development Economic Research.

Khoo, B. T. 2005. *Ethnic Structure, Inequality and Governance in the Public Sector: Malaysian Experiences*. Geneva: United Nations Research Institute for Social Development.

Lee, H. G. 2005. 'Affirmative Action in Malaysia'. *Southeast Asian Affairs 2005*, Institute of Southeast Asian Studies, Singapore, pp. 211–28.

Lee, K. H. and Tan, C. B. (eds) 2000. *The Chinese in Malaysia*. Kuala Lumpur: Oxford University Press.

Lijphart, A. 1977. *Democracy in Plural Societies: A Comparative Exploration*. New Haven, CT: Yale University Press.

Lim, H. H. 2013. 'The Public Service and Ethnic Restructuring under the New Economic Policy: The New Challenge of Correcting Selectivity and Excess'. In E. T. Gomez and J. Saravanamuttu (eds) 2013. *The New Economic Policy in Malaysia: Affirmative Action, Ethnic Inequalities and Social Justice*. Singapore: NUS Press and ISEAS Publishing, pp. 175–203.

Loh, K. W. 2010. 'Restructuring Federal–State Relations in Malaysia: From Centralised to Co-operative Federalism?', *The Round Table: The Commonwealth Journal of International Affairs*, 99(407): 131–40.

Malaysia 2010a. *Tenth Malaysia Plan, 2010–2015*. Kuala Lumpur: National Printing Department.

2010b. *New Economic Model for Malaysia, Part 1*. Putrajaya: National Economic Advisory Council.

Marican, Y. M. 1979. 'Public Personnel Administration in Malaysia'. Research Notes and Discussions Paper No. 12, Institute of Southeast Asian Studies, Singapore.

Means, G. P. 1972. 'Special Rights as a Strategy for Development', *Comparative Politics*, 5(1): 29–61.

1975. 'Malaysia'. In R. N. Kearney (ed.) *Politics and Modernization in South and Southeast Asia*. Cambridge, MA: Schenkman, pp. 153–213.

1998. 'Soft Authoritarianism in Malaysia and Singapore'. In L. Diamond and M. F. Plattner (eds), *Democracy in East Asia*. Baltimore, MD: Johns Hopkins University Press, pp. 96–112.

Meerman, J. 2008. 'The Malaysian Success Story, the Public Sector and Inter-Ethnic Inequality'. In J. M. Nelson, J. Meerman and A. R. Embong (eds), *Globalization and National Autonomy: The Experience of Malaysia*. Singapore: Institute of Southeast Asian Studies, pp. 76–115.

Mohd Nasir, M. A. 2010. 'A New Breed of Civil Servants', *The Star*, 14 August 2010.

mysinchew.com 2010. 'Malaysia Rises to Tier 2 of Trafficking in Persons Report', mysinchew.com, 14 June, available at: www.mysinchew.com/node/40378 (accessed 30 December 2014).

2012. '889 Malaysians Detained Abroad in Past 10 Years for Drugs', mysinchew.com, 30 March, available at: www.mysinchew/node/71944 (accessed 30 December 2014).

National Pharmaceutical Control Bureau (NPCB) 2014a. (Petaling Jaya) 'About the National Pharmaceutical Control Bureau', available at: http://portal.bpfk.gov.my/index.cfm?&menuid=4 (accessed 30 December 2014).

2014b. (Petaling Jaya) 'The Malaysian GLP Monitoring Authority', available at: http://portal.bpfk.gov.my/index.cfm?&menuid=65 (accessed 30 December 2014).

2014c. (Petaling Jaya) 'Cancellation of Notification of Cosmetic Products', available at: http://portal.bpfk.gov.my/index.cfm?&menuid=118&parentid=116 (accessed 30 December 2014).

Ragayah, M. Z. 1988. 'A General Equilibrium Approach to Fiscal Incidence and Redistribution Policies in West Malaysia', PhD thesis, Vanderbilt University.

2014. 'Malaysian Development Experience: Lessons for Developing Countries', *Institutions and Economies*, 6(1): 17–56.

Ramakrishna, K. 2005. 'The Southeast Asian Approach to Counter-Terrorism: Learning from Indonesia and Malaysia', *Journal of Conflict Studies*, 25(1): 27–47.

Sarji, A. 1996. *The Chief Secretary to the Government*. Kuala Lumpur: MPH Publishing.

Sanusi, A., Mansor, N. and Kuddus, A. 2003. *The Malaysian Bureaucracy: Four Decades of Development*. Petaling Jaya: Pearson Prentice Hall.

Schwab, K. (ed.) 2014. *The Global Competitiveness Report, 2014–2015*. Geneva: World Economic Forum.

Shafii, Z., Abidin, N. Z. and Ahmad, A. R. 2009. 'Ethnic Heterogeneity in the Malaysian Economy: A Special Reference to the Ethnic Group Participation in Financial Planning Activities', *Utuslararasi Sosyal Ara Tirmalar Dergisi (Journal of International Social Research)*, 2(8): 394–401.

Shamsul, A. B. 1996. 'The Construction and Transformation of a Social Identity: Malayness and Bumiputraness Re-examined', *Journal of Asian and African Studies*, 52: 15–33.

Snodgrass, D. R. 2002. 'Economic Growth and Income Inequality: The Malaysian Experience'. In M. G. Asher, D. Newman and T. P. Snyder (eds), *Public Policy in Asia: Implications for*

Business and Government. Westport, CT: Quorum Books, pp. 11–31.

The Star 2012. 'Hishammuddin: 10,500 Drug Traffickers Detained since 2009', 19 March.

2013. 'Big Drop in Poverty Rate', 28 March.

Transparency International 2014. (Berlin) 'Corruption Perceptions Index, 1996–2014', available at: www.transparency.org (accessed 30 December 2014).

Van Meter, D. S. and Van Horn, C. E. 1975. 'The Policy Implementation Process: A Conceptual Framework', *Administration and Society*, 6(4): 445–88.

Watts, R. L. 1999. *Comparing Federal Systems*, 2nd edn. Ontario: McGill-Queens University Press.

World Bank 2014a. (Washington, DC) 'Data: GDP per capita (current US$)', available at: data.worldbank.org/indicator/NY.GDP.PCAP.CD (accessed 30 December 2014).

2014b. (Washington, DC) 'Worldwide Governance Indicators, 2013', available at: www.info.worldbank.org/governance/wgi/index.aspx#reports (accessed 30 December 2014).

Yatim, R. 2006. *Cabinet Government in Malaysia*. Kuala Lumpur: DTP Enterprise.

Zarina, O. 2006. 'Human (In)security, Human Trafficking and Security in Malaysia'. In K. Beeks and D. Amir (eds), *Trafficking and the Global Sex Industry*. Lanham, MD: Rowman & Littlefield Publishers, pp. 47–60.

Chapter 4

Dysfunctional bureaucracy, corruption and weak rule of law: a case study of policy implementation in the Philippines

Vicente Chua Reyes, Jr

4.1 Introduction

In 2013, the population of the Association of Southeast Asian Nations (ASEAN) was almost twice that of the United States, one-fifth more than that of the European Union (EU) and nearly five times that of Japan (Haub and Kaneda 2013). Alongside their giant neighbours India and China, the increasing size and influence of ASEAN makes it an attractive destination for investment (Hew and Soesastro 2003). Among the ten very diverse countries of the ASEAN, six nations have emerged with more mature economies: these are the ASEAN-6 comprising Indonesia, Malaysia, Singapore, Thailand, the Philippines and Brunei Darussalam. These six economies within the ASEAN have 'grown rapidly' and 'become industrially competitive' (Severino 2007: 411). The recent history of the region reveals that in terms of 'economic and institutional development' as well as 'global and capital market integration' the ASEAN-6 remain far ahead of Vietnam, Cambodia, Laos and Myanmar (Gates and Than 2001: 3).

However, one country within the famed ASEAN-6 has experienced an ambivalent performance as regards policy implementation – the Philippines. Heralded as a very promising nation in the 1960s and 1970s, the country has been often referred to as the 'sick man of Asia'. Not only has it suffered from chronic deficits in the effective implementation of economic policies, it has also lagged behind most of its neighbours in implementing vital redistributive social policies. The Philippines 'has the highest incidence of poverty measured by the proportion of population living below US$1 per day and the highest income inequality' among the ASEAN-6 (Balboa, Medalla and Yap 2007: 2).

This chapter provides a case study of policy implementation in the Philippines. It describes how a dysfunctional public bureaucracy aggravated by weak rule of law within a context of systemic corruption hinders the implementation of policies. In undertaking an evaluation of policy implementation, this chapter evaluates two specific ASEAN-wide policies from a Philippine perspective: the ASEAN Cosmetic Directive (ACD) and the ASEAN Ministerial Meeting on Transnational Crime/Senior Officials Meeting on Transnational Crime (AMMTC/SOMTC). Recognizing the unique context of the Philippines, this chapter analyses the issues and challenges related to the implementation of these two policies.

4.2 Policy context

In order better to appreciate the issues and challenges that face the Philippines – particularly its civil service, an analysis of the policy context is needed. An analysis of the situation of the Philippine public bureaucracy from a historical and institutional perspective reveals that its trajectory has been typified by discontinuities and contradictions (Imperial 2007). The public bureaucracy is also hindered by an enormous system, the administration of which is 'a daunting task' (Congressional Commission on Education 1991: 60). Using the lens of governance, the Philippine civil service system has been described as suffering from 'systemic corruption' (Reyes 2009b: 95). Systemic corruption becomes worse when the principle of the 'rule of law' and the weaknesses that characterize it predictably make an indelible negative impact on politics and administration (Co et al. 2010: 216).

4.2.1 History

The roots of the crises that face the Philippine public bureaucracy, which is characterized by the interplay of highly centralized power structures, the challenge towards decentralizing power to the local levels and the perennially severe resource restrictions, can be traced to the beginning of the US occupation in the Philippines. Upon seizing control over the majority of the islands in the Philippines, US occupation forces decided to retain the system of government that had existed during the more than 300 years of Spanish colonial occupation of the country. The Spanish governmental system was highly centralized; local political power only rested at the municipal level, where the church, the government offices and the centres of local commerce were located. The *barrios* – composed of one or more *barangays* – which were the pre-Hispanic governmental units, remained isolated from the local power centres. The Americans built on the prevailing Spanish-inherited government system.

It is evident that the occupation of the Philippines was a tumultuous period in terms of political competition and strife within the US government. Partisan politics – evidenced by the historic disputes between the conservative Republicans and liberal Democrats – undoubtedly spilled over to the Philippines creating ripples that not only affected the tenor of political administration in the occupied islands during that era but also generated political implications that are still felt today. Control of the Philippines was a tenuous struggle within American political circles and the confusion and inconsistencies in policies that ensued left behind profound damages on the key Philippine political institutions (Powell and Wyndham 1931: 15). As early as 1930, crises in their incipient forms were already being detected in the Philippine public bureaucracy. Problems in priorities as well as political competition in the American homeland resulted in the establishment of a flawed public bureaucracy in the Philippines – an organization that, in the words of one of the American statesmen, did not have an existing colonial administrative service. The early tremulous history of the Philippine public bureaucracy under the Americans has undeniable repercussions on the contemporary administrative system.

An important legacy of more than three centuries of Spanish colonial rule in the Philippines was the introduction of corruption that resulted from the low salaries of civil servants, the sale of public offices for profit and the appointment of the governor-general and his officials by the King of Spain on the basis of patronage and not merit. By contrast, the legacy of the forty-eight years of American colonial rule was relatively more positive for two reasons: meritocracy was introduced in September 1900 with the enactment of the act

Table 4.1 *Policy context of the Philippines*

Key features	The Philippines
Land area	300,000 sq. km
Population	97,500,000 (2013)
Population growth rate	1.931 per cent (2010)
Fertility rate	3.23 children born/woman (2010)
Net migration rate	1.31 migrants/1,000 population (2010)
Education as percentage of GDP	2.5 per cent of GDP (2005)
GDP per capita	$2,790 (2013)
Geography	Archipelago of 7,107 islands
Literacy rate	92.6 per cent
Type of government	Presidential democracy

Sources: Central Intelligence Agency 2014 and Schwab 2014.

for the establishment and maintenance of an efficient and honest civil service; and corruption declined because the bureaucrats were better paid and corrupt officials were punished (Quah 2011: 115–17). Table 4.1 provides an overview of the policy context of the Philippines.

4.2.2 *Roots of Philippine public bureaucracy*

The historical trajectory of the Philippine public bureaucracy since the American colonial period has been typified by highly fragmented political divisions. A 1931 debate among American officials presiding over the insular government of the Philippines provides interesting insights:

> The policy is partisan and personal, changing with parties and men, and the steady evolution of a form of

> government suitable to Philippine conditions and needs is thus rendered impossible. If the United States had a Colonial Service, these changes would not have so serious an effect. Permanent American officials would inevitably modify home instructions and preserve at any rate the essentials of uniformity. But so long as the Governors of the Philippines come direct from the United States and are subject to changing American political situations, and so long as the Islands are without [a] Colonial Administrative Service, no steady evolution of government is possible. (Powell and Wyndham 1931: 5)

The political struggles that dominated colonial America remained and became a permanent fixture of Philippine public administration. More contemporary Philippine scholars have been much more pointed in their analysis of the political nature of the Philippine public bureaucracy. They go a step further by arguing that it is not the absence of a steady evolution of government that prevails. What actually happens, they argue, is the proliferation of debilitating patronage networks that has besieged the creation and continued existence of Philippine public bureaucracy.

4.2.3 *Legal system*

The backbone of the Philippine legal system is the 1987 Philippine Constitution, described by Desierto (2010: 428) as 'a strong entrenchment of a rights-culture that appears more universalist in character' compared with the four previous versions of the Philippine charter. In relation to the Philippines' recognition of external legal systems such as those espoused by the ASEAN, Article 2, Section 1 of the 1987 Constitution, or the incorporation clause, explicitly states that 'generally accepted principles of international law form part of the law of the land' (Office of the President of the Philippines 1987).

The colonial history of the Philippines having been under the control of Spain and the United States has created a unique legal system. It is a system 'in which three of the world's legal traditions (Roman law, Anglican or common law, and Mohammedan law)' converge and find commonality and 'where two traditions (civil and common) have been blended' into a distinct form unique to the Philippines (Gamboa 1969: 59). Another way of describing it is the union of two 'streams of law – the civil, the legacy of Rome to Spain, and the common, the inheritance of the United States from Great Britain, amplified by American written law' (Bautista 2006: 3) converging into what is the Philippine legal system. Unfortunately, the colonial experience of the Philippines under both Spain and the United States was less than ideal and failed to provide a solid foundation for a legal system that respected the rule of law. Scholars state that corruption became prevalent in the patrimonial system propagated by the Spanish colonizers. This inquiry contends that the inability of America to establish a robust 'Administrative Service' (Powell and Wyndham 1931: 5) in colonial Philippines contributed to the weakened state of the contemporary civil service.

4.2.4 *Geography*

A succinct analysis of one of the major implementation pitfalls plaguing the Philippines is that it operates under conditions of 'extreme scarcity' (Richter 1987: 71). The size, scope and vast differences that characterize the geographic and cultural landscape render the public bureaucracy in a situation where it experiences difficulties in delivering much needed services to its populace.

Comprising 7,107 islands, the Philippines presents itself as a daunting implementation arena. As early as 1987, Richter had already seen the magnitude of implementation challenges that face the extensive and extremely diverse Philippine archipelago. Policy implementation in the vast archipelago is 'characterized by unevenness and discontinuities' exacerbated by the rugged geography. Furthermore, 'while most of the 55 million people live on about ten of these islands, transport between islands and throughout their rugged mountainous interiors is time-consuming, expensive and frequently dangerous' (Richter 1987: 57). Almost thirty years after the Richter article was published, the situation in the Philippines has not improved. Implementation deficits continue to plague various aspects of governance in the country. National government agencies and local government units experience sporadic bursts of implementation successes. However, a sustained ethos of efficient and effective implementation in governance continues to be an elusive objective of achieving positive policy implementation outputs.

4.2.5 *Culture*

Richter has also underscored the limitations of the role of leaders in policy implementation in the Philippines. She unequivocally identifies 'culture' as an important constraint because 'supervisors value personal popularity over a reputation for effective administration' and 'monitor performance only perfunctorily' (Richter 1987: 73). This skewed and unprofessional behaviour (viewed from a Western perspective) of some local leaders – that has been attributed to cultural influences – nevertheless becomes a source of conflict and obstacle in policy implementation.

The literature on Philippine public administration has never failed to identify the impact of the cultural facets of this diverse archipelago on public administration. Varela (1996: 93) clearly stated that: 'the practice of public administration in the country is influenced by the combined effects of Western administrative thought and technology and the local political and administrative culture'. She also mentioned that 'any attempt to improve bureaucratic performance, either through reorganization or value implementation, is met with resistance' (Varela 1996: 95). This resistance to change and particularly the introduction of values as indicated by Varela can be directly traced to the prevalence of local cultural traits like *pakikisama* (fellowship) and *ningas cogon* (starting things but never ending them) that prevail in Philippine bureaucratic environments that are reminiscent of the informal organizations existing within a formal setup that are the basis of the human relations movement in public administration. The influence of 'culture' on leadership in the pursuance of outputs of policy implementation can be seen even more clearly with the concept of 'bureaucratic ambiguity', which is defined by Varela thus:

> The culture of bureaucratic ambiguity is rooted in the multiplicity of conflicting laws, executive orders, judicial

> decisions, civil service and labour relations regulations, auditors' opinions and agency rules which render the organizational environment to be a legal jungle where policies and rules to guide action and behaviour of personnel are unclear and are constantly changing. When this mass of laws, rules and regulations is operationalized in the bureaucracy, confusion in interpretation makes them ambiguous. (Varela 1996: 305)

Varela's 1996 description of the mass of laws, rules and regulations – or red tape – is still very much a valid and relevant observation today. Globally, the Philippines is ranked ninety-fifth among 189 economies on the ease of doing business in 2015 (World Bank 2014: 4). A report generated by several international chambers of commerce in the Philippines has pointed out that 'red tape remains pervasive in the Philippines' (de Vera 2014: 1). Similarly, a survey of firms conducted by the Philippine Institute for Development Studies (PIDS) indicated that 'the most problematic issues indicated are bureaucracy and too much red tape' (Aldaba 2013: 30).

4.3 Profile of the civil service

4.3.1 Legal mandate

The genesis of the Philippine civil service can be traced to the historical period of colonial America. The formal establishment of the civil service system came into effect with the enactment of Public Law No. 5, known as the 'Act for the Establishment and Maintenance of Our Efficient and Honest Civil Service in the Philippine Island' in 1900 by the Second Philippine Commission. One of the key provisions of the establishment of the service was the creation of a Civil Service Board (CSB) composed of a Chairman, a Secretary and a Chief Examiner. The CSB was entrusted with the administration of civil service examinations and was also responsible for setting standards for appointment in the government service. In 1905, the board was reorganized into a Bureau (Civil Service Commission 2010b).

Since 1905, the Philippine public bureaucracy was transformed into one of four constitutional bodies in the Philippine republic. Republic Act No. 2260 changed the Bureau into a Department, which became the Civil Service Commission (CSC) with the ratification of the 1973 Philippine Constitution. The CSC, which serves as the central personnel agency of the government, was further reorganized under Presidential Decree (PD) No. 181 dated 24 September 1972, and again under Executive Order No. 181 dated 21 November 1986. With the new Administrative Code of 1987, Executive Order (EO) 292, the CSC was constitutionally mandated to promote the morale, efficiency, integrity, responsiveness, progressiveness and courtesy in the civil service (Civil Service Commission 2010b).

4.3.2 Evolution and growth of the civil service

The Philippine civil service is the biggest employer of the nation. Civil servants make up approximately 0.2 per cent of the country's population. As of the second quarter of 2010,

Table 4.2 *Growth of the Philippine Civil Service, 1970–2010*

Year	Number of civil servants
1970	430,000
1980	840,000
1990	1,610,000
2000	1,435,468
2010	1,312,508

Source: Civil Service Commission 2010a.

the civil service has 1,312,508 employees.[1] About 834,327 (63.6 per cent) of civil servants belong to the National Government Agencies (NGAs) including State Universities and Colleges (SUCs). Local Government Units (LGUs) have 383,422 (29.2 per cent) of all civil servants while Government Owned and Controlled Corporations (GOCCs) have a total of 94,759 personnel (7.2 per cent) (Civil Service Commission 2010a). Table 4.2 shows the growth in personnel of the Philippine Civil Service from 1970 to 2010.

The civil service has been a target for criticism and this became more pronounced after the institution of the CSC in 1973. Among the most pointed criticism concerning the civil service is its bloated size and inefficient implementation performance. A careful perusal of the statistics of the civil service through the years provides evidence and support for criticisms of it being a bloated and wasteful institution.

[1] This is the latest inventory of official personnel available on the CSC website.

The rate of growth of the Philippine public bureaucracy has been short of phenomenal. Carefully inspecting the inventory of government personnel reveals that 'over the past 35 years, the number of government employees grew at a faster rate than did the population' (Civil Service Commission 2010a). According to the CSC's website:

> Expressed in terms of ratio to the total population, the growth in the size of the Philippine government personnel lends some firm basis for the popular perception of a bloated bureaucracy. In 1970, the ratio of government personnel to the total population is 1:90. By 1990, the ratio stood at 1:52. The most telling indicator of the period of rapid expansion of the bureaucracy is reflected in the growth rate of government's cash disbursements for personal services. Yearly incremental rates from 1980 to 1991 were in double figures, averaging 21 per cent during the 11-year period, and grew as high as 35.8 per cent in 1984–1985. (Civil Service Commission 2010a)

The dramatic increase in the size of the Philippine public bureaucracy can be attributed to two main reasons: political reorganization of the CSC driven by political motives and the phenomenon of hiring casual appointments. This chapter argues that the successive rounds of reorganization that the CSC experienced contributed to a bloated bureaucracy. Although these efforts at reorganization were identified as attempts at generating greater efficiency, most were primarily driven by political reasons, particularly during the Marcos regime. Instead of rationalizing the organizational structure, these changes contributed in preserving those who were already in the service and then bloating this further with the creation of new and politically motivated appointments. A concrete example of this was the creation of the Ministry of Human Settlements, headed by Imelda Marcos, an organization that effectively created another bureaucratic layer above existing local government units.

After the 1986 Revolutionary Constitution was accepted, courtesy of the newly installed Corazon Aquino presidency immediately after the 1986 EDSA revolution that toppled ex-President Marcos, an opportunity to purge the CSC became available. However, President Aquino refused to pare down the organization, electing instead to maintain it by adding another layer of officials by appointing allies who were known as Officers-in-Charge (OICs). In the early 1990s, the Republic Act 7041 or the Attrition Law managed to stem the tide of an expanding public bureaucracy. From 2005 onwards, though, the CSC has reported a continuing increase in the size of its public bureaucracy.

The second reason is due to the hiring of casually employed staff in the CSC. It must be pointed out that the entire Philippine bureaucracy is composed not only of NGAs but of local civil servants found in LGUs as well. In 2008, of a total of 381,502 local civil servants from LGUs, 29 per cent, or 108,892, were non-career officials and almost all were casual appointees (Brillantes and Sonco 2011: 362). In most cases these 'casuals' fail to satisfy employment requirements for the service, and are consequently mostly political appointees. Without a doubt, the civil service and its penchant for being a bloated bureaucracy is an issue that does not easily go away.

4.3.3 Defective public administration and weak rule of law

A highly politicized history, a geography that presents daunting challenges to a weak public bureaucracy and an organization permeated by ambiguity provide the critical backdrop to the prevalence of systemic corruption within the Philippine civil service. *The Global Competitiveness Report, 2014–2015* reinforces this argument when it states that the top four 'most problematic factors for doing business' in the Philippines were: corruption (17.6 per cent); inadequate supply of infrastructure (15.9 per cent); tax regulations (13.3 per cent) and inefficient government bureaucracy (12.6 per cent) (Schwab 2014: 308). This chapter argues that these four problematic factors could be subsumed into corruption and the problems of a dysfunctional public bureaucracy. The same report also provided information on the weak rule of law: in terms of 'efficiency of legal framework in settling disputes' the Philippines garnered a score of 3.5 (i.e., 1 = extremely inefficient and 7 = highly efficient), which is below the international average of 3.7 and a testimony to the difficulty of arriving at fair legal decisions (Schwab 2014: 415).

Systemic corruption becomes aggravated when the supposed safeguards against it, namely the rule of law, are ineffective. However, in order to ensure that the rule of law is safeguarded, steps to curb corruption must be upheld at all times. Co et al. (2010: 215) have argued convincingly about how the weakness of the rule of law is grounded in the ineffective functioning of public administrative institutions. They have identified three vulnerabilities of Philippine public administration that directly contribute to a weak rule of law. The first is the 'insufficiency of budget allocation for the pillars of justice to enable' agencies under the mantle of the Philippine public administration to 'perform effectively and adequately' (215). Secondly, they also point out that 'the constraints on resources including the lack of public attorneys that should respond to the legal needs of the poor, and the slow disposition of court cases' as another important deterrent to the establishment of a robust rule of law (215). The third and final reason points to the existence of systemic corruption that exposes 'legal practitioners, justices, and law enforcers' to vulnerable situations that diminish the effectiveness of a rule of law (216). The Philippine public bureaucracy – buffeted by systemic corruption on the one hand and an ineffective rule of law on the other – is thus enmeshed in a vicious cycle.

The politicization of the public bureaucracy is supported by findings from a study undertaken by the former Secretary of the CSC, Patricia Santo Tomas. She cites the pervasiveness of political patronage at the CSC as a stumbling block to ongoing professionalization efforts:

> The bad news as shown by the numbers is that political patronage remains a stumbling block to professionalization efforts. And this is most evident at the local government level, the most politicized sector of the Philippine bureaucracy . . . We can surmise that heads of LGUs opt to hire people on a casual or contractual basis because the appointees (presumably political protégés) do not meet the qualification standards prescribed for the regular positions. (Santo Tomas 2003: 422–3)

In the history and continuing evolution of the civil service, it may be argued that the most remarkable moments could very well be the adoption of the merit system in the 1935 Philippine constitution as the basis for its corps of professionals and the expansion of its jurisdiction to also include the three branches of government: national, local and government corporations (Santo Tomas 2003: 423). This chapter argues that the adoption of the merit system in 1935 was too late and, more importantly, inadequate in addressing the historical defects of the Philippine civil service. The lack of a colonial administrative service, identified as early as the 1900s, and the continued domination of American governors, who came and went and were greatly affected by the vicissitudes of political contests in the United States, eliminated the chance of creating a deep-rooted, institutionalized and professional bureaucracy (independent of politics) in the Philippines. After the Philippines gained independence from America in July 1946, history continues to be a witness of how a defective public administration and weak rule of law continue to plague the public bureaucracy.

4.4 Policy formulation

Policy formulation occurs within the three branches of government – the executive, legislature and judiciary – in the Philippine context. Before laws are ratified by the bi-cameral Congress (Lower and Upper Houses), a period of consultation occurs that involves the other branches of government, namely the executive as the implementer of enacted laws and the Judiciary carrying out its mandate of ensuring the legality of policies. Consultations with sectoral representatives from non-governmental organizations (NGOs) and other relevant entities also form part of the policy formulation process. The Executive branch, headed by the Philippine President and members of the Cabinet (appointed by the President), possess 'superior power in the budget process' (Civil Service Commission 2010b). In policy formulation, the executive branch provides the impetus as represented, for example, by the Philippine Development Plans and the General Appropriations Act. The other branches of government perform the important function of providing checks and balances to the formulation of policies.

However, a careful analysis of the Philippine public bureaucracy, which is supposed to be composed predominantly of a corps of professionals and career executives, reveals that more often than not they fall prey to the vicissitudes of patronage, spoils or, simply put, politicking. It may be argued that policy formulation in the Philippine context and within the boundaries of the Philippine public bureaucracy is highly politicized. De Dios and Esfahani contend that this phenomenon proliferates 'in the Philippines [because] the bureaucracy is underpaid and deficient in training and qualifications, making it vulnerable both to patronage politics and corruption. It is common practice in the country for winning candidates to treat government appointments as spoils to be distributed' (de Dios 2000: 15).

The observation of how the Philippine public bureaucracy is driven by patron–client networks originated from Carl Landé. He stated that a careful examination of Philippine public administration reveals 'legally prescribed lines of authority within the departments or agencies overlaid by complex networks of dyadic alliances and patron-client relationships' (Landé 1965: 147), which are not only confined within the public bureaucracy but end up in the jurisdictions of prominent politicians. He goes on to suggest that these patron–client relationships have seriously undermined the efficacy of Philippine public administration.

Since the 1960s until today, the public bureaucracy has been condensed into Landé's dominant 'patron–client' paradigm. Lemarchand and Legg built on this patron–client paradigm and extended the analysis to 'paired relationships' in the vein of Landé's 'dyadic analysis' and highlighting the concept of more extended alliances in 'a clientage network'. This network 'involves an aggregate of role sets, serially linked in such a way that a patron also stands in the position of a client toward his superior' (Lemarchand and Legg 1972: 153). Anderson alluded to this when he described the 'cacique democracies' in the Philippines underlining the heavy colonial influence and resulting in a condition where the 'civilian machinery of state remained weak and divided' (Anderson 1988: 11). But the stigma of Philippine public bureaucracy could not solely be attributed to a colonial past. Hutchcroft argued that the worsening condition of Philippine politics has continued to be 'personalistic', coming mostly from an elite class of favoured oligarchs and cronies (Hutchcroft 1991: 415).

Cariño argues that in the field of policy transformation, implementation and governance, two other actors aside from the traditional state have increased in prominence: the market and civil society. Furthermore, she asserts that civil society 'attempt[s] to represent the interests of the inarticulate and the excluded' and also 'get[s] involved in governance to the extent that they contest the power of the state or show alternate ways of service and policy formulation' (Cariño 2003: 69). Cariño depicts a picture of contemporary society that is no longer dominated by the state. On the contrary, it is a scenario where the state's monopoly on governance is being contested by market and civil society. She adds that the participation of market and civil society 'in governance adds a new role to the state – that of building partnerships and linkages to the two sectors'. Moreover, their engagement with the state 'shifts the social picture from elite control to active citizenship' (70). The state is in a situation where policy transformation is no longer seen as its exclusive purview. With the emergence of other actors, it forges partnerships, linkages and alliances that are without a doubt an arena for constant competition and compromise. Cariño underscores an increased role of civil society in the functions of governance and explicitly mentions a new role that states assume: 'building partnerships and linkages' (70).

The participation of civil society in public administration and governance has a legal basis. Bautista (2000: 137) has explicitly identified the provisions within the 1986 Philippine Constitution that ensure this: 'Article II, Sec. 23 of the Philippine Constitution specifies that: the State shall encourage non-governmental, community-based, or sectoral organizations that promote the welfare of the nation'. Bautista clarified that the 1986 Constitution 'identifies people's organizations as entities which could participate in decision-making'. Furthermore, Section 15 of Article XIII defines people's organizations as '*bona fide* associations of citizens with demonstrated capacity to promote the public interest and with identifiable leadership, membership and structure' (Bautista 2000: 137).

4.5 The civil service's role in policy implementation

The civil service serves as the implementing arm of the executive branch of the government. Composed of career civil servants operating through a system of merit, government bureaucrats form the vital frontline of service delivery. Once a particular national policy has been enacted into law together with its Implementing Rules and Regulations (IRR) by Congress or if a Presidential Decree or an Official Declaration from the executive branch has been officially promulgated, these will be sent through the nationwide network of the Philippine public bureaucracy whose role would be to implement these. The current realities in Philippine society serve as intervening factors in policy implementation. A dysfunctional public bureaucracy overcome by lack of capacity and systemic corruption that saps the resources, and the entry of civil society and international organizations, are the conditions that shape policy implementation in the Philippines.

4.5.1 *Conceptual framework*

A major influence in this inquiry is the work of Van Meter and Van Horn (1975) in implementation analysis. According to them, the six important elements of policy implementation are: '(1) policy standards and objectives, (2) resources, (3) inter-organizational communication and enforcement activities, (4) characteristics of the implementing agency, (5) economic, social and political conditions and (6) disposition of implementers' (Van Meter and Van Horn 1975: 462–74). These six variables provide the framework for analysing the effectiveness of the implementation of the ACD and AMMTC/SOMTC as an interactive progression, which not only confines itself to the process but more importantly recognizes the roles of the key stakeholders and the Philippine context of the implementation sites.

Another insightful concept from Van Meter and Van Horn is the relationship between the amount of change and goal consensus. They contend that the conflict of goals occurs when there are major amounts of change involved and where goal consensus is low. They likewise assert the presence of 'incrementalism', where subsequent policy decisions are carried out as a mechanical continuation of previous decisions, which explains why conflicts are less debilitating in cases of minor amounts of change and high goal consensus (465). They theorize that implementation gridlocks occur when the policies are in the quadrant of high change and low consensus, and that implementation successes can be better realized in situations where policies are located in the quadrant of high consensus and minor change.

An analysis of the ACD and AMMTC/SOMTC, which contain analogous and overlapping policy actors but which produce contrasting results, would benefit greatly from using the consensus and change interface of Van Meter and Van Horn. This delicate balance serves as a starting point in the analysis of implementation effectiveness of the ACD and AMMTC/SOMTC policies. The study considers the variations of change and consensus that these two policies require from the stakeholders involved in their implementation.

This chapter extends Van Meter and Van Horn's thesis by contending that implementation analysis must go beyond the study of the effectiveness of policy resulting from the environment that affects the jurisdiction and organization of policy. It asserts that effective implementation analysis must also look at the levels of satisfaction of the target clientele (target beneficiaries) towards the policy being implemented as well as the levels of local actors' participation as a benchmark of the performance of policy. One example of this would be Donald P. Warwick's 'environment of the public organization'. The concepts of 'remote and proximate elements' (Warwick 1975: 61) and his reliance on 'cultural norms, patterns of social stratification', and, more importantly, the use of 'controllers, clientele groups, constituencies, allies and adversaries' (61), provide a starting point for the analytical enrichment of the local actors' perspectives as located in the Philippine case in relation to the implementation of the two selected ASEAN-wide policies. For this chapter, local actors would be synonymous to the stakeholders.

This chapter recognizes that the preconditions for successful policy implementation are appropriate in studying the histories of developing nations like the Philippines. Leadership, a competent public bureaucracy and the presence or absence of corruption (Quah 1987: 91) are characteristics that bedevil not only the Philippines, but similar developing nations that share a history of autocratic regimes in which bureaucracies are instrumentalized for particularistic and elite interests. Another significant factor in the preconditions of successful implementation is the minimal or low level of bureaucratic corruption. A review of the literature in the Philippine setting indicates an acute shortage of implementation studies affected by systemic corruption. This is a research gap that this chapter acknowledges.

This chapter uses the preconditions of successful policy implementation in carefully reviewing the implementation experiences of the ACD and AMMTC/SOMTC in the Philippines. Particular attention is focused on the deficits experienced by the public bureaucracy in meeting the above preconditions. A close scrutiny of the impact of international organizations represented by the ASEAN and civil society organizations on whether they complement or compete with the state in meeting the above preconditions is undertaken. The effects of widespread corruption in the implementation efforts of the public bureaucracy are analysed. A contextual approach is adopted throughout, in order to account for the influence of the unique political, geographic and cultural milieu of the Philippines and its impact on policy implementation.

4.5.2 *Determinants and obstacles in policy implementation*

In order fully to explore the causal linkages between implementation and corruption, a conceptual map has been formulated. The map relies heavily on the points of view of the implementation actors. By combining Chase's 1979 analysis of the obstacles to implementation with Van Meter and Van

Table 4.3 *Factors of implementation*

Operational demands	Nature and availability of resources	Power and shared authority
• policy standards and objectives • inter-organizational communication	• resources • disposition of implementers	• characteristics of the implementing agencies • economic, social and political conditions

Source: Reyes 2009b.

Horn's variables of implementation, the construct 'factors of implementation' is formulated (see Table 4.3). With this construct, the parameters of implementation that describe progress (determinants) and those that lead to problematic implementation (obstacles) are analysed in a systematic manner.

4.5.3 Lack of technological capability and inter-organizational weaknesses

In her study on tourism development and agrarian reform policies, Richter analysed the adverse impact of limited technological capabilities on the policy implementation capabilities of the Philippine public bureaucracy. Recognizing the immense scarcity of resources in the Philippine public bureaucracy she noted that 'training and planning become substitutes for action and policy evaluation. Implementation is often behind schedule and the problem becomes acute when agency coordination is needed and sequencing important' (Richter 1987: 71). Not only does she acknowledge that technological shortfalls prevent successful implementation, she has also noted that the implementation deficit is exacerbated by the difficulties in agency coordination and sequencing. She reinforces this chapter's argument that the lack of technological capabilities contributes to conflict – an implementation deficit – in the carrying out of policy.

A more serious pitfall that ails a highly centralized bureaucracy is the frequent systemic failures in relation to inter-organizational communication. Evidence of this was discovered in an analysis of education reform programmes in the biggest bureaucracy of the Philippines – the Department of Education (DepEd). An analysis of specific programmes revealed a communication gap among the key implementers of DepEd programmes 'seems to be the rule rather than the exception' (Reyes 2009b: 240). But it is not only in education where technology gaps exist. In the comprehensive *Global Competitiveness Report*, the technological status of the Philippines, particularly in its levels of vital infrastructure needed to fuel its economy, remain poor, especially in relation to airport and seaport facilities (Schwab 2014: 28). In a PIDS survey conducted to determine the country's readiness for the ASEAN Economic Community, respondents pointed out fundamental technological weaknesses in the Philippine bureaucracy manifested by 'lengthy procedures, delayed issuance of permits due to slow processing, lack of transparency in the guidelines' (Aldaba 2013: 25). For the Philippine public bureaucracy whose scope spans the entire nation and whose service delivery requirements constitute a vital cog in the country's drive for progress, communication breakdowns severely incapacitate its implementation performance.

4.5.4 *Reorganization and corruption in the public bureaucracy*

The Philippine government has experienced several attempts at reorganization. The very first system-wide change happened with the issuance of the Education Act of 1901. Fifty years later, this was followed by the very first nationwide attempt at reorganization, the Republic Act (RA) 997 or the 1954 Reorganization Act. Twenty years later, the Integrated Reorganization Plan (IRP) of 1972 was drawn up. A relatively recent attempt was RA 6656 or the 1988 Implementation of the Philippine Government Reorganization Act. As can be seen, the civil service has made several attempts at reorganization reform. This study contends that civil service actors in the midst of reorganization manifest important dispositions that have an impact on implementation success. A critique of the reform policies in the DepEd has found that reorganization, streamlining and reforms are usually greeted by affected civil servants with 'lack of compliance' and 'insubordination'. This weakness in the bureaucracy becomes much more apparent in bureaucratic contexts that foster 'high levels of discretion', a situation that can be found, for example, in the Philippine's largest bureaucracy – the DepEd (Aldaba 2013: 25).

Aside from systemic weaknesses, a 'serious attempt to analyse policy implementation deficits in a Philippine setting requires an explicit recognition of the almost ubiquitous impact of corruption' (Reyes 2009b: 3). Scholars and practitioners have identified the debilitating impact that corruption has on the implementation of programmes in the Philippines designed to address basic social needs (Reyes 2009a: 515). Estimates from scholars as well as from the World Bank have identified that 20 per cent of the annual government budget is lost to corruption (Balboa, Medalla and Yap 2007: 13). This amount has been estimated to be about 3 per cent to 4 per cent of the nation's GDP (Johnston 2008: 216). Quah stated that the problem of corruption in the country 'is a way of life' (Quah 2003: 81). In Transparency International's study on the 'Ten Most Corrupt Leaders', the Philippines earned the dubious distinction of having two of its ex-Presidents in the list: Ferdinand Marcos and Joseph Ejercito Estrada (Hodess et al. 2004: 13). Furthermore, corruption and the perennial implementation shortfalls have led to the 'utter failure of the system to deliver economic prosperity and reduce inequality' that has resulted in 'the greatest source of mass alienation' (Bello et al. 2004: 3). International rankings reinforce arguments about corruption's stranglehold in the Philippines. The country averaged a 2.7 score (on a 10-point ascending scale) from 1995 to 2011 and a score of 36 (on a 100-point ascending scale) in the Transparency International's Corruption Perceptions Index, from 2012 to 2014 (Transparency International 2014), positioning it as one of the underperforming countries in its fight against corruption. Surveys conducted by the Political and Economic Risk Consultancy (PERC) on the impact of corruption on the business environment in the Philippines revealed an average score of 8.5 (on a 10-point ascending scale) from 2005 to 2014 (Political & Economic Risk Consultancy Ltd. 2014: 4), placing the nation very near the top of worst performers in relation to anti-corruption efforts.

4.5.5 *Implementing agencies and the advent of civil society and international organizations*

A case study of power and shared authority in the DepEd reveals that the characteristics of implementing agencies determine policy outcomes. Where DepEd reform initiatives are described as problematic, analysis reveals the prominent characteristic of a 'dysfunctional bureaucracy' (Reyes 2009b: 58) typified by a general breakdown of organizational capability. On the other hand, where DepEd reform initiatives have been described as functional, organizational characteristics are typified by the presence of active and engaged 'stakeholder networks' (Reyes 2009b: 119). Another agency, equally noted as a hotbed for corruption and inefficiency, is the Bureau of Customs (BOC). The recent logjam in the port area that has caused major traffic backlogs in Manila as well as delays in the delivery of vital resources to and from the port area have been blamed on the 'lack of clarity in implementation procedures by the BOC' (Aldaba 2013: 26). The labour market of the Philippines, which is managed by multiple agencies such as the Department of Labour and Employment (DOLE), the Philippine Overseas Employment Agency (POEA) and Bureau of Labour Relations, 'suffers from rigidities and inefficiencies' and is yet another example of how government organizations belonging to the public bureaucracy manifest an overall structural weakness (Schwab 2014: 28).

In a situation where systemic weakness and resource scarcity are experienced by the government (the primary source of service delivery in the Philippines) and are aggravated by the prevalence of corruption, two other alternative agents of service delivery emerge: international organizations and civil society. Cariño states that the 'delivery of public goods and services is not limited to the government. Both the private sector and civil society are actively engaged in the production, marketing and distribution of public goods' (2003: 70). One of the most dominant exponents of civil society in the Philippine context without doubt would be the NGOs. Chronic deficits in the provision of services of the state have resulted in the emergence of NGOs as an alternative delivery system for the state. Shigetomi states that 'the existence of people who have been left out by both the market and the state seems to be the most fundamental factor behind the establishment and continued existence of NGOs' (Shigetomi 2002: 2).

It is also within the context of an ineffective government perennially plagued by corruption where international organizations enter the picture: 'as economic globalization proceeds, and as political and administrative relations between countries grow closer and stronger, issues concerning development, which were once domestic problems, are being affected ever more profoundly by international agreements and international consensus' (Shigetomi 2002: 2). Haque (2001: 73), arguing about the decreasing 'publicness' of public bureaucracies, says that international organizations have played a 'significant role in popularizing the "miracle" of market forces and reinforcing an unfavourable public perception of state agencies'. In a period of increased globalization, international organizations have thus become a major factor in the implementation of domestic issues of development concerning nations. Finnemore (1993: 566) has provided empirical evidence to prove that 'organizational innovation was supplied to the state from outside, from an international organization, rather than being the product of any characteristics internal to or inherent in the state itself'. She concludes from her study that an international organization, 'represented by UNESCO', which 'becomes a principal (rather than an agent)', provides an example of how these organizations play dominant roles in promoting and implementing new norms (594). Galicia (2000: 45) has noted that the Philippines, which is indebted to the International Monetary Fund (IMF), provides numerous examples of varying degrees of interventions of international organizations like the IMF, in the implementation of national development goals. The Philippine public bureaucracy provides a case study of how a huge inefficient public bureaucracy functions alongside the influence of civil society and international organizations.

A concrete example of how civil society and international organizations work towards improving the Philippine public bureaucracy is the valuable work undertaken by the 'World Bank, and a consultative group consisting of labour lawyers, employer and employee representatives, experts from the International Labour Organisation (ILO), the Organisation for Economic Cooperation and Development (OECD) as well as the private sector and members of civil society' in their collective efforts to search for ways to improve the limping labour market regulation sector of the Philippines (World Bank 2014: 86).

4.6 Case studies on implementing the ASEAN Cosmetic Directive (ACD) and the ASEAN Ministerial Meeting on Transnational Crime (AMMTC)/Senior Officials Meeting on Transnational Crime (SOMTC)

4.6.1 ASEAN 2015: Lessons in the implementation of specific policies

One of the primary goals in the creation of the ASEAN in 1967 was for geopolitical reasons: 'a firm foundation for common action to promote regional cooperation in South-East Asia in the spirit of equality and partnership and thereby contribute towards peace, progress and prosperity in the region' (ASEAN 1967: 1). However, aside from pursuing geopolitical aspirations, the ASEAN has embarked, painstakingly and ambitiously, on the creation, by 2015, of the ASEAN Economic Community (AEC) (ASEAN 2008: 1). This aspiration was partly inspired after the progress achieved by European nation states in ushering in the institutionalization of the European Union. The AEC provided an optimistic blueprint towards achieving a community strategically connected not only by geopolitical concerns but also united along mutually beneficial economic imperatives. A cornerstone of the AEC would be the implementation of its existing economic initiatives, namely '(i) accelerating regional integration in the priority sectors; (ii) facilitating movement of business persons, skilled labour and talents; and (iii) strengthening the institutional mechanisms of the ASEAN' (ASEAN 2008: 2).

4.6.2 ASEAN economic trade deals: the 'noodle bowl syndrome'

Realistically however, with the wide variety and disparity in their respective political and economic histories, the countries of the ASEAN face daunting challenges as they collectively attempt to implement the pertinent provisions related to AEC 2015. Scholars and practitioners have aptly pointed out that in the specific area of implementing Free Trade Agreements (FTAs), an 'existing large disparity in the level of development will likely lead to divergence or greater disparity in development' (Balboa, Medalla and Yap 2007: 2). Astute observers of the ASEAN regional challenges have described the existing quagmire of trade deals as a 'noodle bowl syndrome' (an unorganized tangle of bilateral trade deals) (Baldwin 2007: 4). The implications of the messy state of the 'noodle bowl (diverse time frames for completion, diverse exclusion lists, and diverse rules of origin and technical and product standards)' would invariably lead to an increase in 'administrative and business transaction costs and discourage utilization of the tariff preferences' (Chia 2011: 62).

Notwithstanding the current state of affairs in relation to complex trade arrangements existing in the ASEAN, the implementation of AEC 2015 was foreseen to be carried out through four interrelated stages. The first stage requires the promotion of transparency and improvement of the notification procedures under all ASEAN economic agreements via the Protocol on Notification Procedures. The second stage is the ratification of all pertinent ASEAN legal instruments made within six months. This would be followed by the third stage, which involved the decision-making processes of economic bodies primarily through consensus. The fourth and final stage underscored the utilization of the Enhanced Dispute Settlement Mechanism (DSM) with the end of promoting a rules-based community (ASEAN 2008: 35).

It is within this context that this chapter is situated. One of the challenges posed by experts on the future of the ASEAN region is the ability of most of its nations, known to be traditionally state-centred, to be able to increase understanding and collaboration with international institutions that are above the level of the state and with civil society that is below the level of the state. This inquiry seeks to study the dynamics of policy implementation, corruption and the interaction of government, civil society organizations and international institutions. The focus is on how the ACD and AMMTC/SOMTC are implemented in the Philippines.

In the Philippine context, the Department of Foreign Affairs (DFA) acts as the agency tasked with the role of a 'clearing house' in matters pertaining to relations with the ASEAN or for other international organizations for that matter. In the implementation of specific ASEAN policies, such as the ACD and AMMTC/SOMTC, the DFA facilitates the communication and linkages with various national departments and offices. Implementation of ASEAN policies are given legal force through Executive Orders emanating from the Office of the President. Inter-Agency Committees (IACs) are created and these are mandated with the implementation of ASEAN-wide policies in the Philippine context. In the subsequent sections, the specific agencies and offices involved in the implementation of the ACD and AMMTC/SOMTC are identified.

4.6.3 *What is the ASEAN Cosmetic Directive?*

On 2 September 2003, the ten-nation ASEAN adopted the ASEAN Cosmetic Directive (ACD) (ASEAN 2006: 8). The ACD is the natural progression from the Principles of Harmonization of Cosmetic Regulations and the Common Technical Documents for Cosmetics. The genesis of these policies derive from the ASEAN Mutual Recognition Agreement of Product Registration Approval for Cosmetics and the 'last resort' Protocol on Dispute Settlement Mechanism, signed on 20 November 1996 (ASEAN 2006: 7). What can be gleaned from a careful perusal of the historical documents within the ASEAN that ushered in the finalization of the ACD is that the economics of free trade in the highly marketable cosmetics industry and the continuous search for mutually beneficial regimes for all participating stakeholders are critical factors that led to the passage of the ACD. One can even argue that the progress of the passage and current implementation of the ACD as well as the issues and challenges that face it lie squarely on the dynamics of interaction between the key stakeholders.

4.6.4 *What is the AMMTC/SOMTC?*

The SOMTC was formalized in 1997, during the first AMMTC, which is the highest policy-making body in the ASEAN region for transnational crime. The SOMTC, as mandated in 1997, is the implementing arm of the AMMTC and is mainly responsible for crafting the implementation of the ASEAN Plan of Action to Combat Transnational Crime (ASEAN 1999). A scrutiny of the ASEAN documents pertinent to the AMMTC and the SOMTC reveals that great strides have been accomplished in relation to the pursuance of diplomacy. However, in the efforts of implementing a systemic and binding rule of law that governs the flashpoints identified in transnational crime (i.e., money laundering, trafficking in persons, drug trafficking, arms smuggling and piracy) the performance of the AMMTC/SOMTC is still very much a work in progress.

A review of the pertinent literature composed of ASEAN official documents, Philippine rulings as well as scholarly studies on the ASEAN and particularly the implementation of the ACD and AMMTC/SOMTC form the bulk of the data sources for this chapter. The literature review was complemented by primary data obtained from interviews with selected stakeholders of the ACD and AMMTC/SOMTC. A total of thirteen stakeholders carrying out duties within the context of the two policies were the respondents for this study.[2] Table 4.4 provides a brief description of the respondents for the two case studies.

4.7 Assessing the implementation of the ACD

Using the factors of implementation as an analytical lens, it can be argued that deliberate efforts on the part of the key stakeholders are made in order to address the operational demands of the ACD. The key stakeholders are also able strategically to manage the nature and availability of resources needed for the functional implementation of the ACD. Power

[2] All the names of the respondents have been changed to maintain confidentiality.

Table 4.4 *Philippine interview respondents*

Names (pseudonyms)	Institutional affiliation	Date of interview
1. R. Cruz	international cosmetics industry executive	19 March 2012
2. I. de la Cruz	international cosmetics industry executive	19 March 2012
3. V. Santos	local cosmetics industry enterprise executive	23 March 2012
4. J. Tan	local cosmetics industry enterprise executive	23 March 2012
5. J. Santos	Food and Drug Administration official	19 March 2012
6. J. de la Cruz	Cosmetic Chamber of the Philippines official	20 March 2012
7. F. Tan	anti-trafficking Philippine NGO official	19 March 2012
8. B. Tan	anti-trafficking Philippine NGO official	19 March 2012
9. H. Flores	Philippine National Police official	21 March 2012
10. F. Bautista	Philippine National Police official	21 March 2012
11. I. Tan	Philippine National Police official	21 March 2012
12. D. Santos	Department of Foreign Affairs	21 March 2012
13. I. Santos	Philippine National Police official	22 March 2012

and shared authority among the key stakeholders remain the most complex component in the implementation of the ACD.

4.7.1 *Operational demands*

Concerted efforts from the different stakeholders are made to uphold the policy standards and objectives of the ACD.

On the whole, the implementation of the ACD from a Philippine experience has been encouraging but real challenges remain. The historical trajectory of the ACD from its genesis to its present form is a testament to the positive experience of the regional organization: the 'ASEAN has thrived in finalizing the ASEAN Harmonized Cosmetic Regulatory Scheme, which consists of two phases: the Mutual Recognition Agreement (MRA) and the ACD' (Horikoshi 2006: 41). In the Philippine context, the implementation of the ACD lies squarely on the Food and Drug Administration (FDA) of the Department of Health (DOH) (House of Representatives 2009). The fundamental policy objective of the FDA in relation to implementing the ACD lies in their role 'to transpose the Directive into national legislation and put in place a notification system for placement of cosmetics' (Chia 2011: 60).

In relation to the consistent transposition of the ACD into national legislation, the key stakeholders from industry and the FDA have claimed that the Philippines have been implementing this task rather diligently (R. Cruz, pers. comm., 19 March 2012). The main issues raised by the key stakeholders – particularly those coming from the cosmetics industry – have been the lack of a binding ASEAN legal framework especially in regard to perceived violations in the transposition by other ASEAN countries (I. de la Cruz, pers. comm., 19 March 2012). In fact, the industry stakeholders have claimed that among the industries in the various ASEAN countries, the integration is not real and that what actually pervades is factionalism (R. Cruz, pers. comm., 19 March 2012). The notion of factionalism is a very strong position advocated by the Philippine-based ACD stakeholders specifically those dealing with traditional cosmetics products and those representing small and medium-sized enterprises (SMEs). These stakeholders argue that the policy goal espoused in the ACD, which is 'harmonization of standards', 'is an advantage to [the European Union] but a disadvantage to small, local manufacturers in the ASEAN' (R. Cruz, pers. comm., 19 March 2012). V. Santos (pers. comm., 23 March 2012) and I. de la Cruz (pers. comm., 19 March 2012) confirm this similar observation. Not surprisingly, even the stakeholders representing the biggest cosmetics industries in the Philippines acknowledge how the current policy standards and objectives of the ACD deter SMEs from entering and flourishing in the planned AEC (J. de la Cruz, pers. comm., 20 March 2012).

One area of strength recognized in this chapter is the 'inter-organizational communication among the key stakeholders of [the] ACD's implementation from a Philippine context' (R. Cruz, pers. comm., 19 March 2012). Government officials as well as the industry partners have very regular communications: as a matter of fact, the senior leaders of the Chamber of Cosmetics Industry of the Philippines (CCIP) 'regularly initiate communications with the FDA as these are related to the approval and marketing of cosmetic products'. The key stakeholders in the implementation of the ACD in a Philippine perspective have indicated that senior government officials and industry representatives are merely 'a phone call or a text away' (J. de la Cruz, pers. comm., 20 March 2012).

4.7.2 *Nature and availability of resources*

With the full-scale implementation of the ACD, the Philippine's DOH had to lobby for the passage of legislation that converted its Bureau of Food and Drugs Administration (BFDA) to an FDA plus the accompanying and necessary additional powers. This needed to be done in order to anticipate the broader and more specialized tasks that the ACD required from the FDA and other national agencies related to cosmetics. In the Philippines, RA 9711 or the Food and Drug Administration Act of 2009 was the answer that the DOH was looking for (House of Representatives 2009).

An implication of the greater powers of the Philippine FDA was the flexibility to modify the registration fees for new products (i.e., some drugs may be considered as cosmetics). The Philippine FDA, indicating that resource mobilization was essential in order for it to carry out its greater role, proposed an increase of a whopping 1004 per cent in the price of a notification licence (J. Santos, pers. comm., 19 March 2012). This massive increase in registration fees can clearly be seen by scrutinizing how product registration for a new drug increased from its original price to its newly stated rate:

> Accordingly, the biggest fee increases are for product registration. A new drug's initial registration used to be 6,667 Philippine Pesos (approximately $144), but is now 210,000 PHP ($4,544). Though initial registration used to be for one year, the FDA has extended it for three years. However, the renewal fee has increased from 20,000 PHP ($432) to 70,000 PHP ($1,515) and only lasts for one year. (Pacific Bridge Medical 2009)

FDA officials rationalized that, with the increased role that the new office needed to perform resulting from the reorganization of the agency, a massive infusion of qualified personnel and state of the art equipment was necessary. One of the most effective ways to generate much needed resources was to increase the charges levied on drug manufacturers. In the FDA's estimation, the huge increase in registration fees was justified.

The key stakeholders possess varying amounts of resources; nonetheless, these are maximized in order to effect the implementation of the ACD. Historically, the cosmetics industry (both in the ASEAN and in the specific countries like the Philippines) carries quite a lot of weight in terms of influence (market share) and impact (economic contribution). In the experience of implementing the ACD in the Philippines, the cosmetics industry has enough leverage so that in 2003 industry partners provided professional training to the then FDA field and central officers free of charge. This is an example of the 'muscle of the cosmetics association in the Philippines' (R. Cruz, pers. comm., 19 March 2012).

4.7.3 Power and shared authority

Power and shared authority in the implementation of the ACD in a Philippine perspective has been a complicated experience. The difficulties arise from the characteristics and capacities of the FDA in implementing the ACD, and the perceptions of other key stakeholders of 'unfairness towards SMEs' resulting from the new regulations that are disadvantageous to those small enterprises with limited capital in the implementation of the ACD.

The FDA as the main implementing agent of the ACD in the Philippines is a lightning rod for criticism. The main complaints that have been raised by key stakeholders about the FDA are: 'lack of manpower – no warm bodies and current staff lack competence (mostly fresh graduates with Bachelor of Science (Pharmacy) degrees who may lack experience) – and leadership'. Stakeholders have pointed out that a change of leadership in 2003, and the drastic policy changes that ensued, unsettled most of the established actors involved in the implementation of the ACD (J. Santos, pers. comm., 19 March 2012).

With the increased roles that the Philippine FDA is supposed to undertake, stakeholders involved in the ACD have questioned – quite legitimately – whether or not the FDA is fully prepared to carry out its newly constituted roles. Previously, the FDA's task was more administrative. However, with the revisions brought about by the ACD, the Philippine FDA would need to have a cadre of trained operatives (such as biochemists, chemical engineers and industrial engineers, as well as qualified and (more importantly) experienced pharmacists) to undertake the required scientific and technical review of products under the ACD. Stakeholders involved in the ACD who are very familiar with the Philippine FDA categorically state that at the moment the FDA is ill-prepared.

The key stakeholders in the implementation of the ACD from a Philippine perspective also lament how some ASEAN nations flout the policy objectives and standards of the ACD. These Philippine cosmetics industry representatives state that this becomes particularly acute during the transposition of the ACD's pertinent rules to the local legislation of some ASEAN nations. Stakeholders have disclosed that 'each country undertakes separate and different transpositions of ACD agreements into local national laws'. For example, a country like Vietnam transposes the ACD agreement pertaining to the need to identify clearly the ingredients used on product labels into their local context. However, in the Vietnamese context, product labels are not strictly required. What happens is that multinational firms entering Vietnam spend a great deal on producing detailed labels consistent with ACD agreements while their Vietnamese competitors do not spend anything at all, as the local context does not require this rule to be implemented. The disparity of transposition of ACD agreements illustrated by this example goes against the objective of standardization (I. de la Cruz, pers. comm., 19 March 2012). This remains one of the complex components of power and shared authority, as it is difficult to achieve common standards and Mutually Recognized Agreements (MRAs) among the ASEAN countries as the more developed countries have imposed more stringent standards than their less developed counterparts (Chia 2011: 52).

Aside from the manpower issues that surface with the implementation of the ACD (from a regime of simple registration to the current stringent submission of more elaborate product dossiers), the key stakeholders have argued that SMEs would find barriers to entry almost impossible to overcome. V. Santos and J. Tan (pers. comm., 23 March 2012) strongly pointed out this negative implication. The existence of barriers to entry to SMEs is a phenomenon that is not only confined to the Philippine context as a result of the ACD. Non-traditional cosmetics stakeholders in different parts of the world, who usually belong to the ranks of the SMEs, have also raised these issues. American and European SMEs have highlighted how intermittent changes that come from national and international agencies can adversely impact their operations:

> SMEs complained that constantly scrutinising changing lists of ingredients put out by authoritative bodies, hiring legal advisors, and reformulating their products to keep up with these changes would force their product costs up, and they would become uncompetitive and collapse. The American situation described above is, of course, similar to that of European SMEs. (Burfield 2010)

The key stakeholders in the implementation of the ACD have indicated that 'corruption still occurs in the system' (R. Cruz, pers. comm., 19 March 2012). Most of the industry partners of the ACD stated that corruption still occurs in the Philippines (e.g., importing raw materials through the Bureau of Customs with the accompanying problems that arise) albeit on a smaller scale. Several measures to make the processes of the Bureau of Customs more transparent (e.g., the installation of closed circuit television in customs-bonded warehouses), and simplifying procedures in order to eliminate complex and multiple interactions with various agents through one-stop shops, have made an impact in slowing down widespread corrupt activities. Other respondents have stated that the Philippine cosmetics industry has 'matured through the decades' to make it less vulnerable to rampant corruption (J. de la Cruz, pers. comm., 20 March 2012).

Perhaps the loudest and most vociferous voices against the implementation of the ACD are two of the respondents who remain vigilant and actively advocate a review of the ACD's implementation. V. Santos and J. Tan (pers. comm., 23 March 2012) are of the strong opinion that corruption prevails but on a scale that happens not in the Philippines alone but with multinational cosmetics manufacturers 'bribing government officials of the FDA' and 'crowding out SMEs'. They also state that the ACD is a 'blatant display of power from multinational agencies' bullying SMEs in the Philippines.

4.8 Assessing the implementation of the AMMTC/SOMTC

Using the factors of implementation as an analytical lens, it can be argued that communication among the key stakeholders is consistently maintained whilst the fundamental laws pertinent to transnational crime undergo renegotiation and refinement in order to address the operational demands of the AMMTC/SOMTC. The key stakeholders have underscored the inherent difficulties faced in managing the nature and availability of resources needed for the implementation of the AMMTC/SOMTC. Power and shared authority among the key stakeholders persist as the most challenging component in implementing the AMMTC/SOMTC.

4.8.1 Operational demands

In the implementation of the AMMTC/SOMTC in the Philippines, inter-organizational communication among the key stakeholders remains highly functional. The AMMTC/SOMTC has mobilized several ASEAN nation-based groups to tackle transnational crime. In the Philippine perspective, this group is composed of the Secretaries of the Department of Justice and Department of Social Work (both sit as co-chairs), Heads of the DFA, DOLE, POEA, the Bureau of Immigration, the Philippine National Police, National Commission on the Role of Filipino Women and three representatives from NGOs as members (B. Tan, pers. comm., 19 March 2012). From the perspective of the DFA, the implementation of the SOMTC has been functional (D. Santos, pers. comm., 21 March 2012). Among the Philippine-based members, the implementation of the AMMTC/SOMTC has been translated to 'diplomacy is taking place' through 'the sharing of information' (B. Cruz, pers. comm., 21 March 2012).

The more tenuous aspect of the operational demands of implementing guidelines from the SOMTC can be found in the contested definitions of transnational crime. Money laundering, piracy and drug trafficking are among the serious problems encountered by the Philippines and other ASEAN countries and by various other nations in the world. One particular transnational crime that has attracted much attention to the ASEAN from other countries is trafficking in persons. The history of the ASEAN region has given it quite an unsavoury reputation in relation to trafficking in persons. This becomes a very urgent and serious issue particularly when one considers the linkage of sex trafficking to the region and the problematic legal approach that is generally pursued in the ASEAN. Cheah elaborates on these contradictions:

> Despite sex trafficking's historical and long-standing roots in the ASEAN region, ASEAN States have failed to deal

> with the problem effectively. This is due to the criminal law model adopted by most ASEAN States in combating sex trafficking. The criminal law model focuses on penalization of the trafficking act and fails to adequately address the socio-economic causes and consequences of sex trafficking. As a result, victims of sex trafficking are neglected or re-victimised by authorities of the destination country, are left in limbo while awaiting repatriation, and upon repatriation are ostracised or marginalized in the States of origin. (Cheah 2006: 47)

In response to the increased pressure for the ASEAN seriously to address the issue of trafficking in persons, a number of the ASEAN nations have already adopted the Trafficking Protocol (United Nations 2000). However, as already pointed out by Cheah, ASEAN's approach to trafficking in persons (particularly sex trafficking) relies on either a criminal law model or a victim-centred approach (Cheah 2006: 47). The varied approach to dealing with trafficking in persons in the ASEAN provides a glimpse of how this serious phenomenon is dealt with in different ways in the region.

In the ASEAN region, there is a clamour to adopt the victim-centred approach. Notably in the Philippines, the implementation of approaches to combat trafficking in persons has been progressing steadily. In 2003, the Philippine Congress was able to put into law anti-trafficking legislation provisions that address this critical issue (House of Representatives 2003). Despite these legal achievements 'on paper', the key stakeholders at the forefront of the implementation of the AMMTC/SOMTC guidelines indicate that 'more needs to be done beyond the mere sharing of information' and that a concerted effort to arrive at a 'universally accepted interpretation of the rule of law is needed' as opposed to the current state of affairs which accommodates varied interpretations within the ASEAN (I. Santos, pers. comm., 22 March 2012).

4.8.2 *Nature and availability of resources*

The key stakeholders have underscored the inherent difficulties faced in managing the nature and availability of resources needed for the implementation of the AMMTC/SOMTC. Government agencies in the Philippines tasked to implement the pertinent guidelines of the AMMTC/SOMTC have lamented the difficulty of acquiring funds. Aside from the initial outlays provided (i.e., allocation of office space for AMMTC/SOMTC officials at Camp *Crame* – the Philippines National Police Headquarters), there are currently no recurrent funds being pumped into AMMTC/SOMTC to address their operational needs. What happens is that the AMMTC/SOMTC officials use the budget allocated originally for the key functions of their agencies and use some of these to fund the AMMTC/SOMTC activities. The key stakeholders have indicated that the accessibility and availability of internally allotted funds for the smooth functioning of their organizations remain a pressing challenge (F. Tan, pers. comm., 19 March 2012 and H. Flores, pers. comm., 21 March 2012).

Civil society representatives implementing the AMMTC/SOMTC have also underscored the phenomenon of 'capacity-building fatigue' that not only saps the energy of volunteers but also threatens to compromise the coffers of civil society (B. Tan, pers. comm., 19 March 2012). Additionally, civil society representatives, who have had vast experience in dealing with specific transnational crimes such as trafficking in persons, have expressed surprise that their knowledge and expertise are only used in a limited way by the government. These civil society representatives are asked to be merely 'resource speakers'. Civil society stakeholders argue that they should form part of a more strategic and integrated approach to transnational crime. They propose that the anti-trafficking curriculum for law enforcers could benefit greatly from civil society as they transform outdated concepts of trafficking specifically to identify 'victims as those that need protection and traffickers as those that need to be tracked down and persecuted' (I. Santos, pers. comm., 22 March 2012).

The disposition of implementers is another source of contention in addressing the implementation of the AMMTC/SOMTC. The key stakeholders have explicitly stated that 'compliance versus real practical decisions that leads to real action is not currently happening in the [AMMTC]/SOMTC'. The experience of the Philippine stakeholders in implementing the AMMTC/SOMTC proves to be constantly a complex issue. An example of this complexity from a Philippine perspective can be seen in the controversial Trafficking Protocol, which Brunei Darussalam and Singapore have not signed or ratified, for several reasons. Singapore and Brunei Darussalam are heavy importers of foreign workers. Commentators have opined that some of the provisions of the proposed Trafficking Protocol have been considered by officials of these nations as disadvantageous to their current national manpower hiring practices. Indonesia, Malaysia, Vietnam, Thailand, Myanmar and Laos have ratified the Trafficking Protocol but have raised reservations. Only Cambodia and the Philippines have signed and ratified the Trafficking Protocol without any conditions, reservations or objections (United Nations 2014). In short, there is no consensus among the ASEAN countries in implementing the Trafficking Protocol.

The key stakeholders have explicitly stated that law enforcement is 'infested' with 'corruption' (B. Tan, pers. comm., 19 March 2012). Civil society stakeholders have unequivocally indicated how in the interventions that they carry out, particularly in relation to efforts addressing trafficking in persons, they encounter 'corrupt practices' (I. Santos, pers. comm., 22 March 2012). These allegations of how corruption worsens the problems of trafficking of persons, particularly in a Philippine context, are supported by various international multilateral agencies. Those engaged in human trafficking usually operate in highly effective networks with considerable resources: the success of their illegal trade is bolstered by corruption (UNICRI & AIC 2000). A specific example provided by I. Santos (pers. comm., 22 March 2012) illustrates that alleged human traffickers whom they have identified and reported to law enforcers still 'magically get away during sting operations'. On several occasions, they have observed how known human traffickers have been 'approached by several law enforcers minutes before a raid' thus escaping from the 'clutches of the law'. A very specific action that civil society has initiated is the preparation of corruption vulnerability maps that they share with all

AMMTC/SOMTC stakeholders to improve vigilance and promote anti-corruption (I. Santos, pers. comm., 22 March 2012). Law enforcers party to the AMMTC/SOMTC have 'acknowledged that there are lawless elements within their ranks' (F. Bautista, pers. comm., 21 March 2012) but these have become much more limited (B. Cruz, pers. comm., 21 March 2012).

4.8.3 Power and shared authority

Power and shared authority among the key stakeholders persist as the most challenging component in the implementation of the AMMTC/SOMTC. Perhaps one of the most troubling aspects that face the implementers of efforts against transnational crime is that most of its existing provisions are non-binding (I. Tan, pers. comm., 21 March). B. Cruz (pers. comm., 21 March 2012), as a law enforcer, is particularly frustrated with how the non-binding nature of the AMMTC/SOMTC dampens the efficacy of their activities. The key stakeholders from across the various representatives of the AMMTC/SOMTC in a Philippine context have openly clamoured for the adoption of the Trafficking Protocol (Melican 2011) – for all the ASEAN countries (R. Cruz, pers. comm., 21 March 2012) – but to date have been unsuccessful.

However, with the current reality of the non-binding nature of its statutes, stakeholders have acknowledged that the AMMTC/SOMTC is 'an opportunity'; as 'coordination is essential to combat transnational crime, shared knowledge is valuable' (I. Santos, pers. comm., 22 March 2012).

Also, stakeholders from both civil society and government have recognized that 'NGOs' decisions, which are by nature "quicker", [are] therefore much easier to make versus government bureaucracy' (B. Tan, pers. comm., 19 March 2012), and have thus worked around arrangements to maximize this type of situation. It can be argued that the very real existing limitations (e.g., non-binding laws) have given birth to novel approaches in implementing the AMMTC/SOMTC. One solution that has arisen from among some of the ASEAN nations is the formation of trans-governmental networks. In this approach, various 'organs within each state – police departments, immigration departments, the military, legislators' have created 'transnational networks' that allow for direct coordination among the ASEAN level counterparts (Renshaw 2008: 3).

4.9 Conclusion: implications for current ASEAN processes and outputs

This chapter provides an analysis of the civil service's role in policy implementation in the Philippines. It argues that the Philippine civil service is currently weak, fragmented and afflicted by systemic corruption. Its current weakened state could be attributed to three main factors. First, owing to its highly political nature caused primarily by its unsteady colonial origins, the Philippine public bureaucracy has been typified by continuities and discontinuities making implementation of policies a haphazard affair. Secondly, the breadth and width that the Philippine Civil Service is mandated to serve remains a daunting challenge: an archipelago of

7,107 islands with still undeveloped infrastructure. Lastly, systemic corruption is a malaise that troubles the civil service and is worsened by the weak rule of law. Consequently, a careful assessment of the implementation of policies would need to be cognizant of these three constraints of the Philippine civil service.

4.9.1 *Change versus consensus*

Consistent with the arguments of Van Meter and Van Horn, implementation gridlock occurs in quadrants where there is great change and very little goal consensus. The Philippine experience of creating the FDA in order to address the mandate of the ACD has produced a situation where the price of product registration has risen by 1004 per cent and a dearth of trained manpower to implement the new requirements of the FDA review has been revealed. These are examples of situations where there are great changes with very little consensus.

The Philippine experience of implementing the AMMTC/SOMTC has been similar to the ACD, although it has occurred at a more deliberate and sustained pace (e.g., non-adoption of the Trafficking Protocol – a policy that requires great change and a lack of consensus among some specific ASEAN nations).[3]

[3] In the issue of Trafficking in Persons, the division among the ASEAN states exists more sharply between 'sending nations' (usually poverty-stricken) and the 'receiving nations' (usually more-developed).

In the Philippine case, the ACD has experienced greater progress. The legal adoption of the key ACD code embodied in the ASEAN Harmonized Cosmetic Regulatory Scheme has undoubtedly hastened this process. Notwithstanding the undeniable fact that the civil service, represented by the FDA, was undermanned and underfunded to take on its new roles, the ACD still moved forward. Based on this assessment, this progress was due mainly to the active participation of other stakeholders – those who do not belong to the civil service, namely the private sector.

By contrast, the AMMTC/SOMTC has experienced a much more belaboured progress. Although non-civil service stakeholders played very active roles, a key element of the policy – the adoption of the Trafficking Protocol – remained unresolved. This uncertainty created a 'foot-dragging effect' where civil service stakeholders found themselves increasingly frustrated and demoralized with what they perceived was a deliberate and inexplicably laggard behaviour of other stakeholders (the civil servants of other ASEAN nations) in relation to the AMMTC/SOMTC.

4.9.2 Achieving a balance between change and consensus

For the ACD, the change that was adopted in the Philippines was drastic. The amount of consensus was moderate. Perhaps as the civil service moves forward the amount of change can be tweaked in order to make it 'slight to moderate'. This could be done by implementing change through stages in order to balance out the moderate consensus. For the

AMMTC/SOMTC, the suggested drastic change was aggravated by the lack of consensus in relation to the Trafficking Protocol. Using Van Meter and Van Horn's change and goal consensus model, one can see the high degree of required change and the low amount of consensus that the Trafficking Protocol required of most of the ASEAN members. Balancing and perhaps repackaging the change to be less drastic (e.g., using staggered phases of implementation instead of a sudden transformation) and then taking realistic efforts to arrive at greater consensus (e.g., allowing for greater and meaningful discussion within the ASEAN in relation to reservations raised by some of the states in relation to the Trafficking Protocol) could mean better progress for policy implementation.

The experience of implementing the ACD and AMMTC/SOMTC provides lessons for ASEAN-wide attempts at policy formulation and implementation. Balancing the need to change (cognizant of the contextual conditions of the member state) with the degree of consensus (familiar with the levels of flexibility of member states) seems a plausible way to ensure that ASEAN policies move forward.

One powerful lesson that the ASEAN countries can learn in relation to arriving at a feasible balance between change and consensus is the region's experience in addressing the transnational crime of terrorism. Scholars and practitioners have identified that the experience of Southeast Asia in addressing terrorism in the region has been met with a 'broad general consensus' (Soeslilowati 2011: 239) among the ASEAN members. It has been suggested that this happened with the astute combination of 'depoliticizing terrorism' (treating terrorism as a technical problem rather than the more sensitive 'nation and ethnicity' problem and thereby arriving at a careful consensus) and the application of 'ASEANization' of counterterrorism policies (the introduction of change via the well-known ASEAN way) (Gerstl 2010: 72).

4.9.3 Policy borrowing and policy transference

The experience of the ACD as it was adopted from the EU provides some critical insights in relation to policy borrowing. The explicit resistance demonstrated by SMEs and the non-traditional cosmetics industries (in the Philippines in particular) as echoed by more established cosmetics industry players may need careful reflection. The words of one of the ACD stakeholders regarding this issue are worth considering: 'In 1996, the policy borrowing of the ASEAN from the EU model was done without a deep understanding. Now, ACD is becoming a threat to established manufacturers as well as SMEs' (R. Cruz, pers. comm., 19 March 2012).

The AMMTC/SOMTC provides a valuable learning experience in policy transference with particular attention to the inherent shortcomings that accompany them. Civil service stakeholders in the Philippines, as well as non-civil service actors, witnessed how policy transference – in the form of key AMMTC/SOMTC policies – varied greatly as they were introduced, interpreted and adopted by the other ASEAN member states. Initial euphoria at the signing of the AMMTC/SOMTC documents turned into dismay when ratification did not follow; worse still, some ASEAN member states neither signed nor ratified the Trafficking Protocol. Philippine stakeholders involved in the AMMTC/SOMTC have expressed frustration at the unpredictability and uncertainty of the AMMTC/SOMTC.

The implementation of the ACD from the perspectives of civil service and non-civil service stakeholders has crystallized the limitations of policy borrowing. For the future, what would be most promising would be contextualized policy borrowing: adopting what works and discarding what does not as these are carefully considered within the unique policy contexts of the member states. More importantly, the effort of policy borrowing must be tempered with a very critical perspective of who benefits and who is disadvantaged, and therefore what compromises are needed in order to move forward.

The difficult implementation of the AMMTC/SOMTC as experienced by the stakeholders has highlighted the drawbacks of policy transference. Different nation states of the ASEAN clearly have different perspectives in relation to the implementation of the AMMTC/SOMTC. Perhaps a more productive way to succeed in policy transference would be to arrive at workable strategies as far as possible so that all the stakeholders see advantages in adopting region-wide policies.

References

Aldaba, R. 2013. 'Getting Ready for the ASEAN Economic Community 2015: Philippine Investment Liberalization and Facilitation', Philippine Institute for Development Studies, Discussion Paper Series No. 3, pp. 1–36.

Anderson, B. 1988. 'Cacique Democracy and the Philippines: Origins and Dreams', *New Left Review* 169 (May–June): 3–33.

ASEAN 1967. 'The ASEAN Declaration'. In *Bangkok Declaration*. Jakarta: ASEAN Secretariat.

1999. '*Joint Communique of the Second ASEAN Ministerial Meeting on Transnational Crime*'. Jakarta: ASEAN Secretariat.

2006. '*ASEAN Cosmetic Directive*'. Jakarta: ASEAN Secretariat.

2008. '*ASEAN Economic Community Blueprint*'. Jakarta: ASEAN Secretariat.

Balboa, J., Medalla, E. and Yap, J. 2007. 'Closer Trade and Financial Cooperation in ASEAN: Issues at the Regional and National Level with Focus on the Philippines'. Discussion Paper Series No. 2007-03, pp. 1–25.

Baldwin, R. 2007. 'Managing the Noodle Bowl: The Fragility of East Asian Regionalism'. Working Paper Series on Regional Economic Integration No. 7, Asian Development Bank, Manila, pp. 1–32.

Bautista, A. 2006. 'Reinventing Philippine Legal Education'. In *9th General Assembly ASEAN Law Association*. Bangkok: ASEAN Law Association, pp. 1–10.

Bautista, V. 2000. 'Public–Private Partnership in Poverty Alleviation: The Case of the CIDSS', Eleventh International Society for Third Sector Research conference, Trinity College Dublin, 5–8 July.

Bello, W., Docena, H., de Guzman, M. and Malig, M. 2004. 'The Political Economy of Permanent Crisis'. In W. Bello, H. Docena, M. de Guzman and M. Malig (eds), *The Anti-Development State: The Political Economy of Permanent Crisis in the Philippines*. New York: Palgrave, pp. 9–32.

Brillantes, A. and Sonco, J. T. 2011. 'Decentralization and Governance in the Philippines'. In E. Berman (ed.), *Public Administration in Southeast Asia: Thailand, Philippines, Malaysia,*

Hong Kong and Macau. Boca Raton, FL: CRC Press, pp. 355–80.

Burfield, T. 2010. 'The Role of Risk Aversion in the Decline of the Perfumery Art', World Perfumery Congress, 44, Cannes, 9 June.

Cariño, L. V. 2003. 'The Concept of Governance'. In V. A. Bautista, M. C. P. Alfiler, D. R. Reyes and P. D. Tapales (eds), *Public Administration in the Philippines: A Reader*, 2nd edn. Quezon City: National College of Public Administration and Governance, University of the Philippines, pp. 66–76.

Central Intelligence Agency 2014. *The World Factbook: The Philippines*. https://www.cia.gov/library/publications/the-world-factbook/geos/rp.html.

Chase, G. 1979. 'Implementing a Human Services Program: How Hard Will it Be?', *Public Policy*, 27(4): 385–435.

Cheah, W. 2006. 'Assessing Criminal Justice and Human Rights Models in the Fight against Sex Trafficking: A Case Study of the ASEAN Region', *Essex Human Rights Review*, 3(1): 46–63.

Chia, S. Y. 2011. 'Association of Southeast Asian Nations Economic Integration: Developments and Challenges', *Asian Economic Policy Review*, 6(1): 43–63.

Chua, Y. 1999. *Robbed: An Investigation of Corruption in Philippine Education*. Quezon City: Philippine Centre for Investigative Journalism.

Civil Service Commission 2010a. 'Inventory of Government Personnel (2nd Quarter) 2010'. Quezon City.

2010b. 'Mandate of the Civil Service Commission'. Quezon City.

Co, E., Malaluan, N., Neame, A., Manuel, M. and Musngi, M. 2010. *Philippine Democracy Assessment: Rule of Law and Access to Justice*. Manila: Action for Economic Reforms and the International Institute for Democracy and Electoral Assistance.

Congressional Commission on Education 1991. 'Governance and Management'. In *Making Education Work: an Agenda for Reform*, EDCOM Report 1991. Manila: Congress of the Republic of the Philippines, pp. 1–80.

de Dios, E. 2000. 'Interest-group Competition, Legislative Obstruction and Executive Power', *Philippine Review of Economics*, 37 (1): 12–35.

de Vera, B. O. 2014. 'Red Tape Continues to Drag Down PH, Say EU Businessmen', *Philippine Daily Inquirer*, September 6.

Desierto, D. 2010. 'A Universalist History of the 1987 Philippine Constitution', *Historia Constitucional*, 11: 427–84.

Finnemore, M. 1993. 'International Organizations as Teachers of Norms: The United Nations Education Scientific and Cultural Organization and Science Policy', *International Organization*, 47(4): 565–97.

Galicia, R. 2000. 'Deep in Debt, Staggering in Debt Payment', *Community and Habitat*, 7: 40–5.

Gamboa, M. 1969. *An Introduction to Philippine Law*. Quezon City: Central Lawbook Publishing.

Gates, C. and Than, M. 2001. 'ASEAN Enlargement: An Introductory Overview'. In M. Than and C. Gates (eds), *ASEAN Enlargement: Impacts and Implications*. Singapore: Institute of Southeast Asian Studies, pp. 1–25.

Gerstl, A. 2010. 'The Depoliticisation and "ASEANisation" of Counter-Terrorism Policies in South-East Asia: A Weak Trigger for a Fragmented Version of Human Security', *Current Research on South-East Asia*, 3(1): 48–75.

Haque, M. S. 2001. 'The Diminishing Publicness of Public Service under the Current Mode of Governance', *Public Administration Review*, 69(1): 3–19.

Haub, C. and Kaneda, T. 2013. '*2013 World Population Data Sheet*'. Washington, DC: Population Reference Bureau.

Hew, D. and Soesastro, H. 2003. 'Realizing the ASEAN Economic Community by 2020', *ASEAN Economic Bulletin*, 20(3): 292–6.

Hodess, R., Inowlocki, T., Rodriguez, D. and Wolfe, T. 2004. *Global Corruption Report 2004*. London: Pluto Press.

Horikoshi, E. 2006. 'Cosmetic Regulatory Harmonization in ASEAN', *Fragrance Journal*, 34(1): 41–6.

House of Representatives 2003. 'Anti-Trafficking in Persons Act of 2003'. In *House of Representatives, 12th Congress*. Quezon City: Information and Communications Technology Service.

2009. 'Food and Drug Administration Act of 2009'. In *House of Representatives, 14th Congress*. Quezon City: Information and Communications Technology Service, pp. 1–18.

Hutchcroft, P. 1991. 'Oligarchs and Cronies in the Philippine State: The Politics of Patrimonial Plunder', *World Politics*, 43(3): 414–50.

Imperial, N. 2007. Keynote Address: 'The Challenges of Educational Reforms in the Philippines: The Case of the EDCOM and PCER', Fourth National Convention of the Philippine Association of Teachers of Education Foundation (PATEF), Bayview Hotel, Manila, 24 November.

Johnston, M. 2008. 'Japan, Korea, the Philippines, China: Four Syndromes of Corruption', *Crime, Law Social Change*, 49(3): 205–23.

Landé, C. 1965. *Leaders, Factions and Parties: The Structure of Philippine Politics*. Yale University Southeast Asia Studies Monograph Series No. 6 New Haven, CT: Yale University Press.

Lemarchand, R. and Legg, K. 1972. 'Political Clientelism and Development: A Preliminary Analysis', *Comparative Politics*, 4(2): 149–78.

Melican, N. R. 2011. 'ASEAN Convention on Human Trafficking Sought', *BusinessWorld*, 13 July.

Office of the President of the Philippines 1987. 'The 1987 Constitution of the Republic of the Philippines'. In *Official Gazette*. Manila: Office of the President, Republic of the Philippines.

Pacific Bridge Medical. 2009. 'Public Hearing for Revised Fee Schedule Issued by Filipino Food and Drug Administration', *Asia Medical eNewsletter*, 25 February.

Political and Economic Risk Consultancy Ltd. 2014. 'Corruption's Impact on the Business Environment', *Asian Intelligence*, 895 (19 March): 1–5.

Powell, I. and Wyndham, H. 1931. 'Colonial Administration in the Philippine Islands'. In *Comparative Methods of Colonial Administration (Record of Fifth Meeting)*. London: Chatham House, pp. 1–30.

Quah, J. S. T. 1987. 'Public Bureaucracy and Policy Implementation in Singapore', *Southeast Asian Journal of Social Science*, 15(2): 77–95.

2003. *Curbing Corruption in Asia: A Comparative Study of Six Countries*. Singapore: Eastern Universities Press.

2011. *Curbing Corruption in Asian Countries: An Impossible Dream?* Bingley: Emerald Group Publishing.

Renshaw, C. 2008. 'The Globalisation Paradox and the Implementation of International Human Rights: The Function of Transnational Networks in Combating Human Trafficking in the ASEAN Region', Law and Society Association Australia and New Zealand (LSAANZ) conference, University of Sydney, 10–12 December.

Reyes, V. C. 2009a. 'Case Study of Implementation amidst Corruption Linkages: The National Textbook Delivery Programme (TDP) of the Philippine Department of Education', *Journal of Educational Policy*, 24(4): 515–35.

2009b. *Corruption and Implementation: Case Studies in Philippine Public Administration*. Quezon City: National College of

Public Administration and Governance, University of the Philippines.

Richter, L. K. 1987. 'Public Bureaucracy in Post-Marcos Philippines', *Southeast Asian Journal of Social Science*, 15(2): 57–76.

Santo Tomas, P. A. 2003. 'The Philippine Bureaucracy: A Question of Numbers'. In V. A. Bautista, M. C. P. Alfiler, D. R. Reyes and P. D. Tapales (eds), *Public Administration in the Philippines: A Reader*, 2nd edn. Quezon City: National College of Public Administration and Governance, University of the Philippines, pp. 415–37.

Schwab, K. (ed.) 2014. *The Global Competitiveness Report, 2014–2015*. Geneva: World Economic Forum.

Severino, R. 2007. 'ASEAN beyond Forty: Towards Political and Economic Integration', *Contemporary Southeast Asia*, 29(3): 406–23.

Shigetomi, S. 2002. 'The State and NGOs: Issues and Analytical Framework'. In S. Shigetomi (ed.), *The State and NGOs: A Perspective from Asia*. Singapore: Institute of Southeast Asian Studies, pp. 1–33.

Soeslilowati, S. 2011. 'ASEAN's Response to the Challenge of Terrorism', *Society, Culture and Politics (Masyarakat, Kebudayaan dan Politik)*, 24(3): 228–41.

Transparency International 2014. (Berlin) 'Corruption Perceptions Index, 1995–2014', available at: www.transparency.org (accessed 10 December 2014).

United Nations 2000. 'Protocol to Prevent, Suppress and Punish Trafficking in Persons, Especially Women and Children, Supplementing the United Nations Convention against Transnational Organized Crime', *Trafficking Protocol*. New York: United Nations.

2014. *'Protocol to Prevent, Suppress and Punish Trafficking in Persons, Especially Women and Children, Supplementing the*

United Nations Convention against Transnational Organised Crime'. New York: United Nations.

United Nations Interregional Crime and Justice Research Institute (UNICRI) and Australian Institute of Criminology (AIC) 2000. 'Human Smuggling and Trafficking: A Desk Review on the Trafficking in Women from the Philippines'. In 10th *United Nations Congress on the Prevention of Crime and the Treatment of Offenders Conference*, Vienna, 10–17 April.

Van Meter, C. and Van Horn, D. 1975. 'The Policy Implementation Process: A Conceptual Framework', *Administration and Society*, 6(4): 445–88.

Varela, A. P. 1996. *Administrative Culture and Political Change*. Quezon City: College of Public Administration, University of the Philippines.

Warwick, D. P. 1975. *A Theory of Public Bureaucracy*. Cambridge, MA: Harvard University Press.

World Bank 2014. *Doing Business 2015: Going beyond Efficiency*. Washington, DC: World Bank.

Chapter 5

Governance and meritocracy: a study of policy implementation in Singapore

David Seth Jones

5.1 Introduction

Over the years, Singapore's public bureaucracy (comprising the civil service and statutory boards) has been recognized for its professionalism and integrity, and for its pivotal role in promoting the country's socio-economic development, which has enhanced Singapore's reputation for high standards of governance and administration.

The country has been awarded high percentile rankings for five of the World Bank's governance indicators for 2013: government effectiveness (99.5), political stability and absence of violence/terrorism (95.7), control of corruption (96.7), regulatory quality (100) and rule of law (95.3) (World Bank 2014). These rankings are corroborated by the high global rankings (often within the first three) on other governance indicators in the World Economic Forum's *Global Competiveness Reports*, the World Bank's *Doing Business* surveys and Transparency International's Corruption Perceptions Index (CPI). Critics of Singapore have argued that such achievements have been won at the expense of individual freedom and open democracy. In fact, the only governance indicator used by the World Bank for which Singapore does not have a high percentile rank is voice and accountability (52.1, in 2013), due in part to controls over the press and broadcast media (World Bank 2014). However, this indicator has not taken into account the complexity and shifting nature of Singapore's political culture in recent years.

This chapter is in two parts. The first part examines policy implementation in Singapore as a key factor in its achievement of a high standard of governance. It focuses on the essential features of policy implementation in Singapore by adopting the framework developed by Van Meter and Van Horn (1975: 462–74). To facilitate the understanding of policy implementation in Singapore, this part analyses the policy context, the profile of the public bureaucracy, the main characteristics of policy formulation, and provides three policy recommendations to address its limitations. The second part of the chapter deals with the implementation of these two ASEAN policies by the public bureaucracy in Singapore: the ASEAN Cosmetic Directive (ACD) of 2003 and the ASEAN Declaration on Transnational Crime of 1997, administered by the ASEAN Ministerial Meeting on Transnational Crime (AMMTC) and the Senior Officials Meeting on Transnational Crime (SOMTC).

5.2 Policy context

This section describes the context which influences how policy is implemented in Singapore by identifying important aspects of its geography, history, society, economy, public finances and the political and legal system.

5.2.1 *Geographical and historical context*

Singapore is a city state comprising a small island with a land area of 718.3 sq. km (including over 123 sq. km of land reclaimed from the sea). It occupies a strategic position between Peninsular Malaysia and Indonesia at the southern tip of mainland Southeast Asia but is lacking in natural resources except for deep water and sheltered harbours and anchorages. Singapore's history is marked by its British colonial past, and influxes of immigrants from China, India, Ceylon, Malaya and the Dutch East Indies. Other important historical occurrences were the Japanese Occupation during 1942–1945, the fight against communism in the 1950s and early 1960s, the granting of self-government in June 1959 and separation from Malaysia in August 1965 (Abshire 2011: 57–158).

The geographical features and historical experiences of Singapore have in a number of ways influenced how it is governed. Its smallness, lack of natural resources and the Japanese Occupation have fostered among the political leaders a sense of vulnerability and a long-held belief that nothing can be taken for granted with respect to safeguarding its prosperity and security. The country's smallness and lack of natural resources have also made the political leaders aware of the need to build the country's human capital through education and meritocracy as the essential path to prosperity and stability. The upshot has been the creation of strong institutional capacity within the public bureaucracy, and a clear commitment to innovation and reform to meet the ever changing economic and social needs of the country.

5.2.2 *Demographic and social context*

The population of Singapore has grown from just over 3 million in 1990 to 5.4 million in June 2013 (Department of Statistics 2014: 23). This has been achieved despite the decreasing rate of marriage and a declining birth rate, which dropped to 1.19 births per woman in 2013 (one of the lowest in the world) (Department of Statistics 2014: 10, 28). Much of the expansion of the population has been due to the influx of large numbers of foreigners who have taken jobs in business and the professions. The population is multi-ethnic, with a large Chinese majority and the remainder mainly being Malays and Indians (see Table 5.1). It is also a religiously diverse population comprising to varying degrees Buddhists, Taoists, Hindus, Muslims and Christians, as well those professing no religious belief (see Table 5.2). This has further reinforced the commitment to meritocracy, discussed below, which does not accord privileges to any one ethnic or religious group.

Table 5.1 *Composition of the Singapore population by ethnic group, 2013*

Ethnic group	**Percentage**
Chinese	74.2
Malay	13.3
Indian	9.1
Others	3.4
Total	100

Source: Department of Statistics 2014: 26.

Table 5.2 *Composition of the Singapore population by religious affiliation, 2010*

Religious affiliation	Percentage
Taoist/Buddhist	44.2
Muslim	14.7
Hindu	5.1
Christian	18.3
Others	17.7
Total	100

Source: Department of Statistics 2011: x.

5.2.3 *Economic and fiscal context*

The economy is characterized by strong real GDP growth rates which averaged 6.04 per cent per year between 2005 and 2013 and is categorized as high income, with a GDP per capita of US$54,776 in 2013 (Schwab 2014: 402). The economy is strongly export-oriented and is mainly based on high-value-added products and services such as advanced technology and professional, business and technical services (Ghesquiere 2007: 152–3; Economic Development Board 2012). Reflecting the trends in the economy, the composition of the workforce has changed over the last ten years with a greater proportion classified as senior white collar and a declining proportion as blue collar (see Table 5.3). With increased prosperity, income inequality has widened. The Gini coefficient has risen from just over 0.43 in 2000 to 0.45 in 2010, and the ratio of average income in the top quintile of employed households to that in the lowest quintile has

Table 5.3 *Composition of the Singapore population by occupational group, 2001 and 2013*

Occupational group	2001	2013
	(percentage of workforce)	
Senior white collar	26.5	31.1
Junior white collar	44.5	47.1
Skilled blue collar	6.4	4.0
Unskilled and semi-skilled blue collar	18.5	14.5
Others	4.1	3.3
Totals	100	100

Source: Department of Statistics 2012: 50; 2014: 61.

increased from 10.1 to 12.9 in the same period (Bhaskaran et al. 2012: 4–5). These measures of income inequality are higher than those of other states in Southeast Asia, except Malaysia (Asian Development Bank 2014: 153).

Further contributing to Singapore's economic development has been a conservative fiscal policy in which government spending has normally remained below 15 per cent of GDP (in fiscal year 2013/14 it was 14.2 per cent of GDP) and fiscal surpluses have been regularly achieved (Ghesquiere 2007: 51–8; Ministry of Finance 2010a: 28; 2014: 1; Asian Development Bank 2014: 283). Regular fiscal surpluses have contributed to the accumulation of substantial foreign reserves, amounting to US$346.5 billion in June 2014 (Monetary Authority of Singapore 2014). Strong revenue flows have also enabled the government to allocate the necessary human and financial resources to the public bureaucracy for effective policy implementation.

5.2.4 *Political and legal context*

The system of government in Singapore is based on the Westminister parliamentary model but with the Elected President as Head of State, instead of being purely titular, exercising limited executive powers. The President, in his personal discretion, may veto the spending of reserves which the government of the day did not accumulate, and must approve key public service appointments, namely the Chief Justice, the Attorney-General, the chairman and members of the Public Service Commission, the Chief of the Defence Force, and the Commissioner of Police. The President may also exercise oversight to a limited extent over the Corrupt Practices Investigation Bureau and the government's use of the Internal Security Act and the Maintenance of Religious Harmony Act.

The executive itself consists of a cabinet of eighteen Ministers assisted by Junior Ministers (Senior Ministers of State and Ministers of State) and Parliamentary Secretaries, collectively responsible to a ninety-nine-member unicameral parliament. Apart from the eighty-seven elected MPs, there are two other types of MPs. First, there are the Non-elected Constituency MPs (NCMPs), who are designed to ensure representation of a minimum number of opposition MPs in Parliament. Their number is nine minus the number of opposition MPs elected and they are drawn from those who have secured the highest percentage of the votes cast for defeated opposition candidates. The second type of MP is the Nominated MP (NMP), designed to reflect an independent and non-partisan view in Parliament. There may be up to nine NMPs who are chosen by a Special Select Committee of

Parliament from names submitted by the public. They must be individuals who have made an outstanding contribution to Singapore or have a distinguished record within their field. There are currently a maximum of nine NMPs. Singapore's Parliament and politics in general are dominated by the People's Action Party (PAP) which has held power since June 1959.

The criteria of appointment to the cabinet are stringent. Those appointed are often talent spotted through informal feedback with major consideration given to professional achievement and high academic attainment. Of the eighteen members of the present cabinet, three have a successful background in the corporate sector, four in the military, seven in the bureaucracy (mainly statutory boards, including the Monetary Authority of Singapore (MAS)), three in the professions and one in academia. In nearly all cases, they had reached a senior management level or had made a noticeable impact within their profession (Government of Singapore 2012). Prior to their career, they attended highly reputable universities, in many cases up to postgraduate level.

The stringent criteria governing full ministerial appointments are also reflected in the small number of Junior Ministers and Parliamentary Secretaries who enter the cabinet. Of the fifty-nine MPs who were appointed as Junior Ministers and Parliamentary Secretaries between 1990 and 2010, only sixteen advanced to a full ministerial position by 2011 (this occurred within a short period of one to five years of their initial appointment) (Ministry of Communications and Information 1990; Ministry of Information and the Arts 1991–2001; Ministry of Information, Communications and the Arts

2002–2011). The emphasis on talent in cabinet appointments points to a political leadership culture in Singapore which is strongly rooted in the principle of meritocracy as measured by academic and career success, and parallels the meritocracy in government administration as discussed below. The extended system of meritocracy to include the political leadership was described by Vogel as 'macho-meritocracy' (1989: 1052–4).

The legal system in Singapore combines common law and parliamentary statutory law. Common law principles may be applied to contract, trust and equity, property and tort law, which are largely judge-made with precedents drawn from cases both in the Singapore courts and in the courts in England and other common law jurisdictions. However, over time these areas of law have also been modified by statutes of the Singapore parliament. Nearly all criminal, company and family law is derived from parliamentary statutes (Bell 1999: 1–5).

Although lacking specialist administrative courts, Singapore has a clearly defined system of administrative law. Ministers, civil servants and public agencies are required to act fairly, reasonably and in accordance with the law. If their actions do not meet such criteria, they can be invalidated and declared unlawful through judicial review, especially in cases of ultra vires and procedural impropriety (Thio 1999: 160–7). In addition, under Singapore's system of administrative law, a great deal of the responsibilities and powers of public agencies have been stipulated in lower-level instruments governing implementation, such as statutory orders, regulations, guidelines, manuals and circulars, which are discussed below. For example, the procurement responsibilities and powers of public agencies are enshrined in detail in the *Instruction Manual* 3, rather than in the Government Procurement Act, which contains only a broad and brief set of provisions.

5.3 Profile of the public bureaucracy

The public bureaucracy consists mainly of the civil service and statutory boards. It does not include government-linked companies and such institutions of public character as universities and community grassroots organizations.

5.3.1 Personnel of the civil service

The Singapore civil service consists of sixteen ministries employing, currently, 81,508 officers (including a small number employed in organs of state), compared with 61,032 in 2001 (an increase of over 33 per cent). This total is supplemented by a further 57,212 employees working in sixty-six statutory boards, with the overall public payroll standing at 138,720 in 2013 (Department of Statistics 2014: 63). The personnel of the civil service are differentiated on the basis of four hierarchical divisions, ranging from Division I at the top to Division IV. Which division a civil servant belongs to depends upon his/her educational qualifications and the nature and level of the responsibility undertaken. Division I officers are graduates involved in management, professional or specialist work. This Division also includes officers in the Administrative Service. Division II includes executive and supervisory grades with a minimum qualification of A levels or a diploma, while Division III consists of clerical, technical and other support grades, with a minimum qualification of GCE O levels. Division IV employees are mainly those who perform manual and routine work (PWC Consulting 2002: vi).

Table 5.4 shows a large increase in Division I officers in absolute and proportionate terms over the last twelve years (they now comprise 57 per cent of all personnel) and an equally large decrease in Division III officers. These shifts are perhaps a response to the changing nature of public administration in Singapore as a result of the expansion of the range of specialist and professional roles to meet the increasingly complex demands of modern policy-making and policy implementation. The decrease in the size of Division III and Division IV may be attributed to the reduced need for straightforward administrative and routine work as a result of automation, use of IT and the streamlining of

Table 5.4 *Size and composition of civil servants in Singapore by division, 2001 and 2013*

Division	**2001**		**2013**	
	Number	Percentage of total workforce	Number	Percentage of total workforce
I	24,765	40.6	46,656	57.2
II	18,227	29.9	25,951	31.8
III	13,772	22.6	5,307	6.5
IV	4,268	7.0	3,594	4.4
Totals	61,032	100	81,508	100

Source: Department of Statistics 2012: 52; 2014: 63.

bureaucratic processes, as well as the outsourcing of certain routine functions to the private sector.

5.3.2 *The Management Associates Programme and the Administrative Service*

The Administrative Service is the elite service within the Singapore civil service. Although its numbers are small (277 officers in December 2010), it exerts a crucial influence upon the formulation and implementation of policy throughout the different ministries and statutory boards. As such, it dominates the senior positions in the civil service and enjoys an exclusive monopoly of the two highest positions, namely Permanent Secretary and Deputy Secretary. Administrative Officers are, as well, seconded to senior positions in statutory boards. Those below the rank of Permanent and Deputy Secretary also occupy important policy-making positions (Jones 2002a: 72–3; Public Service Division 2008: 19).

Entry to the Administrative Service is via a special scheme known as the Management Associates Programme (MAP) introduced in 2002. Those who wish to enter the Service, including scholarship holders, initially apply to join the MAP (they do not apply for a particular advertised position) and are subject to a rigorous selection process (Singapore Administrative Service 2012; Public Service Commission 2002: 1–2; Chan 2009). The majority of those joining the MAP enter directly from a prestigious university and have a strong academic record, many of them holders of government scholarships. In 2010, 52 out of 69 appointees were direct entrants. A small number of entrants are in-service appointees who are nominated by their own ministry (11 in 2010) or recruited from outside the civil service by means of an open advertisement (6 in 2010) (Ong 2011: 1).

Under the MAP, appointees work for two years in a ministry of their choosing, and then work for a further one to two years in other ministries. During and at the end of this period, MAP appointees are carefully assessed, and those who have demonstrated the highest levels of all-round ability are appointed to the Administrative Service. Academic record is still an important criterion of recruitment, but the MAP ensures that proven work ability in different settings is given equal consideration. About a third to half of MAP officers are selected to join the Administrative Service; the others in the MAP are deployed in one of the professional services (Public Service Division 2008: 19; 2009: 23; Chan 2009).

The salaries and bonus packages for the fourteen grades of the Administrative Service are substantial and comparable with those for a commensurate position in the private sector (Singapore Parliament 2007a: cols. 53–136; 2007b: cols. 396–494; Quah 2010: 104–16). Promotion and salary increments depend on a rigorous assessment of Administrative Officers' policy-making, management and leadership skills within the annual appraisal. In addition, they are ranked within a cohort of peers, and given a current estimated potential (CEP) score, which is a measure of career potential in terms of the most senior position an Administrative Officer is expected to reach. The CEP score can be reviewed especially at key milestone points on the Officer's career path (Jones 2002a: 81–2; Quah 2010: 79–82; Saxena 2011: 60; Singapore Parliament 2007a: cols. 53–136). An Administrative Officer who demonstrates significant ability moves up the ladder quickly, and may expect to become Deputy Secretary within seven years of entering the service. For the most effective performers, promotion to Permanent Secretary will occur after a further five to seven years (usually by the age of 40) (Jones 2002a: 80–1; Saxena 2011: 59–60). However, under the so-called 'flow-through' arrangement, Deputy Secretaries and Permanent Secretaries can only enjoy tenure for ten years. This is designed to facilitate rapid promotion of able younger officers (Jones 2002a: 81; Saxena 2011: 60). The prospects of rapid promotion together with the high salaries and bonuses are designed to prevent an outflow of the most able officers to the private sector, and to provide incentives for high level performance. Such an outflow has been a persistent problem over the years (Jones 2002a: 76–7; Singapore Parliament 2007a: cols. 53–136; Quah 2010: 104–22).

During their careers, Administrative Officers are frequently rotated, moving from one ministry to another to gain wide experience of government administration. During the first five years, they may be rotated through three or more ministries (Public Service Division 2008: 34). Given the nature of their work, they are normally concentrated in the headquarters and in the policy planning units of ministries. In addition, at any one time, 15 per cent of Administrative Officers are seconded to positions in statutory boards, the corporate sector, National Trades Union Congress, overseas organizations and the increasingly important third sector (community and grassroots organizations) (Jones 2002a: 73–4; Public Service Division 2008: 34; 2009: 23; Ong 2011: 2–3).

5.3.3 *Professional and non-graduate schemes of service*

Division I of the civil service also includes eight professional schemes of service in addition to the Administrative Service, which are linked to specialist areas (with the exception of the Management Executive Scheme, which is a generalist scheme). The officers in the professional schemes often work alongside Administrative Officers, providing necessary input into policy-making and implementation and day-to-day management, which require professional and specialist knowledge. Some of these officers previously worked in the MAP, and although failing to meet the requirements of the Administrative Service they were still considered able to work in a professional and specialist service. Other professional officers are recruited directly from the university or private sector. During their career they are also subject to rigorous appraisal including CEP ratings (Singapore Parliament 2007b: cols. 396–494; Public Service Division 2008: 34).

Many non-graduates are hired under the Management Support Scheme, and quite a number have progressed to levels of responsibility and remuneration previously reserved for professional graduate officers. From October 2014, non-graduates are able to earn faster promotion, and plans are afoot to merge some of the graduate and non-graduate schemes. This will enable performance and potential together with in-service practical training (as opposed to paper qualifications) to have greater weight in determining upward progression for graduate and non-graduate officers alike. Like the MAP, this is further testimony to a shift to a more flexible and performance-based meritocratic system (Public Service Division 2014).

5.3.4 *Statutory boards*

The public bureaucracy also consists of sixty-six statutory boards, which are established by special Acts of Parliament, and are governed by a board of directors. Statutory boards are separate from the civil service as their employees are not civil servants, and each board, as a corporation, has its own legal personality separate from that of the government. Moreover, in their day-to-day work they enjoy operational autonomy (Sin 1990: 52–3; Worthington 2003: 45; Quah 2010: 41–3, 46–8).

Nonetheless, statutory boards are subject to government control and adhere to government policy. Each is affiliated to a parent ministry and comes under the authority of the responsible minister for that ministry, who makes key policy decisions affecting the board and exercises ultimate executive control (Sin 1990: 52; Worthington 2003: 44–6, 70, 172). Members of the board are appointed by the government, some being Ministers and senior civil servants. In addition, top management positions may be held by Administrative Officers seconded from the civil service (Jones 2002a: 73–5; 2006: 260; Quah 2010: 42). The areas of public administration in which statutory boards figure most prominently are specialist and professional services, requiring management autonomy and technical expertise not normally found in the civil service itself (Sin 1990: 52; Vennewald 1994: 18; Quah 2010: 46–58). Statutory boards may set up subsidiary companies to undertake some of the programmes within their remit (Jones 2006: 261–2, 270–4).

Statutory boards derive their income from several sources to meet their operating and capital expenditure. In the case of operating expenditure, revenue may be generated from fees and charges for the services they provide. Where these cannot meet operating expenditure, income is supplemented by a grant-in-aid from the parent ministry (Jones 2006: 262). In meeting capital expenditure, statutory boards rely on capital grants from the parent ministry (now recognized as equity issued to Minister for Finance Inc.) and loans from either the parent ministry or the market through the issue of bonds (262–70).

5.3.5 *Commitment to meritocracy*

From the early days after self-government until the present, the PAP government has strongly asserted the importance of meritocracy and professional competence in the civil service, in which top positions are awarded only to the 'brightest and best'. This dovetails with meritocracy in the government itself, as mentioned above. Under the meritocracy of the civil service and statutory boards, the Division or scheme of service a civil servant enters is closely linked to his/her academic qualifications, with subsequent promotion depending on proven work performance, as measured by a rigorous appraisal system and CEP assessment. The commitment to meritocracy has resulted in an unwillingness to engage in affirmative discrimination in favour of ethnicity or gender (Jones 2002a: 72–3, 75, 81–2).

5.4 Policy formulation

5.4.1 The civil service's role in policy formulation

The senior civil service, most notably at the higher levels of the Administrative Service, plays a key role in policy formulation. However, the precise details of their responsibilities and how much discretion they exercise are not easy to pin down. Ho (2003: 263–5, 279–81) has emphasized the traditionally subordinate and instrumental role of the civil service over the years, largely concerned with matters of policy implementation, with most policy decisions left to Cabinet Ministers and Junior Ministers. This to some extent is true. The Singapore civil service has never emulated the independent policy-making and veto powers of the Japanese senior bureaucracy; nor those of the *Grands Corps* in France and senior officials in the European Commission. Furthermore, policy-making is rarely constrained by entrenched policy positions within a ministry or department as has happened occasionally in the United Kingdom. The replacement of Permanent Secretaries and Deputy Secretaries every few years, and the frequent rotation of Administrative Officers may prevent them from solidifying a policy position in any one ministry or policy area.

Nonetheless, as policy-making has become more technically complex and specialized in many areas (e.g., financial and corporate regulation, support services for niche businesses, taxation policy, maritime and port services, and integration of land transport), invariably the senior civil service has assumed a greater responsibility in drafting policy papers and undertaking policy analysis. Their policy role includes anticipating and alerting Ministers to impending and future problems and opportunities. This was emphasized by Deputy Prime Minister Teo Chee Hean in an 'Addendum to the President's Address' in 2011 (Prime Minister's Office 2011: 1). A further requirement is to gather and analyse complex information, and provide detailed policy options, including the financial costs of each option. Senior civil servants have been encouraged by government leaders to be innovative and so identify new and untried options, as well as those which can be transferred from other countries. It is also necessary for them to advise Ministers on whether a policy measure is workable, based on a careful assessment of the likelihood of achieving the expected outcomes, and avoiding unintended adverse consequences. In doing this, the senior civil servants may play an important role in evaluating policy proposals submitted by independent policy review committees, and also feedback provided by relevant organizations, individuals and the public at large in public consultations, which will be discussed below. Such analytical and advisory work in policy-making allows top civil servants a degree of influence in shaping policy measures. The influence is more pronounced if the policy is largely shaped by the information gathered, in contrast with a policy shaped by the core values of the government and ruling party.

Of course, Cabinet Ministers and Junior Ministers decide policy strategy, create the policy agenda, determine if a problem needs to be addressed and at what level, make the decision on any significant change in policy direction, and have the final say on the recommendations submitted by the civil servants. It is noticeable how Ministers when speaking in Parliament emphasize how closely they work with their top civil servants, seeing them as partners in the policy team (Ho 2003: 263–5, 276–81).

5.4.2 *Approaches to policy formulation*

The approach to policy formulation by the government and senior civil service in Singapore has been described as essentially pragmatic, entailing a willingness to introduce new policies or modify existing ones as circumstances dictate, regardless of ideological principle. For example, the expansionary budgets introduced in 2008 and 2009 resulted in a rise in public spending and a shrinking of the budget surplus to mitigate the impact of the global recession. Such budgets represented a modest departure from the principles of fiscal conservatism to which the government was strongly committed (Ghesquiere 2007: 86–91; Das 2010: 75–86, 89–95; Asian Development Bank 2012: 268).

Within this pragmatic approach, policy responses to problems have in some cases been proactive and in others reactive. Government leaders in Singapore have occasionally stressed the need to anticipate problems and proactively formulate policy in response. This has been reflected in the creation of a special office in the Public Service Division called the Centre for Strategic Futures, set up in 2009, whose job is, in the words of the Deputy Prime Minister, to conduct 'research on emerging risks and opportunities' and help 'the Public Service think long-term and strategically' (Prime Minister's Office 2011: 1; Public Service Division 2012). For example, measures were introduced between 2002 and 2008 to reduce the amount that can be withdrawn for house purchases from Central Provident Fund (CPF) accounts, to forestall the anticipated shortfall of CPF savings that can be used for retirement. This was seen as a serious problem that was likely to arise in the near future (Jones 2005a: 86–9).

In other cases, the policy response has been reactive, addressing a problem that has existed for some time and is well recognized. The new legislation to improve occupational safety and health (the Workplace Safety and Health Act introduced in 2006) was a response to a poor work safety record over a number of years in certain sectors. Another reactive response were the adjustments to the Ministry of Education's policy in the teaching of the mother tongue, which began in the late 1990s, with the most recent arising from the recommendations of the report of the 2010 Mother Tongue Language Review Committee (MTLRC) (Mother Tongue Language Review Committee 2011: 14–25, 73–6; Lee 2012: 183–201). The adjustments were intended to facilitate the learning of the mother tongue (especially Mandarin) for students who struggled to acquire the necessary proficiency. Many were Chinese students from largely English-speaking households, who had difficulty learning Mandarin. This had been a problem for quite a number of years. Lee Kuan Yew in an interview in 2009 spoke of recent improvements in teaching Mandarin in the schools as becoming 'wise after the event' (Han et al. 2011: 251). The promotion of the mother tongue language has been a bedrock policy of the Singapore government. Perhaps the delay in tackling the problem was a natural caution in modifying such a policy despite a normally pragmatic approach to policy-making.

Policy formulation in Singapore is also characterized by public consultation. This has gradually evolved since the establishment of the Feedback Unit in 1985 and further encouraged by Goh Chok Tong after he became Prime Minister in 1990 (Quah 2010: 208, 228). The Feedback Unit was superseded by the REACH (Reaching Everyone for Active Citizenry @ Home) scheme. Through its web portal, consultations are regularly undertaken on a wide range of policy issues and the feedback given provides an important input into the making of policy. Such consultations are supplemented by open-ended feedback from the general public on issues of concern, through online discussion forums, blogs and e-polls conducted under the REACH web portal. The number of feedback inputs submitted has increased significantly since REACH was set up (see Table 5.5). A discernible rise was recorded after the 2011 general election, with the monthly number of inputs averaging 260 after the election (June–November 2011) compared with 153 before it

Table 5.5 *Number of feedback inputs sent to government agencies through REACH, 2006–2011*

Year	Inputs	Percentage increase
2006	9,400	–
2007	17,000	45
2008	17,000	0
2009	26,900	58
2010	32,000	19
2011	52,000	63

Source: REACH 2011.

(January–May 2011) (REACH 2011). The consultative approach is further reflected in the regular use of independent review committees to evaluate a policy, which gather evidence from a wide range of stakeholders and submit recommendations to the government.

5.5 Policy implementation

5.5.1 Size and competence of staff in implementing agencies

A high proportion of the 138,720 employees working in ministries and statutory boards are involved in different aspects of policy implementation such as operational management and supervision, technical support, service delivery, enforcement, counter services and day-to-day administration. The various schemes involved in these aspects of policy implementation comprise over 70 per cent of the workforce.

The emphasis on meritocracy in Singapore's public bureaucracy, as mentioned above, has resulted in a high level of competence of staff involved in policy implementation. This has been achieved by requiring staff to undergo 100 hours of professional training and skills upgrading per year. The importance of training is reflected as well in the range and frequency of courses offered by the Civil Service College and other training institutions in Singapore that deal with policy implementation issues, and the size of the enrolments for these courses (Public Service Division 2008: 20, 25). The high level of competence is reflected too in the number of positions involving policy implementation functions which require academic and professional qualifications. Advertisements for such positions often specify that applicants must have a university degree or professional diploma.

5.5.2 *Levels of implementation*

The implementation process may be divided into two levels. The first level is the amplification of the operational details of a policy providing the all-important interpretations and minutiae. These may be included in statutory orders and regulations, and, at a more detailed level, in the guidelines, manuals and circulars issued by ministries. For example, the competition policy is based on the Competition Act and is implemented by the Competition Commission of Singapore (CCS) through two statutory orders, six sets of regulations and thirteen sets of guidelines, some of which include a lengthy list of provisions. The guidelines 'indicate the manner in which the CCS will interpret and give effect to the provisions of the Act' and how it 'will apply and enforce the prohibitions against anti-competitive activities under the Act' (Competition Commission of Singapore 2007).

The second level of implementation entails day-to-day operations. This involves dealing with the public by providing services, processing claims and applications, deciding entitlements, issuing notifications, conducting surveillance, inspections and scientific tests, resolving what if any enforcement action is necessary and responding to complaints and receiving feedback. This is undertaken by a large pool of counter-officers, technicians, inspectors, enforcement officers and other street-level officials, together with their supervisors. In addition, much daily operational work is also required in tax administration, land administration, tender management and infrastructure projects.

5.5.3 *Networks of cooperation and communication*

Policy implementation in Singapore, as well as policy formulation, has been characterized by cooperation between different agencies This is reflected in the use of inter-ministerial and inter-agency committees and working groups to examine policy and operational issues and to make recommendations (Public Service Division 2008: 17). The membership of such committees and working groups comprises Ministers and senior and mid-level officials drawn from different agencies, who work together in gathering and analysing evidence, and submitting proposals. Involving different agencies in such an exercise has its benefits especially when the issue is multi-faceted and spans different policy areas. In such cases, sharing of expertise and knowledge, and the articulation of different perspectives, increases the chances of reaching balanced and workable decisions on how best to implement a policy. Recent examples of such cooperation include the inter-ministerial committees on construction safety, sustainable development, climate change, terrorism and the ageing of the population.

Such cooperation has been given added importance with the recent adoption of the 'whole-of-government' or 'networked government' approach. According to the Singapore Public Sector Outcomes Review, this approach emphasizes the need to 'transcend Ministry boundaries', and for public agencies 'to work hand in glove to address any given issue effectively'. In doing this, 'agencies have agreed on a set of common outcomes, with which their priorities have been aligned' (Ministry of Finance 2010a: 1; S. Rajaratnam School of International Studies 2008: 1–3, 5, 10). Thus there has been an explicit commitment under the 'whole-of-government' approach to adopting a holistic view of many complex issues which transcend different policy areas, forging inter-agency cooperation in dealing with such issues, and, where agency functions are related or overlap, developing common outcome indicators.

In addition, policy implementation has involved communication with the public and external organizations through public consultations based on the REACH portal, referred to above. The consultation often covers rules and guidelines governing implementation and everyday operations. A recent example in 2014 is the consultation of food importers and manufacturers on the Agri-Food and Veterinary Authority's (AVA) draft proposals to amend Food Regulations. These concern new additives in food, and also safe mercury levels in fish, intended 'to provide greater transparency to the (food) industry on Singapore's requirements' (Agri-Food and Veterinary Authority of Singapore 2014).

Likewise, consultations undertaken by the independent committees of inquiry concern ways to improve implementation through practical guidelines, and everyday enforcement and service delivery. For example, the recent Censorship Review Committee report recommended the fine tuning of film and video classification and the issue of artistic performance licences (Censorship Review Committee 2010: iv, vi, viii, 8, 23).

However, occasionally communication between the public and government agencies has been undermined when the matter concerned several agencies, resulting in uncertainty about which agency was primarily responsible. This typically arose on issues relating to the upkeep and maintenance of communal living areas such as roads and footpaths, drains and other public facilities. The Singapore government established in October 2014 the Municipal Services Office in the Ministry of National Development (MND) to deal with feedback on such matters and to identify the lead agency or to coordinate the response of different agencies. This also fits into the whole-of-government approach to policy implementation (Ministry of National Development 2014; Sim 2014; Yap 2014).

5.5.4 *Decentralization and hierarchical control*

A significant degree of responsibility for policy implementation has been delegated to statutory boards resulting in their increase from thirty-seven to sixty-six statutory boards from 1989 to 2014. Statutory boards implement the bulk of regulations and also administer a wide range of support services to businesses and the public, including the provision of loans, grants and subsidies. In fact, when such schemes are announced in the budget, the Minister for Finance often will state that the operational details will be drafted by the relevant statutory board. For example, SPRING Singapore, the statutory board with responsibility for enterprise development, developed and publicized operational details for the Angel Investor Scheme announced in the 2010 budget. Under this scheme, wealthy and experienced business leaders were given major tax incentives to sink their personal capital into accredited start-up companies (Ministry of Finance 2010b: 39–40).

Decentralization has also been achieved through the outsourcing of certain services. Service standards are set by the relevant ministry or statutory board and an independent provider is chosen usually through a competitive tender to undertake management and delivery of the service. Within the terms of the contract, the provider has scope to determine how best this can be done. To illustrate, the training programmes in occupational safety and health, which were previously conducted by the Ministry of Manpower (MOM), have been outsourced to independent institutions, the major ones being PSB Academy and various polytechnics (Ministry of Manpower 2012).

The exercise of policy implementation responsibilities by statutory boards and independent providers reflects a decentralized system of implementation, in which it is more clearly separated from policy formulation and centralized hierarchical control by the senior management of ministries. This has been the result of the amount of operational decisions in many areas now requiring specialist and professional expertise, which involves greater operational autonomy. Within a statutory board, top level managers, operational managers and their front-line service staff can more readily enjoy such autonomy (Jones 2006: 261).

In other respects the decentralized system is evident. One is the delegation of budget allocations to ministries under the Block Vote Budget Allocation System (BVBAS). In addition, many recruitment and promotional functions have been transferred from the Public Service Commission (PSC) to Personnel Boards in ministries (the main exceptions being the recruitment of Administrative Officers, and their promotion to Grade 7 or above, which are still the responsibility of the PSC). Of further note is the decentralization of tender management in procurement to ministries and statutory boards (Jones 1998a: 286–7; 2002b: 45–50; Quah 2010: 82–8).

However, within statutory boards and civil service departments that undertake implementation, street level officials dealing with the public and external organizations on a daily basis are often allowed to influence how services should be delivered and laws enforced within specific situations where a professional judgement is necessary. While they are subject to controls within the local hierarchy, such officials are able to use discretion when situations so require or when special cases arise. For example, occupational safety, food safety and environmental health officers may issue warnings at their own discretion rather than summonses if minor offences occur or extenuating circumstances prevail (Jones 1998b: 31–42; 2001a: 192–8).

5.5.5 *Policy standards and objectives*

Standards and objectives have been set in policy implementation through the introduction of performance measurement. Consequently, the statutory boards or operational departments in ministries, which are the implementing agencies, systematically evaluate their performance though the use of key performance indicators and targets. This has been undertaken for the last fifteen years or so, beginning with the Budgeting For Results

(BFR) initiative implemented in 1996. The BFR sought to link, wherever possible, budget allocations to ministries to the measurement of performance (Jones 2001b: 494–506; 2004: 194–6; Quah 2010: 141). In most cases, performance data are provided in a section of a ministry or statutory board's website or in its annual report. From a study by the author of five agencies (the Singapore Prison Service, the AVA, the Ministry of the Environment and Water Resources, the Occupational Health & Safety Division of MOM and the Ministry of Information, Communications and the Arts (MICA)), the indicators adopted measured output in terms of both the amount of work done and the standard of service provided, and also the outcomes of the policy which reveal whether its ultimate goals are being achieved.

The study showed that the Singapore Prison Service (SPS) mainly focuses upon outcomes relating to prisoners becoming well adjusted, law abiding and useful members of society after release. The SPS measures these outcomes by such indicators as recidivism rates for each annual cohort of prisoners released, employability rates (number of prisoners who found a job prior to release), number of prisoners given employment training during their term in prison and percentage of prisoners who completed community-based programmes such as work release programmes, and halfway house and home detention schemes (Singapore Prison Service 2012: 88–92).

The AVA includes all three types of indicators, namely outputs, service standards and outcomes, to measure its performance. For example, in its Veterinary Public Health and Food Safety Programme, it has adopted two outcome indicators concerned with food security and food safety, namely the total number of cases of food-borne illnesses per 100,000 population and the number of key food items of which less than 50 per cent of the supply is obtained from a single country. Alongside these were five output indicators, including the total of food samples tested and the number of laboratory tests conducted, and three indicators to assess service standards, all of which measured timeliness (an example being the proportion of applications for a food licence processed within seven days) (Agri-Food and Veterinary Authority of Singapore 2011: 86–7). Performance measurement is designed to provide sectional managers, senior officials, government leaders and members of the public with a precise disclosure of how well an agency is implementing its policies and delivering its services, and what improvements are necessary.

However, the study of the five agencies shows that performance measurement has not been comprehensively developed and provides an uncertain basis to evaluate agency performance. The main limitation has been the limited criteria by which performance scores can be assessed. All the agencies relied on comparison with performance in previous years. Only one, the AVA, adopted target-setting, although this is widely recognized as an important means to assess performance based on how far the target was achieved or not. Even then, most of the AVA's targets were regularly met, and, in some cases, easily exceeded. This was compounded by the absence of any upward adjustment of targets in the AVA in response to regularly meeting or exceeding them (Agri-Food and Veterinary Authority of Singapore 2011: 86–7).

A further limitation in the assessment of performance scores was the lack in all five agencies of benchmarking against the performance of similar agencies in other jurisdictions with which relevant comparisons can be made (such as some of the developed states of East Asia). There was no system of rating performance scores using a rating scale (usually a five- or three-point scale), often linked either to target achievement or to comparisons of performance through benchmarking. A rating scale readily identifies weak performance (below expectations), average performance (meets expectations) and good performance (exceeds expectations). Benchmarking and ratings may of course be developed in the future as greater importance is attached to performance measurement as a tool of agency evaluation.

5.5.6 *Disposition of implementers*

Achieving intended policy outcomes may rest in part on the disposition of the implementers towards the policy itself and towards the public and groups to whom the policy applies. By and large, policy implementers in Singapore have interpreted and applied policy in a way consistent with policy objectives. This applies to the interpretation of the policy when translated into more detailed and specific requirements through statutory orders, regulations, guidelines, manuals and circulars. Consistency is also reflected in the application of the policy in everyday operations, although, as mentioned above, discretion is permitted when professional judgement is called for or special cases arise. There is little evidence of policy implementers holding values contrary to the policies they administer and seeking to frustrate the achievement of the intended outcomes. Consequently, corruption is not a serious problem in Singapore.

The disposition of policy implementers towards the public at large and to the individuals and organizations they deal with, has been marked in recent years by a greater emphasis given to customer service. To foster better quality customer service, the Service Improvement Unit (SIU) was set up in April 1991, which drew upon feedback from the general public. The objective of better customer service was incorporated into PS21 (Public Service for the 21st Century), introduced in May 1995, which mapped out the vision and future direction for the Singapore public service (Haque 2009: 255–6; Quah 2010: 147–9; Saxena 2011: 88–94). Several steps have been taken to enhance customer service under the guidance of the SIU and the Service Quality Committee of PS21. One is to improve transparency by providing a greater range of information and guidance to members of the public about regulations, schemes and entitlements. Another is to trim red tape and paperwork with respect to the submission and processing of requests, applications and claims, an example being the now streamlined procedures in applications to purchase a Housing and Development Board (HDB) apartment (Housing and Development Board 2012). An additional benefit is to reduce the time taken in processing such applications and claims, often used as an indicator to assess agency performance, as discussed above. To achieve greater customer orientation, emphasis has been given under the guidance of the SIU to training and incentivizing counter staff so that they are amenable to the public, provide relevant advice and display a generally courteous and helpful attitude to the public (Quah 2010: 148–50, 189; Saxena 2011: 91–4, 139–41).

A further initiative in streamlining services was the setting up of the Cut Waste Panel (CWP) in September 2003. It invites suggestions from the public on eliminating unnecessary procedures and resource usage with a view to making cost savings and achieving greater efficiency. The suggestions, which may include clarification of existing practices, are submitted by email to the CWP portal. The panel then identifies those suggestions which relate to cutting waste and forwards them to the relevant agency. The agency's reply, which is vetted by the CWP, is sent within twenty-two days to the suggestor (Cut Waste Panel 2012a). From 2003 to December 2011, 3,592 suggestions were received which concerned cutting waste. Among these suggestions, 3.1 per cent were accepted, 20.5 per cent were already being undertaken, and 14.9 per cent were considered unsuitable for implementation. A further 61.5 per cent were requests by suggestors for clarification on how specific concerns were being addressed. Since 2003, the savings in costs from cutting waste through the CWP scheme have been over SGD11.5 million (Cut Waste Panel 2012b; Quah 2010: 162–3).

Another important scheme to improve the practices and services of the public bureaucracy are the Work Improvement Teams (WITs), which were first set up in 1987. These are work groups comprising six to ten staff members in the same office or section, who are given the task of identifying areas of work where improvements could be made or problems exist, and then to determine, plan and implement a solution. Awards are given for viable solutions with the best projects given a gold award. The WITs programme is based on the idea that agencies must and can continuously improve, and has become an integral part of PS21. Over the years WITs have encountered various challenges. Not least is the need to sustain the momentum in implementing projects and to continue identifying new problems in working practices and determining viable solutions. A further challenge is to ensure that team members remain involved in a WITs project when demands are made on their working time by everyday duties (Civil Service College 2006: 8–56; Public Service Division 2008: 25; Quah 2010: 159–65).

Improved customer service and more efficient and faster operations have been made possible through the development of e-government. A wide range of online services are now available which benefit the public. These provide information and guidance, entail streamlined procedures and facilitate transactions and payments, usually involving a simply constructed single access window. Examples are the Government Electronic Business (GeBiz) as the e-procurement portal and the online business licensing service (Quah 2010: 153–5; GeBiz 2014; EnterpriseOne 2014).

One of the consequences of improving customer service has been the streamlining of bureaucratic regulations and procedures for the business sector. According to the World Bank's Doing Business Survey, in 2014, Singapore was ranked first among 189 countries for the ease of doing business. This assessment in part covers regulatory requirements, bureaucratic procedures and red tape, which can impede doing business across different business activities. It is evident from the survey that such regulations and procedures have been kept to a minimum by the Singapore civil service. For example, only three bureaucratic procedures are involved in starting a business (i.e., obtaining a business registration), taking two and a half days to complete, giving Singapore fifth place in the global ranking of ease of starting a business (World Bank 2013: 222).

Three reasons may be given for Singapore's high rankings. The most important is a commitment by the government that bureaucratic impediments to business activity should be no more than are necessary. The second reason is the desire to keep public agencies lean and efficient, avoiding unnecessary and wasteful paperwork and procedures. The third reason is the provision of online services and single access windows to make it easier for businesses to meet regulatory and procedural requirements. This increases Singapore's competitiveness in attracting foreign investment and reinforces its policy of zero tolerance for corruption by reducing the opportunities for corruption caused by red tape.

5.5.7 Policy resources

Substantial revenue resulting from strong economic growth and an efficient system of tax collection has ensured that the spending requirements of implementing agencies are properly met, as well as generating a budget surplus. A key reform of public spending was the BVBAS introduced in 1989, under which, budget allocations for individual programmes, hitherto decided by the Ministry of Finance, were delegated to the parent ministry and authorized by its Permanent Secretary. This has enabled ministries in their own right to allocate operational spending according to the funding needs of their programmes and of their affiliated statutory boards. The BVBAS has also provided the ministries with the flexibility to transfer funds from one programme to another as operational spending priorities change even during the course of the financial year. One of the benefits of this is to reduce the possibility of programmes being overfunded or underfunded. Similar flexibility has been given to ministries in relation to their capital budgets, allowing them to adjust funding allocations within a capital project and allocate funding from year to year during the course of the project as its progress and circumstances dictated (Jones 1998a: 286–7; 2001c: 142–4; Quah 2010: 141).

Although funding for operational and capital spending has been forthcoming, managers in ministries and statutory boards are expected to make savings, avoid waste, and so secure a greater return for each dollar spent. An example is the system of procurement. Ministries and statutory boards now undertake their own purchasing, with the exception of bulk purchases and information technology systems, but are required to achieve value for money through open and competitive tenders, in which they must choose the lowest or most advantageous bid. Further, to ensure efficient use of resources, accrual accounting has been adopted to varying degrees in both the civil service and statutory boards. This necessitates that non-cash costs are recognized in the accounts, such as depreciation, imputed rentals, deferred capital grants, costs of capital (return on equity) and records of expenditure when goods and services are received (not when payments are made). It is reasoned that accrual accounting enables the managers to be informed of the full costs of their programmes and therefore better enables them to make savings where necessary (Jones 2005b: 109–15; 2006: 266–7).

Accountability in the use of financial and physical resources is enforced through the Office of the Auditor-General (AG). The AG's audits of public accounts cover ministries, statutory boards, government funds, certain government-owned companies and government-regulated accounts. Audits of statutory boards are often undertaken by commercial auditors with the approval of the AG (Auditor-General 2014: 2). The regular annual audit by the AG, known as the financial statements audit, is concerned with the extent of compliance with the relevant statutes and stipulated procedures, and assesses whether a proper disclosure of accounts has been published which reflects fairly and accurately all the financial transactions undertaken. A further concern is to determine whether proper accounting and transactional records have been kept, and if adequate controls were exercised to prevent non-compliance and irregularities in revenue collection and spending (Auditor-General 2014: 1–4; 2011: 8). In addition, from time to time, the AG undertakes an in-depth audit, known as a 'selective audit'. This provides a more detailed assessment of compliance, and highlights, too, 'excess, extravagance or gross inefficiency leading to waste and whether measures to prevent them are in place' (Auditor-General 2014: 1; 2011: 9–10, 14). As a measure of how rigorous the audit can be, the AG's report of 2013/14 highlighted lapses by five ministries and thirteen statutory boards. The audit revealed lapses in the administration of grants, commitment of public funds, administration of schemes and projects, management of land and assets, and procurement (Auditor-General 2014: i–iv, 3). Referring to the procurement lapses in one government agency, the AG's report for 2013/14 highlighted 'instances of contracts awarded through waiver of competition without compelling reasons. There were also irregularities in sourcing for quotations, lapses in evaluation of quotations, and payments without adequate evidence that the goods or services had been received.' The report continued: 'as a result there was no assurance that this entity had obtained value for money for its purchases. The failure to ensure open and fair competition could also subject the entity to allegations of unfairness and lack of transparency' (Auditor-General 2014: 6).

Accountability in policy implementation and the use of resources is reinforced through the Corrupt Practices Investigation Bureau (CPIB), which is part of the Prime Minister's Office and responsible for implementing the Prevention of Corruption Act. Its task is to investigate complaints regarding alleged corruption by public officers, and any other evidence that indicates malpractice and misconduct. The CPIB has wide powers of investigation, and thereby spares no effort to unveil corrupt dealings. It can arrest suspects, cross-examine them, question witnesses, search premises, seize assets and recommend prosecutions to the Public Prosecutor. As part of its investigation, it can inspect bank, share and purchase accounts. If there is insufficient evidence to mount a prosecution, suspected officials may be referred to their Head of Department for disciplinary action with the concurrence of the Public Prosecutor (Corrupt Practices Investigation Bureau 2014; Quah 2003: 114–19).

Furthermore, the CPIB reviews controls within ministries, statutory boards and other public bodies to ensure that evidence of corruption can be brought to light and opportunities for corrupt dealings are minimized. If the review shows failings in work methods and practices that could lead to corruption, the CPIB can recommend that remedial measures are taken (Corrupt Practices Investigation Bureau 2014; Quah 2003: 118). The CPIB may also investigate evidence of corruption in the private sector. As part of its work to prevent corruption, it regularly conducts lectures and seminars to educate public officers, especially those who come into contact with the public, on how corruption can occur and what their responsibilities are in avoiding and reporting corrupt dealings (Corrupt Practices Investigation Bureau 2014). The CPIB has been over the years an effective instrument in combating corruption in both the public and private sectors, and has been one of the key factors contributing to Singapore's low level of corruption (Quah 2003: 124–6; 2010: 184–90).

5.6 Singapore's implementation of two ASEAN agreements

The second part of the chapter deals with the ASEAN context influencing governance in Singapore and has two objectives. First, it will examine the overall role and contribution of Singapore in shaping and implementing ASEAN agreements. The second objective is to discuss the implementation of the ACD and AMMTC/SOMTC in Singapore. Over the years, Singapore has closely identified with ASEAN and fully supported agreements promoting ASEAN cooperation and integration. This arises from its small size and its lack of resources and self-sufficiency necessitating dependence on and cooperation with other states. This section deals with the Singapore government's role in the formulation and implementation of these agreements in Singapore.

5.6.1 Singapore government's contribution to ASEAN measures

Singapore has contributed substantially to dialogue and agreements fostering closer cooperation and integration within the ASEAN. This has included the involvement of Singapore representatives sometimes making a significant contribution in various steering and coordinating committees, task forces and working groups, and regularly attending regional meetings, forums, seminars and workshops. In so doing, the Singapore government has played its part in shaping a wide range of ASEAN agreements, such as treaties, directives, protocols, actions plans, working programmes and other commitments where harmonization is sought. The input is all the more valuable when elements of such measures are already well established in Singapore, allowing the Singapore government to draw upon its experience in the drafting of key provisions.

In addition, at meetings dealing with the practical implementation of ASEAN initiatives, Singapore delegates are sometimes in a good position to impart the relevant knowledge and skills. Such input is particularly useful when matters of a specialist and technical nature are under consideration, in which Singapore government agencies may have more experience than the agencies in other member states. This may be described as capacity building.

An example of Singapore's role in capacity building was provided by the tenth meeting of the ASEAN Experts Group on Competition, which was held in Brunei Darussalam in November 2012.[1] The remit of the meeting was to consider how best to implement a plan to harmonize competition law across ASEAN. This included reviewing the progress made so far to this end, to develop the competencies required in framing and implementing competition law, and to lay the groundwork for a manual spelling out the operational requirements that could be used by the member states. Although the official status of the Singapore delegation (officers from the CCS) was the same as that of the other delegations, it was specifically called upon in the plenary and breakout sessions of the meeting to explain the application of competition law in Singapore (the Competition Act and its implementing regulations and guidelines). The Singapore delegates had a specific knowledge of how to apply competition law whilst in many of the other member states competition law did not exist or was in its infancy (*Borneo Bulletin* 2012: 1; *Borneo Post* 2012).

A further contribution of the Singapore government to the implementation of ASEAN agreements is the provision of technical assistance, based on the resources and expertise of the relevant agencies. An example is the technical assistance provided by the Meteorological Service of the National Environmental Agency of Singapore (MSNEAS) to the ASEAN

[1] The meeting was attended by the author.

Specialized Meteorological Centre (ASMC) as part of the ASEAN programme to combat trans-boundary haze pollution in the region (Jones 2005c: 65–84). The responsibilities of the MSNEAS are, from the analysis of weather patterns, to predict and provide early warning of outbreaks of forest burning in neighbouring states, most notably Indonesia. When they occur, it then identifies, classifies and maps the areas of burning (hotspots) and measures the extent and direction of the resultant haze pollution. This work is undertaken by the meteorologists of MSNEAS through its remote sensing and satellite reception facilities. The information is then sent to the ASMC and subsequently forwarded to the relevant authorities in Indonesia (Chiam 2010). Another example are the laboratories in Singapore authorized by SPRING for testing products from other ASEAN states to ensure that they meet the technical standard required in ASEAN free trade arrangements (SPRING 2014: 59–72).

5.6.2 *Singapore's implementation of ASEAN agreements*

For its part the Singapore government has been committed over the years to implement effectively within its jurisdiction any ASEAN instrument to which it has been a signatory. There are a number of aspects of the implementation worth noting.

If the instrument is legally binding, it is of course submitted to Parliament for ratification and converted into an appropriate domestic legal instrument. This normally takes the form of an amendment to an existing statute or of new subsidiary legislation such as a statutory order or regulation. An example is the

ASEAN Trade in Goods Agreement (ATIGA) of 2010 under the ASEAN Free Trade Area (AFTA) Agreement, which has been translated into domestic law through the amendments to the Customs (Duties) Order under the Customs Act (International Enterprise Singapore 2014; Singapore Customs 2011). ATIGA is the main instrument for implementing the Common Effective Preferential Tariff whereby goods produced within ASEAN entering Singapore (and a number of other ASEAN states) are zero rated for customs purposes.

The implementation of ASEAN arrangements is also undertaken at the administrative level through specific and detailed guidelines, circulars and programmes provided by the ministries and statutory boards. An example is the circular sent to manufacturers and traders by Singapore Customs in 2010, spelling out in detail the procedures and guidelines to be followed when importing goods from other ASEAN states under ATIGA. These include the forms to complete, cost statements to be disclosed and the certificates to be submitted (Singapore Customs 2010). The circular also contained an explanation of ATIGA, reflecting a commitment to raising awareness in the business community about the agreement.

Facilitating the implementation of ASEAN agreements is the existence of high levels of organizational, technical and personnel capacity in the Singapore public bureaucracy. This applies where implementation involves complex and technical processes such as product standard testing under ATIGA (SPRING 2014: 1–23). Furthermore, low levels of corruption remove major obstacles to fair and impartial implementation. For example, the absence of bribery in customs administration ensures a genuinely free flow of goods from other ASEAN states as stipulated by ATIGA (International Enterprise Singapore 2014).

Decisions on ASEAN matters which affect Singapore are to a certain extent decentralized. The Ministry of Foreign Affairs (MFA) has an ASEAN Directorate with seventeen officers, and, together with a number of other regional Directorates, comes under the purview of the Deputy Secretary (International) of the MFA. The ASEAN Directorate handles foreign policy and general matters relating to ASEAN. Other more specialized matters concerning specific sectors are dealt with by the relevant ministry or statutory board. This is reflected in the attendance at many of the ASEAN meetings, forums and workshops within a specific sector by delegates from the competent ministry or statutory board. For example, the Ministry of Trade and Industry (MTI) has an ASEAN Division that handles trade negotiations with ASEAN (Ministry of Trade and Industry 2012). In addition, there are no parliamentary committees with responsibility for vetting the translation of ASEAN measures into domestic legal instruments. Instead, each ministry or statutory board is responsible for the instruments by which ASEAN arrangements relevant to its policy area are implemented.

5.7 Implementing the ASEAN Cosmetic Directive (ACD)

5.7.1 *The ACD*

The ASEAN Cosmetic Directive (ACD), signed in 2003, provides a common set of rules, applicable to all member states, for controlling the manufacture and distribution of cosmetics products. It was subsequently amplified by a list of appendices and guidelines. The purpose of the ACD is to ensure protection against the health hazards posed by certain of these products. The ACD is binding and, as such, each state was required to incorporate the various provisions into its domestic law. In so doing, it had discretion to amplify and interpret those provisions for the purpose of implementation (ASEAN 2003). This first case study examines: (1) how the ACD and its appendices have been implemented in Singapore; and (2) what factors have influenced the effectiveness of the implementation.

5.7.2 *Regulatory scheme based on the ACD*

The ACD was incorporated into Singapore law in 2007 with the passing of the Health Products Act, and the issue of the Health Products (Cosmetic Products – ASEAN Cosmetic Directive) Regulations, 2007 (amended in 2010) (Attorney-General's Chambers 2008; 2010). The latter were supplemented by a set of regulatory guidelines (revised in 2011), which also include in their annex two of the appendices of the ACD (Health Sciences Authority 2011a). Responsibility for implementing the Act and for drafting and implementing the regulations and guidelines is undertaken by the Health Sciences Authority (HSA), which is a statutory board. Day-to-day implementation and enforcement are undertaken by the Health Products Regulation Group of the HSA.

The HSA regulations and guidelines cover all the main aspects of controlling cosmetics manufacture and distribution as laid down in the ACD. In nearly all cases, they replicate the relevant provisions in the ACD and its appendices and guidelines, although the sequencing and wording of some of the provisions differ. In formulating its cosmetics regulations, the HSA added a stipulation, not in the ACD, that judicial penalties may be applied when companies breach the regulations and guidelines (Attorney-General's Chambers 2008; 2010: ss. 4–11). However, in other respects, the appendices and guidelines of the ACD are more extensive and detailed than the HSA regulations and guidelines, such as how a cosmetics product should be tested and what may be claimed as a benefit of a cosmetics product (ASEAN 2007: 3–14).

5.7.3 *Monitoring and enforcement*

The HSA monitors the cosmetics industry to ensure compliance with both the ACD and its own regulations and guidelines. The monitoring function requires the manufacturer or distributor to notify the HSA of each product accompanied by 'such particulars, information, documents and samples of the cosmetics product as the Authority may require' (Attorney-General's Chambers 2010: s. 4; Health Sciences Authority 2009a: 33; 2009b: 1–2; 2011a: 8). If there is a possibility that it contains prohibited ingredients, the HSA may require the company to send the product for testing (this can be done voluntarily at any time). In 2008/09 there were 108,200 notifications, and since then the number has exceeded 130,000 in each year, with 138,745 recorded in 2012/13 (Health Sciences Authority 2009a: 39–40; 2010: 43; 2011b: 45; 2012: 78; 2013: 86).

The second aspect of the monitoring function of the HSA is the auditing of manufacturers' and distributors' product information files (PIFs) to check if the information about the product is in order. Audits are conducted 'routinely or on an ad hoc basis'. Ad hoc audits are normally carried out when a sample test has shown the product to contain a banned ingredient, or when an adverse event has occurred or when a complaint based on credible information is received from a member of the public (Health Sciences Authority 2009a: 33; 2009b: 2; 2011a: 24–32).

A further aspect of the monitoring process is selective sampling and laboratory testing of cosmetics products after they have been placed on the market, to check if they contain ingredients that pose a health risk (Health Sciences Authority 2009a: 33; 2009b: 2; 2010: 36, 60; 2011a: 10). Laboratory testing is undertaken regularly, but will be conducted too if the product notification, PIF audit, and an adverse event report suggest that a health risk exists (Attorney-General's Chambers 2010; Health Sciences Authority 2009a: 33).

Through its monitoring programme, the HSA is responsible for taking enforcement action when the product is found to be unsafe, or when the rules laid down in the ACD itself and the HSA regulations and guidelines have been violated. Failure to submit a notification, compiling an incomplete or inaccurate PIF, or not reporting an adverse event may be penalized through a fine or jail term under the HSA regulations (Attorney-General's Chambers 2010: ss. 4, 10, 11; Health Sciences Authority 2011a: 13). In practice, where such offences are committed for the first time and do not lead to harm to the consumer, the offender would more probably be given a warning.

In addition, when the cosmetics product is proven to be unsafe or to contain a banned substance, the HSA, in accordance with the ACD, has powers requiring its withdrawal from the market (Health Sciences Authority 2011a: 13). Products too may be withdrawn if evidence is gathered from other countries that particular ingredients not yet prohibited may be harmful (Health Sciences Authority 2011b: 37). Withdrawal of the product is the most common type of enforcement action taken by the HSA. In 2008/09, 270 products were withheld/withdrawn; in 2009/10, the figure was 425 products (Health Sciences Authority 2009a: 40; 2010: 43).

5.7.4 *Educational outreach*

The HSA has also favoured a preventive approach to ensure compliance with the ACD, based on educational outreach to the cosmetics industry. This has been done in partnership with the Cosmetic, Toiletry and Fragrance Association of Singapore (CTFAS), which is generally the principal organizer of an outreach event. Other government agencies and private businesses may participate as partners.

The purpose of such events is to familiarize manufacturers and distributors with the requirements of the ACD and the HSA regulations and guidelines, and the steps necessary to achieve compliance. The events in the main take the form of workshops and, on a more informal level, 'tea talks'. Since 2008, quite a number of events have been held. These events explain the requirements of the ACD and also provide hands-on training to enable companies to achieve compliance and offer advice in response to queries in question-and-answer sessions (Cosmetic, Toiletry and Fragrance Association of Singapore 2014a; 2014b). The educational outreach is consistent with the spirit of the ACD since many of the provisions in the appendices and guidelines, as mentioned above, contain explanations and advice.

5.7.5 Factors influencing the ACD's implementation

Despite minor divergences, the regulatory system for cosmetics products in Singapore based on the ACD, as described above, and the monitoring, enforcement and outreach activities which are regularly undertaken, attest to largely effective implementation. This has been due to four factors. First, Singapore has both the resources and expertise for testing cosmetics products. Of particular importance is the cosmetics laboratory of the HSA, which is internationally accredited and provides a wide range of testing services, including spectrometry and liquid and gas chromatography (Health Sciences Authority 2010: 60; 2011b: 62; 2013: 59). The second factor is the widespread consumption of cosmetics products amongst the local population. With increasing affluence and rising incomes in Singapore, the consumption of non-essential or luxury goods, which enhance appearance and status, such as cosmetics items, inevitably rises. Given that some cosmetics products may carry a risk, such mass consumption obviously calls for a degree of control. The third factor is the willingness of the HSA to enter into a partnership with the cosmetics industry through the CTFAS for purposes of education and feedback. The fourth factor responsible for the effective implementation of the ACD is the existence of regulatory schemes administered by the HSA for other health products over a number of years. These include pharmaceutical products, health supplements, homeopathic and traditional medicines, and Chinese proprietary medicines. Such schemes may have perhaps provided a guide and the necessary experience for a similar scheme for cosmetics.

5.8 Implementing the ASEAN Ministerial Meeting on Transnational Crime (AMMTC)/ Senior Officials Meeting on Transnational Crime (SOMTC)

5.8.1 ASEAN agreements on transnational crime and AMMTC/SOMTC

In response to the growing threat of transnational crime, the member states of ASEAN drew up an agreement in 1997 entitled the ASEAN Declaration on Transnational Crime. The agreement, signed by the Minister for Home Affairs or Minister for the Interior, committed the member states to a common effort in fighting transnational crime. Subsequently, the Declaration was amplified by two further agreements relating to implementation: the ASEAN Plan of Action to Combat Transnational Crime in 1999 and the Work Programme to Implement the ASEAN Plan of Action to Combat Transnational Crime in 2002. The body responsible for reviewing and overseeing the implementation of the ASEAN agreements on transnational crime is the ASEAN Ministerial Meeting on Transnational Crime (AMMTC), which is described as 'the highest policy making body on ASEAN cooperation in combating transnational crime' (Sovannasam 2011: 78–83). The AMMTC is supported by the ASEAN Senior Officials Meeting on Transnational Crime (SOMTC), mainly senior level officials in the Ministry of Home Affairs or the Ministry of the Interior (79–83).

This second case study examines the implementation of the ASEAN agreements in Singapore and resolutions of the AMMTC/SOMTC with respect to two contrasting cases. One is combating terrorism in which implementation has been largely effective, and the other is combating trafficking in persons in which implementation has been less effective.

5.8.2 Terrorism

For many years, the Singapore government has been alert to the possibility of terrorist attacks in the country and in recent years has focused on the threat posed by the terrorist group *Jemaah Islamiyah* (JI). It has been equally concerned that Singapore as a communications hub could be used as a transit for terrorists to carry out attacks elsewhere. For this reason the government has spared no effort in ensuring that the police and armed forces have the requisite legal powers, resources and expertise to prevent terrorist attacks and to track down terrorists (Weatherbee 2009: 170–7; Hor 2012: 272–89).

The powers and responsibilities to combat terrorism are laid down in several statutes and regulations. These include the United Nations (Anti-terrorism Measures) Regulations of 2001 and subsequent amendments; the Terrorism

(Suppression of Bombings) Act of 2007 and the Singapore Armed Forces (Amendment) Act of 2007, which enhances the role of the military in searching and detaining terrorist suspects (Attorney-General's Chambers 2003; 2007a; 2007b). Under these and other measures, priority is given to gathering intelligence about terrorist networks, ensuring constant surveillance at check points, vital installations and vulnerable public places, and detaining terrorist suspects. No less important are enhancing public awareness of the dangers of terrorism and ensuring public authorities and the community are well prepared in the event of a terrorist attack. The involvement of the community is part of the concept of 'total defence' which is at the heart of Singapore's security strategy. Much of the responsibility in preventing terrorist attacks and tracking down terrorists is undertaken by special enforcement units, namely the Singapore Special Operations Force, Special Operations Command and Chemical, Biological, Radiological and Explosive Defence Group (Hor 2012: 272–9). Such measures to combat terrorism closely correspond with, and in some respects go beyond, the provisions relating to terrorism in the ASEAN agreements and the resolutions of the AMMTC/SOMTC.

Furthermore, as prescribed in the ASEAN agreements and the resolutions of the AMMTC/SOMTC, Singapore has cooperated with its ASEAN neighbours through intelligence sharing about terrorist networks, passing on information about an intended terrorist attack and tracking down terrorists and deporting them to a member state where they are wanted. This has been exemplified by several instances of cooperation between Singapore and its closest neighbours, Indonesia and Malaysia, which have involved sharing of information and handing over of wanted persons. One example was the tracking down and arrest by the Malaysian authorities in early 2012 of three members of the JI network wanted in Singapore, to which country they were soon after deported (Chen 2012).

5.8.3 Trafficking in persons

The ASEAN agreements identify trafficking in persons (TIP) for purposes of prostitution and forced labour as a growing transnational crime (Weatherbee 2009: 190–5). However, until recently, only limited progress had been made in Singapore in implementing many of the recommendations relating to TIP. Little was done to undertake a country study or self-assessment and provide case studies of TIP, or to enhance awareness of it in the enforcement and judicial community. Although several laws exist that prohibit TIP, they do not reflect the complexity of TIP offences, which remain ill-defined, nor do they stipulate penalties commensurate with the offences. Nor had much been done to build capacity through specialized enforcement teams and by information sharing and cooperation amongst different agencies. Moreover, low priority had been given to prevention and to the rehabilitation of victims. This was perhaps due to the limited numbers of victims who were reported or detected. Lastly, there was little evidence of initiatives to liaise and develop joint exercises with other member states to combat TIP (Singapore Inter-Agency Taskforce on Trafficking in Persons

2012). Such actions had all been proposed in the ASEAN Plan of Action and Work Programme.

However, in 2010, mindful of the growing need to address TIP crimes, an inter-agency task force, the Singapore Inter-Agency Taskforce on Trafficking in Persons (SITTP), was set up by the Singapore government to identify measures to combat them. It comprised several government agencies and private associations. After a public consultation, the task force drafted a National Plan of Action which was announced in March 2012 to be implemented over the following three years (Singapore Parliament 2011: col. 14; Durai 2012; Singapore Inter-Agency Taskforce on Trafficking in Persons 2012).

The National Plan includes measures to improve the collection of data, with reports to be regularly compiled about trends in TIP. Attention is to be given to defining in more detail TIP offences and determining appropriate penalties, to be incorporated into possible new legislation (Singapore Inter-Agency Taskforce on Trafficking in Persons 2012: 9, 11). At the same time, enforcement is to be strengthened through expediting investigations and prosecutions and setting up a specialized enforcement unit (11). Equally important is the intention to raise awareness about TIP in enforcement agencies, the judiciary and the business community, as well as amongst the general public (4–5, 8–9, 11). Emphasis is to be given to the care and rehabilitation of victims through medical and counselling services, improved management of shelters and the provision of legal advice. It is also planned that training programmes will be enhanced to improve detection of trafficking offences and to provide care for victims. What is more, references are made in the National Plan to 'stronger collaboration with foreign governments and embassies', with the intention of 'engag[ing] enforcement agencies of source countries for joint-investigation and sharing of information' (14–15). Overall, the National Plan of Action will bring Singapore in line with the majority of the requirements of the ASEAN Action Plan and Work Programme and also with the provisions of the United Nations Protocol to Prevent, Suppress and Punish Trafficking in Persons, Especially Women and Children.

Many of the measures advocated in the National Plan have now been converted into legislation in the Human Trafficking Bill passed by the Singapore Parliament in November 2014 (Singapore Parliament 2014). Despite the National Plan and the Bill, Singapore has yet to sign and ratify the United Nations Protocol to Prevent, Suppress and Punish Trafficking in Persons, Especially Women and Children. But, speaking at the second reading of the Bill, the Senior Minister of State for Home Affairs announced that 'we intend to ratify [the Protocol] after the proper requirements are met' (Singapore Parliament 2014). Although combating TIP is still a work in progress, the new legislation is a significant step forward.

5.8.4 *Explaining the difference*

The differences in the progress made in implementing the provisions of the ASEAN Declaration, Action Plan and Work Programme and resolutions of the AMMTC/SOMTC with respect to terrorism and TIP may be attributed to the degree of threat posed by the two types of transnational crime.

Terrorism has posed an ever present and serious threat to the population of Singapore, which could also undermine its economic well-being. This is due to the existence of terrorist networks in the region and Singapore's role as a transport and communications hub. The threat posed by TIP is less imminent, due to a relatively small number of TIP offences, although in the long term it could affect Singapore's reputation for ethical standards, effective law enforcement and low crime.

5.9 Conclusion

5.9.1 Policy implementation in Singapore

Policy implementation in Singapore is characterized by these eight features: (1) strong institutional capacity in implementing agencies through a proper framework of rules and responsibilities, high standards of professional competence, based on meritocracy and the availability of resources and funding to meet operational requirements; (2) decentralization in service delivery, budget allocations, personnel management and procurement; (3) emphasis on efficiency, cost saving and avoidance of waste in the use of resources, which is reflected in competitive procurement, reducing unnecessary procedures (exemplified by the Cut Waste Panel) and the use of accrual accounting; (4) inter-agency cooperation in implementing policies (the 'whole-of-government' or 'networked government' approach); (5) performance measurement of the implementing agencies through indicators that measure output, service standards and outcomes; (6) public consultation over how policy is implemented through REACH and independent inquiries; (7) customer-centred disposition of implementing agencies, based on minimizing red tape, streamlined procedures, responsive counter services and online services to facilitate both the public and business sectors; and (8) rigorous audit scrutiny which focuses on both compliance and value for money and strong anti-corruption measures to deter bribery, embezzlement and other forms of corruption.

Three of the above features of policy implementation are also evident in policy formulation, namely meritocracy, public consultation and the 'whole-of-government' approach, including inter-agency cooperation. However, it should be pointed out that in contrast with the decentralized system of implementation, policy formulation is highly centralized, being largely exercised by Ministers, Junior Ministers and Permanent and Deputy Secretaries at the headquarters of the ministries. In addition, whilst meritocracy is common to both policy formulation and implementation, it is much more elite-based through the Administrative Service in the case of policy formulation.

5.9.2 *Policy recommendations*

One of the weaknesses of policy implementation in Singapore has been performance measurement, as indicated above. In view of the limitations identified, three recommendations may be made. First, more attention should be focused on setting targets and making those targets demanding. In addition, comparisons of performance with other developed countries could be introduced, and a three- or five-point rating system should be adopted. The purpose of these three recommendations is to provide a more adequate basis for assessing performance.

A further question concerns the future of public consultation. The rate of acceptance of suggestions submitted has varied a great deal. For example, for some consultations undertaken by the Ministry of Law and Ministry of Manpower, the rate of acceptance was very low, whereas in consultations by the Ministry of Finance with regard to taxation, a significant number of suggestions submitted were accepted. Of course, there may be good reasons to reject suggestions, such as budgetary constraints or divergence from core policy objectives. However, in the future it may be a good idea to avoid low acceptance rates if suggestions indicate a degree of unanimity amongst respondents, especially if they reflect informed views of the business, professional and voluntary associations.

It was mentioned above that the promotion of Administrative Officers to Deputy and Permanent Secretaries was tied to certain age thresholds. A recommendation may be made to allow greater flexibility in this matter. While age tagging of promotion may favour those who show early promise within the fast promotion stream, it may work against those 'late-bloomers' who realize their potential at a later stage, in their mid-career. The latter may thus be denied the opportunity of reaching top positions despite their high calibre. In addition, flexibility may be shown in the application of the flow-through arrangement which limits the tenure to ten years of Permanent and Deputy Secretaries. In certain situations, it may be appropriate to extend the tenure of these positions where experience and institutional memory would be a valuable asset in making policy and operational decisions.

5.9.3 *Singapore's contribution to and implementation of ASEAN agreements*

In discussing Singapore's contribution to and implementation of ASEAN agreements in general, it is noteworthy that Singapore has in the main been fully supportive of measures to promote ASEAN cooperation and integration. Its contribution has entailed three key roles. One is to provide guidance in shaping the details of ASEAN agreements, where it possesses the necessary experience and expertise. The second is to contribute to capacity building for other states of ASEAN to enable them to implement the agreements. The third is to provide technical assistance to further facilitate their implementation by other states. In implementing ASEAN agreements, Singapore has developed the necessary legal and operational frameworks, and has benefited from the high level of institutional capacity of its government agencies, created by its meritocratic system, as well as from the low level of corruption. However, the implementation process has not been centralized in any one agency.

The case studies have focused on how Singapore has implemented the ACD and the AMMTC/SOMTC. They show how the implementation of both instruments reflects the features of mainstream policy implementation, as indicated in this chapter. First, the ability of the Singapore government to implement both instruments stems again from the strong institutional capacity in various regulatory and enforcement agencies. This has been achieved as a result of the meritocratic system with its emphasis on qualifications, training, performance appraisal and specialized knowledge and skills

In applying the ACD, the HSA engages in a partnership with the CTFAS to promote educational outreach and provide feedback. Such partnerships are evident in combating other types of transnational crime such as drug abuse and sea piracy. The emphasis on partnership dovetails with the consultative approach that the government has adopted in policy-making and implementation discussed earlier. In promoting partnership and consultation, the public and external organizations are seen as a resource which may provide specialist information and feedback to help in making or reviewing policy and operational decisions.

The implementation of the ASEAN agreements with respect to combating terrorism depends on the coordination of different agencies. These include the Singapore Special Operations Force, Special Operations Command and the Chemical, Biological, Radiological and Explosives Defence Group. In addition, the formulation of the National Action Plan to address the problem of TIP was the responsibility of an inter-agency task force comprising eight agencies, which is also tasked with its implementation. Similar inter-agency cooperation has occurred in tackling other transnational crimes such as cyber-crime and money laundering. This reflects the 'whole-government' or 'networked government' approach in formulating and implementing policy, referred to above, which has become an important feature of governance of Singapore.

Lastly, in implementing the ACD, the HSA, as a statutory board, enjoys operational autonomy with regard to regulation, surveillance and enforcement. Statutory boards are also involved in combating other forms of transnational crime, under the ASEAN agreements, such as cyber-crime, money laundering and sea piracy, and enjoy similar operational autonomy. This exemplifies the decentralization which characterizes policy implementation in Singapore, as discussed earlier.

There are, though, a few important differences that are worth noting between the implementation of the ACD and its appendices, and the ASEAN agreements and resolutions of the AMMTC/SOMTC on combating terrorism and TIP and other transnational crimes. The ASEAN agreements on transnational crime and resolutions of the AMMTC/SOMTC cover a diverse set of issues and contain often general and discretionary provisions, which do not create binding and precisely defined responsibilities requiring translation into domestic law. This is not so surprising in view of the desire of the ASEAN states to protect their sovereignty, not least in matters relating to law and order and criminal justice. By contrast, the ACD covers a single issue and creates a clear and precise set of mandatory obligations which must be enshrined into domestic law (in Singapore by the Health Products Regulations of 2007). For this reason the ACD is more readily implementable than the more complex and discretionary ASEAN agreements on transnational crime.

A further point of contrast is the extent of interdependence of member states in the application of the two ASEAN instruments. To be effective, implementation of the

ACD does not depend upon compliance in other ASEAN states. Thus, the Singapore government has been able successfully to implement the ACD regardless of the progress of implementation in the other ASEAN states. By contrast, the ability in Singapore to implement the ASEAN agreements on combating terrorism and other transnational crimes depends upon the ability of other states in the region to do so together with a strong commitment to engage in cross-border cooperation. Given the nature of transnational crime, which may involve criminal networks that span national boundaries, shortcomings in combating it in one state may impact on the ability to do so in Singapore itself. For example, the failure to deal effectively with terrorists groups or drug cartels in other states of the region will increase the possibility of terrorism or drug-related crime in Singapore itself. Also, a cautious approach of the ASEAN states to everyday cross-border cooperation in enforcement and capacity building, indicated in the ASEAN agreements, may likewise hinder enforcement agencies in combating transnational crime in Singapore.

References

Abshire, J. 2011. *The History of Singapore*. Santa Barbara, CA: Greenwood Publishing Group.

Agri-Food and Veterinary Authority of Singapore 2011. *Above and Beyond: Annual Report, 2010/2011*. Singapore.

2014. *Consultation on Proposed Amendments to the Food Regulations Regarding Food Additives and Contaminants*. Singapore.

ASEAN 2003. *Agreement on the ASEAN Harmonized Cosmetic Regulatory Scheme: Schedule B: ASEAN Cosmetic Directive*,

Jakarta: ASEAN Secretariat, available at: www.asean.org/communities/asean-economic-community/item/agreement-on-the-asean-harmonized-cosmetic-regulatory-scheme-phnom-penh-2-september-2003 (accessed 17 June 2015).

2007. *ASEAN Cosmetic Directive Guidelines for the Safety Assessment of a Cosmetic Product*. Jakarta: ASEAN Secretariat, available at: www.asean.org/.../1.a.1%20&%201.a.2%20-%2007-06-10%20-%20PIF%20Asean%20 Guidelines.pdf (accessed 17 June 2015).

Asian Development Bank 2012. *Key Indicators for Asia and the Pacific 2012*. Manila.

2014. *Key Indicators for Asia and the Pacific 2014*. Manila.

Attorney-General's Chambers 2003. United Nations (Anti-terrorism Measures) Regulations Revised Edition, 2003. Singapore.

2007a. Terrorism (Suppression of Bombings) Act, 2007, Cap. 324A. Singapore.

2007b. Singapore Armed Forces (Amendment) Act, 2007, Cap. 295. Singapore.

2008. Health Products Act, Cap. 122D, rev. edn. Singapore.

2010. Health Products (Cosmetic Products – ASEAN Cosmetic Directive) Regulations, 2007 (Amended 2010). Singapore.

Auditor-General 2011. *What is Public Accountability?* Singapore.

2014. *Report of the Auditor-General for the Financial Year 2013/2014*. Singapore.

Bell, G. 1999. 'Singapore Legal System in Context – Whither the Concept of the National Legal System'. In K. Tan (ed.), *The Singapore Legal System*, 2nd edn. Singapore: National University of Singapore Press, pp. 1–25.

Bhaskaran, M., Ho, S. C., Low, D., Tan, K. S., Vadaketh, S. and Yeoh, L. K. 2012. 'Background Paper: Inequality and the Need for a New Social Compact'. Paper presented at 'Singapore

Perspectives 2012. Singapore Inclusive: Bridging Divides', Institute of Policy Studies, Singapore, conference, 16 January.

Borneo Bulletin 2012. Bandar Seri Begawan, Brunei, 6 November, p. 1.

Borneo Post 2012. Kuching, Sarawak, 6 November.

Censorship Review Committee 2010. *2010 Report: Censorship Review Committee*. Singapore: Media Development Authority.

Chan, T. 2009. *PSD: MAP Your Future as a Leader*. Singapore: Jobs Central Community, available at: http://smf.jobscentral.com.sg/main/article/53 (accessed 24 February 2012).

Chen, Z. 2012. '3 Terrorist Suspects Arrested, Deported Back to Singapore', Xinhua News Agency, 2 March, available at: http://news.xinhuanet.com/english/world/2012-03/02/c_131442087.htm (accessed 10 June 2015).

Chiam, K. O. 2010. 'Role of the ASEAN Specialized Meteorological Centre (ASMC) in Regional Haze Monitoring'. Paper presented at the Technical Workshop on the Development of the ASEAN Peatland Fire Prediction and Warning System, Kuala Lumpur, 15 July.

Civil Service College 2006. *WITS Guide Book*. Singapore.

Competition Commission of Singapore 2007. (Singapore) *Legislation*, available at: www.ccs.gov.sg/legislation (accessed 28 February 2012).

Corrupt Practices Investigation Bureau 2014. (Singapore) 'Legislation' and 'About Us', available at: www.cpib.gov.sg (accessed 6 September 2014).

Cosmetic, Toiletry and Fragrance Association of Singapore 2014a. (Singapore) 'About Us', available at: www.ctfas.org.sg (accessed 6 September 2014).

2014b. 'Activities Archive'. (Singapore), available at: www.ctfas.org.sg/content.php?c=197&desc=Activities+Archive (accessed 6 September 2014).

Cut Waste Panel 2012a. (Singapore) 'About Us', available at: http://web.archive.org/web/20110522141033/http://www.cutwaste.gov.sg/aboutus.html (accessed 2 March 2012).

2012b. (Singapore) 'Suggestion Statistics', available at: http://web.archive.org/web/20110522141130/http://www.cutwaste.gov.sg/statistics.html (accessed 2 March 2012).

Das, S. B. 2010. *Road to Recovery: Singapore's Journey through Global Crisis*. Singapore: Institute of Southeast Asian Studies.

Department of Statistics 2011. *Census of Population 2010 Statistical Release 2: Households and Housing*. Singapore: Ministry of Trade and Industry, available at: www.singstat.gov.sg/publications/publications-and-papers/cop2010/cop2010-sr2 (accessed 5 April 2012).

2012. *Yearbook of Statistics Singapore, 2012*. Singapore: Ministry of Trade and Industry.

2014. *Yearbook of Statistics Singapore, 2014*. Singapore: Ministry of Trade and Industry.

Durai, J. 2012. 'Singapore to Fight Human Trafficking in "A More Strategic" Way', *Straits Times*, 21 March.

Economic Development Board 2012. (Singapore) 'Industries', available at: www.edb.gov.sg/content/edb/en/industries.html (accessed 5 July 2012).

EnterpriseOne 2014. (Singapore) online business licensing service, available at: https://licences.business.gov.sg (accessed 5 September 2014).

GeBiz 2014. (Singapore) 'About Us', available at: www.gebiz.gov.sg/ (accessed 5 September 2014).

Ghesquiere, H. 2007. *Singapore's Success: Engineering Economic Growth*. Singapore: Thomson Publishing.

Government of Singapore 2012. (Singapore) 'Cabinet: Cabinet Appointments', available at: www.cabinet.gov.sg/content/cabinet/index.html (accessed 23 December 2012).

Han, F. K., Ibrahim, Z., Chua, M. H., Lim, L., Low, I., Lin, R. and Chan, R. 2011. *Lee Kuan Yew: Hard Truths to Keep Singapore Going*. Singapore: Straits Times Press.

Haque, M. S. 2009. 'Public Administration and Public Governance in Singapore'. In P. S. Kim (ed.), *Public Administration and Public Governance in ASEAN Member Countries and Korea*. Seoul: Daeyoung Moonhwasa Publishing Company, pp. 246–71.

Health Sciences Authority 2009a. *Impetus: Health Sciences Authority Annual Report 2008/09*. Singapore.

2009b. *Cosmetic Products HSA Consumer Guide*, available at: www.hsa.gov.sg/content/hsa/en/Health_Products_Regulation/Consumer_Information/Consumer_Guides.html (accessed 12 March 2012).

2010. *Focus: Health Sciences Authority Annual Report 2009/10*. Singapore.

2011a. *Guidelines on the Control of Cosmetic Products, January 2011 to June 2011*. Singapore.

2011b. *Transformation through Synergy: Health Sciences Authority Annual Report 2010/11*. Singapore.

2012. *Health Sciences Authority Annual Report 2011/12*. Singapore.

2013. *Health Sciences Authority Annual Report 2012/13*. Singapore.

Ho, K. L. 2003. *Shared Responsibilities, Unshared Power: The Politics of Policy-making in Singapore*. Singapore: Eastern Universities Press.

Hor, M. 2012. 'Singapore's Anti-terrorism Laws: Reality and Rhetoric'. In V. Ramraj, M. Hor, K. Roach and G. Williams (eds), *Global Anti-Terrorism Law and Policy*, 2nd edn. Cambridge: Cambridge University Press, pp. 271–89.

Housing and Development Board 2012. (Singapore) 'HDB Info-web: Buying a Flat', available at: www.hdb.gov.sg/ (accessed 5 April 2012).

International Enterprise Singapore 2014. (Singapore) 'Singapore FTAs: Overview of ASEAN (AFTA)', available at: www.fta.gov.sg/sg_fta.asp (accessed 7 September 2014).

Jones, D. S. 1998a. 'Recent Budgetary Reforms in Singapore', *Journal of Public Budgeting, Accounting and Financial Management*, 10(2): 279–310.

1998b. 'Law Enforcement in Singapore: An Analysis of the Compliance Strategy', *Asian Journal of Public Administration*, 20(1): 30–56.

2001a. 'Inspection and Enforcement Strategies in Singapore: Food Safety, Pollution Control and Industrial Safety'. In L. Low and D. Johnston (eds), *Singapore Inc.: Public Policy Options in the Third Millennium*. Singapore: Asia Pacific Press, pp. 179–203.

2001b. 'Performance Measurement and Budgetary Management in the Singapore Civil Service', *Journal of Public Budgeting, Accounting and Financial Management*, 13(4): 485–511.

2001c. 'Budgetary Policy in Singapore'. In L. Low and D. Johnston (eds), *Singapore Inc.: Public Policy Options in the Third Millennium*. Singapore: Asia Pacific Press, pp. 131–56.

2002a. 'Recent Changes in Singapore's Administrative Elite: Responding to the Challenges of a Rapidly Growing Economy', *Asian Journal of Political Science*, 10(2): 70–93.

2002b. 'Procurement Practices in the Singapore Civil Service: Balancing Control and Delegation', *Journal of Public Procurement*, 2(1): 29–54.

2004. 'Measurement in the Public Sector: Lessons from Singapore and New Zealand'. In J. Barry, J. Chandler and M. Dent (eds), *Beyond New Public Management*. Aldershot: Ashgate, pp. 191–205.

2005a. 'The Central Provident Fund Scheme in Singapore: Challenges and Reform', *Asian Journal of Political Science*, 13(2): 75–102.

2005b. 'Recent Changes in the Financial Management of the Singapore Civil Service: The Adoption of Resource Accounting, Internal Charging and Revenue Retention'. In A. B. L. Cheung (ed.), *Public Service Reform in East Asia: Reform Issues and Challenges in Japan, Korea, Singapore and Hong Kong*. Hong Kong: Chinese University Press, pp. 105–25.

2005c. 'ASEAN and Transboundary Haze Pollution in Southeast Asia'. In R. Molina (ed.), *Asia-Europe Cooperation on the Environment: Towards Sustainable Forest Management*. Singapore: Asia-Europe Foundation, pp. 65–84.

2006. 'Financial Reforms of Statutory Bodies in Singapore: Control and Autonomy in a Centralized State', *Public Organization Review*, 6(3): 259–76.

Lee, Kuan Yew 2012. *My Lifelong Challenge: Singapore's Bilingual Journey*. Singapore: Straits Times Press.

Low, L. and Johnston, D. (eds) 2001. *Singapore Inc.: Public Policy Options in the Third Millennium*. Singapore: Asia Pacific Press.

Ministry of Communications and Information 1990. *Singapore Government Directory*. Singapore.

Ministry of Finance 2010a. *Singapore Public Sector Outcomes Review: Meeting Challenges of Tomorrow with a Whole of Government Approach*. Singapore.

2010b. (Singapore) 'Singapore Budget 2010: Budget Speech', available at: mof.gov.sg/singapore_budget_archives.aspx (accessed 27 January 2012).

2014 (Singapore) 'Budget 2014: Analysis of Revenue and Expenditure', available at: www.singaporebudget.gov.sg/budget_2014/ (accessed 6 September 2014).

Ministry of Information and the Arts 1991–2001. *Singapore Government Directories*. Singapore.

Ministry of Information, Communications and the Arts 2002–2011. *Singapore Government Directories*. Singapore.

2010. (Singapore) 'Government's Response to the Report of the Censorship Review Committee 2010', available at: www.mci.gov.sg/mobile/news/media/the-governments-response-to-the-censorship-review-committees-recommendations (accessed 10 March 2012).

Ministry of Manpower 2012. (Singapore) 'Workplace Safety & Health: Training', available at: www.mom.gov.sg/workplace-safety-health/training/ (accessed 2 September 2012).

Ministry of National Development 2014. (Singapore) 'Municipal Services Office to Improve Service Delivery', available at: www.mnd.gov.sg/mso/press-municipal-services.htm (accessed 4 September 2014).

Ministry of Trade and Industry 2012. (Singapore) 'About MTI: Divisions and Departments', available at: www.mti.gov.sg/AboutMTI/Pages/Divisions-and-Departments.aspx (accessed 14 January 2013).

Monetary Authority of Singapore 2014. (Singapore) 'Statistics Room: Official Foreign Reserves', available at: www.mas.gov.sg/Statistics/Reserve-Statistics/Official-Foreign-Reserves.aspx (accessed 6 September 2014).

Mother Tongue Language Review Committee 2011. *Nurturing Active Learners and Proficient Users: 2010 Mother Tongue Languages Review Committee Report.* Singapore: Ministry of Education.

Ong, P. 2011. 'Opening Address by Mr Peter Ong, Head, Civil Service, at 2011 Administrative Service Dinner and Promotion Ceremony, 28 March 2011'. Singapore: Public Service Division.

Prime Minister's Office 2011. 'Addendum to the President's Address'. Singapore.

Public Service Commission 2002. (Singapore) 'Management Associates Programme (MAP) Background Factsheet', available at: app.psd.gov.sg/data/MAP%20factsheet.doc (accessed 24 February 2012).

Public Service Division 2008. (Singapore) *National Goals, Global Perspectives: The Singapore Public Service*, available at: www.psd.gov.sg (accessed 22 February 2012).

2009. (Singapore) *The Singapore Public Service: One Career, Infinite Opportunities*, available at: www.psd.gov.sg (accessed 25 February 2012).

2012. (Singapore) 'Our Clusters', available at: http://web.archive.org/web/20130629220019/http://www.psd.gov.sg/content/psd/en/aboutpsd/organisation_chart.html (accessed 27 August 2012).

2014. (Singapore) 'Public Service Improves Career Prospects for Non-Graduates', available at: www.psd.gov.sg/media/press-releases (accessed 4 September 2014).

PWC Consulting 2002. (Hong Kong) 'Appendix D: Singapore Country Summary'. In PWC Consulting (ed.), *Interim Report to the Task Force on the Review of Civil Service Pay Policy and System*, available at: www.jsscs.gov.hk/en/publications/pwc/appendix_d.htm (accessed 20 February 2012).

Quah, J. S. T. 2003. *Curbing Corruption in Asia: A Comparative Study of Six Countries*. Singapore: Eastern Universities Press.

2010. *Public Administration Singapore-Style*. Bingley: Emerald Group Publishing.

REACH 2011. (Singapore) 'What Singaporeans are Talking about in 2011', available at: www.reach.gov.sg/portals/0/MediaRelease/REACH%20Media%20Release%20for%205th%20Anniversary%20(12Dec).pdf (accessed 4 June 2012).

2012. (Singapore) *REACH Reaching Everyone for Active Citizenry@home: Public Consultations*, available at: www.reach.gov.sg/YourSay/EConsultationPaper.aspx (accessed 10 March 2012).

S. Rajaratnam School of International Studies 2008. *Networked Government and Homeland Security Workshop: Conference Report*. Singapore.

Saxena, N. C. 2011. *Virtuous Cycles: The Singapore Public Service and National Development*. Singapore: United Nations Development Programme and Civil Service College.

Schwab, K. (ed.) 2014. *The Global Competitiveness Report, 2014–2015*. Geneva: World Economic Forum.

Sim, W. 2014. 'Municipal Services Office to Open Oct[ober] 1, says Grace Fu', *Straits Times*, 24 August.

Sin, B. A. 1990. 'Statutory Board Privatization: Some Issues of Accountability and Control (1)', *Malayan Law Journal*, 2: 50–7.

Singapore Administrative Service 2012. *Management Associates Programme: A Career Like No Other*. Singapore: Public Service Division, available at: http://web.archive.org/web/20120316070000/http://www.adminservice.gov.sg/MAP/Career Path (accessed 24 February 2012).

Singapore Customs 2010. (Singapore) 'Circular: Implementation of ASEAN Trade Agreement in Goods, 09/10', available at: www.customs.gov.sg/topNav/new/cir/ (accessed 27 December 2012).

2011. (Singapore) 'Legislation', available at: www.customs.gov.sg/topNav/ (accessed 27 December 2012).

Singapore Inter-Agency Taskforce on Trafficking in Persons 2012. *National Plan of Action against Trafficking in Persons, 2012–2015*. Singapore: Ministry of Manpower.

Singapore Parliament 2007a. *Singapore Parliament Reports*, vol. 83 (9 April). Singapore.

2007b. *Singapore Parliament Reports*, vol. 83 (11 April). Singapore.

2011. *Singapore Parliament Reports*, vol. 88 (22 November). Singapore.

2014. *Singapore Parliament Reports*, vol. 92 (3 November). Singapore.

Singapore Prison Service 2012. (Singapore) 'Annual Statistics', available at: www.prisons.gov.sg/ (accessed 2 March 2012).

Sovannasam, U. 2011. 'ASEAN Efforts in Dealing with Transnational Crime'. In Y. Y. Lee (ed.), *ASEAN Matters: Reflecting on the Association of Southeast Asian Nations*. Singapore: Lee Kuan Yew School of Public Policy, National University of Singapore and Institute of Policy Studies, pp. 77–84.

SPRING 2014. *Conformity Assessment: Information Booklet*, rev. edn. Singapore.

Thio, L. A. 1999. 'Law and the Administrative State'. In K. Tan (ed.), *The Singapore Legal System*, 2nd edn. Singapore: Singapore University Press, pp. 160–229.

Van Meter, D. and Van Horn, C. 1975. 'The Policy Implementation Process: A Conceptual Framework', *Administration and Society*, 6(4): 445–88.

Vennewald, W. 1994. *Technocrats in the State Enterprise System of Singapore*, Working Paper No. 32. Perth: Asia Research Centre, Murdoch University.

Vogel, E. F. 1989. 'A Little Dragon Tamed'. In K. S. Sandhu and P. Wheatley (eds), *Management of Success: The Moulding of Modern Singapore*. Singapore: Institute of Southeast Asian Studies, pp. 1049–66.

Weatherbee, D. 2009. *International Relations in Southeast Asia: The Struggle for Autonomy*, 2nd edn. Lanham, MD: Rowman & Littlefield Publishers.

World Bank 2013. *Doing Business 2014: Understanding Regulations for Small and Medium-Size Enterprises*. Washington DC.

2014. (Washington, DC) 'Worldwide Governance Indicators 1996–2013', available at: info.worldbank.org/governance/wgi/index.aspx#reports (accessed 5 October 2014).

Worthington, R. 2003. *Governance in Singapore*. London: Routledge Curzon.

Yap, C. 2014. 'What Municipal Services Unit Aims to Achieve' (Letter to Forum Page), *Straits Times*, 30 August.

Chapter 6

Vietnam's public bureaucracy and implementation of two ASEAN policies

Jairo Acuña-Alfaro and Anh Tran

6.1 Introduction

This chapter examines the formulation, implementation and monitoring of policies by the public bureaucracy in Vietnam. It presents a discussion of the main features of Vietnamese public bureaucracy and its recent evolution arising from the promulgation of the Law on Civil Servants and Public Officials. It describes the hierarchically structured process of policy formulation, which involves a monolithic process of discussion and deliberation among the policy-makers. While there is formalistic cohesion among the policy-makers after policy formulation, there are bottlenecks in policy implementation and policy monitoring because of dispersion among public officials and civil servants, their limited capacities and the prevalence of patronage and nepotism in the Vietnamese public bureaucracy.

The processes of policy implementation in Vietnam have been characterized by some scholars as 'purposively complicated' and 'frequently unclear and overlapping' (Gainsborough, Dang and Tran 2009; Gainsborough 2010),

We thank Hoang Manh Chien for providing very useful and detailed policy information that has been used in this chapter.

'gloomy with a large gap between intention and implementation' (Fritzen 2005) and 'manifold and dispersed' (Woodside 2006; Acuña-Alfaro 2009a).

This chapter is divided into five sections. The following section focuses on the policy context and identifies the salient features that influence policy formulation and implementation in Vietnam. The second section provides background information on Vietnam's public bureaucracy and describes its 'waved' approach to reform and implementation. The third section discusses the distinctions between public officials and civil servants in Vietnam. The fourth section looks into recent efforts to differentiate and develop a more meritocratic system in order to enhance policy implementation.

The fifth section focuses on the challenges of linking policy intention with implementation by presenting two case studies which continue the analysis in the previous sections regarding the role of the public bureaucracy in policy implementation. These case studies examine the processes related to policy implementation by the public bureaucracy in Vietnam and identify a hierarchically structured and formalistic process of policy formulation. However, given the dispersed network of public officials and civil servants and their limited skills and capacities, policy implementation and policy monitoring are found to be bottlenecks.

6.2 Policy context in Vietnam

Vietnam has a land area of 331,114 sq. km and borders the Gulfs of Thailand and Tonkin as well as the South China Sea

(*The Economist* 2013: 240). It also shares boundaries with China, Laos and Cambodia. It has an s-shaped figure with a coastline of 3,260 km. The distance from the north to the south is 1,650 km, and is about 50 km wide at the narrowest point.

The country has a population of 89,710,000 (General Statistics Office 2014a). This means that Vietnam is the third most populous country in Southeast Asia and the thirteenth in the world. The population structure is predominantly rural (70.4 per cent) and has even gender distribution: 49.5 per cent male, 50.5 female. The average annual population growth rate from 1999 to 2009 was only 1.2 per cent. The country's population density is 259 persons per sq. km and has a mix of fifty-four different ethnicities in which the *Kinh* group represents the majority, with about 85 per cent of the population.

This section analyses those salient factors influencing policy formulation and implementation in Vietnam. In particular, the discussion includes features related to: (1) an emerging economy that has recently experienced high rates of economic growth and a transition from low- to middle-income country status; (2) increasing activity in the private sector, but limited advances in the public sector apparatus; (3) a one-party communist regime and unitary and collective government structure marked by the leadership of the party and implementation by the government; and (4) the recent institution in 2009 of the Law on Public Officials and Civil Servants and the implied emergence of differentiation in public sector roles.

Historically, Vietnam's bureaucracy was influenced by the French, Soviet and Chinese bureaucratic models. The colonial parliamentary system was introduced by the French in the early 1900s and was modified and improved in later regimes. Most leaders and high-ranking bureaucrats in this early period were trained in local French-speaking schools and influenced by the French bureaucratic culture. After 1975, the executive branch was formed in close concert with the Soviet system, with the Council of Ministers forming the government's 'cabinet'. The number and even the names of ministries followed the Soviet system faithfully. The current Ministry of Investment and Planning is a clear legacy of this system. On the other hand, the structure of the Communist Party of Vietnam (CPV) shows a significant resemblance to that of its Chinese counterpart. Many of Vietnam's current leaders have been trained either in the Soviet Union or China or both.

Vietnam has engineered and implemented a remarkable economic and social transition that has put the country into the low- to middle-income category in less than three decades. The reforms undertaken since the 1980s have transitioned the country from a centrally managed framework to a more market-oriented one in order to realize human development objectives and improve living conditions. The country has made impressive gains in poverty reduction and has substantially improved social development indicators at the aggregate levels. Vietnam has witnessed the rapid emergence of a strong private sector, a GDP income per capita of approximately US$1,910 in 2013, from a low of US$285 in 1985 (World Bank 2014).

Most recently, the 2011 *Vietnam Human Development Report* prepared by the United Nations Development Programme (UNDP) placed Vietnam among the world's medium human-development countries. In fact, from 2001 to 2011, Vietnam's Human Development Index (HDI) increased by nearly 12 per cent, from 0.651 to 0.728 on a scale of 0 to 1. The HDI is made up of three dimensions: income (GDP per capita at purchasing power parity), life expectancy and education (adult literacy rates and gross enrolment rates). This is impressive progress, and it reflects Vietnam's significant achievements in generating economic growth and improving living standards (UNDP 2011).

As part of this reform process, Vietnam has also formulated an ambitious and comprehensive set of policies in order to improve the performance of its public sector. In the context of a single-party ruled socialist state the public sector is inevitably large. It covers different players, including the ruling CPV and its political–social arms as well as the executive, the judicial, the legislative and the state economics sectors. All of these players take up a considerably large proportion of total employment and state budget, and they also adopt a hierarchical approach to policy formulation.

The state budget for the public sector in 2010 was projected to be at approximately 38 per cent, excluding budgeting for national defence, public security and special sectors (Ministry of Finance 2010). Yet, the Politburo is the main policy-making organ and currently is composed of fourteen members elected by the Central Committee of 175 members. In January 2011, the CPV held its 11th National Party Congress in which members elected a new leadership, most prominently a new General Secretary and a new

Politburo. The Communist Party Congress was followed in May 2011 by the holding of national and local elections, which brought changes in the composition of the National Assembly and the local legislatures, the appointment of a new President, the reconfirmation of the incumbent Prime Minister and the appointment of a new cabinet with seventeen new members out of twenty-six.

Improving the policy-making process in such a large public system requires numerous policies, including public administration reforms, judicial reforms, legislative reforms and political reforms. For instance, Vietnam is in the process of implementing different sector-specific reforms. Public administration reform has completed its first ten-year phase (see Decision 136/2001/QD-TTg, dated 17 September 2001 deciding the Overall Programme on State Administrative Reform from 2001 to 2010) and on 8 November 2011 the government ratified Resolution 30c/NQ-CP promulgating the Master Programme on State Administration Reform from 2011 to 2020. Judicial reform started in 2005 with Resolution No. 49-NQ/TW dated 2 June 2005 of the Politburo of the Communist Party of Vietnam on the Strategy on Judicial Reform towards 2020. State-owned enterprise reform has been in process for two decades since the 10 May 1990 Decision No. 143/HDBT of the Ministers Council, which was later legislated in the Law on Enterprises 2005. These policy reform efforts to improve the provision of public service, especially for the poor and vulnerable, have brought good dividends to Vietnamese citizens in the last two decades. In addition, these efforts, together with the ongoing processes to improve public administration, have increased the quality of services available to citizens, allowing for greater access to science, technology, educational opportunities and healthcare facilities.

These have been achieved within a decentralized structure and with limited institutional coherence and coordination, in which three main actors – the CPV, the government (and in particular its executive branch) and the Vietnam Fatherland Front (VFF), including its mass organizations – have played different but often overlapping roles. Within the confines of a unitary political system, major policies come from the Politburo and its Central Committee and are distilled down in a hierarchical manner.

In a nutshell, the remarkable transformation experienced by Vietnam in its transition to higher development standards has been characterized by clearly defined policies. The first policy involved the transition from a centrally planned economy towards a socialist-oriented economy. A second policy included the reform of the public administration system, together with increases in the quantity and availability of public services. These policies allowed Vietnam to transition from a lower- to a low- to middle-income status. This shift implies that Vietnamese children enjoy greater freedoms and opportunities for higher levels of education, health and income than did their parents. These efforts also aim to bring up citizens as subjects of development; they imply a shift in the way citizens are mobilized and encouraged to participate in local affairs.

This transition is also remarkable in terms of the recent evolution in the public bureaucracy of Vietnam. As Poon, Nguyen and Do (2009: 202) suggest, 'it can be said that in-depth discussions about the Vietnamese bureaucracy began only when *doi moi* [renovation] started'. But this transition is also rooted in three historical features of Vietnam's public bureaucracy. First, the public bureaucracy evolved from a long French colonial period that emphasized a 'mandarin' structure, which was followed by long wars that prevented the construction of a proper system. In addition, the political context and the long period of conflict limited opportunities for building the capacity of the public bureaucracy to implement public policies. Secondly, from this centralized planning system followed a Soviet 'cadre' system, which did not define differences in appointments, grades and ranks. And thirdly, the single-party system has meant a derogation of civil servant neutrality (202–3).

6.3 Profile of Vietnam's public bureaucracy

This section discusses a 'waved' approach in terms of reform and its implementation in Vietnam's bureaucratic system. A first 'wave' is marked by a 'mandarin' system, followed by the enforcement of a 'cadre' system typical of communist regimes in the second wave. The third and most recent wave relates to the transition towards a socialist-oriented market economy. This section will discuss the public bureaucracy's dual-appointment system as well as recent attempts to make the transition towards a bureaucratic system that is both 'career-based' and 'position-based'.

The evolution of Vietnam's public bureaucracy has followed a waved approach: from its French legacy to a communist regime and recently from a centrally planned regime to a socialist-oriented market economy. A look at the normative documentation on bureaucracy and related issues suggests four historical periods: (1) the 'mandarin' original structure (Woodside 2006); (2) the pre-1945 era when the bureaucracy was developed under the French; (3) the 1945–95 period of central planning when the communist 'cadre' system took root; and (4) the transition starting in 1995 towards a socialist-oriented market economy.

According to the 2014 Labour Force Survey, Vietnam's state sector employs a total of 5,389,900 people, equivalent to 10.2 per cent of the total workforce. This is an increase compared with 4.8 million people in state employment in 2009 (see Table 6.1). Patterns of employment are also quite diverse in the rest of the economy. Overall employment during 2009 was concentrated in the agricultural industry (47.6 per cent) and to a lesser extent in manufacturing (14.5 per cent) and retail and wholesale trading (11.9 per cent). State employment is concentrated in public services, especially education (32 per cent of total state employment), public administration (23 per cent) and health and social work (7.7 per cent). In addition to these, manufacturing (probably from state-owned enterprises) employs a substantial share of state workers (10.3 per cent) (Warren and Pham 2010: 4–5).

According to the historical account of institutional development, the public bureaucracy has changed in a way that reflects institutional circumstances over six decades of development. It has embedded three key features: (1) a 'mandarin' structure tailored to ruling society, rather than a public bureaucracy aimed at serving the general public; (2) a Soviet-styled central planning 'cadre' system that did not clearly distinguish civil servants from other public officials; and

Table 6.1 *Employed population in Vietnam by economic sector, 2009–2014*

	September 2009	July 2010	July 2011	October 2012	October 2013	April 2014
Self-employed	37.717 million (78.6%)	38.820 million (78.5%)	39.164 million (77.8%)	–	–	–
Cooperative	0.226 million (0.5%)	0.364 million (0.7%)	0.138 million (0.3%)	–	–	–
Private enterprise	3.865 million (8.0%)	3.745 million (7.6%)	4.100 million (8.1%)	–	–	–
Non-state	–	–	–	45.057 million (86.5%)	45.288 million (85.8%)	45.349 million (85.8%)
State	4.794 million (10.0%)	4.780 million (9.7%)	5.251 million (10.4%)	5.273 million (10.1%)	5.466 million (10.3%)	5.390 million (10.2%)
Foreign-invested enterprise	1.398 million (2.9%)	1.756 million (3.5%)	1.700 million (3.4%)	1.664 million (3.2%)	1.896 million (3.6%)	1.904 million (3.6%)
Unspecified	–	–	–	0.120 million (0.02%)	0.143 million (0.02%)	0.196 million (0.03%)
Totals	48.000 million (100%)	49.466 million (100%)	50.352 million (100%)	52.114 million (100%)	52.793 million (100%)	52.838 million (100%)

Sources: General Statistics Office 2012a; 2012b; 2014b.

(3) a one-party-ruled dual-subordination system in which the CPV takes the leading role and the public bureaucracy follows (Poon, Nguyen and Do 2009).[1]

This evolution of the public bureaucracy's legal foundations can be seen through the lens of path dependency. In 1945, the interim government led by Ho Chi Minh removed the 'mandarin' regimes, which had been under French public administration, and moved those officials who were still capable and ethical to the interim government's new public bureaucracy (Official Order No. 18-SL/1945 of the President of the Interim Government of Vietnam Democratic Republic on 18 August 1945). This was followed in 1948 by the establishment of a regime of civil servants, which regulated civil servants working in government agencies and excluded officers working for the army and defence forces (Official Order No. 32-SL/1948 of the President of Vietnam Democratic Republic on 29 May 1948). The French style of public administration was inherent in the interim government.

In 1950, President Ho Chi Minh defined civil servants as those 'citizens delegated with specific tasks in the people's state apparatus' and who are 'ultimately put under the supreme leadership of the Government' rather than under partisan leadership (Official Order No. 76-SL/1950 of the

[1] See also the discussion by senior Member of the CPV's Central Party's Committee on Organization and Personnel, Prof. Dr Le Minh Thong (2009: 20): 'The Party assumes united leadership over personnel issues and team management . . . In Vietnam, cadres and civil servants are attached to the Party, trained by the Party, exercising trains [*sic*] and loyalty to the Party's goal and ideology as well as following the leadership and management of the Party through Party units at all levels.'

President of Vietnam 1945). The Official Order set out principles for civil servants' management (e.g., recruitment of civil servants based on competency, including experience and educational qualifications as well as recruitment and examination placement), while also providing for a system of grade-based remuneration and rewarding outstanding performers. The intentions underlying these principles were clear, yet implementation was difficult, as Vietnam had fallen back into continuous war and the public bureaucracy was regulated by myriad secondary normative documents (Nguyen and Nguyen 2010: 68). Soviet-style state management with a system of 'cadres' started to take shape in both political and public administration arenas as soon as Vietnam embarked on the path to a communist political system.

No by-law document was issued to govern Vietnam's public bureaucracy as a whole until 1991 (Decree No. 169-HDBT dated 25 May 1991). The then Council of Ministers did not aim to regulate elected people holding senior management positions in the legislative, executive and justice branches; temporary contracted staff and unclassified trainees; people working in state-owned enterprises and people working in agencies of the CPV and mass organizations (who were subject to regulations by the CPV or mass organizations). Such regulation would have been largely contrary to preceding and succeeding legal documents.

The most significant new policy formulated in this third period was the 1998 Ordinance on Public Officials and Civil Servants, a higher legislative document regulating the bureaucracy. The goal of the Ordinance was to build a force of public officials and civil servants (including public employees and excluding army and defence professional officers) who were 'ethically qualified, professionally capable and competent, diligent in serving citizens, and loyal to the Socialist Republic of Vietnam' (quoted from the Preamble of the Ordinance). The Ordinance's scope of regulation includes public officials, civil servants and public employees. Personnel and organization of the public bureaucracy were put under the unified leadership of the CPV and human resource management were set to be in compliance with delegation regulations provided for by the CPV and the state.

The Ordinance was put into force through a series of four government decrees (Nos. 114–17). One major change was seen in the separation of public officials and civil servants working in state agencies (including political, socio-political organizations and state agencies at all levels in Decree No. 117) from those working in state-owned enterprises and public service delivery units (Decree No. 116). Another change was the introduction of commune-level public officials and civil servants (Decree No 114) and stand-by civil servants (Decree No. 115). Despite clearer definitions of the four major groups of public employees in general terms, confusion remained regarding how to understand and apply the terms within state agencies and in public life.

This Ordinance was recently replaced by a higher-legal normative document: Law No. 22/2008/QH12 on Public Officials and Civil Servants. The aim of this new Law is to: 'regulate public officials and civil servants' election, recruitment, instatement, employment and management of public officials and civil servants; obligations, rights and responsibilities of public officials and civil servants and conditions to ensure the performance of official functions and duties' (Article 1).

The Law marks a move from a scattered by-law system to a legislation governing bureaucratic personnel. In principle, the law upgrades the Ordinance's normative hierarchy (i.e., turning the Ordinance into a law) rather than making more substantial or radical changes; the upgrade, however, can be seen as a necessary attempt to professionalize the bureaucracy without involving public service delivery sectors. In fact, the new Law excludes public employees (or *viên chức*) who work for state-run professional institutions (e.g., research institutes and think tanks) and state-run public services (e.g., public schools, public hospitals, libraries and museums) from the public bureaucracy.

According to the Law, the public bureaucracy's personnel system is rooted in communist government structure and is characterized by the coexistence of both political and non-political public officials. Public officials (or *cán bộ* in Vietnamese) are those who are elected or appointed to hold positions in the state, political or socio-political apparatus, executing the CPV's directions and visions as part of a one-party system (Article 28). Remuneration for public officials comes from the state budget. There is no provision regarding the classification or categorization of public officials.

Civil servants (or *công chức*) are those who are recruited according to their examination scores to work in agencies of the CPV and socio-political organizations; hold leadership or management positions in public service delivery agencies; work in agencies and units of the People's Army (but not as military officers, professional servicemen and servicewomen or national defence workers); and agencies and units of the People's Public Security Forces (but not as officers or professional non-commissioned officers). The inclusion of *cán bộ* and *công chức* in one law shows the unified nature of the political system, which exercises its overall leadership over both the political and public administration systems.

Regarding categories and grades, the Law regulates the categorization of civil servants but not of elected or appointed public officials. Accordingly, there are three ways of categorizing *công chức*, based on position and authority, on qualifications and on professional grades in management roles and pay roll. The current grading system, together with the existing career-based approach to personnel management allows little room for ranking or evaluating individual performance against overall, generic grading requirements, despite the fact that each sub-grade has different implications in terms of the nature of jobs and tasks.

The Law also reincorporates the principle of 'merit', though it is not yet as prominent or central as it was in late-1940s official regulations. Another addition is the gradual incorporation of position-based elements together with the current career-based system. These two elements go hand in hand with Vietnam's pursuit of improved professionalism. This can also be seen as a departure from the earlier communist-style 'cadre' system in normative terms. The prominent concern now is how effectively and practically to implement these regulations in the face of existing confusion regarding the difference between political and non-political public officials in the bureaucracy. The existing mantra, 'Party leadership, state management', attempts to explain to whom these concerns are addressed (Nguyen and Nguyen 2010: 40, 69).

6.4 Policy formulation

This section connects the previous sections by considering the distinctions between public officials and civil servants in Vietnam as stipulated in the current Law on Public Officials and Civil Servants. In particular, this section discusses the role of policy-makers and the processes and networks in which they are implicated while performing their public duties. It discusses the Vietnamese understanding that 'Party leads and Government implements', and analyses the dual top-down and decentralized processes of policy-making. The section also highlights the elements of 'formalistic' policy-making, in which the policy-makers tend to have a more reactive rather than proactive response to policy issues. For instance, policy-makers pay close attention to policy formulation by issuing normative legal documents (laws, decrees and resolutions), but they tend to leave implementation adrift. The consequence of this is that policy-makers spend most of the time issuing new or amended normative documents.

The above historical and institutional developments have led to a hierarchically structured public bureaucracy where seniority takes precedent. This hierarchical nature is evident in the Law's tendency to split provisions for different groups of public employees into different levels. The Law dedicates one chapter to public officials from the central to provincial level, one to civil servants from central to provincial level and another to civil servants at the commune level.

One area of reform aimed at strengthening the linkages between policy intention and implementation has tried to clarify the roles and functions of the public sector's workforce. In that regard, the bureaucratic reform process of the past five years has marked a move away from a scattered by-law system towards legislation governing personnel management in the public bureaucracy. In principle, the reform brings neither substantial nor radical changes; it only upgrades its normative hierarchy. In practice, however, the current Law primarily attempts to centralize a previously scattered system of decrees and other normative documents.

It is difficult to explain the ways in which public policies are formulated in Vietnam, as formulation involves a grey area of politics and governance arrangements. Most policies are developed as part of a 'black-box' process in which it is difficult to ascertain attribution and to trace prevailing practices back in time, step-by-step. Therefore, rather than try to speculate on how policy happens, the following discussion will consider the effects and underlying intentions of the most recent and significant public policies regarding Vietnam's public bureaucracy. Resolution 30c on the State Administration Reform Master Programme for 2011 to 2020 implies a commitment to and continuation of public sector reform efforts. It aligns with the decisions from the 11th National Party Congress, including the adoption of the 2011–2020 Socio-Economic Development Strategy, with calls for the development of strong human resources in the private and public sectors; accordingly, several training and scholarship programmes have been put in place in recent years. Undoubtedly, appropriate incentives and remuneration are necessary conditions for achieving these objectives and must be put in place in a transparent, fair and accountable manner.

Resolution 30c signals important shifts in three key areas. First, the resolution attempts to spell out clearer objectives and assign more concrete roles and responsibilities to line ministries and implementing agencies. This means opportunities for greater institutional accountability, as respective agencies are now benchmarked in terms of expected results. Secondly, it emphasizes the development of human resources. This is in line with the ongoing bureaucratic reform efforts and measures aimed at addressing the issues of incentives and dispersed salary structures. And thirdly, it aims to enhance public service delivery, a shift in line with the country's recent transition to middle-income status, and also to look at organizations' and individuals' satisfaction with outputs, rather than relying on processes and procedures. A starting point is the ongoing effort to institutionalize more-rigorous performance-monitoring tools.

The second and third shifts are important since better-quality service delivery requires better-quality human resources. And, for both, a proper, transparent and fair system of incentives and remuneration is necessary. This discussion reinforces the importance of linking intention with implementation. Intentions to reform the public administration system have intensified in the last ten years. Yet, while progress has been achieved in some areas (for example, the institutionalization of one-stop shops across all sixty-three provinces, the reclassification of administrative procedures and enhanced user satisfaction regarding select administrative procedures), overall, citizens seem satisfied with their experiences regarding different administrative procedures, in particular, certification procedures and the obtainment of personal documents and construction permits. One procedure that clearly falls behind in citizen satisfaction involves the acquisition of land-use rights certificates (LURCs). As observed in the Vietnam Governance and Public Administration Performance Index (PAPI), the process of obtaining a LURC consistently scores the lowest of all administrative procedures, not only in terms of overall satisfaction but also regarding the attitude of public officials and the number of necessary requirements (UNDP et al. 2012). The transition from intention to implementation has had its challenges and limitations. Additionally, when discussing incentives and salaries in the public sector, the discussion has revolved around mutually reinforcing elements of the public bureaucracy that need to be considered during the implementation of Resolution 30c.

Indeed, Resolution 30c highlights the importance of improving human-resource matters within the bureaucracy. Yet, while progress has been made since 2009 with the Law on Public Officials and Civil Servants and its subsequent guiding normative documents, citizens' perceptions regarding the importance of personal connections for getting jobs in the public sector remain constant. Practices of nepotism, dispersed remuneration and the opacity of 'incentive' provision remain widespread. The PAPI survey found that less than a quarter of Vietnamese citizens (23 per cent) think connections are not important in order to work in the public sector, as opposed to 50 per cent who think connections are important. The PAPI policy research also suggests that bribes for jobs in the public sector are prevalent and that personal relationships are important to the pursuit of public sector careers.

The second and third shifts are also among the key challenges for ensuring greater and more sustained reforms because they explicitly refer to the system of remuneration and incentives. The spirit of the 1999 Party Central Committee Resolution 7th (VIII session) requires that 'wages must be closely attached to the country's economic development'. In that spirit, public sector remuneration is considered an investment for development, a motivation for individual economic development and an indispensable element of improving policy-making processes (Do 2009).

Resolution 30c calls for the modernization of Vietnam's policy-making processes. This implies the realization that policy formulation regarding Vietnam's social and economic development goals of building a prosperous, democratic society and a thriving market economy will require a public administration that can address the challenges and deliver the promise of a higher standard of living and greater prosperity for all citizens. Modernization of the public sector necessitates the undertaking of greater efforts in human resource management and in mainstreaming the principles of a meritocratic and efficient public administration system with staff that are motivated, skilled and capable of managing the economic, social and environmental challenges facing Vietnam as it graduates to a higher middle-income status.

6.5 Public bureaucracy's role in policy implementation

This section examines recent efforts to differentiate and move towards a more meritocratic public bureaucracy. The discussion is grounded in the 2009 Law and its attempt to distinguish between categories. It includes a discussion of the five variables of Van Meter and Van Horn's (1975) model of policy implementation, namely policy standards and objectives, policy resources, inter-organizational communication and enforcement activities, characteristics of implementing agencies and disposition of the implementers.

In terms of institutional arrangement, the public bureaucracy is put under the overall leadership and direction of the CPV while it is managed and administered by the state. More specifically, state management of public officials and civil servants is undertaken by relevant agencies of the CPV responsible for appointees and recruited staff within the political system; of the National Assembly for elected and recruited staff in the National Assembly system; of the government for appointed, elected and recruited staff in the government system; and of mass organizations for appointed, elected and recruited staff in mass organizations. The Office of the State President, State Audit, the Supreme People's Procuracy and the Supreme People's Court will manage public officials and civil servants working in these state bodies (see Law No. 22/2008/QH12, Articles 65–9). That is, the CPV exercises leadership in defining the policy standards and objectives. For instance, any key personnel planning or management proposal from the government, state agencies or political–social organizations must be reviewed by the CPV and in particular by its Central Committee for Organization and Personnel (CCOP). The first principle for the management of public officials and civil servants is set forth in the Law No. 22/2008 on Public Officials and Civil Servants as 'ensuring the leadership of the CPV and the management of the state' (Article 5[1]). Insofar as it is subordinate to the Party in the planning and management of senior public officials, the state may face hurdles in meeting requirements for impartial and technically competent human resources to run agencies (Le 2009: 20; Poon, Nguyen and Do 2009: 203). The Politburo also issues regulations on the criteria for evaluating public-official and civil-servant performance (*Tuoi Tre* 2010).

Public officials and senior civil servants are under the administration of the CPV, the government and political–social organizations. For civil servants in general, the Ministry of Home Affairs is delegated by the government to manage civil servants working in the government system nationwide (Government Decree No. 71/2003). Ministries, ministerial-equivalent agencies and provincial People's Committees undertake state management of civil servants under government delegation. District-level People's Committees, which are delegated by provincial People's Committees, manage civil servants working at the district level. These agencies manage civil servants working in agencies of the CPV and political–social organizations to make sure that the government delegates the management.

The evolving Vietnamese public bureaucracy has singular characteristics that in terms of institutional arrangements fall within a 'hybrid' system. That is, following the typology of civil service differences developed by Aberbach, Putnam and Rockman (1981), the Vietnamese system is marked by the disappearance of distinctions between politicians and bureaucrats, and can be described as a sort of politicized bureaucracy or bureaucratized politics. Traditionally, bureaucratic systems can be classified according to the nature of interactions between policy-makers (politicians) and bureaucrats (career-based). Variations exist, and Vietnam is not an exception. However, such exercises in definition may aid in deepening understanding and in avoiding some of the mistakes made in the 1990s by post-communist states in Eastern Europe, where bureaucratic development was mostly limited to the development of legislation as a panacea for addressing other problems (Verheijen 2007).

On the issue of policy-resource assignment, a previous study has identified a 'roller coaster' approach for budgeting public administration resources in Vietnam. In particular, this 'type of expenditure might be considered an indication that [public administration reform], while remain[ing] the top discourse priority, in terms of budget allocation signals hesitation that may influence continuity and stability of the reform process' (Acuña-Alfaro 2009b: 25). For instance, the budget line 'general public administration' can be considered one of the main categories for allocating resources to the bureaucracy in order to implement policies. However, expenditures on this category have fluctuated in important ways: they decreased between 2000 and 2002 (from 7.42 per cent to 5.8 per cent of the state budget); remained constant from 2004 to 2005 (7.42 per cent and 6.76 per cent, respectively) and were further reduced in 2006 and 2007 (6.01 per cent and 7.31 per cent) to pre-2000 levels. This fluctuation, which is also tied to the limited fiscal transparency on budget allocation in the country, makes it difficult to assess the assignment of policy resources.

An additional element relates to the incentives system that currently prevails in the bureaucracy. The remuneration and incentives systems in the public sector need to be rationalized. Not only are salary and payment reform necessary, but it will also be crucial to transition from undesirable behaviours (such as nepotism and patronage, which are pervasive in the civil service) to new methods of performance management based on civil servant abilities, a performance culture, competent and meritocratic human resources and transparency in human resource matters (Acuña-Alfaro 2012).

In practice, the current remuneration regime in the public bureaucracy is said to be one of the main reasons that civil servants quit their public sector jobs. This seems to confirm the assumptions about the 'tendency in Vietnam to view public office as a vehicle for personal enrichment', which 'happens in a variety of ways whether it is officials charging for their services, running businesses, or exploiting their position for private gain in other ways' (Gainsborough, Dang and Tran 2009).

A non-randomized online survey by VietnamNet in 2012 identified perceptions regarding the different bureaucratic problems and practices rooted in the current incentives system. These practices to some extent reflect performance limitations and the obstacles to policy implementation, as they promote dispersion as opposed to concentration and professionalism. For instance, out of 14,108 online respondents, 77 per cent believe that civil servants' salaries are not sufficient to cover living expenses. This contrasts with the 3 per cent who assume that they can set aside savings from their salaries. Out of 15,106 online respondents, 35 per cent suggested that civil servants use their working time to do extra work for additional income, 31 per cent claimed that they took their positions in hopes of receiving additional informal payments, and 25 per cent said that they did extra work using their positions and networks. Answers to another question, which attracted 10,973 online respondents, suggested that the vast majority of civil servants join the civil service because of its perceived stability. In particular, 30 per cent choose to enter the civil service because it offers job stability until retirement; 26 per cent do so because they do not know where to work and 18 per cent opt for employment in the public sector because they hope to be promoted to higher positions. Some 12 per cent of the respondents suggested that they would join in order to contribute to the development of the state sector, while 7 per cent aimed to study and improve their capacities. Also, out of 10,745 online respondents, 37 per cent suggested that civil servants remain in their jobs because they allow for numerous opportunities to seek extra incomes, while only 3 per cent suggested that public sector agencies provide inspiring working environments (Acuña-Alfaro 2012: 13–15).

In terms of inter-organizational communication and enforcement activities, Van Meter and Van Horn (1975: 465–7) argue that effective implementation requires that policy objectives and standards be understood by those responsible for their achievement. In principle this is straightforward in the Vietnamese case, given the nature of the single-party regime in which, as mentioned earlier, the Party leads and the government implements. That is, the Party makes the important policy decisions and then the complex machinery of the public sector puts in place the normative framework, which is then followed by implementation on the part of responsible government agencies at the central or local levels. However, as mentioned earlier, all too often the processes of inter-organizational communication and enforcement in Vietnam face purposively complicated, frequently unclear and overlapping rules and regulations.

Gainsborough (2006; 2010) pointed out that regulations in Vietnam are frequently unclear and overlapping. This results from the fact that inexperienced and incapable officials draft such regulations. It is also due, however, to a logic inherent in the policy formulation process that requires this lack of clarity in order to create opportunities for private gain.

This lack of clarity and unevenness of implementation is to a large extent tied to the characteristics and disposition of implementing agencies. When referring to the Vietnamese bureaucratic characteristics some remarks can be made in terms of the capacities and disposition of implementers. For instance, a study by the Institute of State and Law, Vietnam Academy of Social Sciences (VASS) estimated that 60 per cent to 70 per cent of civil servants have not been trained on state management issues; 50 per cent of staff in key positions at the communal level have only finished primary or secondary school education and 79.2 per cent of staff in key positions in communes have not received professional training in state management (Uc 2007). Also, it has been said that among the top students in Vietnam's national universities, less than 10 per cent opt for careers in the public sector, while, according to the Ministry of Home Affairs (MHA), between 2003 and 2007, over 16,000 public and civil servants resigned from the public sector (0.8 per cent of the total number of public and civil servants). Most of the 'brain drain' was from the central level agencies, including the Ministry of Finance, where more than 1,000 people quit their jobs. This brain drain is also occurring at the provincial level: Ho Chi Minh City (HCMC) ranks first amongst provinces, with approximately 6,500 people having left their positions (Acuña-Alfaro 2008). This departure of capable people should be a central concern for the public sector (not in terms of quantity of staff, but rather in terms of quality).

As the retention of highly qualified bureaucrats is a crucial challenge for Vietnam, the policy discussion must be placed in the overall development context. As Vietnam shifts to higher levels of development and adapts to market-oriented reforms, citizens increasingly have options regarding the ways in which they contribute to development processes. It is understandable that talented public officials hope to make a difference wherever they can, and, as Vietnam grows economically, new jobs are created in the non-profit and private sectors. While this shift creates new opportunities for public officials, it also forces the government to be more competitive in attracting its share of talent from a much more mobile and far less loyal labour market. The public sector, therefore, needs to compete with the private sector in order to attract talented people.

In addition, analysis of the Labour Force Survey in 2009 suggests that one driver for this drain is the nature of 'multi-employment' in the state sector. That is, the share of workers with more than one job is heavily concentrated in state employment. On average, 14.4 per cent of state employees have more than one job. Multi-employment in the state is more prominent in public administration services (37 per cent), education (32.4 per cent) and health (10.1 per cent) (Warren and Pham 2010: 5–6). This tendency is motivated by dispersed and inefficient salary structures, in which salary is only a fraction of the income composition of public officials and civil servants. Income also extends to allowances, bonuses, envelopes and other supplementary income, including other jobs. A study has suggested that official salaries only amount to about one-third of public sector members' total income (National Academy of Public Administration and Central Institute of Economic Management 2006).

Also important are the perceptions that citizens must pay bribes to obtain jobs in the public sector and that personal connections are necessary for getting public sector jobs. A nationwide survey found that only 20 per cent to 23 per cent of citizens think that connections are not important when it comes to getting a job in a people's committee office or as a land registrar, primary school teacher or justice officer, while about 50 per cent think that connections are important for these jobs. In addition, the same survey found that 40.33 per cent of citizens believe that it is unnecessary to pay bribes in order to obtain public sector employment (UNDP et al. 2012: 25–32).

These practices reflect the disposition of the implementers, as suggested in the framework developed by Van Meter and Van Horn (1975: 465–7) and represent one of the greatest challenges ahead for the professionalization of the public bureaucracy in Vietnam. The obstacles to the reformation of Vietnam's public bureaucracy are associated with instituting a more transparent and simple system of incentives and remuneration and with bringing a culture of service delivery to the administrative system. Currently, it seems that the implementers consider these practices normal and to some extent necessary when it comes to getting a job in the public sector.

Data and evidence from citizens' experiences captured by PAPI and other surveys suggest that negative incentives in the public sector are a recurrent problem. These practices distort the provision of public services and limit the capacities of human resources (i.e., public administrators). For this, a more transparent and simple system of incentives and remuneration is required, as well as stronger and bolder efforts to clarify income-making opportunities for public sector workers beyond official salaries and regulated allowances. In addition to recruitment and promotion practices aimed at ensuring that the most capable and talented should be rewarded accordingly, those lagging behind should be handled properly, whether that means enhanced training and capacity-building opportunities or dismissal.

6.6 Implementation of two ASEAN policy initiatives

Following the other four country chapters in this book, two case studies are selected and analysed in the next two sections. The cases focus on the implementation of the ASEAN

Cosmetic Directive (ACD) and the ASEAN Ministerial Meeting on Transnational Crime (AMMTC) and Senior Officials Meeting on Transnational Crime (SOMTC) in Vietnam. These cases will identify those responsible for policy formulation and policy implementation and describe the ways in which implementation is undertaken and monitored, the relationships and networks (political and hierarchical) existing between policy-makers and implementers and the type of resources devoted to implementation.

To deal with ASEAN matters and to improve the quality and efficiency of Vietnam's participation in ASEAN, each Vietnamese ministry is responsible for the issues under its main jurisdiction. The Ministry of Foreign Affairs (MFA) plays an important role, as it is the national coordinating body, assisting the Prime Minister in directing all activities related to ASEAN cooperation. It does so with help from the National Secretariat of ASEAN, which is essentially the ASEAN Department within the MFA.

ASEAN generally emphasizes 'three pillars' for regional cooperation, which are security, economic integration and socio-cultural integration. In Vietnam, these three pillar areas are assigned to the MFA, the Ministry of Industry and Trade (MOIT) and the Ministry of Labour, War Invalids and Social Affairs, respectively. First, the MFA is the main government agency responsible for activities related to the ASEAN Coordinating Council (ACC) and the Council of the ASEAN Political and Security Community (APSC). The MFA is also responsible for coordinating preparation for ASEAN Summits, ASEAN Community Council Meetings and ASEAN Coordinating Council Meetings. Second, the MOIT is the main agency responsible for the ASEAN Economic Community Council (AEC). Third, the Ministry of Labour, War Invalids and Social Affairs is mainly responsible for the ASEAN Social Culture Community (ASCC).

These ministries have to contact and coordinate regularly with other relevant agencies in order to ensure consistency and uniformity in the exchange and processing of information, advice and suggestions as well as the implementation of guidelines and policies. In participating in ASEAN cooperation, each Vietnamese ministry is required to have one official or one department devoted to ASEAN-related matters. This official or department is responsible for coordinating within the ministry as well as with other ministries. If necessary, officials and departments establish joint working groups at the Ministry, to handle more complex cooperation activities.

Finally, the National Secretariat of ASEAN is the focal point for coordinating the activities of the agencies. It advises and recommends policies related to ASEAN cooperation and ensures that other government bodies develop and implement initiatives suggested by Vietnam. The ASEAN National Secretariat is responsible for keeping and updating the list of related departments and officials in charge of ASEAN matters in the various ministries and agencies. It is also the local focal point for updating the situation regularly as well as maintaining network operations in order to help strengthen the sharing of information and the coordination of activities among participating agencies within ASEAN.

A caveat is that there are differences between Vietnam's legal system and those of other ASEAN countries, including differences in the legal enforcement mechanisms. Moreover, ASEAN cooperation programmes (both bilateral and multilateral) must comply with international regulations. In such a complicated institutional setting, it is challenging to ensure swift and efficient implementation of the ACD and AMMTC/SOMTC initiatives.

6.7 Implementing the ASEAN Cosmetic Directive (ACD)

The Agreement on the ASEAN Harmonized Cosmetic Regulatory Scheme was signed by all ASEAN member countries on 2 September 2008, and came into effect on 1 January 2009. The ASEAN Cosmetic Agreement opened up a new period for cosmetics management in Vietnam. The health sector became the first sector to be fully integrated into ASEAN cosmetics management.

The formulation of management policies for the cosmetics sector is assigned to the Ministry of Health (MOH). Accordingly, it promulgates a list of cosmetics products, which must be registered as to their quality. After the Circular came into force, the Minister of Health signed Decision No. 2063/BYT-QD on 4 November 1996 promulgating the list of cosmetics products that are required to register the quality at the MOH. Since then, the MOH has issued and replaced five legal documents stipulating the professional management for cosmetics products.

Under the MOH, all the policies and management documents must be grounded in actual situations. For the policy-making process or the promulgation of new regulations, documents must comply with required procedures to ensure transparency and feasibility. The process of issuing a document or a new policy includes a series of steps, such as a proposal on the part of the agency in charge to revise a legal document and obtainment of leadership approval for discussion of the proposal at sub-committees, including approval by the respective legal departments. The completion of these steps is followed by a process of review and discussion across different agencies which itself precedes formal approval, issuance of policy documents and dissemination. Thus, from 1997 to the present, the MOH has been the highest-level professional management agency responsible for formulating policies aimed at regulating the cosmetics sector. It bears full government responsibility for these policies. However, cosmetics enterprises are subject to inspection and supervision by other authorities such as the Market Management Agency (MMA), which is under the MOIT as well as the Police Department and Customs Department.

The Prime Minister signed the decision to establish the 127 members of the Management Board. This board includes representatives from the MOH, the MOIT, the Customs Department and the Police Department, as well as authorities from the People's Committees. Among all these parties, the market management department is the leading agency. The management board is authorized to supervise and prevent low-quality products from being circulated in the market. The board coordinates at the inter-ministerial management level and appoints a supervision unit to check the market. The supervision unit requires the participation of authorities in related agencies.

Upon the promulgation of new policies or regulations, the MOH makes plans for the dissemination of documents and conducts training for agencies involved in implementing newly issued policies. The propagation and dissemination of policies are considered routine activities and are conducted annually. Such activities not only help enterprises and agencies get updates regarding the new regulations, but they also help management agencies promptly answer any questions relating to the new regulations. The management agencies consequently identify contents that are inadequate for and incompatible with the real situation. Accordingly, they can make plans for timely revision.

The agency authorized to implement the ACD is the Drug Administration of Vietnam (DAV). This agency is under the direct management of the MOH, but it has its own stamp and account. It acts as consultant to the Minister of Health regarding the policies and initiatives associated with the management of the cosmetics and drug sector. The DAV was established in 1996 and now has ninety-eight employees.

Policy-making is an ongoing process, and in order to meet real-world requirements and avoid being out-dated it requires continuous improvement. Therefore, each policy is planned for a certain period. Management agencies must be in consistent dialogue with enterprises in order to make plans and fully prepare the necessary resources for the policy-making process, especially in the context of today's rapid globalization.

6.7.1 Policy formulation

On 9 February 2003, the Minister of Industry and Trade signed the Agreement on the ASEAN Harmonized Cosmetic Regulatory Scheme. The Cosmetic Council meets twice a year, and one senior staff member of the cosmetic-management department is appointed to be Vietnam's representative and team leader to the Vietnamese delegation. After initiatives aimed at harmonizing the management of the cosmetics sector in the regional countries are passed, the MOIT played the role of the focal representative of the Vietnamese government. The MOIT led negotiations, holding meetings with relevant agencies to discuss the agreement terms and taking the initiative for building a harmonious agreement beneficial to all member countries.

To ensure transparency, all recommendations are sent out by two methods: direct dialogue and formal written documents certified by the head of each agency unit. After each round of negotiation, the working group meets and discusses new issues. The process is considered complete when all of the terms are adopted.

Planning new policies is relatively a new challenge for management agencies in the cosmetics sector in Vietnam. At this time, Vietnam is still subject to old management methods that focus more on the controlling role of management agencies than the role of the business sector. Making policies that focus on post-inspection in light of the ACD has required changes in the mindset of the management authorities. The management agencies must clearly define the autonomy of enterprises and create clear mechanisms for the cosmetics business. On the business side, they also have to identify their responsibility and accountability towards management agencies and consumers regarding the safety and quality of products. In response to these challenges, many workshops have been organized by the MOH to propagate the ACD and to collect comments from businesses as well as other relevant agencies. This is to ensure the highest practicability of the regulation once it is actually implemented.

Central and local supervision bodies are equipped with technical systems and personnel to ensure the management of the cosmetics sector. The exchange of information and coordination among authorized agencies, including technical agencies and supervising agencies, are promoted. The two key features of this mechanism are: (1) the annual appointment of supervising agency staff members to attend a training course conducted by the ASEAN Secretariat, in which they learn about new standards and testing measures for cosmetics products; (2) an annual meeting of representatives from the management agencies, supervising agencies and testing agencies to evaluate the standards of cosmetics management in Vietnam.

To prepare human resources for the implementation of the ACD, the MOH coordinates with the People's Committees at the local and provincial levels to complete its organization and empower the qualified staff to supervise and manage cosmetics manufacturing businesses in the region. More specifically, these activities include: (1) close coordination between the MOH and the People's Committees at the city and provincial levels as equal partners in information exchange, and initiation of the action plans; (2) implementation of the MOH's plans and policies by the Department of Health; (3) the annual appointment of the supervising unit by the MOH to review the activities of the Department of Health and to provide feedback to the MOH on its own performance; (4) management of the

Department of Health's budget and human resources by the People's Committees in coordination with the MOH, which allocates the resources and personnel for meeting cosmetic-management requirements.

The transformation from pre- to post-inspection requires strengthening the inspection of cosmetics at the sales departments. Therefore, the establishment of an inter-sectoral coordination mechanism in cosmetics market management has been essential. This system was established from the central to local levels. The interdisciplinary inspection team is composed of representatives from market-management agencies, police and customs departments. The exchange of information between these agencies has increasingly been strengthened as well.

The policy formulation process has encountered many challenges. Changing the mindset of managers and enterprises about cosmetics management has been the greatest challenge for policy-makers, as the ACD's goal has been to replace pre-supervision of cosmetics products with post-supervision. In the past, the management agencies were appointed to review the application documents and make decisions regarding which products met the legal requirements to circulate in the market. Once the products were approved for circulation in the market by the management agencies, the supervision and follow-up activities were not fully considered. In contrast, the 'post-supervision' system follows the reverse process, as the management agencies must place special focus on supervision and checking the products in their market circulation. Enterprises must bear full responsibility for the safety and quality of these products.

As such, enterprises are given autonomy by the management agencies. The fact that management agencies do not have absolute power in determining whether the products can be circulated in the market is also a great challenge. For the management agencies, it is necessary to ensure the autonomy of enterprises and to reduce red tape and unnecessary paperwork. The management agencies also need to ensure the quality of products without the discrimination of domestic or imported products. These agencies also need to strengthen consumer propaganda to help citizens to make wise choices when using cosmetics products. And, when it comes to enterprises, it is important to help them become aware of their responsibilities towards the management agencies and consumers. Enterprises must take active prevention measures to restrict poor-quality products. These difficulties can be solved only by appropriate propagation along with the application of appropriate sanctions for the enforcement of regulations.

6.7.2 *Policy implementation*

The MOH is responsible for assessing and announcing product quality. The processing time for assessment is three working days. The application files do not require technical documents. This process is also simpler than before, as the management agencies do not need to organize appraisal records. The MOH will not certify products that do not meet the regulations (for example, products that use ingredients containing substances banned for cosmetics use, or products not classified as cosmetics). For the remaining cases, the DAV issues quality certifications for cosmetics products. The ACD has set a rule that management agencies have three working days to resolve all application documents. However, the huge number of application files for both domestic and imported products poses great challenges to these management agencies. This has resulted in the increased decentralization of authority to the local management level. Each Provincial Health Department is responsible for receiving and handling dossiers applied in that province. This not only significantly reduces the workload for the central administration bodies but also helps business firms save money and time. In principle, the quality certification issued by the DAV (the central management) or the Provincial Health Department (the local management) has the same legal value.

When cosmetics are circulated in the market, both the central and local management agencies will undertake the post-trade monitoring activities. High-risk products are selected for testing. If there is any doubt about the product quality, the product is passed to the testing agencies for further examination. Those products not meeting standard requirements will be withdrawn, depending on the level of violation. Certain cases may be transferred to inspection agencies for penalties as prescribed.

Inspection and monitoring activities for cosmetics sales are done on a regular basis to enforce legal implementation and also to help businesses fully understand legal requirements. Not all enterprises involved in the cosmetics business fully understand the technical characteristics of their products. Very few of these enterprises are manufacturers, since they are involved mostly in marketing or distributing products. If the management agencies find evidence that a given product does not meet quality standards, they will inform the product's manufacturers. It is clear that after each test these enterprises have become more aware of the legal requirements and their responsibilities to consumers.

The ACD has also issued a regulation that has had a great impact on the operation of enterprises, especially local cosmetics manufacturers. According to the ACD, all cosmetics manufacturing facilities must conform to the principles and standards of the ASEAN's 'Cosmetics Good Manufacturing Practices' (CGMP). In fact, most firms have consciously developed a scientific production model that is closely related to the principles of the CGMP. However, they are worried about their own capacity to deploy fully and thoroughly the CGMP as the requirements are only feasible for large production scales. This fact makes the managers of enterprises increase the dissemination of information and training on the CGMP. Annually, the DAV organizes training courses on the CGMP for all cosmetics companies. At these training sessions, the management agencies, experts and businesses have open dialogue and exchanges regarding their experiences. The results are relatively optimistic, since most participants' CGMP awareness has been enhanced. However, there is still a gap between awareness and implementation, as the enterprises need time to change existing models and adjust their activities accordingly.

All provisions of the ACD are fully applied in Vietnam. Regulations on cosmetics labelling are also implemented thoroughly. This has created certain difficulties for management agencies and enterprises. At present, the Vietnam government has issued general regulations on labelling for goods exchanged in the market. However, there exist other provisions regulating product labelling that overlap with the ACD's requirements. Hence, businesses do not know exactly which rules to follow. Such overlapping in regulations happens not only in Vietnam but also in other countries in the region.

There are also other challenges in implementing the ACD. The most noticeable challenge is linguistic because the ACD is written in English, and its contents must be translated into Vietnamese. Translation from English into Vietnamese is difficult, as certain issues are not easily translated into Vietnamese. To resolve this problem, the DAV (as an agency at the central management level) has issued guidelines for the publication of cosmetics features. Such guidelines are applied to all the provinces in order to avoid any discrepancies in management by the Department of Health in different localities.

Any new regulation applied in practice will meet with certain difficulties, and the ACD is no exception. There are a number of provisions in the old regulations that are no longer suitable for the current situation. Some provisions are also unclear or inconsistent with the provisions of the ACD. These shortcomings are detected in time thanks to the constant interaction between the management bodies and enterprises. On 25 January 2011, the MOH issued Circular No. 06/2011/TT-YT regulating cosmetics management. This Circular replaced Decision 48/2007/QD-BYT. The adoption of the new policy has required the continuous improvement of working methods. Enhancing staff capacity, collecting recommendations from business sectors and updating changes in market practices are all essential to the policy-making process.

Regular participation in ASEAN Cosmetic Council meetings also enables the managers to exchange experiences with their counterparts in other countries in the region. As such, the managers can draw lessons which are applicable to Vietnam and make the regulations more viable.

6.7.3 Conclusion

More than four years after the implementation of the Agreement on the ASEAN Harmonized Cosmetic Regulatory Scheme, the management agencies have granted more than 54,000 quality certificates for cosmetics products. These certificates recognize that these cosmetics products circulate in the market. However, 54,000 certificates do not reflect all quality aspects of the products. A majority of applicants are granted certificates. Only a few products violate the regulations and are thus rejected. Applications are rejected, for instance, when products contain forbidden chemicals or when they are not categorized as cosmetic, among other reasons. Of the 54,000 certificates awarded to applicants, the DAV granted 3,000, and the Department of Health granted the rest.

The total of 54,000 certificates is an impressive figure that is achieved by strong efforts on the part of management agencies at both the central and local levels. In addition, close coordination between the agencies and People's Committees of the provinces and cities aids in the prompt resolution of difficulties encountered in the implementation process. Necessary resources, including human resources, financial resources and facilities have been mobilized to consolidate the management apparatus.

Thus far, funds for the implementation of the ACD have been provided from the state budget. The government guarantees the necessary funds for the effective implementation of the ACD. In turn, the government requires transparency in all activities. In addition, the World Health Organization also funds a number of activities related to the establishment and dissemination of policies. These activities include specialized training on inspection, testing CGMP and monitoring cosmetics sales departments. Some activities receive funds from the ASEAN Secretariat, especially funding for specialists.

At present, the coordination and cooperation scheme has several weaknesses. First, financial resources are not allocated appropriately. Supervising agencies are responsible for the purchase of cosmetics samples, but they are incapable of fulfilling their obligations. The management bodies can spend 80 per cent of their revenue earned from collected fees (the fees that enterprises must pay to obtain certificates for their products) in order to conduct their activities. The rest of the revenue must be transferred to the state budget.

The policy-making process is a regular and continuous activity. A policy is feasible only for a certain period. This requires policy-makers to exchange information and coordinate regularly with policy implementation agencies. The introduction of new policies must be grounded in practical situations. Once a policy is issued, a corresponding regulation is put into implementation. Such regulations govern all activities related to issues under consideration. Market inspectors for cosmetics businesses and other management agencies monitor the implementation process. This monitoring of different stakeholders helps to ensure strict legal enforcement as well as management transparency.

Besides its benefits, the ACD also poses challenges to both management agencies and enterprises. The post-inspection mechanism requires authorities to strengthen post-trade monitoring activities. Under the current situation, the number of management staff in the cosmetics field is too limited to meet inspection requirements. On the other hand, the mechanisms for coordination and information exchange between agencies are not fully developed. Though the Vietnamese government is pushing for administrative reform, many cumbersome administrative procedures still undermine the effectiveness of inspections.

For the business sector, especially small-scale enterprises, the deployment of CGMP in accordance with the ACD also creates many difficulties due to limited financial and human resources. Many efforts have been made to facilitate the exchange of experiences, information and training, but the successful implementation of the ACD requires close cooperation from the authorities and efforts on the part of the enterprises themselves as well.

Agreement on the ASEAN Harmonized Cosmetic Regulatory Scheme was reached over six years ago. In situations like this, however, any member country will face certain difficulties in applying the agreement provisions in practice. For this reason, the ASEAN Cosmetic Council holds regular biannual meetings that provide opportunities for countries to exchange experiences and work together to overcome difficulties. Vietnam is trying hard to develop a cosmetics sector that is fully integrated with those of the other countries in the region.

6.8 Implementing the ASEAN Ministerial Meeting on Transnational Crime (AMMTC)/ Senior Officials Meeting on Transnational Crime (SOMTC)

This second case study begins with a brief update on transnational crimes in Vietnam, followed by a detailed description of the coordination of the Vietnamese authorities and agencies involved in implementing the AMMTC/SOMTC initiatives. It concludes with a discussion of the challenges faced by Vietnam in implementing the AMMTC/SOMTC.

In recent years, transnational crimes, which are crimes involving foreign elements in Vietnam, have become more organized and complicated. These crimes have increased in magnitude and seriousness. Increasingly, international crime groups collude with domestic criminal gangs. Information exchange concerning transnational crimes through the Interpol channel increased significantly in 2011. Among these transnational crimes, the most serious are drug trafficking, human trafficking, assisting illegal migrants to third countries and internet crimes.

Dealing with these crimes requires a chain of complex efforts coordinated at all branches and levels of government. In the past, Vietnam had a general National Committee on Preventing and Fighting Crimes. Later, this committee was divided into separate committees to deal with specific major crimes. These committees include the National Committee on Preventing and Fighting Drug Trafficking and the National Committee on Preventing and Fighting Human Trafficking. The Ministry of Public Security (MPS) coordinates these committees. Within the MPS, the General Department of

Police is usually the liaison party coordinating the activities of the other ministries and local authorities. It makes requests, collects information and analyses and develops action plans for the Prime Minister's approval.

Generally, in committing crimes, criminals take advantage of the land common to and the sea bordering the ASEAN countries. This heightens the necessity of cooperation in fighting transnational crime in each country as well as in the ASEAN community. Since joining ASEAN in 1995, Vietnam has been working with the organization's other members to combat transnational crimes in the region and in the world. For each ASEAN agreement that Vietnam participates in, the government establishes a national steering committee or inter-ministerial working group to coordinate related activities and draft national reports on the implementation of each agreement. Usually, the MPS also coordinates these steering committees (with the exception of the United Nations Convention against Corruption). The MPS has established an office to support each of the committees.

6.8.1 Coordination for implementing the AMMTC/SOMTC

Responsibilities for dealing with transnational crimes under the AMMTC/SOMTC are divided among several government departments. The MPS is the key agency in charge of all activities related to the prevention and combating of transnational crimes under the ASEAN coordination schemes and in general. The Ministry of National Defence manages the Border Guard, Coast Guard and the Navy, which are involved extensively in these activities. The Customs Department is responsible for dealing with such illegal transnational activities as smuggling, drug trafficking, weapons smuggling and money laundering. The MFA coordinates the detection, extradition and transfer of criminals. The Financial Intelligence Unit (State Bank) provides support for the prevention of money laundering and terrorism financing. The Ministry of Finance's Budget Division allocates the government budget for the prevention of transnational crimes. The Supreme People's Procuracy prosecutes criminals in court and presides over all the procedures regarding extradition and transfer of criminals. The Ministry of Justice supports the preparation of mutual judicial assistance on transnational crimes at the multilateral and bilateral levels. The Ministry of Communication and Information is responsible for the propagation and dissemination via mass media of information regarding the AMMTC/SOMTC meetings, especially when these meetings discuss transnational crime issues in Vietnam and the region. Further support comes from other organizations such as the Committee on National Drug Control, which assists in the fight against drug trafficking, and the Vietnam Women's Union, which plays an important role in preventing the trafficking of women and children. The MPS coordinates support from these agencies and relevant government organizations at all levels.

Within the MPS, the General Department of Police coordinates the implementation of policy initiatives by ASEAN by assigning responsibilities to its seven functional units. First, the Interpol Vietnam Office (IVO) is responsible for promoting cooperation between the police force of Vietnam and ASEANAPOL, INTERPOL and the police forces of all countries in joint efforts to prevent crimes. The IVO is the lead agency for drafting national reports and policy initiatives launched at the AMMTC/SOMTC meetings. Its other functions include: making proposals for research projects and institutions for AMMTC/SOMTC operations, appointing senior Vietnamese police officials to special working groups or as consultants, providing suggestions to the Vietnamese government and to the MPS regarding their participation in resolutions for preventing transnational crime, providing support to the Vietnamese delegation in the AMMTC and chairing meetings to prepare the convening of the AMMTC/SOMTC in Hanoi.

The Immigration Administration Department implements activities for the detection and prevention of transnational crime. It also coordinates the processing of cases of expulsion and extradition as well as the transfer of Vietnamese offenders. The Criminal Police Department chairs the detection and investigation of transnational organized crimes by groups in Vietnam. It is in charge of investigating serious criminal offences such as murder, robbery, kidnapping, extortion, gambling, drug trafficking and money laundering. The trafficking of women and children are significant issues closely related to recent ASEAN policy initiatives. On the other hand, the Drug Crime Police Department coordinates with the entire public security system to detect and investigate the manufacture, transportation and sale of drugs in Vietnam. Drug deals are mostly tied to transnational organized crimes. This department must closely cooperate with other agencies in Vietnam and with the police forces of ASEAN countries as well to effectively fight this sort of crime. The Economic Police Department coordinates with the

Financial Intelligence Unit of the State Bank and the National Interpol in order to investigate organized money laundering crimes. It also cooperates with the Custom and Tax Department to prevent transnational smuggling activities like counterfeit goods transactions. The Internet Crime Police Department focuses on criminals using high technology (namely, the Internet) to commit crimes such as internal network attacks and credit card information theft and is concerned with detecting and removing international crime syndicates. Finally, the Anti-Terrorism Department conducts activities for the detection and investigation of terrorism as well as for the coordination of internal and international cooperation in combating such crimes.

Besides the General Department of Police, the General Department of Security handles cases of terrorism and immigration, especially crimes related to foreign citizenship, human trafficking and internet crimes. The Legal Department improves the international legal instruments related to the combating of transnational crimes in collaboration with the Ministry of Justice. Local authorities in the country, especially those in provinces that share borders with other neighbouring countries such as China or the ASEAN countries, also play a significant role. Based on the regular coordination results, these agencies must take action for the implementation of ASEAN policy initiatives.

6.8.2 Dissemination of policy initiatives

After reporting to the Prime Minister on the results of the AMMTC and getting approval for the National Action Plan, the MPS assigns tasks to its functional units, which include the General Department of Police and General Department for Combating Crime. These functional units will exchange information and coordinate with other relevant ministries and industries about the implementation of the policy initiatives. In addition to formal written notifications, the dissemination of ASEAN policy initiatives is also conducted in the following manner: first, meetings are organized with key leaders to communicate the new policy initiatives, while each subunit continues to disseminate the basic contents of the new policy initiatives to their officers; second, the General Department for Combating Crime holds meetings to discuss the new initiatives, assign specific tasks and propose new measures to improve the policy initiatives; and third, information about the policy initiatives is posted in magazines and newsletters such as the *Journal of the People's Police* and the Interpol newsletter.

Information on transnational crimes is disseminated through internal media channels within the branches and functional agencies. This helps to improve awareness of transnational crimes and to enhance cooperation within the system. Through the press, radio, television and all other media, information dissemination alerts the public to issues regarding transnational crimes and contributes to the fight against these crimes.

6.8.3 *Reporting system*

Various departments cooperate to prevent and combat transnational crime, and each is responsible for its own assigned performance.[2] All associated departments must submit periodical reports including monthly, quarterly, six-month and annual reports on the results of the implementation of policy initiatives. These reports are sent to the leadership of the MPS and other police units.

The Advisory Department assists the General Department of Police in compiling all reports, preparing a final version and then seeking out the Minister of Public Security's approval. Each department's reports (especially the annual and biannual reports) describe difficulties and obstacles encountered in the implementation of the policy initiatives and propose specific measures and recommendations for improving implementation. The report also includes suggestions on the measures taken and requests assistance with human resources, budget allowance and enhanced cooperation between involved sectors and levels. The MPS then finalizes the ministerial report on transnational crimes, which is approved and signed by the Minister and then sent to the Prime Minister and other related ministries for implementation.

6.8.4 Difficulties in implementing the AMMTC/SOMTC

Like most other international institutions, the AMMTC/SOMTC do not have effective enforcement mechanisms in

[2] Although police departments are considered units of the armed forces and therefore follow a top-down command management in which all units follow orders and are instructed and supervised from above, these units can actively implement their assigned tasks and responsibilities.

Vietnam (or in other member countries) and therefore face challenges in implementing their initiatives. Further, the intervening periods between AMMTC and the SOMTC meetings are too short (two years and one year, respectively) for the proper implementation of initiatives. As a result, implementation sometimes remains on the surface and on paper rather than having real impact in the fight against transnational crimes.

Another challenge for Vietnam in implementing the AMMTC/SOMTC is the lack of staff proficient in foreign languages, experienced in conducting surveys or skilled in technology and finance. To overcome this difficulty, the most common solution has been to conduct more training programmes, which are led by specialists in relevant fields of expertise. Such training also requires participation from consultants with expertise in different areas, including financial analysts (who help find solutions to curb money laundering activities).

When encountering technical investigation problems, such as determining the method of processing chemicals, homemade bombs for terrorist purposes, preparation of synthetic drugs and the assessment of DNA in blood samples, hair and saliva, the relevant departments in Vietnam often seek support from the more advanced ASEAN partners or professional associations. Certain cases have even been sent to United Nations' experts or to developed countries for technical assistance.

One major issue with implementing the AMMTC/SOMTC is the dominance of political factors over other factors. Therefore, bilateral cooperation with China, Laos and

Cambodia has been more effective than with other countries because of their political ties with Vietnam. Vietnam and China (which plays an 'observer' role in both the AMMTC and SOMTC) have collaborated very fruitfully in dealing with transnational crimes, particularly in drug trafficking and the cross-border escapes of domestic criminals. Geopolitical conditions contribute to the effective cooperation among the police, customs and border guard forces of these two countries.

However, cooperation between Vietnam and China in preventing transnational crimes still faces three problems. First, persons from China have migrated illegally to Vietnam, mainly in order to go to other ASEAN countries. After they are deported to China by the Vietnamese police force, they often come back to Vietnam shortly after their deportation. Second, when Vietnam requests Chinese assistance for the search and rescue of trafficked Vietnamese women in China, China is often very slow with cooperation and support. Third, detecting facilities that produce counterfeit products or laundered money from China is not an easy task. Attempts to prevent the illegal importation into Vietnam of counterfeit goods made in China have not been effective.

Similarly, cooperation between Vietnam, Laos and Cambodia has also been effective because of their close political ties. Laos even allows Vietnam's police force to enter its territory to arrest criminals. During the past ten years or so, the three Indochina countries have organized annual meetings in order to improve the joint operations of the police and public security forces at the borders regarding transnational crimes. In cooperation with Laos, however, there have been problems with the investigation of drug deals along the Vietnam–Laos border.

Many members of ethnic minorities (particularly the H'mong) in Laos are involved in these drug deals, and it is difficult to manage them. Regarding Vietnam's cooperation with Cambodia, too, the ease of crossing the borders between the two countries has presented obstacles to joint efforts aimed at preventing the trafficking of women. The police force also faces challenges in preventing Vietnamese people from crossing the border to gamble in casinos in Cambodia.

There are also many difficulties associated with the mechanisms of coordination between Vietnam and other ASEAN countries. There are always delays in the assessment stage and loopholes in the supervision and management processes. The functions of government agencies are not always clear-cut in Vietnam. This leads to the overlap of functions among the government's different branches. Consequently, the process for implementing transnational crime prevention has not been as swift as it needs to be. It is important to have a specific plan to increase the accountability of the local authorities. The domestic laws regulating transnational crimes should be compatible with international law. Member countries need a legal system to lay out the mechanisms for the effective enforcement of transnational crime prevention. Member countries should set strategies for addressing policy planning to ensure effective working mechanisms and supervision.

6.9 Conclusion

Bureaucratic reform in Vietnam has experienced a 'waved' approach in terms of implementation and reform. The policy formulation process has also impacted these 'waves'. During the first wave, the 'mandarin' system was abolished. The second wave includes the application of the 'cadre' system typical of communist regimes. The third and most recent wave of reform has amounted to a critical turning point, especially in combination with the country's transition towards a socialist-oriented market economy. In this third wave, the most significant changes have been the introduction of the 1998 Ordinance on Public Officials and Civil Servants and its enactment as a law in 2009.

To a certain extent, the public bureaucracy has become more professional than it has been in the past. The new public bureaucracy has not inherited the confused state-management functions and public service delivery of a centrally planned economy, which has resulted in the sense that public employees are, in normative terms, no longer a subject of regulation of the new Law. Other than that, there has been no dramatic change in the way in which public officials and civil servants are managed, promoted, rewarded and motivated. This is a key challenge that Vietnam's public bureaucracy will face unless strong political reform is envisioned and embarked upon.

A key question now involves the facilitation of reforms towards a modernized and more professional public bureaucracy: what needs to be done? Would a more modern public bureaucracy require greater distinction between the two subjects of public governance (i.e., public officials and civil servants)? Would the public bureaucracy require more competitive remuneration packages in order to motivate civil servants and avoid the brain drain to the private sector?

Would it require increased impartiality and a nepotism-free, personal bias-free working environment in which civil servants could feel equally treated? Or would the public bureaucracy require a stronger merit-based approach to personnel management in order to encourage and reward talented individuals for joining it? Further thought and research should take into account questions of clearer power divisions, stronger institutional reforms, more available resources in both personnel and financial terms and robust agents for change in the public bureaucracy.

The case studies of the implementation of the two ASEAN policy initiatives underline these challenges. In Vietnam, the MOH and MPS are the two organizations responsible for implementing the ACD and the AMMTC/SOMTC respectively. The 'waved' approach of public administration reform has had both desirable and undesirable effects on the implementation of these initiatives. Both organizations face considerable political influence in their policy-making and implementing tasks, which dominate professional expertise. The political heads of these organizations are promoted internally, indicating no distinction between politician and public servant career paths. This gives the leadership of the organizations professional expertise, which somewhat offsets the political influence mentioned above. The waves of reform did not create a merit-based incentive system to motivate employees to implement these initiatives well. Uncompetitive pay does not attract talented individuals to work in these organizations and diverts existing staff to focus instead on private income making activities. These problems hinder significantly the implementation and monitoring of these two ASEAN initiatives.

In order to effectively implement policies, the dual-system in public-personnel management must be carefully reviewed and the demarcation lines between relevant authorities in personnel administration and political appointment need clarification. In Vietnam, it seems that the personnel authorities at both the central and local levels are blurred at present, and it is suggested that the secondary legislation should contain provisions protecting the bureaucracy from political or other kinds of interference. That is, to draw the demarcation line between the CPV and the central personnel management agency is a challenging matter. Nevertheless, it must be considered for the further development of the public bureaucracy in Vietnam. The recent approval of the secondary legislation is a positive step in that direction as it focuses on regulating the second tier of government officials. Yet changes in normative documents will not be a panacea for successful implementation because the process is more manifold, and tougher political decisions regarding differentiation, merit and incentives will be needed to successfully implement the intended reforms and changes.

References

Aberbach, J. D., Putnam, R. D. and Rockman, B. A. 1981. *Bureaucrats and Politicians in Western Democracies*. Cambridge, MA: Harvard University Press.

Acuña-Alfaro, J. 2008. 'Where Does Bureaucracy Reform Fit in?', Policy brief on public administration reform and anti-corruption. UNDP Vietnam, Hanoi.

(ed.) 2009a. *Reforming Public Administration in Vietnam: Current Situation and Recommendations*. Hanoi: National Political Publishing House.

2009b. 'Overview: Addressing Governance and Public Administration Reform Effectively in Vietnam'. In J. Acuña-Alfaro (ed.), *Reforming Public Administration in Vietnam: Current Situation and Recommendations*. Hanoi: National Political Publishing House, pp. 21–40.

2012. 'Incentives and Salaries in Vietnam's Public Sector', *Vietnam Law and Legal Forum* (January–February): 11–15.

Do, P. D. 2009 'Wage Policy for Cadres and Civil Servants in Vietnam'. In Institute for Personnel Organizational Sciences and Fafo (eds), *Civil Servants Policies Norwegian and Vietnamese Experiences: Workshop Proceedings*. Hanoi, pp. 100–20.

The Economist 2013. *Pocket World in Figures, 2014 Edition*. London: Profile Books.

Fritzen, S. 2005. 'The "Misery" of Implementation: Governance, Institutions and Anti-Corruption in Vietnam'. In N. Tarling (ed.), *Corruption and Good Governance in Asia*. London: Routledge, pp. 98–120.

Gainsborough, M. 2006. *National Integrity Systems Transparency International: Country Study Report of Vietnam*. Berlin: Transparency International.

2010. *Vietnam: Rethinking the State*. London: Zed Books.

Gainsborough, M., Dang, N. D. and Tran, T. P. 2009. 'Corruption, Public Administration Reform and Development: Challenges and Opportunities as Vietnam Moves towards Middle-Income Status'. In J. Acuña-Alfaro (ed.), *Reforming Public Administration in Vietnam: Current Situation and Recommendations*. Hanoi: National Political Publishing House, pp. 377–427.

General Statistics Office 2010. 'The 2009 Vietnam Population and Housing Census: Major Findings'. Central Population and Housing Census Steering Committee, Hanoi.

2012a. 'Report on the 2011 Vietnam Labour Force Survey'. Ministry of Planning and Investment, Hanoi.

2012b. 'Report on the Labour Force Survey: First Nine Months of 2012'. Ministry of Planning and Investment, Hanoi, available at: www.gso.gov.vn (accessed 9 January 2013).

2014a. 'Media Brief: Socio-economic Situation in 2013'. Ministry of Planning and Investment, Hanoi, available at: www.gso.gov.vn (accessed 2 December 2014).

2014b. 'Report on the Labour Force Survey: Quarter 2, 2014'. Ministry of Planning and Investment, Hanoi, available at: www.gso.gov.vn (accessed 2 December 2014).

Le, Minh Thong 2009. 'Current Issues Regarding Development and Implementation of Personnel Policy for Cadres and Civil Servants in Vietnam'. In Institute for Personnel Organizational Sciences and Fafo (eds), *Civil Servants Policies Norwegian and Vietnamese Experiences: Workshop Proceedings.* Hanoi, pp. 6–19.

Ministry of Finance Vietnam 2010. 'Decision 3234/QD-BTC on Publicizing State Budget Estimates for 2010'. Hanoi.

Ministry of Home Affairs Vietnam 2005. *Lịch sử Bộ Nội vụ* [The History of the Ministry of Home Affairs]. Hanoi: National Political Publishing House.

2008. 'Report on General Review of the Implementation of the Ordinance on Public Officials and Civil Servants from 1998 to 2008'. Hanoi.

2010. 'Report on Review of the Implementation of the Public Administration Reform Master Plan (2001–2010) and Orientation and Tasks for Public Administration Reform for the

Period of 2011–2020', draft report for submission to the Government for approval of issuance, Hanoi.

Ministry of Home Affairs Vietnam, Asian Development Bank and Vietnam Competitiveness Initiative 2008. 'Regulatory Impact Assessment (RIA): Report of the Draft Law on Public Officials and Civil Servants'. Hanoi.

National Academy of Public Administration (NPA) and Central Institute of Economic Management (CIEM) 2006. 'The Current Salary System in Vietnam's Public Administration: Need for Decentralized Approach', report prepared for the Deutsche Gesellschaft für Internationale Zusammenarbeit (GTZ) [German Technical Cooperation Agency], Hanoi.

Nguyen, H. T. and Nguyen L. P. 2010. *Public Administration*. Hanoi: Science and Technology Publishing House.

Nguyen, M. P. 2009. 'Process to Establish Public Service: Public Staff Mechanism in Viet Nam and Current Emerged Issues'. In Institute for Personnel Organizational Sciences and Fafo (eds), *Civil Servants Policies Norwegian and Vietnamese Experiences: Workshop Proceedings*. Hanoi, pp. 83–6.

Painter, M. 2006. 'Sequencing Bureaucracy Pay Reforms in Vietnam: Transition or Leapfrog?', *Governance*, 19(2): 325–46.

Painter, M., Ha, H. H. and Chu, Q. K. 2009. 'Institutional Reform for Public Administration in Contemporary Vietnam'. In J. Acuña-Alfaro (ed.), *Reforming Public Administration in Vietnam: Current Situation and Recommendations*. Hanoi: National Political Publishing House, pp. 318–76.

Poon, Y., Nguyen, K. H. and Do, X. T. 2009. 'The Reform of the Bureaucracy System as Vietnam Moves into the Middle-income Country Category'. In J. Acuña-Alfaro (ed.), *Reforming Public Administration in Vietnam: Current Situation and Recommendations*. Hanoi: National Political Publishing House, pp. 197–249.

Tuoi Tre [newspaper] 2010. 'Ba nội dung đánh giá cán bộ, công chức' [Three Sets of Criteria for Evaluation of Performance of Public Officials and Civil Servants], 26 February, available at: http://tuoitre.vn/tin/chinh-tri-xa-hoi/20100226/ba-noi-dung-danh-gia-can-bo-cong-chuc/365332.html (accessed 8 January 2015).

Uc, D. T. (ed.) 2007. *Evaluation of the Results of Public Administration Reform and Solutions to Acceleration of Public Administration Reform in Vietnam*. Hanoi: Institute of State and Law, Vietnam Academy of Social Sciences (in Vietnamese).

United Nations Development Programme (UNDP) 2011. 'Vietnam Human Development Report: Social Progress for Human Development'. UNDP Vietnam, Hanoi.

United Nations Development Programme (UNDP), Centre for Community Support and Development Studies (CECODES), Vietnam Fatherland Front (VFF) and Commission on People's Petitions (CPP) 2012, 'The Vietnam Governance and Public Administration Performance Index (PAPI): Measuring Citizens' Experiences', joint policy research paper, Hanoi, available at: www.papi.vn (accessed 9 January 2013).

Van Meter, D. S. and Van Horn, C. E. 1975. 'The Policy Implementation Process: A Conceptual Framework', *Administration and Society*, 6(4): 445–88.

Verheijen, A. J. G. 2007. 'Public Administration in Post-Communist States'. In B. G. Peters and J. Pierre (eds), *The Handbook of Public Administration*, London: Sage Publications, pp. 311–19.

Warren, A. and Pham, T. L. P. 2010. 'An Analysis of Employment in the State Sector in Vietnam: Main Findings', unpublished draft version of UNDP Vietnam Technical Note, Hanoi.

Woodside, A. 2006. *Lost Modernities: China, Vietnam, Korea and the Hazards of World History*. Cambridge, MA: Harvard University Press.

World Bank 2009. *Vietnam Development Report 2010: Modern Institutions*. Hanoi: World Bank.

2014. (Washington DC) 'World Development Indicators', available at: http://data.worldbank.org/country/vietnam#cp_wdi (accessed 12 December 2014).

Chapter 7

Policy implementation in ASEAN and the European Union: the problem of asymmetric compliance

Giulio Napolitano

7.1 The public bureaucracy's role in implementing international policies

Policy-makers and scholars around the world are aware of the problems that arise when public bureaucracies must execute the statutes approved by parliaments and follow the guidelines decided at the political level. The political system, economic development, geographical conditions, administrative culture and civic traditions are all factors responsible for the different levels of administrative performance in policy implementation within every nation (Pressman and Wildavsky 1984). From this general starting point, specific attention has been devoted to the following reasons for the failures in policy implementation in the Third World, namely the lack of qualified personnel and funds; insufficient direction and control from political leaders; resistance; corruption; and social indiscipline (Quah 1984).

Apart from the specific national context, rational choice approaches make clear why, all over the world, policy implementation is so difficult. Policy-makers, who are usually elected, act as principals, delegating implementation to expert agents, the bureaucrats. In every principal–agent relationship, principals suffer agency losses, because agents might drift in order to maximize their personal interests rather than perfectly accomplishing the mandate (Shepsle 1992; Horn 1995; Huber, Shipan and Pfahler 2001). If principals wish to reduce the risk of such losses, they must pay the costs of establishing and making effective a proper system of control, which usually is shaped by 'administrative law' (McCubbins, Noll and Weingast 1987; Mashaw 1990; Macey 1992; Posner 2001). This explains why the problem of policy implementation is also one of the key issues of political and scientific debate in the developed countries.

Public bureaucracies also play a fundamental – even if often neglected – role in implementing international norms and policies. Signing a treaty and then adopting coherent national legal rules in the execution of an international obligation is often insufficient for that purpose. And even when courts, at both the national and supranational levels, enforce individual rights arising from international agreements, as in the case of the European Convention on Human Rights, they do just a part of the work (protecting rights is not simply a matter of *ex post* enforcement on a case-by-case basis; it requires an active policy *ex ante* too).

In an international context, problems of policy implementation become harder to resolve because they also involve compliance and not just implementation. In other words, countries may be unable to implement international policies because of a lack (depending on various factors) of administrative capacity. But these countries can also be deliberately non-compliant. They can show a willingness to cooperate, signing a treaty or adopting a collective decision. And, then, they can avoid limitations and negative effects coming from that, through ineffective policy implementation at the national level. In such a case, non-compliance is a rational and opportunistic strategy through which a country maximizes the benefits of being part of an international cooperative environment without bearing the subsequent costs. This is a typical free rider strategy.

Problems of implementation and compliance change according to the kind – bilateral or multilateral, simple or complex, 'organized' or not – of the international legal framework considered. In some cases, there is a simple bilateral relationship between an international organization and a country, as illustrated in the World Bank's programmes in developing countries. The World Bank and the recipient country sign an agreement to promote economic growth through specific actions and projects specified in the contract. Policy implementation by the recipient country is relevant only within the contractual link with the World Bank.

In other cases, on the contrary, there is a multilateral relationship arising from an international treaty, which has been signed by several countries. The treaty may be a single purpose one, when it is related to a specific policy goal (like the Protocol of Kyoto); or a multi-purpose one, when it refers to a plurality of connected policies (like the Treaty of Rome establishing the European Economic Community, and the Treaties of Lisbon on the European Union and its functioning). Policy implementation, in those cases, requires active cooperation by multiple actors. Matters become even more complex when there are several games on the table, with each one different from the others.

Another relevant distinction is between the cases in which the proper implementation of the treaty occurs under simple breach of contract rules or the oversight of a purely intergovernmental setting (a body composed of representatives of national governments, like the Security Council); or is in the hands of a truly supranational organization with an administrative 'infrastructure' (like the European Commission (EC)). In the first case, implementation oversight is less effective. Infringements procedures are long lasting. And, in a purely international setting, each national representative tries to protect its own country from a negative judgment of non-compliance.

According to the different legal frameworks existing at the international level, problems of policy implementation change. In a purely bilateral relationship, the outcomes are fundamentally either compliance or non-compliance (of course, in the middle, there are many intermediate cases of partial compliance). Apart from the issue of administrative capacity, the implementing country has to decide whether its dominant strategy is to comply or not. In assuming such a decision, it will evaluate the costs of effective compliance and the risk of being detected for any infringement.

In a multilateral relationship, on the contrary, we might have, beyond compliance or non-compliance, also the case of asymmetric compliance. The asymmetry may be across countries, when some of the stipulating parties are compliant and others are not; and between different policies covered by the same 'multi-purpose' treaty. Administrative capacity may differ from one country to another and from one policy to another. Countries have different administrative traditions and performance. However, bureaucratic quality is not homogeneous, and varies in the different countries. Furthermore, strategies of compliance and non-compliance in a multi-party and multi-game setting are also more complex. Some countries might be tempted to free ride on other countries' loyal cooperation: or to adopt a strategy of selective cooperation according to the kind of policy. Moreover, private stakeholders influence in different ways implementation and compliance; but not with the same intensity in all policies. Their pressure is supposed to be stronger in market areas, where they can benefit from the removal of national barriers, than in non-market ones.

In such a context, the existence of a truly supranational organization with an administrative infrastructure might limit agency losses: partly because it can directly perform some implementation tasks and partly because it is better equipped to monitor effective compliance by member states and national administrations. Promoting administrative convergence and regulating national administrations can reduce ineffective implementation and non-compliance too.

7.2 Asymmetric compliance: ASEAN and the European Union compared

As shown in the previous six chapters of this book, the case of asymmetric compliance, across both countries and policies, is particularly relevant in the case of the Association of Southeast Asian Nations (ASEAN). This is not a surprising outcome because ASEAN is a typical multi-purpose legal entity, arising from an international treaty signed by different sovereign governments. ASEAN has ten members: the founding five members of 1967 (Indonesia, Malaysia, the Philippines, Singapore and Thailand) and the other five members, which joined ASEAN in the 1980s and in the 1990s: Brunei Darussalam, Myanmar, Cambodia, Laos and Vietnam. In November 2007, the ASEAN members signed the ASEAN Charter, which governs their relations and establishes ASEAN as an international legal entity.

The complex structure of ASEAN provides a favourable environment for asymmetric compliance. ASEAN is both a geopolitical and an economic organization. Its aims include economic growth, social progress, cultural development and protection of regional peace and stability. In particular, regional cooperation is organized according to these three pillars: the ASEAN Political Security Community; the ASEAN Economic Community; and the ASEAN Socio-Cultural Community.

Another distinctive feature of ASEAN is the clear separation between policy formulation and policy implementation. In the ASEAN institutional system, policy formulation is in the hands of Heads of State or Government who constitute the ASEAN Summit. The ASEAN Coordinating Council, consisting of the Foreign Affairs Ministers, prepares the meetings of the ASEAN Summit, coordinates the implementation of the ASEAN Summit decisions, enhances policy coherence among the ASEAN Community Councils and monitors the Secretary-General's activities. Each one of the three ASEAN Communities is governed by its own Council. Every member state shall designate its national representation for each ASEAN Community Council meeting. The ASEAN Sectorial Ministerial Bodies shall implement the agreements and decisions of the ASEAN Summit and strengthen cooperation in their respective fields.

Policy implementation, on the contrary, is mainly delegated to the civil services of the participating countries, even if under the supervision of the Secretary-General of ASEAN. In particular, the Secretary-General, appointed by the ASEAN Summit for a non-renewable term of office of five years, facilitates and monitors the progress in the implementation of ASEAN agreements and decisions.

According to Article 13 of the ASEAN Charter, each ASEAN member state is required to establish an ASEAN National Secretariat, which shall: (1) serve as the national focal point; (2) be the repository of information on all ASEAN matters at the national level; (3) coordinate the implementation of ASEAN decisions at the national level; (4) coordinate and support the national preparations of ASEAN meetings; (5) promote ASEAN identity and awareness at the national level; and (6) contribute to ASEAN community building. In each ASEAN member state, the Ministry of Foreign Affairs (MFA) is usually the lead ministry that is responsible for dealing with ASEAN matters and implementing ASEAN agreements working together with the relevant ministries depending on the issues.

As a matter of fact, the analysis of the policy implementation of the ASEAN Charter, rules and guidelines reveals problems of asymmetric compliance between countries and policies. What are the causes of such a 'double' asymmetric compliance, between countries and policies? What remedies can be introduced to increase the effectiveness and coherence of policy implementation?

To address these questions a good reference point is the experience of the European Union (EU). However, the relevance of the EU's experience must not be overemphasized because ASEAN and the EU represent different models of regional integration. Even if the EU is older, it is not necessarily an example to follow, for two reasons.

First, Southeast Asian countries have adopted the so-called 'ASEAN way' model of cooperation based on the ideals of non-interference, informality, minimal institutionalization, consultation and consensus, non-use of force and non-confrontation. As it was observed, the 'ASEAN way' indicates 'a process of regional interactions and cooperation based on discreteness, informality, consensus building and non-confrontational bargaining styles' that contrasts with 'the adversarial posturing, majority vote and other legalistic decision-making procedures in Western multilateral organizations' (Acharya 2001: 64).

The EU, on the contrary, is a very complex institutional and legal machine, with twenty-eight member states. European Treaties, regulations and directives are the sources of law, producing legal effects in all the member states. Power is divided among the Council, representing Heads and members of national governments, the European Parliament, directly elected by citizens and the Commission, serving exclusively the European interest. The Court of First Instance and the European Court of Justice solve disputes and ensure the uniform interpretation of European Law.

Second, the EU's attractiveness and reputation are changing. For a long time, it was viewed all over the world as the most successful case of supranational integration in a sort of never-ending process ('an ever closer Union') (Börzel and Risse: 2012). However, in recent years, the Eurozone crisis has greatly reduced the confidence in the European institutional system, and has also undermined its influence over other regional integration experiences.

Serious dysfunctional aspects of the EU have emerged, including asymmetry in implementation. Vast differences in bureaucratic capacity have emerged since the beginning and increased after the enlargement to Eastern Europe. All the member states are subject to an incredibly high amount of infringement procedures initiated by the EC, acting as a watchdog of the Treaties. Italy, Greece and Belgium are often among the worst performers. Nonetheless, in the recent past, even the two largest member states failed to comply with the core provisions of the Treaty. As a matter of fact, in 2005, France and Germany departed from the Stability and Growth Pact (SGP) requirements in the Treaty of Maastricht (budget surpluses/deficits to range from + 3 per cent to − 3 per cent of GDP). This led eventually to more flexible rules for interpreting the SGP. Ironically, some of the countries which are now the subject of bailouts and financial assistance, complied with the SGP requirements at that time.

Nonetheless, in ASEAN's recent evolution, there were several, even if selective, transplants of the specific institutional devices adopted in the EU: the purpose of an 'internal market'; the establishment of a three 'pillars' system; and the role of the

Committee of Permanent Representatives (CPR), similar to the one played in Europe by the Coreper (Jetschke and Murray: 2012). In the future, ASEAN might decide to face its policy implementation problems by looking at practical and legal devices that were adopted by the EU to overcome, or at least to reduce, similar difficulties (not always achieving full success, as previously noted).

7.3 Causes of asymmetric compliance across countries

There are many causes of implementation failure and asymmetric compliance among countries. The political context, legal system, administrative culture, economic development and geographical conditions play relevant roles in shaping bureaucratic performance and cooperation capacity, as shown in the previous six chapters in this book.

Beginning with the political context, empirical research has shown that the public bureaucracy in a stable, democratic and incorrupt political system with rule of law will be more effective in policy implementation than its counterpart in an unstable, authoritarian and corrupt political system without rule of law. There are many differences in the political systems in the ASEAN countries. In the five countries examined in this book, there are four different institutional regimes: presidential democracy in Indonesia and the Philippines, parliamentary democracy in Singapore, constitutional monarchy in Malaysia and communist state in Vietnam. Levels of competition in party system and change in governmental leadership also differ too.

According to several indicators, Singapore has the most stable and least corrupt political system with the highest degree of rule of law. The political systems of Malaysia and Vietnam are second and third in terms of political stability, perceived level of corruption and the rule of law. In Chapter 6, Jairo Acuña-Alfaro and Ahn Tran indicated that Vietnam's major problem is the high level of political interference and the absence of a clear demarcation between the Communist Party and the public bureaucracy. However, the Philippines and Indonesia are politically unstable and perceived to be very corrupt countries with a low degree of rule of law.

The different roles played by the legal systems in the ASEAN countries must also be noted. Singapore, notwithstanding its common law tradition, has developed a coherent system of administrative law. According to David Seth Jones in Chapter 5, public law bodies and civil servants in Singapore are required to act fairly, reasonably and in accordance with the law. If their decisions and actions do not meet such criteria, they can be invalidated and declared contrary to law through judicial review, even if by ordinary (non-specialist administrative) courts. Statutory orders, regulations, guidelines, manuals and circulars detail responsibilities and powers of public agencies.

On the other hand, Acuña-Alfaro and Tran show in Chapter 6 that the public bureaucracy in Vietnam has only been regulated by legislative documents during the last fifteen years. A law adopted in 2008 has transformed a scattered by-law system to legislation governing bureaucratic personnel, with the establishment of obligations, rights and responsibilities of public officials and setting conditions for ensuring the performance of their official functions and duties.

Size and population matter too. The public bureaucracy in a geographically large country tends to face more difficulties in policy implementation, especially in its provinces, than the public bureaucracy in a small country. Likewise, the public bureaucracy in a country with a small population will encounter less difficulty in policy implementation than the public bureaucracy in a country with a large population. Jon Quah shows in his comparison of the policy contexts of the five ASEAN countries in Chapter 1 that the differences between Singapore (land area 716 sq. km; population 5.4 million) and Indonesia (land area 1,904,443 sq. km; population 248 million) are enormous. In such a context, the size of public bureaucracy is different too. In absolute terms, the number of bureaucrats ranges from 4,375,009 for Indonesia to 138,720 for Singapore. However, for population, the country with the highest ratio of civil servants is Malaysia, which has forty-three civil servants per 1,000 population compared to the fourteen civil servants per 1,000 population in the Philippines.

The public bureaucracy in a poor country is supposed to encounter more problems in policy implementation than the public bureaucracy in an affluent country if the former does not have adequate financial and technical resources. For example, Singapore with a per capita GDP of US$54,776 is the most affluent among the five countries while Vietnam is the poorest with a per capita GDP of US$1,902. Jones contends in Chapter 5 that Singapore's comparative advantage is twofold.

First, strong revenue flows in Singapore enable the allocation of human and financial resources to the public bureaucracy. Singapore's second advantage is that a conservative fiscal policy minimizes the waste of public money and creates powerful incentives for bureaucratic efficiency.

In Southeast Asian countries, civic traditions and administrative culture are deeply influenced by their colonial legacy. This factor can be positive or negative for the public bureaucracy's role in policy implementation in terms of promoting meritocracy, developing infrastructure and investing in the educational system. The colonial legacies of the five countries are different as they were colonized by Britain, France, the Netherlands, Spain and the United States. Only the British legacy has played an important role in developing techniques and skills for the public service. This influence, in Jones's view, together with the influx of large numbers of foreigners at work in recent years and the existence of a multi-ethnic population, explain the commitment to professionalism that distinguishes the civil service in Singapore from its counterparts in the other four ASEAN countries.

As a consequence of all these factors, administrative performance varies from one ASEAN country to the other. The most widespread, even if controversial, governance indicators clearly show that. Government effectiveness refers to the quality of public service provision, the quality of the bureaucracy, the competence of civil servants, the independence of the civil service from political pressures, and the credibility of the government's commitment. In Chapter 1, Quah stresses that, according to the World Bank's governance indicator on government effectiveness from 1996 to 2013,

Singapore is the most effective, with an average percentile rank of 98.9, followed by Malaysia (82.2 percentile rank), Vietnam (43.6 percentile rank), Indonesia (42.5 percentile rank) and the Philippines (40.6 percentile rank).

Similarly, for regulatory quality, which refers to the incidence of market-unfriendly policies such as price controls or inadequate bank supervision, as well as perceptions of the burdens imposed by excessive regulation in areas such as foreign trade and business development, Singapore is again the best performer, followed by Malaysia, the Philippines, Indonesia and Vietnam. The World Bank's *Doing Business* 2014 shows that Singapore is ranked first among 189 economies in terms of the ease of doing business, followed by Malaysia (ranked 6th), Vietnam (ranked 99th), the Philippines (ranked 108th) and Indonesia (ranked 120th) (World Bank 2013: 3).

According to Quah in Chapter 1, the World Bank's evaluation of the government effectiveness and regulatory quality of the five ASEAN public bureaucracies confirms the PERC's assessment of their effectiveness from 1998 to 2012 in Table 1.11, which shows that Singapore's public bureaucracy is ranked first, with an average score of 2.24, followed by Malaysia (6.51), the Philippines (7.79), Vietnam (8.13) and Indonesia (8.22).

In sum, as shown in Chapters 1–6, the five ASEAN public bureaucracies vary considerably in terms of their size and effectiveness. Singapore has the smallest but most effective public bureaucracy according to three indicators. Malaysia's public bureaucracy of 1.2 million employees is the second most effective after Singapore. On the other hand, the larger public bureaucracies of the Philippines, Vietnam and Indonesia are less effective than their counterparts in Singapore and Malaysia.

Different levels in administrative capacity, of course, seriously undermine the possibility of a coherent and homogeneous implementation of ASEAN policies and rules. Furthermore, differences in the political and economic context also influence the incentives and strategies of compliance. Competitive economic systems, technologically advanced industries and exporting producers will exert pressure on their respective governments to implement fairly supranational policies and ensure proper compliance by other member states. The opposite will happen in less developed countries.

From the preceding analysis, it might seem that the differences between the ASEAN countries are more pronounced than those existing between the EU countries. This explains why the asymmetries in policy implementation seem to be deeper for the ASEAN countries than the EU countries. Nonetheless, such differences must not be overemphasized. In Europe, too, homogeneity is not the dominant issue.

The political context in the EU countries has become similar to a certain extent. Multi-party free competition is now present in all the EU member states but the constitutional settings are different. Monarchies, presidential or semi-presidential republics, and parliamentary regimes are all present among the EU countries. Levels of economic development, geographical conditions, legal systems, administrative cultures and civic traditions are also different. Civil law countries coexist with common law ones. Among the civil law countries, only some of them, like France and Italy, have as a distinctive feature an administrative law tradition, based on the creative role played by the special judge for administrative disputes. Germany and Italy enacted in the 1970s and 1990s general laws regulating the administrative decision-making process. However, even though France and the United Kingdom have not relied on this option their quality of administrative democracy and transparency appear to be superior, because of special regulations relating to public inquiries and public debate before the adoption of 'sensible' decisions (such as the allocation of noxious facilities).

The political and administrative culture of the EEC founding countries differs from that of the EEC/EU's more recent member states, especially those in Eastern Europe. The EEC countries assisted the newer member states to enable them to join the EU. Even though laws have been harmonized, effective and homogeneous policy implementation is still far away. In recent years, some empirical data show that a distinction of civic tradition has emerged between northern Europe and southern Europe in relation to public debt management, level of public expenditure, tax loyalty and protection of future generations. However, while some north European countries are highly compliant in fiscal sustainability standards and rightly expect the same from their European partners, they still resist opening their market to other European enterprises, especially in the sector of services. Moreover, France and Germany were the first two countries to infringe the Stability and Growth Pact, without paying serious consequences for such a breach.

7.4 Causes of asymmetric compliance across policies

Asymmetries occur not only among countries but also among policies. Consequently, the role of the public bureaucracies in policy implementation is illustrated by focusing on the ASEAN Cosmetic Directive (ACD) and the ASEAN Ministerial Meeting on Transnational Crime (AMMTC) and Senior Officials Meeting on Transnational Crime (SOMTC) agreements and resolutions.

The ACD was signed by the ASEAN countries in September 2003 and came into effect on 1 January 2008. Its objective is to protect consumers in the ASEAN countries from the health hazards posed by cosmetics products by conducting post-market surveillance of these products instead of relying on pre-market approval. Each ASEAN country has to incorporate the ACD into its domestic laws, but it has the discretion to amplify and interpret the ACD provisions for implementation.

Unlike the ACD, the AMMTC/SOMTC is multifaceted and covers various issues. In 1997, the ASEAN Declaration on Transnational Crime was signed by the ASEAN countries to combat transnational crime. The Declaration was followed by the ASEAN Plan of Action to Combat Transnational Crime in 1999 and the Work Programme to Implement the ASEAN Plan of Action to Combat Transnational Crime in 2002. The 1997 ASEAN Declaration on Transnational Crime focuses on the following eight aspects: terrorism, trafficking in persons, sea piracy, drug trafficking, money laundering and terrorism financing, cyber-crime, economic crime, and arms smuggling. The AMMTC was convened in

November 1997 to implement the ASEAN agreements on transnational crime. It is supported by the SOMTC, which meets annually to coordinate and cooperate with other ASEAN bodies dealing with transnational crime. The AMMTC/SOMTC has recommended that the ASEAN countries enhance their efforts in combating transnational crime by sharing intelligence, tracking and deporting wanted persons and conducting joint operations.

The comparison of the implementation of the ACD and AMMTC/SOMTC in the five ASEAN countries by Quah in Chapter 1 confirms that the national public bureaucracies have been more effective in implementing the ACD than the AMMTC and SOMTC, for three reasons. First, the ACD focuses on a single issue while the AMMTC/SOMTC deals with eight types of transnational crime. Second, the narrower scope of the ACD means that fewer agencies are involved in its implementation in contrast with the implementation of the AMMTC/SOMTC, which requires more implementing agencies because of its wider scope. Third, while both policies have encountered problems in implementation, the problems in implementing the AMMTC/SOMTC – in particular the limited capacity of enforcement agencies, coordination failure and corruption – are more serious than those faced in implementing the ACD. In short, the five ASEAN countries have been more effective in implementing the ACD than the AMMTC/SOMTC because the former involves a single issue and fewer implementing agencies and have faced fewer implementation problems.

Successes and failures, of course, depend also on the specific conditions existing at the national level. In the case of Singapore, Jones concludes in Chapter 5 that the ACD's effective implementation was the outcome of these different positive converging factors: quality of cosmetics laboratory of the Health Sciences Authority; widespread consumption of cosmetics products among the local population; cooperation with the cosmetics industry; and developed bureaucratic experience on similar matters. However, he contends that the implementation of the ASEAN Action Plan and Work Programme on the Trafficking in Persons (TIP) is still a work in progress because the threat posed by TIP is less imminent, due to a relatively small number of such offences at the moment. The opposite is true in the case of the fight against terrorism, which became an important issue for Indonesia, Malaysia and Singapore after the 2002 Bali bombing, according to Pramusinto in Chapter 2.

Different outcomes between policies, even in good performing countries, are not surprising. Usually, market integration policies are more successful than cooperation in the exercise of traditional 'sovereign' functions in both the ASEAN and EU countries, for several reasons. The first reason is the importance of history as national governments are particularly jealous of their sovereign prerogatives. They are instinctively against sharing and even coordinating functions and powers in matters like security, criminal prosecution, immigration policies and foreign affairs.

Secondly, integration practices, especially in Europe, are much more long-lasting in the market field than in the case of typical sovereign functions. The establishment of a common market without internal barriers was at the core of the European project since the beginning in 1957. Cooperation in the fields of justice and security, on the contrary, started only in 1992, with the Maastricht Treaty and the building up of those two other pillars in the European construction. Even after 1992, legal integration in the economic sector was much stronger than in the fields of justice and security.

What must be stressed, however, is that other relevant factors are also related to the problem of policy implementation and to the different roles played by the private stakeholders. During the initial stage, market integration policies do not need a wide delegation of powers to national administrations to be effective. They simply require the abolition of legal barriers to trade and free circulation. However, administrative integration and coordination become fundamental during a later stage (European Commission 2011). Cooperation in the exercise of sovereign functions, on the contrary, since the beginning, requires a continuous bureaucratic activity of exchanging data and information, joint operations and other activities.

Private stakeholders also play a very important role in enforcing market integration provisions by taking immediate advantage of the freedom of circulation rights and liberalization measures. Furthermore, they can act before the national and supranational courts to obtain the full respect of the rights deriving from those measures. Even in the less institutionalized framework of the ASEAN countries, case studies examined in this book provide evidence of the relevant role played by private stakeholders. In Chapter 4 on the Philippines, Reyes observed that even though the cosmetics industry was involved in all stages of the implementation process and even provided professional training to public officers, interest groups can nevertheless use their influence to oppose a market integration policy. Similarly, in Chapter 2, Pramusinto demonstrates clearly the conflict in Indonesia between the large cosmetics companies, which push for the proper implementation of the ACD, and the small companies which resist this policy. In the case of Vietnam, which is analysed by Acuña-Alfaro and Tran in Chapter 6, the constant interaction between the management bodies of the implementing agencies and the enterprises plays an important role in making clear the provisions of the ACD and in ensuring their effective implementation.

The complete opposite is the situation with the common or the coordinated exercise of sovereign functions, because in most cases citizens do not derive direct benefit or advantage from those functions or policies. These functions usually produce, in economic terms, public goods, not private goods. This explains why there is no specific legal tool, or even a rational incentive, to act and push for more effective supranational integration. Consequently, it is not surprising that private stakeholders have failed to improve vigilance and promote anti-corruption efforts as shown in the ineffective implementation of the Trafficking Protocol in the five ASEAN countries.

7.5 Remedies for policy implementation failure and asymmetric compliance

The analysis, even if necessarily partial, reveals the existence of relevant policy implementation failures and asymmetric compliance. Reasons for such an outcome are different. Many factors, being closely linked to political, historical and cultural elements, are difficult to manage or overcome, at least in the short term.

Nonetheless, there are some possible remedies that could be usefully introduced. The most important ones are legal, which can be extracted from the toolbox of administrative law. For the reasons indicated at the outset of this chapter, administrative law specializes in addressing the problems arising from the principal–agent relationship existing between the policy-makers and policy implementers.

In an international setting, however, the principal–agent relationship existing between the policy-makers and policy implementers is much more complex. The evolution of the EU's administrative system and law represents an interesting reference point for reflecting on the forms and techniques of administrative cooperation and integration in a supranational context (Schwarze 2012).

Examining the European experience, there are three most important techniques developed to ameliorate policy implementation and reduce asymmetric compliance: (1) promoting the development of a common administrative culture and practice; (2) enhancing a stronger common regulation for national administrations; and (3) strengthening the roles and powers of a common supranational administration. These techniques cannot be easily transplanted for two reasons: first, they are only partly successful and required a long time to be introduced and fine-tuned; and second, as previously noted, the ASEAN's legal framework remains very different from the EU's framework. However, three useful suggestions can be derived from examining the European case.

7.5.1 The development of a common administrative culture and practice

The first way to improve policy implementation is through the promotion of a common administrative culture and practice among the ASEAN countries. Hence, it is important to analyse and compare their administrative performance in order to identify their strengths and weaknesses. The chapters in this book represent a preliminary attempt in this sense. Best practices could then become the object of training and educational activities. The importance of creating a common administrative culture should not be underestimated. Administrative performance concerns not only organization and rules but also includes the skills, capacity and civic attitudes of all public servants and managers.

Good practices, of course, can be stimulated by good rules too. Legal solutions experimented with in one country, where they are particularly efficient in enhancing good performance and compliance, could be imitated or transplanted. Such a choice is a voluntary one, freely made by a sovereign country. Peer reviews and rankings, nonetheless, represent a powerful incentive to transplant successful legal solutions, both for internal consensus and for external reputation reasons. Such an approach could be useful in the case of the ASEAN countries.

Even in the much more 'legalized' order of the EU, the integration through voluntary even if induced convergence plays an important role, in particular in the field of public administration and policy implementation. In many policy areas, EU member states formulate their own national policies rather than having an EU-wide policy laid down in law. However, under the Open Method of Coordination (OMC), governments learn from each other by sharing information and comparing initiatives. This enables them to adopt best practices and to coordinate their national policies.

The OMC provides a framework for cooperation between the member states, whose national policies can thus be directed towards certain common objectives. Under this method, the member states are evaluated by one another, with the European Commission's role limited to coordination and surveillance. The OMC takes place in these sectors of economic or social activity of the member states, namely employment, social protection, social inclusion, education, youth or training.

As policy implementation and cooperation falls within this area, Article 197 of the Treaty on the Functioning of the EU states that 'effective implementation of Union law by the member states, which is essential for the proper functioning of the Union, shall be regarded as a matter of common interest'. Consequently, 'the Union may support the efforts of member states to improve their administrative capacity to implement Union law. Such actions may include facilitating the exchange of information and of civil servants as well as supporting training schemes' (Article 197, para. 2).

The OMC deals with measures which are binding on member states in varying degrees, but which do not take the form of directives, regulations or decisions. It is based principally on four steps: (1) joint identification and definition of objectives to be achieved (usually in Council summits and meetings); (2) joint establishment of data sets, training techniques and measuring instruments (statistics, indicators, guidelines); (3) transposing guidelines into national and regional policies adopted by the member states; and (4) benchmarking, i.e., comparison of the member states' performance and exchange of best practices (monitored by the Commission).

The OMC, in conclusion, rests on soft law mechanisms such as guidelines and indicators, benchmarking and sharing of best practices. This means that there are no official sanctions for laggards. Rather, the method's effectiveness relies on a form of peer pressure and naming and shaming, as no member state wants to be seen as the worst in a given policy area.

In the ASEAN case, the introduction of something similar to the European OMC could be extremely useful. Without any change to the ASEAN Charter and to other legally binding provisions, it could be possible to enhance convergence between the national administrations of the member states. To that purpose, the Secretary-General of ASEAN, together with the ASEAN Secretariat, could play a very important role in stimulating good practices and transplanting successful legal devices. The civil services in Indonesia, Malaysia, the Philippines, Singapore and Thailand have organized regional seminars for their civil servants to meet and exchange information on best practices.

Their tasks greatly evolved from the origins of ASEAN in August 1967 to the present day. The ASEAN Secretary-General is asked to report the progress of the Communities to the relevant ministerial meetings and the Summit. The Roadmap for the ASEAN Community is also tasked with mobilizing resources from the member states. Along with the concerned ASEAN sectorial ministerial bodies, the Secretary-General is responsible for its implementation. In exercising all these functions, the Secretary-General can focus on the need for promoting good administration through measuring performance, blaming and shaming, favouring transplants of relevant legal and organizational features.

7.5.2 A stronger common regulation for national administrations

Political, economic and geographical factors are difficult to change. Each country will retain its political system, and is bounded by historical borders and natural features, with its own development and growth model. Administrative institutions, rules and procedures, on the contrary, can be more easily harmonized through law.

More frequently, nonetheless, harmonization is achieved through a complex mix of different legal solutions adopted in several countries. It is not achieved through imitation or transplantation. A patchwork of different legal and administrative traditions may be desirable. In Europe, for example, the solutions adopted are often a mix of French and German traditions, while the British models often inspire recipes for modernizing the system of public management. Harmonization affects both organizational and procedural issues.

First, a useful rule is the one obliging member states to establish independent authorities to implement supranational policies and rules. Independent authorities are expected to be more loyal to the Union in ensuring a proper execution of common purposes and rules than public bureaucracies directly depending on national governments. For example, in many network industries, traditionally run by public enterprises, regulatory measures necessary to open the market to competition must be adopted by national authorities fully independent from governmental and private influence. This is the case of the telecommunications and energy sectors. Following the last generation of European regulations and directives, each member state must designate a national regulatory authority. Its institutional design – related to appointment mechanisms, no revocation clause, organizational and financial autonomy – must avoid any influence from political bodies and economic actors. However, such a design was not easily implemented as the EU needed several rule-making acts and the opening of various infringement procedures (one against Germany, in the case of the regulations of the next generation's network that was adopted by Parliament and not by the national regulatory authority, in violation of the EU law).

Second, national administrations charged with the implementation of supranational policies and rules may be required to follow common procedural requirements. Among them, 'notice and comment' procedures equally protect the rights of all interested parties, irrespective of their nationality. These procedures are also conceived as an important tool to activate fire-alarm signals when national administrations fail to comply with supranational policies. Following those signals, the EC can better decide if and when to exercise its veto powers or follow an infringement procedure. The mechanism described here is particularly effective in the sector of electronic communications, where the Commission has become the regulatory master and private actors play a double role before the national regulatory authority and the Commission.

Paradoxically enough, the EU's experience shows that a stronger common regulation for national public administration might not require a specific legal basis in the treaty. Actually, in the European treaties, there are no specific provisions regarding the harmonization of administrative law rules as such. Nonetheless, the EU succeeded in shaping national administrative institutions, because that was necessary to make effective the creation of a truly internal market. According to the European Court of Justice (C-359/92), a directive can oblige member states to establish national authorities required to implement coherently the European legal framework. Among the approximation measures that a European directive can enact, there are also those affecting the organization of the public bureaucracies.

Similarly, in the case of the ASEAN countries, some degree of harmonization could be reached without any Charter amendment. Sector by sector, specific agreements and directives could require the member states to adopt similar organizational and procedural devices in order to enhance the quality and coherence of policy implementation.

7.5.3 Strengthening tasks and powers of supranational administrations

The harmonization of the national administration regulations could be accompanied by the establishment of a stronger supranational administration and the strengthening of its tasks and powers. However, the administrative infrastructure of the ASEAN is quite poor at the moment, at least when compared to the European Union. The ASEAN Secretariat is conceived only as the staff service of the General Secretary of the organization. As a matter of fact, the member states resist any allocation of substantial competence to the ASEAN Secretariat: 'any hint of supranational authority is anathema' (Termsak 2009: 144). Member states always intended to keep control of the ASEAN Secretariat and not allow it to evolve into anything resembling the EC. Also, the space for the development of a decentralized administrative system appears to be limited. According to the Charter, each ASEAN Sectorial Ministerial Body may have under its purview the relevant senior officials and subsidiary bodies to undertake its functions.

Such a structure is completely different from the one existing in the EU, based on the EC and some decentralized agencies. The EC is the executive body of the EU responsible for proposing legislation, implementing decisions, upholding its treaties and daily operations. The EC operates as a cabinet government, with twenty-eight members. There is one member per member state, though members are bound to represent the interests of the EU as a whole rather than their home state.

The EC was set up from the start to act as an independent supranational authority separate from the governments. The members are proposed by their member state governments, one from each country. Once appointed, they are bound to act independently – neutral from other influences, including those coming from member states. This is in contrast with the Council of Ministers, which represents governments, the European Parliament, which represents citizens, and the Economic and Social Committee, which represents organized civil society. Through Article 17 of the Treaty on European Union the EC has several responsibilities: develop medium-term strategies; draft legislation and arbitrate in the legislative process; represent the EU in trade negotiations; make rules and regulations, for example, in competition policy; draw up the EU's budget; and scrutinize the implementation of the treaties and legislation.

Before the Treaty of Lisbon came into force, the EU's executive power was held by the Council: it conferred on the EC such powers as it could exercise. However, the Council was in principle allowed to withdraw these powers, exercise them directly or impose conditions on their use. This aspect has been changed by the Treaty of Lisbon, after which the EC exercises its powers just by virtue of the treaties.

Once legislation is passed by the Council and Parliament, the EC has the responsibility to ensure that it is implemented. It does this through the member states or through its agencies. In adopting the necessary technical measures, the EC is assisted by committees made up of representatives of member states (a process known in jargon as 'comitology'). In particular, the EC has a duty to ensure the treaties and laws are upheld, potentially by taking member states or other institutions to the Court of Justice in a dispute. In this role, the EC is known informally as the 'guardian of the treaties'.

In its administrative structure, the EC is divided into departments known as Directorates-General (DGs) that are similar to departments or ministries. Each DG covers a specific policy area, such as agriculture or justice and citizens' rights, or internal services, such as human resources and translation, and is headed by a Director-General who is responsible to a Commissioner. A Commissioner's portfolio can be supported by numerous DGs, who prepare proposals for them and, if approved by a majority of Commissioners, such proposals are sent to the Parliament and Council for consideration. In September 2012, 23,803 persons were employed by the EC as officials and temporary agents. In addition to these, 9,230 'external staff' (e.g., contractual agents, detached national experts, young experts, trainees etc.) were also employed by the EC. The EC's civil service is headed by a Secretary-General. The EC today is a powerful administrative body, even if its dimension cannot be compared with those of the national governments.

The European administrative system is integrated by more than thirty agencies, located in different EU countries. They have an important role in implementing EU policies, especially tasks of a technical, scientific, operational and/or regulatory nature. This frees up the EU institutions, especially the EC, to concentrate on policy-making. They also support cooperation between the EU and national governments in important policy areas, by pooling technical and specialist expertise from both the EU institutions and the national authorities.

The decentralized agencies are independent legal entities under European public law, distinct from the EU institutions (Council, Parliament, Commission etc.). They are established through specific regulations. The treaties do not even mention these agencies because they were set up on a case-by-case basis over the years to respond to emerging individual policy needs and operating in different conditions. In 2012, the EU rectified this by adopting a comprehensive set of guiding principles – a 'common approach' – to make the agencies more coherent, effective and accountable.

Creating its own supranational administrative system, the EU succeeded in reducing the risks of poor implementation and non-compliance at the national level. However, the positive outcomes of the EU must not be overemphasized because the area of European direct administration is still very limited. There is a huge difference in the administrative capacity of the EC, which has binding and effective powers, and its various agencies. There are also different levels of performance and success among the DGs of the EC.

The history of the European administration seems to be completely different from the ASEAN one. However, a careful analysis reveals some interesting similarities. The growth of the EC's administrative structure was a gradual process, taking more than thirty years. And, for a long time, until the Treaty of Lisbon, there was no significant treaty amendment. The EC's powers were reinforced through sectorial directives, and ad hoc regulations established European agencies in many regulatory fields. Only the Treaty of Lisbon recognized the existence of a truly 'European administration', requiring it to be 'open, efficient and independent' (Article 298, Treaty on the Functioning of the EU).

Also in the ASEAN system, the role of the ASEAN Secretariat and other supranational bodies could be extended in a pragmatic way, without any formal change of the ASEAN Charter. Specific agreements and directives can delegate implementation and supervisory tasks to the ASEAN Secretariat or other instrumental bodies, on a case-by-case basis. The strengthening of a supranational administrative system could take place without any general and explicit rejection of the 'ASEAN way' to common policy implementation. In principle, member states could continue to deny any conferral of authority to the ASEAN Secretariat or other related bodies. In practice, however, they could recognize, through specific agreements, that giving limited executive and supervising powers to supranational administrations could be the best way to pursue a proper and coherent implementation of common rules and policies.

References

Acharya, A. 2001. *Constructing a Security Community in South East Asia: ASEAN and the Problem of Regional Order*. London: Routledge.

Börzel, T. A. and Risse, T. 2012. 'When Europeanisation Meets Diffusion: Exploring New Territory', *West European Politics*, 35(1): 192–207.

European Commission 2011. *Better Governance of the Single Market through Greater Administrative Cooperation: A Strategy for Expanding and Developing the Internal Market Information System*. Brussels: European Commission.

Horn, M. J. 1995. *The Political Economy of Public Administration*. Cambridge: Cambridge University Press.

Huber, J. D., Shipan, C. R. and Pfahler, M. 2001. 'Legislatures and Statutory Control of Bureaucracy', *American Journal of Political Science*, 45(2): 330–45.

Jetschke, A. and Murray, P. 2012. 'Diffusing Regional Integration: The EU and Southeast Asia', *West European Politics*, 35(1): 174–91.

Macey, J. 1992. 'Organizational Design and the Political Control of Administrative Agencies', *Journal of Law, Economics and Organization*, 8: 93–110.

Mashaw, J. L. 1990. 'Explaining Administrative Process: Normative, Positive and Critical Stories of Legal Development', *Journal of Law Economics and Organization*, 6: 267–98.

McCubbins, M., Noll, R. and Weingast, B. 1987. 'Administrative Procedures as Instruments of Political Control', *Journal of Law Economics and Organization*, 3: 243–77.

Posner, E. A. 2001. 'Cost-Benefit Analysis as a Solution to a Principal Agent Problem', *Administrative Law Review*, 53: 289–97.

Pressman, J. and Wildavsky, A. 1984. *Implementation, How Great Expectations in Washington are Dashed in Oakland*, 3rd edn. Berkeley, CA: University of California Press.

Quah, J. S. T. 1984. 'The Public Policy-Making Process in Singapore', *Asian Journal of Public Administration*, 6(2): 108–26.

Schwarze, J. 2012. 'European Administrative Law in the Light of the Treaty of Lisbon', *European Public Law*, 18(2): 285–304.

Shepsle, K. A. 1992. 'Bureaucratic Drift, Coalitional Drift, and Time Consistency: A Comment on Macey', *Journal of Law, Economics and Organization*, 8(1): 111–18.

Termsak, C. 2009. 'Institutional Reform: One Charter, Three Communities, Many Challenges'. In D. Emmerson (ed.),

Hard Choices: Security, Democracy, and Regionalism in Southeast Asia. Singapore: Institute of Southeast Asian Studies, pp. 91–131.

World Bank 2013. *Doing Business 2014: Understanding Regulations for Small and Medium Size Enterprises*. Washington, DC: World Bank.

EXECUTIVE SUMMARY

Jon S. T. Quah

The public bureaucracy is a key institution in the Association of Southeast Asian Nations (ASEAN) countries because it is usually the largest employer and is also responsible for the implementation of public policies. How effective are the public bureaucracies in the ASEAN countries in policy implementation? This book focuses on the public bureaucracies' role in policy implementation in Indonesia, Malaysia, the Philippines, Singapore and Vietnam. Its purpose is twofold: (1) to analyse the role of the public bureaucracies in policy implementation in these five countries; and (2) to compare and explain their different levels of effectiveness.

There is great diversity in the policy contexts of the five ASEAN countries. First, the size of these countries in terms of land area and population ranging from the smallest (the city state of Singapore) to the largest (the world's largest archipelago of Indonesia) are two important aspects which influence greatly the public bureaucracy's effectiveness in policy implementation. Second, the colonial legacy is another significant factor as the legacy of former British colonies like Singapore and Malaysia appears to be more positive than the colonial legacies of the Dutch for Indonesia, the Spanish and United States for the Philippines, and the French for Vietnam. Third, there is a wide disparity in GDP per capita between

Singapore's GDP per capita of US$54,776 in 2013, and the other four ASEAN countries, with Vietnam having the lowest GDP per capita of US$1,902 for the same year. Finally, except for Vietnam, which is a communist state, the other four countries have democratic political systems: Indonesia and the Philippines are presidential democracies, Malaysia is a constitutional monarchy and Singapore is a parliamentary democracy. The most important factor for effective policy implementation is perhaps the political will or commitment of both the incumbent government and the implementers. Thus, the policy contexts of the five ASEAN countries have a tremendous impact on their public bureaucracies' role in policy implementation, as a favourable policy context will enhance their role while an unfavourable policy context will undermine it.

To ensure consistency and enhance comparative analysis, Van Meter and Van Horn's model of policy implementation involving these six variables is adopted in the five country chapters, namely the 'economic, social and political conditions' (or policy context), clarity of the policy standards and objectives; their communication to the implementers; availability of policy resources; effectiveness of the implementing agencies; and disposition of the implementers. A common approach is employed for these chapters, beginning with an analysis of the country's policy context and a profile of its public bureaucracy before analysing the public bureaucracy's role in policy implementation according to Van Meter and Van Horn's framework. The implementation of two ASEAN policies – the ASEAN Cosmetic Directive (ACD) and the ASEAN Ministerial Meeting on Transnational Crime

(AMMTC)/Senior Officers Meeting on Transnational Crime (SOMTC) – are analysed as case studies in the five countries to facilitate comparison. This book is divided into seven chapters, consisting of the comparative overview in Chapter 1, the five country chapters on Indonesia, Malaysia, the Philippines, Singapore and Vietnam, and Chapter 7, which compares the experiences of the ASEAN and European Union (EU) in policy implementation.

In Chapter 1, Jon S. T. Quah compares the performance of the public bureaucracies in policy implementation in the five ASEAN countries and concludes that their effectiveness depends on (1) whether their policy contexts are favourable or unfavourable, especially in terms of the commitment of the governments and disposition of the implementers to the policy; and (2) whether their public bureaucracies are effective or ineffective. This means that a country with a favourable policy context and an effective public bureaucracy will be more effective in policy implementation than a country with an unfavourable policy context and an ineffective public bureaucracy. Singapore is the most effective in policy implementation because of its favourable policy context and its effective public bureaucracy. Conversely, Indonesia is the least effective in policy implementation because of its unfavourable policy context and its ineffective public bureaucracy. Malaysia, Vietnam and the Philippines occupy intermediate positions between Singapore and Indonesia and are ranked second, third and fourth respectively, depending on the nature of their policy contexts and the levels of effectiveness of their public bureaucracies.

Furthermore, a comparative analysis of the implementation of the ACD and the AMMTC/SOMTC in the five ASEAN countries shows that their public bureaucracies are more effective in implementing the ACD than the AMMTC/SOMTC for three reasons. First, the ACD focuses on a single issue while the AMMTC and SOMTC deal with eight types of transnational crimes. Second, the ACD's narrower scope means that fewer agencies are involved in its implementation in contrast with the implementation of the AMMTC/SOMTC, which requires more implementing agencies because of their wider scope. Third, while both policies have encountered problems in implementation, the problems in implementing the AMMTC/SOMTC are more serious than those faced in implementing the ACD. In sum, the five ASEAN countries have been more effective in implementing the ACD than the AMMTC/SOMTC because the former involves a single issue and fewer implementing agencies, and has encountered fewer implementation problems than the latter.

In Chapter 2, Agus Pramusinto contends that the Indonesian public bureaucracy's role in policy implementation has been adversely affected by the democratization of its political system, which has transformed the hegemonic party system into a multi-party system. During the New Order regime, the public bureaucracy formulated the laws, which were easily approved by the National Assembly because President Suharto relied on Presidential Instructions to expedite the policy formulation process. However, the policy formulation process during the post-Suharto period became less efficient and more time-consuming because of the need for public consultation, the representation of many political parties and the longer agenda in the National Assembly. More importantly, the implementing agencies in Indonesia are ineffective because of their incompetent personnel, the disparity in span of control among ministries and their vulnerability to political pressures from members of the National Assembly.

The role of the Malaysian public bureaucracy in policy implementation is analysed by Nik Rosnah Wan Abdullah in Chapter 3. She argues that while the public bureaucracy in Malaysia has been effective as reflected in the increase of its percentile rank on the World Bank's governance indicator on government effectiveness from 76.1 to 81.8 from 1996 to 2013, its role in policy implementation has been hindered by these two weaknesses: (1) its ethnic preference for Malay or *Bumiputera* candidates and discrimination towards the Chinese and Indians in recruitment and promotion in the civil service; and (2) the problem of corruption which is manifested in Malaysia's mediocre performance on Transparency International's Corruption Perceptions Index as it was ranked fiftieth among 175 countries in 2014 with a score of 52 on a scale ranging from 0 (highly corrupt) to 100 (very clean).

Vicente Chua Reyes, Jr shows in Chapter 4 that the public bureaucracy in the Philippines is dysfunctional and ineffective in policy implementation because it suffers from systemic corruption and operates in an environment characterized by weak rule of law. Among the five ASEAN countries, the Philippines is perceived to be among the most corrupt, according to five indicators of corruption. Similarly, in terms of the World Bank's rule of law governance indicator, the Philippines' percentile rank has decreased significantly from 50.7 in 1996 to 41.7 in 2013.

As Singapore has the most stable and least corrupt political system with the highest degree of rule of law, its public bureaucracy is, not surprisingly, the most effective in policy implementation as reflected in its average percentile rank of 98.9 on the World Bank's governance indicator on government effectiveness from 1996 to 2013 (see Table 1.9) and its average score of 2.24 on the Political and Economic Risk Consultancy's (PERC's) evaluation of its effectiveness from 1998 to 2012 (see Table 1.11). In Chapter 5, David Seth Jones attributes the effectiveness of Singapore's public bureaucracy in policy implementation to these five factors: its policy of meritocracy with the retention of the Public Service Commission; the Corrupt Practices Investigation Bureau's effectiveness in curbing corruption; the availability of resources and funding to meet operational requirements; decentralization in service delivery, budget allocations, personnel management and procurement; and inter-agency cooperation in implementing policies.

Chapter 6, which is written by Jairo Acuña-Alfaro and Anh Tran, focuses on the public bureaucracy's role in policy implementation in Vietnam, a communist state under the absolute control of the Communist Party of Vietnam (CPV), which is responsible for the formulation and implementation of personnel policies of the cadres and civil servants. This means that, unlike their politically neutral counterparts in Indonesia, Malaysia, the Philippines and Singapore, most Vietnamese public officials and civil servants are party members who remain loyal to the CPV's goals and ideology. Indeed, Vietnam's public bureaucracy is ineffective in policy implementation because of these four problems: its general performance appraisal system does not assess actual staff performance; the difficulty in enforcing disciplinary action against incompetent civil servants; the limited capacity of its civil servants, which is reflected in their lack of training in state management and their low level of education; and the low salaries of civil servants, which not only encourages corruption but also leads to their brain drain to the private sector and their holding of several jobs to supplement their low wages.

Finally, in Chapter 7, Giulio Napolitano observes that some EU policies or agreements are not implemented by the member states not only because of their limited administrative capacity but more importantly because of deliberate or selective non-compliance, which he describes as 'asymmetric compliance'. As the complex structure of ASEAN provides a favourable environment for asymmetric compliance, he recommends that the ASEAN countries can enhance policy implementation and minimize asymmetric compliance by adopting these three suggestions from the experience of the EU countries: (1) promoting the development of a common administrative culture; (2) developing stronger common regulations for the public bureaucracies; and (3) strengthening the roles and powers of a common supra-national organization such as the ASEAN Secretariat. However, it might be difficult for the ASEAN countries to transplant these ideas because of the long time taken by the EU countries to introduce and fine-tune these solutions, and also because of their different legal systems.

INDEX

Printed in Singapore by Markono Print Media Pte Ltd